"Written by a transatlantic team of expert women, *Luxury Marketing and Brand Strategy* illustrates how to craft a luxury marketing strategy innovative enough to satisfy the dreams of the world's most demanding customers amidst a changing global landscape. Highly recommended!"

Hana Machková, *Professor, Prague University of Economics and Business*

Luxury Marketing and Brand Strategy

This text provides a comprehensive and strategic overview of luxury marketing and brand management, guiding brands to balance tradition with innovation as they navigate modern challenges and seize opportunities in a rapidly evolving global market.

The book explores the core aspects of luxury branding, including the defining traits of luxury brands, the dominance of major luxury groups and the resilience of independent brands with storied histories. It explores the delicate balance required to maintain a brand's luxury status amidst evolving consumer expectations, technological advancements and sustainability concerns. Students will gain insight into innovative marketing strategies, from the use of NFTs and blockchain to the integration of AI and the metaverse in enhancing customer experiences. Offering a clear and engaging pathway through the complexities of luxury brand management, the authors draw on their extensive academic and professional experience, presenting a rich blend of theoretical insights and real-world global and cross-industry case studies from prestigious brands like Cartier, Van Cleef & Arpels, Chanel, Ferrari, Orient-Express and many others.

This textbook is designed to be the cornerstone for advanced undergraduate and postgraduate courses in luxury marketing and luxury brand management. With a focus on the latest trends and future directions in luxury marketing, *Luxury Marketing and Brand Strategy* is not only an academic resource but also a practical guide for navigating and succeeding in the dynamic luxury market.

Online resources include PowerPoint lecture slides for each chapter, sample answers for discussion questions, and a test bank. Please visit www.routledge.com/9781032973951.

Květa Olšanová is Associate Professor at the Prague University of Economics and Business. Dr. Olšanová has an extensive marketing background and close connections with the luxury industry.

Gina Cook is Professor in the College of Business at Metropolitan State University of Denver in Colorado, USA, where she teaches international business and marketing courses.

Marija Zlatić taught marketing for many years at Prague University of Economics and Business and has recently transitioned into the private sector, focused on luxury strategy and technology.

Mastering Luxury Management

The luxury sector is a rapidly evolving and competitive global industry, requiring premium brands to be dynamic and innovative in their business and management decisions to remain relevant. This series meets the need for thorough yet practical and accessible textbooks that address the complexity of the luxury industry and challenges facing its management.

Mastering Luxury Management is a valuable resource for Luxury Management courses, helping readers to acquire an in-depth understanding of contemporary theories and how they apply in practice, alongside recognizing trends and developments that may shape the future marketplace. Individually, each text provides essential reading for a core topic. A range of consistent pedagogical features are used across the series, including international case studies that demonstrate practical applications in the luxury context.

Each text will be invaluable reading for advanced undergraduate and postgraduate students, in particular those studying for a Master's or MBA in Luxury Management or Luxury Brand Management, as they provide tools and strategies for a successful future career in luxury.

Strategic Luxury Management
Value Creation and Creativity for Competitive Advantage
David Millán Planelles

Contemporary Issues in Luxury Brand Management
Edited by Sylvie Studente and Eleonora Cattaneo

Research Methods in Luxury Management
Michael J.G. Parnwell, Kelly Meng

Luxury Marketing and Brand Strategy
Theory and Practice for a Changing World
Květa Olšanová, Gina Cook and Marija Zlatić

For more information about this series, please visit: www.routledge.com/Mastering-Luxury-Management/book-series/LM

Luxury Marketing and Brand Strategy

Theory and Practice for a Changing World

Květa Olšanová, Gina Cook
and Marija Zlatić

Routledge
Taylor & Francis Group
LONDON AND NEW YORK

Designed cover image: ilbusca/Getty Images

First published 2026
by Routledge
4 Park Square, Milton Park, Abingdon, Oxon OX14 4RN

and by Routledge
605 Third Avenue, New York, NY 10158

Routledge is an imprint of the Taylor & Francis Group, an informa business

British Library Cataloguing-in-Publication Data
A catalogue record for this book is available from the British Library

ISBN: 978-1-032-97433-0 (hbk)
ISBN: 978-1-032-97395-1 (pbk)
ISBN: 978-1-003-59370-6 (ebk)

DOI: 10.4324/9781003593706

Typeset in Sabon
by Apex CoVantage, LLC

Access the Support Material: www.routledge.com/9781032973951

Contents

Preface

This book, *Luxury Marketing and Brand Strategy: Theory and Practice for a Changing World*, represents the culmination of a long period of research and professional cooperation by our international team of authors. Our partnership was initiated through opportunities created via globalization, and we have happily cooperated for a number of years. In this text, our team – Květa Olšanová, Gina Cook and Marija Zlatić – proposes a guide for anyone intrigued by the complex world of luxury marketing. Students, luxury brand managers and professionals looking to update their knowledge can use this book to gain a comprehensive overview of the unique characteristics and challenges of the luxury industry. Marketers of non-luxury brands can find the strategies applied here as inspiration for adjusting various parts of the marketing mix to increase profitability or reach alternative target groups.

This book is a significantly updated and expanded English edition of the original Czech title published in 2023 in Prague by Grada Publishing. It offers an in-depth exploration of luxury brand management, incorporating a more international perspective. This edition includes the latest market developments, recent brand trends and the use of innovative examples, with new mini-cases added. In addition to the core segment of personal luxury goods, the text also includes snapshots of other lux segments, such as luxury cars and hospitality, providing readers with a broader view of the luxury industry.

The title is designed as the foundation for undergraduate or graduate students in luxury marketing courses. Readers can join a straightforward yet engaging journey through the complexities of managing luxury brands. Drawing on the authors' extensive academic and professional experience, a rich mix of theoretical insights and real-life mini-case studies from prestigious brands, such as Cartier, Van Cleef & Arpels, Chanel, Ferrari, Orient-Express and many others, is presented.

The book is based on the foundational aspects of luxury brand business strategy. It characterizes the defining features of luxury brands, the dominance of large luxury groups and, at the same time, the resilience of independent brands having rich histories. It explores the delicate balance required to maintain a brand's luxury status amid evolving consumer expectations, technological advances and sustainability concerns. Readers will gain insight into innovative marketing strategies, from the use of NFTs and blockchain to integrating AI and the metaverse in improving the customer experience.

The authors' focus on the latest trends and potential future directions in luxury marketing positions *Luxury Marketing and Brand Strategy: Theory and Practice for a Changing World* as a key academic resource and practical guide for orientation and potential success in the dynamic luxury market. In sum, the text provides a strategic framework for luxury brand management. It guides brands in balancing tradition with innovation as they navigate modern challenges and seize opportunities in a rapidly evolving global market.

Organization

The content is organized into seven chapters profiling the specifics of luxury brand management. Each chapter is a blend of theoretical approaches from academic sources and credible consultancy reports as well as examples of how the approaches are reflected in the business practices of the leading luxury brands and groups. The theory is applied in numerous cutting-edge mini-cases, illustrating current challenges facing the top global luxury brands, and how the organizations and brands have adapted (or not) to succeed creatively in a period of challenging market dynamics. The text has a global geographic scope, and special effort has been made to include current research and cover emerging trends. Each chapter is accompanied by keywords, an explanation and a set of application questions to reflect the theoretical foundations and provide opportunities to apply critical thinking.

The first chapter – "Flashback to the origins of luxury" – includes a short introduction to luxury from the historical point of view, illustrating how the concept has evolved while staying closely tied to status, power and exclusivity. Understanding the historical context helps explain how owning luxurious items and lux lifestyles have shaped societies, from ancient civilizations up to the modern day. Starting with its spiritual roots in the Paleolithic era, the text follows luxury's journey through history, including the extravagant lifestyles of ancient Egypt, Greece and Rome. Philosophers during the Renaissance celebrated luxury as a form of artistic and cultural excellence. The Enlightenment, however, questioned its moral impact and criticized its excesses. Later, the Industrial Revolution brought about changes that made luxury more accessible. Today, the ownership of luxury goods in the broad sense is often tied to ideas of heritage, with brands using their histories to create stories that feel exclusive and timeless. The chapter suggests that understanding these historical shifts is key to appreciating how luxury now functions, which in turn enables the effective management of luxury brands.

Chapter 2 – "The worlds of luxury" – overviews the complex nature of the global luxury industry, emphasizing its historical evolution as well as the segmentation of its principal markets. The luxury industry is categorized into eight primary sectors: luxury cars, hospitality, fine wines and spirits, gourmet food, high-end furniture, fine art, private jets and yachts and cruises. These sectors constitute a substantial share of the luxury economy, with personal luxury goods, luxury cars and hospitality accounting for 80% of the market in 2023. Special attention is paid to the personal luxury sector, including its consolidation during the 1990s, driven by key corporations such as LVMH, Richemont and others that now dominate the sector. The chapter emphasizes strategies that differentiate luxury brands from premium and mass offerings and luxury business strategies that underpin the distinct positioning of luxury brands.

The third chapter – "Luxury geography and demographics: Understanding the basics of 'who' and 'where'" – provides an understanding of the socioeconomic profiles and geographic concentrations of luxury consumers needed for effective brand management. The luxury sector is not the exclusive domain of older, affluent consumers whose behaviors are well known and predictable; it is now significantly shaped by younger generations, particularly Gen Z and Gen Alpha. They will potentially evolve into luxury customers whose individual values, preferences and expectations may challenge traditional luxury business strategies, since reaching them may demand innovative approaches in branding, communication and product offerings. The geographic distribution of luxury consumption is also shifting. Asian markets (China in particular) are increasingly becoming dominant. This move demands that luxury brands, including the most traditional ones, adapt to accommodate these markets' cultural contexts while remaining true to well-established identities based on long heritage and typically European culture.

The principles that define luxury brand management as distinct from traditional marketing are explored in Chapter 4, titled "The enduring principles specific to luxury brand management." It emphasizes that luxury brands are built through a unique strategy, often different from the rules of the fast-moving consumer goods (FMCG) market. Critical aspects of luxury brand management include cultivating emotional connections with consumers, maintaining the rarity and exclusivity of products and preserving heritage and craftsmanship. The chapter introduces the *anti-laws* of luxury, which guide the industry away from competitive positioning and mass marketing, focusing instead on incomparable identity and exclusivity. Through case studies (Panthère du Cartier, Ferrari, Van Cleef & Arpels) and many examples, the chapter demonstrates how luxury brands maintain their aura of exclusivity, scarcity and being desired by clients, ensuring their long-term success.

"Distribution: Balancing traditional channels and e-commerce," Chapter 5, explores the evolution of distribution strategies within the luxury goods market. The main focus is committed to the mix between traditional retail and e-commerce. Brick-and-mortar stores remain dominant in luxury, but the rapid rise of digital channels impacts the sector. Major players like Kering and Richemont have reported significant growth in online sales, driven by the pandemic and generational shifts toward millennials and Gen Z. The chapter highlights the rise of mono-brand stores and experiential retail as important recovery strategies, complemented by the integration of omnichannel CRM systems, particularly in Asia. It explores the continuous development of social commerce (s-commerce) and live stream shopping in some geographies, underscoring their appeal to younger, digitally native consumers. Examples and case studies, such as Smartzer's live shopping technology, illustrate the industry's ambitions toward exploring digital personalization and omnichannel strategies. Finally, the chapter provides insights into how luxury brands balance exclusivity and accessibility in a digitally-driven era, ensuring brand loyalty and long-term market relevance.

Chapter 6 – "Corporate social responsibility and sustainability" – presents incorporating corporate social responsibility (CSR) and sustainability in the luxury sector, determined mainly by younger consumers' demand and evolving investor expectations. The paradox between luxury and sustainability is discussed, as well as the industry's historical resistance to sustainability and its gradual transition toward environmentally and socially responsible practices. Luxury brands increasingly align their strategies with the United Nations Sustainable Development Goals (SDGs), particularly climate action (SDG 13) and responsible production (SDG 12). The mini-case studies of the Stella McCartney and Chanel brands illustrate innovative approaches to environmental protection. The Hermès case study is focused on the importance of incorporating CSR targets into the company's strategy from the highest levels of the management hierarchy. Implementation of digital product passports for supply chain tracking and counterfeiting prevention are outlined, and the potential of the second-hand markets in luxury is highlighted. The chapter also underscores the importance of CSR in brand communication and how it impacts purchase intention.

Finally, the seventh chapter – "Emerging technologies in the management of luxury brands" – explores the impact of technological developments on brand management. It highlights the potential for luxury brands to engage younger consumer segments by integrating digital innovations while still preserving traditional brand values – a necessity in order to retain the exclusivity in line with luxury business strategy. As technology investment rises in the luxury sector, brands leverage artificial intelligence (AI), blockchain and the metaverse to offer more immersive and personalized experiences. The chapter discusses various examples, such as the Aura Blockchain Consortium, which enhances transparency and authentication in product purchases, as well as innovative collaborations such as Tiffany's CryptoPunk NFTs, which combine art, rarity and technology to appeal to digital-native consumers. The chapter also addresses the role of NFTs in digital ownership, the potential of the metaverse as a space for experiential luxury and the challenges of aligning digital initiatives with the exclusivity and heritage of luxury brands. The chapter demonstrates that luxury brands must deal with complex digital landscapes to remain relevant and innovative, engaging future generations through new digital experiences and web3 technologies.

Luxury is forever – thus, it was not this book's intent to capture every single ever-evolving aspect of this industry and its customers. Rather, it was our goal to focus on the timeless principles within the context of today's challenges facing the industry. Numerous examples and mini-cases highlight that the basic principles of the luxury business strategy are valid despite the evolving technological or communication tools. The *savoir-faire* that demands time to develop and produce luxury items remains a necessary condition to succeed among demanding luxury customers.

As a whole, the chapters illustrate the evolution and complex dynamics of the global luxury industry while emphasizing historical context together with modern day market dynamics. The text explores the socioeconomic profiles and geographic concentrations of luxury consumers, examines key elements of luxury brand management and illustrates the impact of emerging technologies. The importance of sustainability and corporate social responsibility is emphasized. Through the use of various mini-case studies and examples, the book considers how lux brands maintain exclusivity while adapting to contemporary challenges to ensure long-term success.

About the authors

Květa Olšanová is an academic and professional with an extensive background in business and marketing and close connections with the luxury industry in Czech Republic. She graduated from Prague University of Economics and Business, the top business school in the region, and built a successful career in marketing with global brands in companies like Kraft Foods (now Mondelēz International) and Citibank. In 2015, she earned her PhD from the same university and transitioned into academia. Dr. Olšanová teaches International Marketing, Luxury Marketing and Marketing Management at the Faculty of International Business at Prague University of Economics and Business, sharing her extensive industry experience with students at both the undergraduate and graduate levels. Her dedication to education and research led to her appointment as Associate Professor in 2023. Dr. Olšanová publishes in both national and international journals, and her monograph, published by Grada Publishing in 2023, became the cornerstone for this book published by Routledge under the title *Luxury Marketing and Brand Strategy: Theory and Practice for a Changing World.*

Gina Cook's professional background includes more than 25 years of cross-functional, cross-industry and multinational experience. She is a professor in the College of Business at Metropolitan State University of Denver in Colorado, USA, where she teaches international business and marketing courses. Dr. Cook also serves as the Director of the International Business programs at MSU and is a member of the board at the World Trade Center Denver. She previously lived in the Czech Republic for 15 years, where she was a faculty member teaching graduate courses at the Prague University of Economics and Business. Dr. Cook has also served as an international visiting professor on several occasions, most recently at Shandong University of Finance and Economics in Jinan, China. She has lived, worked, studied and traveled in more than 70 countries. Dr. Cook publishes in both American and international journals and has been a contributing author in two textbooks.

Marija Zlatić is an accomplished academic and business professional who completed her doctoral work at Prague University of Economics and Business in 2012. Dr. Zlatić built a successful academic career, establishing a new subject of luxury marketing for international students and teaching marketing communications and luxury marketing. In 2022, she transitioned into the private sector, co-founded a start-up and now works in the entrepreneurial space. In particular, Dr. Zlatić is currently focused on building strategic marketing practices which combine principles of luxury business and the tech field. Her main research interest is in the area of luxury with an emphasis on human-centric business experience design.

Acknowledgments

We are profoundly grateful to our colleagues and friends who kindly provided their time and shared thoughts to help us clarify concepts and make this text an engaging and cutting-edge resource. We are very grateful to the reviewers for their constructive and insightful comments. And thank you – students, professors and professionals alike – for selecting our text. We look forward to working with you!

The Moser and TATIANA brand teams provided us invaluable help not only by granting permissions but also with their countless consultations regarding the success factors of domestic luxury brands. Deep appreciation goes to the SHANG XIA brand team for providing permission to use a photo as well as their helpful attitude when consulting on the text. We would also like to extend our appreciation to Yuga Labs for the profound insights into digital collectibles and permission to use the image of one of the rare CryptoPunks. Further thanks go to the ŠKODA Auto company for sharing valuable perspectives on the automotive industry.

We are deeply grateful to Grada Publishing for their cooperation in the development of a previous version of this book (published in the Czech language) and their kind generosity in allowing us to present an English version to a broader, more global audience.

Heartfelt thanks to Sophia Levine and Nicole Doyle, the editorial team at Routledge. Their high standards, perceptive feedback and constant availability were instrumental in bringing this book to fruition.

The authors would also like to extend gratitude to their academic institutions – the Department of International Business, Faculty of International Relations, at Prague University of Economics and Business as well as the Management Department, College of Business, at Metropolitan State University of Denver – for the unwavering support and commitment to professional development. Their resources and guidance have been pivotal in achieving this professional goal.

Most of all, we would like to thank our friends and families, who have participated in the long process of bringing this project to life. Their patience and kind support were invaluable and enabled us to bring this text forward. We are also profoundly grateful for the highly productive cooperation among our team!

Chapter 1

Flashback to the origins of luxury

Luxury is a phenomenon. Luxury is an ideology. Luxury is a philosophy that questions the notions of virtue, morality, indulgence, conspicuousness, progress and development. The concept of luxury is rich and has evolved to become complex and multivariable. Plato and Socrates acknowledged that luxury would not only be an "inevitable element of civilized society, but a defining one" (Quartz, 2017). People's relationship with luxury has always been volatile, confronting values and priorities, right and wrong, good and bad and necessity vs. wastefulness. Luxury doesn't necessarily refer just to a specific category of products because it indicates a conceptual and symbolic dimension which is identified in the cultural values of society of a particular historical period (Brun & Castelli, 2013). Finally, luxury is a concept as old as humankind, and it has been an integral part of the history of civilizations.

To fully understand luxury, one needs to unveil many layers hidden in the history of this societal, economic, cultural and business phenomenon. Authors usually question the definition of luxury and the origin of the word itself. However, the historical perspective of luxury is rarely in focus. The history of luxury is the history of human society. It tells the story of the political and cultural expressions of luxury among different social strata as well as the rise of human wealth, appreciation of the extraordinary and collective indulgence (Lakovic, 2023).

The relevance of exploring the history of luxury is as important as the etymology of the word or defining the term. What luxury represented over the different ages provides us with valuable insights into the essential functions of luxury like status, success or power signaling. By understanding luxury as a manifestation of human desires, perceptions and social norms, we can appreciate its complexities and implications in contemporary society (Turunen, 2017). Thus, forms of luxury often tell a delicate story about the evolution of luxury within society over centuries.

Today's manifestations of luxury in products, brands and services differ from their historical manifestations (Turunen, 2017). Still, denying the history of luxury would be as harmful as denying the identity of any heritage brand we consume today. What are genuine luxury brands without roots? Kapferer and Bastien (2009) debated that the roots are, in fact, relevant to today's brands. According to them, history enabled the brands to build a cult of inherited values, making them stand out as unique and authentic. When you look more closely,

DOI: 10.4324/9781003593706-1

you will see that the brands use history to leverage tradition and heritage. People buy into that pedigree and are willing to pay for the time embodied in the ingredients, pieces that have rare know-how, are preserved and were made with skills worth paying for and collecting. The authors concluded that it is not only the history but the myth created around luxury that counts. For example, writing "Est. 1889" or "Founded 1889" or "Since 1889" on a brand is not luxury. Instead, creating a story and status symbols signaling some epic moment is what bridges the gap between the academic understanding of luxury and the practical application of its signals (Kapferer & Bastien, 2009).

This is why the next part takes a chronological view of the historical evolution of luxury, clarifies many misconceptions and hopefully contributes to a better contextual understanding of the true origins of luxury per se – luxury not only as a business and marketing term but as an ideological engine of societal growth and prosperity. In addition, it also helps to understand how the codes of luxury business were sourced.

1.1 Just how old is luxury?

The exact "birth" of luxury is hard to determine. Some forms of luxury are believed to have existed in the first organized, hierarchical societies. Luxury goods have been symbols of power and status, differentiating those higher up the hierarchical ladder. Looking at how past societies were organized, we find various examples of unique items, ornaments, materials and artifacts only accessible to specific members or groups. Over centuries, owning particular objects or acquiring unique goods was regarded negatively. Thus, luxury has been historically seen as a divider.

Throughout history, mankind has developed philosophies and mechanisms to utilize the power of luxury (Pinkhasov & Nair, 2014), posing the dilemma of whether the existence of luxury is a pointless extravagance or a powerful driver of artistic and technical discoveries. Some of the first manifestations of luxury artifacts tell us much more than what we can naively equalize with money, showoff or bling. Luxury products represent symbols, the whole universe of rituals and the vision of self-affirmation, but they are also at the forefront of creativity and innovation. Examples are numerous: the first writing instruments, the first bottle to preserve perfume, extracting colors, pyramids and soap.

1.1.1 Early manifestations of luxury: Lavish spiritual luxury

The earliest indications of luxury as a societal phenomenon can be found in the **Paleolithic period,** which spanned approximately 2.5 million years ago to 10,000 B.C. During this era, luxury was exclusively perceived as a collective spiritual concept, taking on a predominantly non-material and spiritual essence (Lakovic, 2023). This marks the genesis of luxury as something extraordinary, godlike and distinct from the everyday. Early societies expressed luxury through ceremonial practices such as communal singing or praying. However, with the emergence of the first civilizations, such as the Mesopotamians, Maya and early Chinese, luxury began to adopt a more tangible and materialistic form. Early civilizations also showcased their power and affluence by possessing grandiose palaces, sculptures, ornaments, gold, precious jewelry and opulent clothing.

Ancient Egypt stands out as an example of opulence and is characterized as a hierarchical society governed by specific rules. The pharaohs and priests represented the top of the social pyramid in Egypt. Their lifestyles involved extravagant, ostentatious luxury, which is also one of the ways status and power were expressed. They had access to excessive goods, far out of the reach of the general population. This, in combination with the rituals surrounding the afterlife, illustrate how possessions emerged as symbols of power, prestige and personal achievement. Luxury filled every aspect of Egyptian upper class life, from the extravagant homes decorated with gold to the use of rare perfumes reserved for the highest of society. Ostrich feathers (shown in Picture 1.1) and eggs were considered luxury items for the Ancient Egyptians. Hunting the giant birds was a royal sport enabling rulers to demonstrate their control over nature (Euronews, 2017).

In death, the pursuit of extravagance continued with the belief that one's possessions would accompany the deceased into the afterlife. Consequently, tombs were over-decorated, filled with jewelry, horses, ships, weapons and other luxurious items alongside the deceased. A connection between material opulence and mortality was established by the practices closely linking luxury with the concepts of the afterlife and funeral ceremonies.

Moving forward to the ancient worlds of **Greece and Rome**, one sees a new approach surrounding the morality of luxury. Some viewed obtaining a luxurious lifestyle as a driving force for societal progress, but others considered it a threat to both integrity and morality. This debate over the qualities as well as immoralities of luxury sparked considerable social disruption, with tensions escalating into civil unrest.

The Ancient Romans used the term *luxuria* to describe sinful excess and rebellious living. This debate reached new heights as the elite confronted contrasting visions of asceticism versus lavishness. Opulent displays of wealth, from exquisite jewelry to fine silverware, became markers of social status and influence – valuable insight into the complex social relations of the Empire. Among the ultimate symbols of prestige were robes dyed in Tyrian purple, a color derived from the rare secretion of sea snails (Picture 1.2). These luxurious garments epitomized the height of Roman opulence and power (Euronews, 2017).

1.1.2 The prosperous hereditary luxury: Middle Ages, Renaissance and Enlightenment age

During **medieval times**, luxury was associated with hereditary succession as birthright and social standing determined access to luxury. Inheritance laws articulated the passing down of wealth, estates and prestigious titles from one generation to the next, ensuring the preservation of familial privilege. Symbols of noble life were seen in luxurious clothing made from rare, imported materials, lavish feasts, exotic spices, indulgent leisure activities and courtly entertainment.

Picture 1.1 Ostrich feather fan. By Daderot, licensed under the Creative Commons CC0 1.0 Universal Public Domain Dedication, available at (Wikimedia Commons, 2024).

Picture 1.2 *Haustellum brandaris* as a source for Tyrian purple. By M. Violante, licensed under the Creative Commons Attribution 2.5 Generic license, available at (Wikimedia Commons, 2007).

Alongside the royal families and nobility, the Church demonstrated considerable influence in medieval society and played a significant role a consumer of luxury. Religious leaders adorned artifacts and garments with elaborate decorations, including golden embroidery, to symbolize the spiritual wealth and authority of the Church. Those in society who pursued aspects of luxury were also seen as deviating from the common "good practices" of moral men and women. Practices of hedonism or "earthly pleasures" were considered sinful. This perception was reinforced as the word *luxury* entered the English language from French, initially carrying a sexual connotation as early as 1340 (Gurzki, 2020).

The Renaissance and Enlightenment were two distinct periods in European history characterized by significant cultural, intellectual and social developments. The Renaissance and Enlightenment offer contrasting perspectives on the nature and significance of luxury. The Renaissance, from the 14th to 17th century, was marked by a rebirth of classical learning, artistic innovation and flourishing culture. It celebrated artistic splendor and opulence. In Renaissance Italy, particularly in city-states like Florence and Venice, luxury was synonymous with refinement and creative excellence. The upper classes commissioned recognized artists and architects to create magnificent palaces with extravagant artwork and decorative gardens. Fashion also played a crucial role, with rare fabrics, complex embroidery and extravagant garments serving as symbols of wealth and status. Luxury during the Renaissance was deeply intertwined with the patronage of the arts, as wealthy merchants and noble patrons competed for prestige through their support of artistic endeavors. Luxury was shown generously – often and everywhere.

The Enlightenment, or the Age of Reason, flourished in the 17th and 18th centuries. It was an era of intellectual inquiry, scientific progress and social reform. The Enlightenment critiqued excessive luxury consumption and advocated for moderation and rationality in all aspects of life. Philosophers such as Voltaire, Rousseau and Montesquieu critiqued the excesses of the aristocracy and advocated for a more egalitarian society (Gurzki, 2020). Luxury during the Enlightenment was viewed with skepticism because it was seen as a potential threat to social equality and moral integrity. The enlightenment ideals promoted a more refined view of physical wealth. Nevertheless, the upper classes continued to enjoy extravagant lifestyles, accompanied by ownership of luxury goods.

Picture 1.3 Elisabeth Vigée-Lebrun – Marie-Antoinette dit "à la Rose." By DcoetzeeBot, public domain, available at (Wikimedia Commons, 2011).

All of this brought profound social shifts, including the American and French revolutions and the collapse of the French monarchy. These events influenced the concept of luxury from the economic and philosophical points of view. It was then that promotion of free market economics was widespread among philosophers and economists alike.

Among the voices that emerged during this era, philosopher David Hume was particularly noteworthy for examining luxury in his essay "Of Luxury." Hume distinguished between what he termed *good* and *bad* luxury. He associated *good* luxury with the refinement and advancement of the arts, contrasting it with *bad* luxury, which he deemed excessive and harmful. Hume advocated for a balanced perspective, suggesting that a society could engage with luxury in a virtuous, moral and ethical manner (Cunningham, 2005).

1.1.3 The path towards "democratized" luxury

After the French Revolution, which marked the end of the monarchy, the hereditary approach to luxury diminished. The Industrial Revolution brought the rise of the bourgeoisie, profound changes to the distribution of wealth and rise in living standards. This socio-economic shift was discussed in the *Theory of the Leisure Class* from 1899. Here, the economist Thorstein Veblen coined the term "conspicuous consumption." He recognized the changes in production and the growth of the middle class. Thanks to the increase in wealth, they now had an insatiable need for luxury consumption and also to show it. He argued that people of means now engaged in meaningless pursuits (studying dead languages or collecting racing horses) to differentiate themselves from the working class. Those spared from manual labor purchased items primarily aimed at enhancing their status. For instance, a man might invest in a top hat, while a woman might opt for high heels. Female emancipation throughout the late 19th and 20th centuries also contributed to the democratization of luxury. However, luxury was still reserved for a small elite group, since most people lived in underdeveloped economies.

The 20th century saw societal shifts; post-war, people valued life differently, and women gained independence and additional rights. Fashion became more inclusive as the gap between exclusive haute couture and affordable ready-to-wear lines gradually narrowed. Luxury brands broadened their appeal with more accessible products like perfumes. By the century's end, luxury fashion was a global phenomenon. Kapferer and Bastien (2009) suggest that the luxury market of the 20th century was marked by three significant factors: the rise in purchasing power, the democratization of luxury goods and the globalization forces that established the basis for the current luxury scene. As a result, luxury became more widespread across various strata of society, prompting the development of new consumer markets. The introduction of "ready-to-wear" items further democratized luxury by making it accessible to an even broader audience. Luxury brands also extended their reach by introducing entry-level luxury items such as perfumes and accessories (Kapferer & Bastien, 2009).

Paris was at the center of this development, with iconic brands such as Chanel and Dior making it their home. These brands redefined fashion and luxury. Designers like Gabrielle Chanel promoted simple, strong styles, while others like Christian Dior or Jeanne Lanvin emphasized femininity and elegance. These brands not only shaped fashion but also became influential names, each bringing revolutionary perspectives on fashion, luxury and the representation of women's bodies.

1.2 Summary: History of luxury

The perception of luxury has developed over the course of human history and has reflected the social values and aspirations of the various periods. From the spiritual extravagance of ancient Egypt to the moral debate of Greece and Rome, luxury has remained a symbol of status, aspiration and power. As Coco Chanel once said, "Luxury is a necessity that begins where necessity ends" (Picardie, 2017, p. 110).

Interpreting luxury manifestations over time revealed the perpetual nature of luxury. What was regarded as a luxury and had symbolic value at a specific time tells a lot about the desires and pursuits of people on a personal level. Once people fulfill their dreams, those desired objects or products become everyday necessities. As Turunen points out,

> No matter if social development creates social necessities or because living standards rise at a personal level, many goods that were once attainable only to a small group of people can become attainable to all. Therefore, understanding what is regarded as luxury today may indicate tomorrow's necessities.
>
> (2017, p. 27)

Once, even soap was a luxury, similar to having a mobile phone when they were first developed.

The history of luxury discloses a lot about the functions and meanings of luxury goods. From the perspective of today's luxury brand manager, understanding these functions and their evolution can help in setting the direction for brand creation, management and growth. To quote Kapferer and Bastien (2009), "History gives depth to a brand and timelessness to its objects" (p. 87). Does this mean that we cannot have any new luxury brands without history? Not at all. The trick is that history doesn't always have to be that of the brand itself. Codes for luxury brands can be created from various social, temporal, cultural or environmental contexts or different levels of the imagination. Thus, we can distinguish between three types of history: true history, allocation of true historical elements in a new and different way and creation of a new contemporary legend. The latter was the strategy used by many American brands such as Ralph Lauren, Donna Karan or Calvin Klein (Kapferer & Bastien, 2009).

As we continue to explore the fascinating history of luxury, we are reminded of its enduring significance in shaping human societies and cultures across the ages. In conclusion, to reference the famous words inscribed on every dial of the Rolex Oyster watch, as history shows, luxury is perpetual.

Key terms

Conspicuous Consumption: A term created by Thorstein Veblen, referring to displaying wealth by acquiring luxury goods to increase social status.
Cultural Significance of Luxury: How luxury influences societal values, aspirations and power dynamics throughout history.
Democratization of Luxury: The process by which luxury goods and services became more accessible to a broader audience, particularly through the rise of the middle class and mass production.
Hereditary Luxury: A concept prevalent in the Middle Ages, where access to luxury was determined by birthright and social standing, passed down through generations.
Historical Evolution of Luxury: The development of luxury from old civilizations through the Middle Ages to the present. It includes the changing functions and meanings of luxury.
Spiritual Luxury: The earliest form of luxury, characterized by non-material, spiritual practices such as communal rituals and ceremonies in ancient societies.
Status Symbol: A consistent approach to luxury through different historical periods. The use of luxury items to signify social status, success and power.

Discussion questions

1. How has the concept of luxury evolved throughout history? What factors have driven these changes?
2. In what ways does the democratization of luxury impact the traditional notions of exclusivity and status associated with luxury goods?
3. How do historical and cultural contexts influence the perception and value of luxury in different societies?
4. Discuss the extent to which luxury can exist without historical roots, or is a brand's history essential to its luxury status?
5. How do philosophical perspectives on luxury, such as those from the Enlightenment, continue to influence modern views on consumption and materialism?

Reference list

Brun, A., & Castelli, C. (2013, November). The Nature of Luxury: A Consumer Perspective. *International Journal of Retail & Distribution Management*, 41, 823–847.
Cunningham, A. (2005). David Hume's Account of Luxury. *Journal of History of Economic Taught*, 3(27), 231–250.

Euronews. (2017). *A Brief History of Luxury*. Retrieved April 2024, from euronews.com: https://www.euronews.com/green/2017/09/18/a-brief-history-of-luxury

Gurzki, H. (2020). A Brief History of Luxury and Consumption. In *The Creation of the Extraordinary*. Springer Gabler.

Kapferer, J. N., & Bastien, V. (2009). *The Luxury Strategy: Break the Rules of Marketing to Build Luxury Brands*. Kogan Page.

Lakovic, I. (2023). *The Luxurist*. Retrieved March 2024, from luxury integrated.com: www.luxuryintegrated.com

Picardie, J. (2017). *Coco Chanel: The Legend and the Life*. London: HarperCollinsPublishers.

Pinkhasov, M., & Nair, R. J. (2014). *Real Luxury: How Luxury Brands Can Create Value for the Long Term*. Palgrave Macmillan.

Quartz. (2017). *Quartz*. Retrieved April 2024, from qz.com: https://qz.com/quartzy

Turunen, L. L. (2017). *Interpretations of Luxury*. Palgrave Macmillan.

Wikimedia Commons. (2007, March 18). *File:vHaustellum brandaris 000.jpg*. Retrieved September 2024, from commons.wikimedia.org: https://commons.wikimedia.org/wiki/File:Haustellum_brandaris_000.jpg

Wikimedia Commons. (2011, February 19). *File:Louise Elisabeth Vigée-Lebrun – Marie-Antoinette dit « à la Rose » – Google Art Project.jpg*. Retrieved September 2024, from wikidata.org: https://www.wikidata.org/wiki/Q47365#/media/File:Louise_Elisabeth_Vigée-Lebrun_-_Marie-Antoinette_dit_«_à_la_Rose_»_-_Google_Art_Project.jpg

Wikimedia Commons. (2024, February 26). *File:Brisé Fan, Ostrich Feathers, Tortoise Shell, Whale Bone, and Silk, 1880–1900, from the Cooper Hewitt, Smithsonian Design Museum – CHSDM-1954-36-1MattFlynn.jpg*. Retrieved September 2024, from wikimedia.org: https://commons.wikimedia.org/wiki/File:Brisé_fan,_ostrich_feathers,_tortoise_shell,_whale_bone,_and_silk,_1880-1900,_from_the_Cooper_Hewitt,_Smithsonian_Design_Museum_-_CHSDM-1954-36-1MattFlynn.jpg

Chapter 2

The worlds of luxury

In addition to personal luxury goods, the overall luxury market covers the following eight segments: luxury cars, luxury hospitality, fine wines and spirit, gourmet food and fine dining, high-end furniture and housewares, fine art, private jets and yachts and finally luxury cruises. The proportion of the particular segments is shown on Figure 2.1.

Together, luxury cars, hospitality and personal luxury goods make up 80% of the market. In 2023, the luxury overall market's retail sales value increased by 8%–10% vs. 2022, reaching €1.5 trillion; this is 18%–20% above 2019 levels. All segments grew in 2023, including luxury hospitality and cruises, which have been the slowest to reach pre-COVID levels. In 2023, spending continued to favor tangible luxury goods. The highest absolute growth between 2019 and 2023 was in personal luxury goods, experience-based goods (like fine art, wines and spirits, private jets and yachts, luxury cruises) and luxury cars. The smallest growth was experienced in the luxury hospitality segment (Bain & Company, 2024).

2.1 Defining personal luxury: The essence of excellence

The personal luxury goods market is central to the luxury industry and is often considered "the luxury" among the general public since the brands of personal luxury are widely visible and recognized. The personal luxury industry only consolidated as a sector in the late 1990s, mainly thanks to the visions of companies such as LVMH (Moët Hennessy-Louis Vuitton SE) and Richemont. Bernard Arnault started applying the fundamentals of strategic management when building the LVMH conglomerate. From a $20 billion market, it grew – thanks to globalization, new wealth creation opportunities, new customer segments, new markets, digital communications, the growth of international tourism and cultural convergence – into a segment where the Top 100 luxury goods companies generated $387 billion in revenues in 2022. The largest groups are shown in Table 2.1 (Okonkwo-Pézard, 2017; Deloitte, 2023; Som & Blanckaert, 2021).

DOI: 10.4324/9781003593706-2

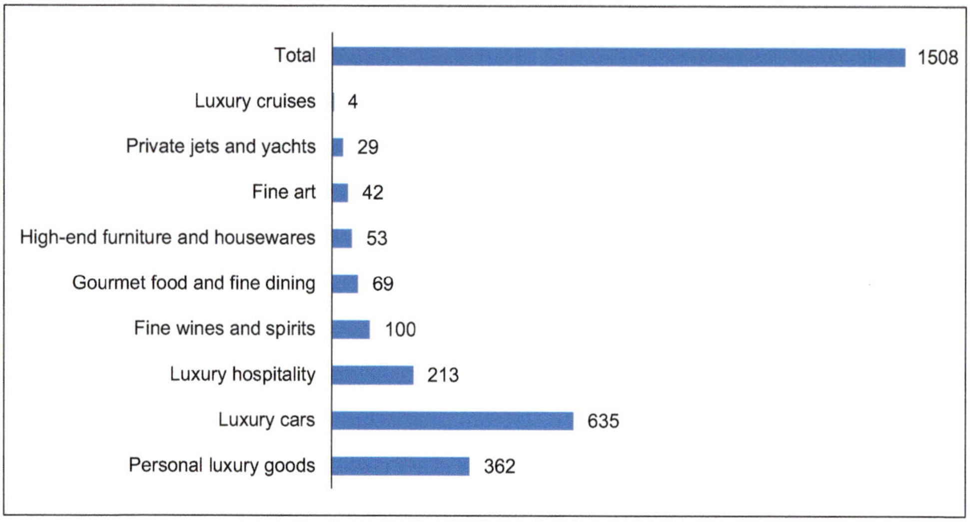

Figure 2.1 Worldwide luxury market, 2023E purchases value (in billions EUR). Authors based on data available from (Bain & Company, 2024).

During FY2022, the Top 100 luxury goods companies generated composite sales of $347 billion, up from the $305 billion registered in FY2021. This sales increase signals the excellent state of the luxury industry after the pandemic years. The importance of the biggest luxury companies demonstrates that the Top 10 generate 57% of the total Top 100 luxury goods revenues. The minimum revenue threshold to enter the Top 100 was $284 million. The minimum sales size for a company to enter the Top 10 was nearly $8.4 billion, compared to nearly $7.2 billion in 2021.

LVMH continues its leadership position through its sales contribution to the Top 10 sales (31%), followed by Kering (11%) and Richemont SA (10%). Hermès International was in the top ten for the first time in the fiscal year 2020, reaching 9th place, currently in 8th place. On the other hand, the Swatch Group dropped three places and ended up in 13th place in 2021 and in 12th place in 2022.

All of the Top 10 companies reported growth in sales, remained profitable and collectively achieved a higher profit than the combined Top 100 organizations in the ranking. Several smaller companies reported losses.

The major acquisitions were done by Kering (Maui Jim eyewear, Creed luxury fragrance and Valentino (30% with 100% option), Richemont (Italian shoemaker Gianvito Rossi), Estée Lauder (TOM FORD brand) and L'Oréal (Aēsop brand). Finally, Tapestry was reported as potentially the next Top 10 member due to the acquisition of Capri Holdings Limited (Michael Kors, Versace and Jimmy Choo brands) (Deloitte, 2023).

2.2 Characteristics of luxury brands in the personal luxury segment

From an etymological perspective, the word luxury comes from Latin *luxuria*, meaning extravagance and excess. *Luxuria* was used to describe rebellious living and sinful excess, as discussed previously. It still has an ambivalent meaning – positive in terms of deviating from

Table 2.1 Ranking of luxury brand groups by sales in 2022. Authors based on data available at (Deloitte, 2023, p. 17).

Sales rank	Group name	Country of origin	FY2022 sales (US$M)	FY2022 Total revenue (US$M)	FY2022 Net profit margin	FY2019–2022 Luxury goods sales CAGR
1	LVMH Moët Hennessy-Louis Vuitton SE	France	59,869	83,241	18.6%	19.4%
2	Kering SA	France	21,394	21,394	18.3%	8.6%
3	Compagnie Financière Richemont SA	Switzerland	19,248	22,276	10.8 %	11.5%
4	The Estée Lauder Companies Inc.	US	17,737	17,737	13.6%	6.1%
5	Chanel Limited	France	17,224	17,224	26.7%	12.0%
6	L'Oréal Luxe	UK	15,388	15,388	n/a	9.9%
7	Chow Tai Fook Jewelry Group Limited	China/Hong Kong SAR	12,563	12,709	7.0%	14.0%
8	Hermès International SCA	France	12,196	12,196	29.1%	19.0%
9	Rolex SA	Switzerland	10,336 e	10,336 est.	Not available	13.8%
10	PVH Corp.	US	8,364	9,155	10.4%	1.2%
Top 10*			**194,319**	**221,656**	**17.5%**	**12.8%**
Top 100*			**346,989**	**386,963**	**13.4%**	**8.4%**
Top 10 share of Top 100			**56.0%**	**57.3%**	**76.4%**	

the norm, innovative and beautiful, negative in terms of profusion, extravagance, greediness and excessiveness. In the English language, the word lost its pejorative meaning stemming from licentiousness and debauchery in the 17th century, when it began to be used as "something comfortable beyond the necessities of life" (Online Etymology Dictionary, 2022).

The term *luxus* signifies "all that is exuberant, expensive, refined, and sumptuous" (Som & Blanckaert, 2021, p. 30). According to Kapferer, *luxury* is an "elusive concept"; hence the ambiguity of its definitions (Kapferer & Bastien, 2012, pp. 45–46). When trying to define this concept, it is first necessary to distinguish between the **absolute and relative concepts of** luxury, **one's own or personal luxury**, luxury as a **sector** and, last but not least, **luxury as a business model and strategy**.

Typical spontaneous associations with the word luxury include yachts, private jets or residences around the world. In this concept of **absolute luxury**, these are goods inaccessible to most people in today's society. In the past, art, parallel to today's luxury brands, was created primarily for the church, the nobility or later for the rich bourgeoisie, and it was absolutely inaccessible to ordinary people. Nowadays, the concept of absolute luxury is attributed to a latent social function of restoring social stratification, especially in countries that position themselves as an otherwise classless society, the USA, for example. The concept of **relative luxury** is based on the provision of utility in the form of a small pleasure, which is not a functional necessity for a person. For example, a weekend visit to a more expensive restaurant is a relative luxury for families in many countries and one they consciously indulge in and enjoy. People who decide to fulfil their own dreams and undertake an expedition to Antarctica or Kilimanjaro perceive the trip as a personal luxury with which they fulfil their dreams. The concept of personal luxury is highly emotional and also referred to as experiential. Perceiving **luxury as an industrial sector** is another way of seeing it, usually defined by consulting firms such as Bain & Co. or Deloitte. Usually, luxury is associated with expensive products, which are not necessarily always related to luxury brands as discussed in this publication. The reason for this is the availability of data, which is easier to obtain for expensive or premium products; however, for purely luxury brands, their availability is limited or published in incomparable formats. There is often a mix of premium and truly luxury brands. Finally, luxury exists **as a business strategy**, which works with luxury brands according to rules that are significantly different from premium or other brands that do not meet the criteria of luxury (Kapferer & Bastien, 2012).

Given the existence of different definitions of luxury, Kapferer formulated their intersection in the form of six criteria that a luxury brand, unlike premium brands, should meet (Kapferer & Bastien, 2012):

1. A luxury brand means a high-quality **hedonistic experience** or a product made to last a long time, which distinguishes a luxury product from a fashionable one (timelessness vs. contemporary fashion);
2. It is offered at a **price that far exceeds** what its mere functional value would require, it is incomparable with an alternative brand (on the contrary, premium brands are often compared and comparable with each other);
3. It is linked to heritage, unique **know-how** and a specific **culture**;
4. It is available in a **targeted and controlled distribution**;
5. It is offered with personalized accompanying **services**; and
6. It is **a social indicator** that makes the owner or recipient feel exceptional and privileged (unlike premium brands) (Kapferer & Bastien, 2012).

These criteria do not include one characteristic often mentioned in connection with luxury strategy, and that is scarcity or rarity. According to Kapferer, scarcity is part of a luxury strategy, but for some brands, maintaining it is too big a drag on long-term growth, which is why he doesn't specifically list it in his criteria (Kapferer & Bastien, 2012).

The luxury branding system described in the following contains Kapferer's earlier term *griffe* as referring to products at the top of the luxury brand's pyramid. *Griffe* is an untranslatable term in the context of luxury and haute couture. It is based on the French *le griffe* (claw) and in the context of luxury brands means the non-transferable creative signature of the author: "whose reference world is art, whose production is handmade, and whose obsession is to create a work unsurpassed, striking and rendered in such perfection as to strike you in the face" (Kapferer, 1997, pp. 254–255). Dior can therefore be both a *griffe* brand and a luxury brand. Therefore, in the luxury context, the branding pyramid has four layers:

- The base of the imaginary pyramid represents **mass-market brands.** These brands produce goods in large quantities, with a focus on cost efficiency and mass appeal;
- The second tier represents **upper-range brands.** These brands focus on high-quality goods, but their production takes place in factories, often at a larger scale compared to luxury brands;
- The third tier are **luxury brands.** They are known for their craftsmanship and exclusivity, often producing goods in small series in craft workshops. The products are typically handmade, and the craftsmanship is of very high quality;
- And finally, the top of the pyramid is "***The Griffe,***" which refers to the most exclusive level of brands. These brands are known for their unique and highly perfected designs, with the products often viewed as works of art (Kapferer, 1997, pp. 254–255).

It is not possible to change the order of the individual layers of the pyramid. From a *griffe* brand, you can go to mass production if you manage it badly, but it doesn't work the other way around. Luxury brands Dior or Cartier, producing in small series with perfect craftsmanship, also produce perfumes that represent the highest quality in their category. Here the interaction between the individual floors is obvious, as the development of the *griffe* brand's haute couture collection requires investments that mass-producing products of a higher price level can earn.

Keller (2017), unlike Kapferer, who strictly distinguishes between premium and luxury brands, also uses terms related to premium for price or brand image. The definition of luxury brands is based on ten key characteristics, which focus primarily on the architecture of luxury brands and brand equity (BE):

1. Essential to the management of a luxury brand is the maintenance and control of a premium, strong, compact and **long-term consistent image,** which alone can justify the high price of a luxury brand in the eyes of the consumer;
2. Branding a luxury brand involves creating many **intangible associations with the brand and its image,** which are aspirational not only for current customers but also potential new ones who want to imitate existing users or enjoy rewards in the form of the feeling of using or owning a luxury brand;
3. For a high-end customer experience with a luxury brand, all **parts of its marketing mix must be balanced** with absolutely flawless execution;
4. In the case of a luxury brand, its elements play a major role in the value of the brand, that is, in addition to the brand name, the logo, symbols associated with the brand, packaging and so on also influence the image;
5. Important factors in building the value of luxury brands can be **secondary associations with personalities, events or even countries** that have their own positive image and their own positive associations;
6. Retail distribution of luxury brands is highly **selective** and strictly controlled by brand management;
7. Luxury brands use **a premium pricing strategy,** often without significant discounts that could send the wrong signal to customers about brand quality;
8. A clear **emphasis on the architecture of luxury brands** with regard to their exclusivity within the portfolio. When lengthening or deepening a product line, it is necessary to carefully consider which brand elements, current or new, to use for a new product;

9. **Broad definition of competition or reference framework** for luxury brands. Luxury customer spending is far from necessity oriented and is interchangeable across luxury sectors (fashion vs. real estate vs. luxury holidays, etc.); and
10. Brands in the luxury sector are highly vulnerable to the spread of counterfeits. Knowing the protection of their customers and brand image, luxury brand managers must devote considerable effort to **the legal protection of all trademarks** and actively and aggressively intervene against the production and distribution of counterfeits (Keller, 2017, pp. 179–184).

To provide a cleaner methodological definition of the term luxury brands and clarify the definitions, Miller and Mills (2012) examined existing definitions published between 1990 and 2010 using a so-called multiple lens approach. This included the best-known studies by authors such as Kapferer and Bastien (2009), Tynan et al. (1964), Berthon et al. (2009), Vigneron and Johnson (1999, 2004) and 11 other authors or teams of authors. Based on a structured comparison of individual approaches and definitions, they created the optics of seven criteria, the content of which they further defined and created lexical items distinguishing a luxury brand from a premium brand. **The terms related to luxury are magnificence, extravagance, opulence, sumptuous and lavishness, while the items related to premium brands are reputation, honor, esteem, kudos and high regards** (Miller & Mills, 2012).

This provides a basic vocabulary for comparing a luxury and premium brand; in other words, what branded luxury is and how it differs from a premium brand. Another term encountered in luxury theory is a **fashion brand.** A summary of the criteria distinguishing between luxury, fashion and premium brands was summarized by Kapferer and Bastien (2012) into a so-called luxury, fashion and premium positioning triangle. Fashion brands distinguish the wearer from the crowd, adding him/her to the clan indulging in the same brand, but they do not provide social stratification or social promotion. **Fashion collections are ephemeral, while luxury brands are characterized by timelessness, incomparability and rarity.** Premium brands are of high quality with a good price vs. quality ratio. A fashion brand is about seduction based on permanent renewal – every season needs a new bestseller that will go out of fashion in a few years. Therefore, according to this business model, product quality is not a core value in fashion, and it does not make sense for companies to invest fundamentally in it. That is why most fashion brands reduce production costs by outsourcing their production to Southeast Asian countries. Unsold inventory is quickly sold off at the end of the season (Kapferer & Bastien, 2012). Fashion brands are further characterized by the use of licenses to penetrate other categories to increase financial income faster (Bastien & Kapferer, 2013).

In order to define luxury brands, it is still necessary to specify the dimensions of luxury scales used to measure the perception of them. De Barnier et al. (2012) combined three well-known scales to identify the perceived level of luxury of each brand (Dubois et al., 2001; Vigneron & Johnson, 1999; Kapferer & Bastien, 2009) and identified common factors, which are, simply put:

- **Elitism** (measured by product attributes such as: expensive, inaccessible to everyone);
- **Creativity** (exceptional brand, created by genius, excellent artistic and craftsmanship . . .);
- **Uniqueness** or magnificence (with attributes such as selected, rare, magnificent and unique brand);
- **Difference** (e.g. brand ownership makes me different from other people; a brand dreamed of . . .);
- **Refinement** (e.g. a dazzling, refined, attractive brand);

- **Exceptional quality** (tradition, know-how, excellent product, long history);
- **Hedonistic** experience (exceptional brand, good taste of the owners of the brand); and
- **Strength** (e.g. leading, successful, powerful brand).

Based on these scales, the authors demonstrated the difference of three groups of luxury brands on the example of selected brands: available (represented by Montblanc and Chanel), mid-range (Rolex) and unavailable (Ferrari and Van Cleef & Arpels); (De Barnier et al., 2012).

The brands of the top 20 groups or conglomerates are listed in Table 2.2. Historical milestones of brands of the leading groups will be presented in the following subsections.

For the sake of completeness, it should be added that this ranking includes groups and brands of so-called personal luxury, including selected wine and spirits brands, which, according to Bain and Company (2022), represent approximately 32% of the volume of the entire luxury world. Other segments include luxury cars (48%), hospitality (7%), select gourmet food (4%), luxury furniture and housewares (4%), art (3%) and private jets and yachts (2%) (Bain & Company, 2022).

Luxury world brands are characterized by their easily recognizable style, strong identity and high awareness, as well as strong emotional and symbolic associations with the brand. Additional common features include controlled distribution, high quality and premium price (Okonkwo-Pézard, 2017), as will be seen in the examples of the largest groups in the personal luxury segment.

2.3 Main groups in the world of personal luxury

In the literature, terms related to groups of luxury brands are often confused. Essentially, there are two types of companies: the first applies luxury as a business strategy, while the second operates in markets with luxury brands but mixes luxury, premium and fashion brands together (Kapferer & Bastien, 2012). For both groups of companies, the reference framework of brands is the luxury market. On the contrary, the biggest difference is the way the brands are managed in luxury groups applying a business strategy, where the brand strategy dominates or is superior to the corporate strategy. Cartier is a brand; Richemont is a corporation. Richemont's profits come from the profits of individual brands, not from economies of scale of the entire group, and this is true for the entire first group of players in luxury (Ijaouane & Kapferer, 2012).

An example of the **first group** is the conglomerate Moët Hennessy-Louis Vuitton SE (LVMH) (more in 2.3.1), which pioneered luxury strategy in the 1980s. Initially, Louis Vuitton and Moët Hennessy did not merge due to problems. Both grew and were solidly managed and profitable. They decided to merge to keep control in the hands of both families and to make it easier for them to resist attacks from other companies. LVMH's headquarters consisted of a relatively small finance department that managed the Group's substantial cash flow and relationships with shareholders outside the founders' families. Although Bernard Arnault later took over the management of LVMH, he remained faithful to the independence of the individual brands. LVMH has not resisted the appeal of economies of scale, like firms from the second group of luxury brands such as L'Oréal or Swatch Group, as was demonstrated by the acquisitions of Sephora or DFS (Duty Free Shops). In the first group, the luxury brands are separated into individual companies; they have their own CEOs, their own brand marketing and limited influence from headquarters. Synergies that arise from corporate management include especially those on the side of human resources management (Kapferer & Bastien, 2012).

Table 2.2 Brands of individual groups of luxury manufacturers from the Top 20 by sales FY2022. Authors based on data available at (Deloitte, 2023).

Rank	Group name	Brand selection
1	LVMH Moët Hennessy-Louis Vuitton SE	Louis Vuitton, Christian Dior, Celine, Tiffany & Co., Fendi, BVLGARI, Loro Piana, Emilio Pucci, Off-White, Acqua di Parma, Loewe, Marc Jacobs, TAG Heuer, Benefit Cosmetics
2	Kering SA	Gucci, Saint Laurent, Bottega Veneta, Balenciaga, Alexander McQueen, Brioni, Pomellato, Boucheron
3	Compagnie Financière Richemont SA	Cartier, Van Cleef & Arpels, Buccellati, Piaget, Montblanc, Jaeger-LeCoultre, Vacheron Constantin, IWC, Chloé, Panerai
4	The Estée Lauder Companies Inc.	Estée Lauder, Tom Ford Beauty, Bobbi Brown, La Mer, Jo Malone London, Aveda
5	Chanel Limited	Chanel
6	L'Oréal Luxe	Lancôme, Kiehl's, Biotherm, Urban Decay, IT Cosmetics, Mugler, Azzarro fragrances; Licensed brands including Giorgio Armani, Yves Saint Laurent, Valentino
7	Chow Tai Fook Jewelry Group Limited	Chow Tai Fook, Hearts on Fire, T Mark, Enzo, Soinlove, Monologue
8	Hermès International SCA	Hermès, John Lobb
9	Rolex SA	Rolex, Tudor
10	PVH Corp.	Tommy Hilfinger, Calvin Klein
11	Lao Feng Xiang Co., Ltd.	Lao Fengxiang
12	The Swatch Group Ltd.	Omega, Longines, Breguet, Harry Winston, Rado, Blancpain
13	China National Gold Group Gold Jewelry Co., Ltd	China Gold, Jin-Rujin, Jin-ShangYin
14	Tapestry, Inc.	Coach, Kate Spade, Stuart Weitzman
15	Ralph Lauren Corporation	Ralph Lauren, Polo Ralph Lauren, Lauren Ralph Lauren
16	Capri Holdings Limited	Michael Kors, MICHAEL Kors, Jimmy Choo, Versace
17	Shiseido Company, Limited	SHISEIDO, clé de peau BEAUTÉ, NARS, Drunk Elephant, IPSA, THE GINZA; Licensed fragrance brands
18	Prada Group	Prada, Miu, Church's, Car Shoe
19	Malabar Gold & Diamonds	Malabar, Mine, Precia, Era, Starlet
20	Burberry Group plc	Burberry

Firms from the **second group** are characterized by four types of synergies, which are their typical features and differentiation from the first group. These are **operational synergies, synergies arising from market power, financial synergies** and **those associated with corporate management.** Synergies in corporate operations arise, for example, from a joint R&D

department for a certain market segment (L'Oréal perfumes). Synergy in the distribution of brands or in the development of new products no longer corresponds to luxury strategy as a method of management; on the contrary, it is typical for FMCG products. Synergies resulting from market power are realized by groups that sell, for example, a brand important for selected chains or department stores. They can use such market power to negotiate distribution, placement or listing fees for other portfolio brands. The financial synergy from corporate finance management stems from the ability of brands to take advantage of, for example, a better rating of the parent company and to use its credit lines for their expansion under much more favorable conditions than the brand itself. As with the first group of companies, the synergies associated with corporate management are related to HR and talent acquisition, people development and the offer of career growth that the group or parent company can offer to job seekers or employees. The possibility of further acquisitions of the parent company, supply chain control or expansion in distribution are other examples where the benefits of corporate management of these companies can be realized (Kapferer & Bastien, 2012).

In addition to the two previously defined groups, some important luxury brands are still run by the founding families and resist the offers of luxury conglomerates. The most famous are Chanel, Hermès, Rolex, Patek Philippe and others. Many of the original family brands became part of conglomerates, but many of them also disappeared, and the names of the originally family luxury brands are no longer known (e.g. the Parisian hat shop Gelot or luxury robes of designer Jean Dessès, which were very popular in the 1950s and 1960s). Historically, family businesses with luxury brands were, and some still are, firmly tied to a particular region, to its culture, and in the case of strong brands, their identity is integrated into the image of the country or region. Som and Blanckaert (2021) list five reasons for incorporating originally separate brands into conglomerates in the 1980s:

- Family management of a company is much **more complex** because of emotional and personal relationships;
- Difficulty **attracting top managerial talent** to the management of a family business;
- **Relationships between siblings or extended family** can lead to quarrels, riots and legal battles;
- **The informal nature of family businesses** leads to ad-hoc decisions without formal management processes; and
- Insufficient attention paid to **succession planning** in the company or attracting new talent (Som & Blanckaert, 2021).

2.3.1 LVMH: Moët Hennessy-Louis Vuitton SE

Sales of LVMH, the largest group of luxury brands, reached almost $60 billion in 2022, with 19% cumulative growth (CAGR FY2019–22) and 22.6% YOY growth. In April 2023, LVMH became the first European company with a market value of more than $500 billion (Deloitte, 2023). Bernard Arnault became the wealthiest person on the planet in 2023 with a $211 billion fortune value (Forbes, 2023). "Our long-term vision model values our brands' heritage and sparks creativity and excellence. It is the driving force behind the Group's success and the guarantor of its future," says Bernard Arnault, CEO and founder of the LVMH Group (LVMH, 2022b). According to his statement to CNBC, while in the process of building the company in the last decades of the previous century, he was criticized many times for putting together so many independent brands (because the competitors thought this did not make sense); however, many of them later copied the strategy (CNBC, 2018).

According to B. Arnault, the LVMH Group is based on the heritage of the brands that it has merged during its relatively short history under its group; the history and key milestones are chronologically illustrated in Table 2.3.

Table 2.3 Key milestones in the history of LVMH-owned brands. Adapted by authors based on data from (LVMH Group, 2022; The Fashion Law, 2021; Bengtsson, et al., 2021).

1593	The Sauvage family acquires the Château d'Yquem and transforms it into a wine estate that earns a reputation as an exceptional vineyard.
1729	Nicolas Ruinart founds the very first champagne brand, which still bears his name.
1780	Marie-Etienne Nitot founds the jewelry brand Chaumet.
1803	Establishment of the Jean Vincent Bully brand.
1816	Barbe Nicole Clicquot Ponsardin invented the sludge table, a special counter for shaking off sludge or sediment for fermentation in champagne, and thus revolutionized the world of champagne and its commercialization.
1828	Establishment of the Guerlain brand, which was managed by the family of founder Pierre-Francois-Pascal Guerlain (1798–1864) throughout its existence until 1994 (acquisition of LVMH).
1837	Founding of Tiffany & Co.
1846	Loewe is founded in Madrid, focusing on selecting the finest leathers and creating iconic pieces of leather and ready-to-wear.
1852	Aristide and Marguerite Boucicaut found Le Bon Marché in Paris, defining the concept of a department store.
1854	Louis Vuitton establishes its workshop in Paris.
1859	Hennessy, which has focused on international customers since the very beginning, supplies its cognac to China for the first time.
1869	Founding of the Tag Heuer brand.
1884	Establishment of the BVLGARI brand.
1889	Created by Aimé Guerlain, Jicky becomes the first fragrance in the world to use synthetic raw materials in its composition. Eugène Mercier placed second behind the Eifel Tower at the World Exhibition in Paris with his gigantic barrel containing the equivalent of 200,000 bottles of champagne.
1895	Alessandro Berluti founds the eponymous workshop. The Alessandro model is still in the brand's shoe offer.
1914	Creation of the Jean Patou brand.
1924	Pietro Loro Piana, an Italian engineer originally from Piedmont, founds his textile company focused on wool products.
1925	Establishment of the Fendi brand.
1945	Establishment of the Céline brand.
1946	Founding of the Christian Dior brand.
1947	Designer Christian Dior, who considered fragrance the finishing touch of every outfit, launches Miss Dior perfume during the launch of his first ready-to-wear collection. Establishment of the Emilio Pucci brand.

(Continued)

Table 2.3 (Continued)

1952	Founding of the Givenchy brand.
1957	Hubert de Givenchy asked his muse, Audrey Hepburn, to pose for a L'Interdit ad as the first brand ambassador in the history of the perfumery. Founding of the Italian jewelry store Repossi.
1960	The snake is marked as the main symbol of the BVLGARI brand and the beginning of the 1960s is considered the birth of the success of her Serpenti collection. American entrepreneurs Charles Feeney and Robert Warren Miller create DFS (Duty Free Shops), which is currently the world leader in selling luxury products to international travelers.
1969	TAG Heuer presents a collection of Monaco watches with a square dial. Zenith launches El Primero, a watch with the first fully integrated, high-frequency automatic chronograph movement. Establishment of the retail brand Sephora.
1970	Establishment of the Kenzo brand.
1977	Creation of the Rossimoda brand.
1979	The Krug champagne brand produced the first vintage of Clos du Mesnil from Chardonnay grapes grown on an area of 1.85 hectares in the heart of the French region of Champagne.
1984	Creation of the Marc Jacobs brand. Creation of the Thomas Pink brand. Creation of the DKNY brand.
1987	LVMH is formed by the merger of Moët Hennessy and Louis Vuitton.
1988	Acquisition of Givenchy.
1989	Creation of the Rimowa brand.
1992	Acquisition of Berluti.
1993	Acquisition of Kenzo.
1994	Acquisition of Guerlain.
1996	Acquisition of Céline. Acquisition of Loewe.
1997	Acquisition of Marc Jacobs. Marc Jacobs became creative director of Louis Vuitton in the year of the LVMH acquisition and worked in the women's clothing division until 2013. Acquisition of the retail brand Sephora.
1999	Acquisition of Thomas Pink. Acquisition of the Tag Heuer brand. An unsuccessful attempt to acquire the Gucci brand, which was taken over by Pinault-Printemps-Redoute (now Kering).
2000	Acquisition of the Emilio Pucci brand. Acquisition of Rossimoda brand.

(Continued)

Table 2.3 (Continued)

2001	Acquisition of the Fendi brand. Acquisition of DKNY (sold to G-III Apparel Group in 2016). An unsuccessful attempt to acquire the Hermès brand, which was only completed in 2015 when LVMH announced the distribution of the acquired 23% stake to Hermès shareholders and institutional investors.
2004	Establishment of the Nicholas Kirkwood brand.
2010	Completion of the acquisition of La Samaritaine, which began in 2001. Acquisition of Moynat, a 19th-century luggage manufacturer.
2011	Entering the BVLGARI brand, the Bulgari family acquired 3% of LVMH shares for a 50.4% stake in the company.
2013	Acquisition of the Loro Piana brand. Acquisition of the Nicholas Kirkwood brand. Acquisition of a minority stake in the J.W. Anderson brand. Virgil Abloh founds the brand Off-White.
2015	Acquisition of the Italian jewelry store Repossi.
2016	Acquisition of luxury luggage manufacturer Rimowa.
2017	Acquisition of the Christian Dior brand.
2018	Acquisition of the Jean Patou brand.
2019	Creation of a new brand Fenty, a joint venture with Rihanna. A joint venture with Stella McCartney; according to available data, Stella McCartney was still the majority owner of the brand.
2020	Acquisition of Tiffany & Co., LVMH's largest investment to date (approximately $15.8 billion).
2021	Former creative director Céline founds the Phoebe Philo brand, in which LVMH has a minority stake. Acquisition of the Off-White brand. Its founder, Virgil Abloh, continues as the brand's creative director until his unexpected death in 2021. Acquisition of Officine Universelle Buly 1803 (Jean Vincent Bully brand).

From today's point of view, construction of the empire began in 1984 when the then-35-year-old Bernard Arnault took the opportunity to buy the company Boussac, owner of Christian Dior Haute Couture. Boussac was under state control after the company had to declare the largest bankruptcy in post-war French history. At that time, Arnault had approximately ten years' of experience in managing the family construction company founded by his grandfather. To buy Boussac, he used $15 million from the family fortune and $45 million from the French financial institution Lazard Frères. Within two years, he laid off 9,000 employees, sold the disposable diaper division and most of its textile operations for $500 million and got Boussac into the black (The New York Times Magazine, 1989; Som & Blanckaert, 2021).

In 1987, he invested in LVMH, a conglomerate that merged Louis Vuitton, led by Henry Racamier, and Moët Hennessy, represented by Alain Chevalier. The June 1987 merger was preceded by fears of a takeover of Moët Hennessy, as members of the Moët, Chandon and

Hennessy families owned only 22% of the voting rights. But after the merger, Henry Racamier – who had run the company since 1977 – needed allies against Alain Chevalier. Chevalier assumed the position of managing director of the new company, while Racamier was his deputy and head of strategy. The second position in the new company did not match his experience, and initially Arnault was to be his ally with his purchase of 24% of LVMH shares. However, Arnault soon increased his stake to 37.5% and then to 43.5%, which meant control over the entire LVMH.

Over the next two decades, the company grew organically through new product launches and other acquisitions of brands with significant traditions and histories that it currently controls, listed chronologically in Table 2.4. Not all acquisitions were successful. In January 1999, Bernard Arnault targeted Italian fashion house Gucci, which issued additional shares in its defense and offered a 40% stake to Pinault-Printemps-Redoute (PPR, later Kering) for $2.9 billion. Arnault offered $4.9 billion for a 100% stake, and the dispute between him and Pinault (PPR) was only ended by a court ruling in favor of Kering, to which Arnault eventually sold all the remaining shares in 2000. Similarly, Arnault failed in his bid for a gradual (and cited as violent) takeover of the Hermès brand in 2013. His efforts resulted in stubborn and courageous actions by members of the Hermès family, who blocked more than 51% of the shares. Other initially promising acquisitions did not meet LVMH's expectations. The most famous are Michael Kors, which was sold in 2003 and Christian Lacroix, sold in 2005 (Som & Blanckaert, 2021).

What are the key success factors for LVMH that have contributed to its stable and long-term growth for more than three decades, with the only exception being the COVID year 2021? In the literature, the key success factors include **the independence or separation of portfolio brand management** and **creativity**, exemplified by Arnault's trust in John Galliani's creations for Dior. "Our entire business is based on the freedom of our designers to create without any limits," said Arnault in an interview with HBR (*Harvard Business Review*, 2001). **Selecting creative talent** for the positions of creative brand directors is also seen as a company strength. However, the independence in the management of individual brands, providing each of them with a unique brand identity, is balanced by absolute cost control in other management areas, such as **synergies** in media purchasing, advertising, retail lease, logistics or purchasing (Som & Blanckaert, 2021; Cavender & Kincade, 2014). Another important element in the strategic management of the Group's brands is the strict **adherence to quality management.** The Group oversees the production of almost all products, with minimal outsourcing, while **controlling supply chains and distribution networks.** Louis Vuitton is one of the few companies that owns and operates 100% of its retail network. Last but not least, an important success factor is **the emphasis on innovation.** Despite a certain rigidity of the luxury sector, the group is not afraid to embark on innovative materials (e.g. color-changing optical fibers in LV bags or personalized packaging for Guerlain lipsticks) (Som & Blanckaert, 2021). Finally, **the internationalization of its brands** is key. Louis Vuitton was one of the first to enter China and to invest and develop its business there, opening a flagship shop in Beijing's Palace Hotel in 1992. Hennessy made its initial shipment of cognac to China back in 1859. Other *Maisons* followed, and their interest was reflected in multiple projects, including the opening of Louis Vuitton and Dior shops in Shanghai's first mall – the prestigious Plaza 66 (LVMH, 2023b).

These success factors were confirmed by Cavender and Kincade (2014) in a case study dedicated to the management of luxury brands, where they systematically studied available literature, interviews with LVMH representatives, websites and official documents using the example of LVMH. The study focused specifically on the Louis Vuitton brand, as the authors consider it an archetypal representative of luxury brands. In the conclusions, they identified indicators of successes and failures of brand management to manage brand strategy:

1. **Trust in independent brand management.** Bernard Arnault's absolute trust in the CEO of Louis Vuitton, which faced declining profits and sales in the 1990s: Yves Carcell was a visionary manager who capitalized on the identity of the LV brand by emphasizing its craftsmanship but further enriched it to realize its full potential, above all by creating artificial scarcity, diversifying the brand portfolio by introducing products with innovative design and material and thus managing to restore his former exclusivity;
2. Protection or **separation of brands within the portfolio.** Thanks to minimal interaction between the company's individual brands and between the brands and the LVMH Group, the identities of individual brands were not compromised;
3. **Transfer of knowledge between brands** to retain existing stars (i.e. Louis Vuitton, Moët & Chandon, Hennessy, Parfums and Christian Dior) and future potential portfolio stars (i.e. Fendi, Celine) by implementing best practices from portfolio stars across the Group. As the portfolio expands, it is clear that the communication of best practices between brands presents an opportunity to improve the performance of all brands;
4. The communication of luxury brands can take **advantage of the already existing high awareness** in a more abstract and avant-garde way compared to everyday brands. A product can be fundamentally sidelined, such as Louis Vuitton's "Core Values" campaign, whose visuals radiate the essence of the brand, reflect its symbolic nature and try to transport customers into the brand's dream world;
5. Integrating the **marketing vision into all levels of the company:** Arnault himself stated in an interview with the *Harvard Business Review* that "the last thing you should do is allocate ad creation to the marketing department of that brand. If you do that, you lose the proximity between the designers and the message to the marketplace," because that would mean losing connection between the designer's idea and the customer (*Harvard Business Review*, 2001);
6. Experiential marketing in the sense of **creating customer experiences**, for example, through the involvement of artists, designers and architects in the architecture and design of brand flagships, with the aim of creating a connection with the customer not only through the brand identity but by intensively creating impressive experiences in the presentation of products (Manlow & Nobbs, 2013);
7. Brand architecture. LVMH cares about traditional brands in the star-studded portfolio but also skillfully **diversifies the portfolio** by including brands that have a greater opportunity to engage younger target groups (Urban Decay, Benefit in Cosmetics, Off-White). The extension of the product line (brand extensions) and sub-branding within a given brand architecture in the innovation process occurs sensitively, with regard to not damaging the brand image;
8. **Long-term return on investment.** In the early stages of LVMH's build-up, sales and revenues grew in an attempt to outperform the company's competitors primarily through acquisitions, but profitability declined. It is reported that the price of some acquisitions did not match the strength of the brands, and some brands were not in the shape that LVMH had anticipated. In contrast to the strategy of buying new brands in the 1990s, in 2002, Arnault made a turn towards long-term growth through a return to a focus on internal growth and investment in the development of the portfolio's star brands (Louis Vuitton, Moët & Chandon, Hennessy, Parfums and Christian Dior). This strategy included a focus on creativity and **continuous innovation,** targeted investments and the liquidation of non-strategic assets;

9. **Roofing of brands with corporate know-how.** In the early years of the conglomerate, until approximately 2002, brands remained autonomous from numerous activities, which alleviated the stress of acquisition and helped to maintain existing brand identities. Later, however, LVMH began to implement integration activities to support individual brands and especially to realize economics of scale. The credibility of individual brands was preserved, and the original designers enjoyed the support of their creativity, but at the same time, the company began to provide a structure and **corporate support system** that most independent designers did not have. LVMH also introduced the LVMH House, a corporate development function that supported and developed working relationships between brand managers; and
10. **Adaptability:** LVMH's corporate strategy in times of crisis focuses on strengthening star brands such as Louis Vuitton, taking into account their roots, long-term heritage and tradition (Cavender & Kincade, 2014).

In order to stay relevant with the younger target audience, the brands (mainly Louis Vuitton) are **developing digital brand identities** for the web3 platforms, leading to development of virtual products or digital twins (both physical and virtual products) on their own platform.

Finally, to introduce the largest group of luxury brands – LVMH – we can return to their philosophy: "Passionate about creativity" (LVMH, 2022a). This includes know-how (*savoir-faire*), creativity and passion stemming from the family's tradition of individual brands, as well as Arnault family traditions – quality, heritage and passion for new brands. This helps foster a closer connection between LVMH and younger target groups. In keeping with the anti-laws of luxury (outlined later), it offers customers unexpected variations of traditional products: "You can't charge a premium price to give people what they expect, so you'd never develop such groundbreaking products that cause people to line up around the block. We have them. And we only have them because we give our artists and designers freedom," said Bernard Arnault (*Harvard Business Review*, 2001).

2.3.2 Kering SA

Kering SA's sales in 2022 reached almost $21.4 billion, up 15.3% YOY. The Group operated with a margin of 18.3%, with a 47% share of the Gucci brand. The second most important brand is Yves Saint Laurent, with reported sales at $3.3 billion, followed by Bottega Veneta, Balenciaga and Alexander McQueen (Deloitte, 2023). The year 2023 was important for the group due to establishment of Kering Beauté, aiming to help the group's Houses (Bottega Veneta, Balenciaga, Alexander McQueen, Pomellato and Qeelin) to develop their beauty businesses (Kering SA, 2023). The Kering Beauté establishment was followed by acquisition of historic high-end fragrance house Creed, founded in 1760, including the iconic Aventus brand. This step provided Kering Beauté with the scale and platform for the development of other fragrance brands leveraging Creed's global distribution network (Deloitte, 2023).

The history of Kering SA begins in 1963, when François Pinault founded Établissements Pinault (Pinault SA) in Brittany, specializing in the B2B and B2C timber trade. It was much later, in 1999, that Pinault entered the luxury market. Pinault SA grew both organically and through acquisitions and was listed on the Paris Stock Exchange in 1988.

A fundamental strategic change occurred in the early 1990s (Kering SA, 2022). In 1989, Pinault SA acquired a 20% stake in a French distribution conglomerate operating mainly in Africa (CFAO). Later, Pinault SA and CFAO merged into a new group led by François Pinault, which continued to expand through acquisitions in the retail sector. In 1991, it acquired the French furniture retailer Conforama; in 1992, the Printemps department stores (which owned 54% of the retail company La Redoute); and in 1994, the French bookstore Fnac. In 2013, the group was renamed Kering (Kering SA, 2022; Som & Blanckaert, 2021).

The year 1999 was crucial for the luxury group as we know it today. PPR acquired a controlling stake in Gucci (42%) and a 100% stake in Yves Saint Laurent for $3 billion, creating a luxury brands division that the company further developed through additional brand acquisitions, whose historic milestones are shown in Table 2.4, emphasizing luxury brands and their heritage as the cornerstones of the group's shift towards luxury (Kering SA, 2022).

Table 2.4 Key milestones in the history of brands owned by Kering SA. Authors based on (Kering SA, 2022; Som & Blanckaert, 2021; Kering SA, 2023).

1858	Frédéric Boucheron opens his first shop at the Galerie de Valois, under the arcades of the Palais Royal, in the heart of the Parisian world of luxury. In 1893, Boucheron became the first jeweler to set up a shop on Place Vendôme.
1917	Cristóbal Balenciaga founds the Balenciaga store in San Sebastian, Spain. Twenty years later, Balenciaga opens a shop in Paris.
1921	Guccio Gucci opens a leather goods store in Florence, combining craftsmanship combined with a very contemporary creative vision, inspired by the refinement of the equestrian world.
1945	Foundation of the Brioni tailoring brand in Rome.
1961	Yves Saint Laurent and Pierre Bergé set up their own shop on Rue La Boétie in Paris, which will become one of the most famous fashion brands of the 20th century.
1963	François Pinault founds the "Établissements Pinault" in Rennes, a timber trading company.
1966	The Bottega Veneta brand is founded in Vicenza, referring to the tradition of Italian leather craftsmanship with a leather binding known as "intrecciato," the future trademark of the brand.
1967	Pino Rabolini, a descendant of a goldsmith family in Milan, creates the Pomellato brand.
1988	The Pinault Group is listed on the Paris Stock Exchange. After the acquisition of Le Printemps and the acquisition of an ownership stake in La Redoute, Pinault Printemps Redoute became Pinault in 1994 and in 2005 the name of the company changed to PPR.
1992	Lee Alexander McQueen, a graduate of the prestigious St. Martin's College of Art and Design in London, opens a fashion house in London and founds the Alexander McQueen brand.
1995	Pomellato introduces the concept of affordable miniature jewelry DoDo, each made from a single gram with a message of love, happiness, freedom and friendship.
1999	PPR begins its transformation into a group of luxury brands, buying a 42% stake in Gucci. Acquisition of Boucheron.

(Continued)

Table 2.4 (Continued)

2001	Acquisition of Bottega Venetta. Acquisition of Balenciaga. Strategic partnership with Alexander McQueen.
2004	Creation of the Qeelin brand, inspired by ancient Chinese culture (e.g. Bo collection with panda diamonds). Increases Gucci's stake to 99.4%.
2012	Acquisition of Brioni brand. Purchase of a majority stake in the Sowind Group (with the Girard-Perregaux brand dating back to 1771).
2013	PPR changes its name to Kering with a new visual identity, including a logo with the emblem of an owl, a symbol of wisdom, protection and foresight. Acquisition of the 2013 Qeelin brand. Acquisition of the Pomellato and DoDo brands.
2014	Acquisition of the Ulysse Nardin brand (founded in 1846).
2015	Kering Eyewear (design, development and distribution of Gucci, Cartier, Saint Laurent, Balenciaga, Bottega Veneta, Alexander McQueen, Stella McCartney, Alaïa, Courrèges, Montblanc, Brioni, Boucheron, Pomellato, McQ, Puma).
2022	The sale of the stake in Sowind Group, which owns the Girard-Perregaux brand, as part of the transaction was the sale of the Ulysse Nardin brand. Kering thus ceases to operate in the luxury watch market.
2023	Launch of Kering Beauté – to support the Group's Houses, namely Bottega Veneta, Balenciaga, Alexander McQueen, Pomellato and Qeelin, as they develop their beauty businesses to become growth drivers. Kering Beauté acquires high-end fragrance house Creed; founded in 1760, including the iconic Aventus. Kering's acquisition of 30% stake at Valentino.

At the time of its acquisition of a major stake in Gucci and its takeover of Yves Saint Laurent, Pinault-Printemps-Redoute was not focused solely on luxury products. It was not until 2003 that they sold Pinault Bois et Matériaux to the British company Wolseley for €565 million and in 2004 also the manufacturer of electrical installation materials Rexel. In the following year, the company simplified its name to PPR and continued with acquisitions, such as the gradual acquisition of a controlling stake in the Puma brand (62.1% in 2007). However, other acquisitions have already focused on the luxury sector, as can be seen from the previous overview.

In 2003, François Pinault handed over to his son François-Henri Pinault – who had worked in various positions in the group since 1987 – the position of managing director of Artemis (the holding company controlling PPR, which François had founded in 1992 as a tool for managing family assets). Two years later, François-Henri also became chairman and CEO of the PPR Group. Despite his confidence in luxury brands, he added the sports and lifestyle segment to the luxury pillar by joining Puma, believing that the luxury and sports pillars would be the foundation for further growth. Puma was seen as a promising and bold part of the portfolio. From a strategic perspective, it could mark the path to expansion into the affordable luxury market, where relatively less competition and fewer opportunities for higher growth were foreseen in the coming years. Puma – as one of the most fashionable and design-intensive sportswear brands – provided a platform to which PPR's specific skills in the management of fashion and luxury brands, leather goods, fragrances and cosmetics could significantly contribute (Solca, 2007). Since 2013, when the group changed its name to Kering, it has gradually divested itself of brands outside the luxury sector, and since 2019, when it sold the American sports brand Volcon, it has been exclusively operating in the field of luxury brands (Som & Blanckaert, 2021). The Puma brand is still controlled by the Pinault family through Group Artémis S.A., which owns approximately 41% of Kering's shares. The rest of Kering's shares are split between international (44.7%) and French (8.4%) institutional investors, individual shareholders (4.8%), equity (1.0%) and employee shares (0.1%) (Som & Blanckaert, 2021).

What are the key success factors of Kering SA? Like LVMH, Kering is one of the dominant multi-brand groups managing luxury brands, **providing each brand with a high degree of autonomy**. François-Henri's approach to further acquisitions is influenced by a clear perception of the market from both a luxury customer and a luxury brand management perspective, as evidenced by his statement to the *Harvard Business Review*:

> Theoretically, we could have tried to expand Gucci to cover many more segments [rather] than to acquire other brands, but we think that would be at the expense of what makes Gucci unique – what we call its DNA. We decided to allow more brands to complement each other rather than compete with each other. When considering an acquisition today, we strive to ensure that the brand fulfils a clear mission within our group and matches a different market segment.
>
> (2014)

In addition, the Group allows brands **a diversified approach to their communication strategy**. Gucci, for example, is quite active on social media and digital media, while Bottega Veneta is experimenting with abandoning all social networks (Som & Blanckaert, 2021; Forbes, 2021). At the same time, the group has many CSR activities and is considered a **pioneer of social responsibility in the luxury industry**. For example, they announced that from 2022, none of the group's brands will use animal fur (Kering SA, 2022). After the sale of non-luxury assets, the company transformed into a multi-brand luxury group and, despite strong organic growth and acquisition activities, is able to respond to market changes. Last but not least, the group's founder, François Pinault, **resolved the succession issue (i.e. who the successor will be)** relatively early and unequivocally, which can be the source of problems and inconsistencies in strategic planning in many family businesses. Under the leadership of François-Henri Pinault, the company has transformed from the PPR retail group into a group of luxury brands whose ambition is to be the world's most influential luxury group in the field of creativity, sustainability and long-term economic performance (Kering SA, 2021).

2.3.3 The Estée Lauder Companies Inc.

The founder of the company, Estée Lauder, was born at the beginning of the 20th century as Josephine Esther Mentzer in New York to a mother originally from Hungary and a father originally from Bohemia. Cosmetics became her passion during childhood, when she and her Hungarian uncle prepared their first creams in the kitchen. She founded the cosmetic empire with her husband Joseph Lauder in 1946, and in the 1960s there was a gradual internationalization (Som & Blanckaert, 2021; Estée Lauder Companies, 2022). It currently operates in more than 150 countries with luxury goods sales of $17.7 billion. The company sells its brands such as Estée Lauder, Clinique, Origins, M·A·C, Bobbi Brown, La Mer and others (detailed overview in Table 2.5). In addition to their own brands, they hold licenses for fragrances, cosmetics and/or related products sold under the brands of various designers.

The Lauder family still has a key position in the company, with approximately 85% of the voting rights (Estée Lauder Companies, Inc., 2021). The third generation, William, Aerin and Jane, is actively involved in the management of the company in cooperation with its executives. Jane Lauder, granddaughter of Estée Lauder, has been a leading and recognized voice in the beauty industry for more than 20 years. As executive vice president, she leads (among other things) a company-wide strategy to create digitally focused priorities to accelerate growth (Estée Lauder Companies, 2022).

Each brand has its own specific position in the market of cosmetics and other cosmetic products. Skin care products (58%), make-up (26%), fragrances (12%) and hair care (4%) account for the largest share of turnover (Estée Lauder Companies, Inc., 2021). In its annual report, the company divides its brands into heritage (Estée Lauder, Clinique and Origins), luxury brands (La Mer, Jo Malone London, Tom Ford Beauty, AERIN, Le Labo, Editions de Parfums Frédéric Malle and Kilian Paris), make-up artists (M·A·C and Bobbi Brown) and perfumes of brands licensed by the company (Tommy Hilfiger, Donna Karan New York, DKNY, Michael Kors and Ermenegildo Zegna) (Estée Lauder Companies, Inc., 2021). Licensed and make-up artist brands are not luxury brands in accordance with the context of this publication, but it is important to assess the company's portfolio with regard to the volume these brands bring.

Table 2.5 shows the **intensification of the company's acquisition efforts** over the last decade. At the same time, according to its website, the company did not renew the licenses for fragrances of Tommy Hilfiger, Donna Karan New York, DKNY, Michael Kors and Ermenegildo Zegna and stopped selling the brands Becca, RODIN olio lusso and Prescriptives. A growth strategy is also emerging, focusing on acquiring minority stakes in companies, after which the company gives them autonomy in management and at the same time provides them with the know-how of a corporate partner. Such minority investments include an Indian-based company that manufactures and sells Ayurvedic skincare under the Forest Essentials brand (Estée Lauder Companies, Inc., 2021) and British cosmetics brand Haeckels, which may need Estée Lauder management experience for international expansion (Forbes, 2022a).

In 2020, the company announced a joint collaboration agreement with biotech company Atropos Therapeutics to identify and develop age-modulating chemicals (Cosmetics Business, 2020). The focus on innovation is also evident in the involvement in the world's largest innovation platform Plug and Play to identify and support emerging brands and business models not only through funding opportunities, but also through mentorship by experienced Estée Lauder managers and developers (Plug and Play, 2021).

Emphasis on research and development is another factor in the company's success. R&D investments totaled $307 million in fiscal year 2022 (compared to $243 million in 2021 and $228 million in 2020), and they employ approximately 1,250 R&D employees. In fiscal year 2021, the company began construction of a new innovation center in Shanghai, with commissioning in 2023, indicating increased interest in the Chinese market and specific products (Estée Lauder Companies, Inc., 2022).

Digital innovations, namely early adoption of potential benefits of the Metaverse, brought the Estée Lauder brand to the world of virtual fashion shows. In 2022, it participated in a show organized by the platform Decentralized. The brand was the exclusive beauty partner of Metaverse Fashion Week in March 2022, collaborating with Dr. Box (identity designer and one of the first women to pioneer the concept of beauty futurism) to create an original non-fungible token (NFT) wearable inspired by the brand's #1 serum, Advanced Night

Table 2.5 Key milestones in the history of Estée Lauder Companies, Inc. Authors based on data available at (Estée Lauder Companies, Inc., 2021; Estée Lauder Companies, 2022; Som & Blanckaert, 2021; Deloitte, 2023).

1946	Estée Lauder brand is founded.
1947	First big order from Saks Fifth Avenue worth $800.
1964	Launch of the Aramis brand (men's fragrances and care).
1968	Launch of the Clinique brand.
1987	Introduction of the Lab Series (skin care line for men).
1990	Launch of the Origins brand, known for effective natural skin care, under a license agreement to develop and market cosmetic products under the name Dr. Andrew Weil.
1995	Leonard A. Lauder (son of Estée Lauder) lists the company. Acquisition of Bobbi Brown (a brand with artistic roots that focuses on creating a teaching and learning community of women around the world). Acquisition of La Mer.
1997	Acquisition of the Aveda brand.
1998	Completion of the acquisition of the Canadian professional cosmetics brand M·A·C.
1999	Acquisition of luxury fragrance brand Jo Malone London.
2003	Acquisition of Parisian cosmetics brand Darphin.
2005	Conclusion of a license agreement for the development, production and distribution of Tom Ford fragrances and cosmetic products.
2006	Acquisition of Bumble and bumble, a New York-based hair care professional brand.
2010	Acquisition of the Los Angeles brand Smashbox Cosmetics.
2012	A luxury brand of cosmetics and fragrances AERIN Beauty inspired by the style of Aerin Lauder, granddaughter of Estée Lauder, was launched on the market.
2014	Acquisition of Le Labo, a slow perfumery brand that produces personalized fragrances.
2015	Acquisition of the fragrance brand Les Editions de Parfums Frédéric Malle. Acquisition of GLAMGLOW brand.
2016	Acquisition of the perfume brand Kilian Paris. Acquisition of make-up brand Too Faced.
2019	Acquisition of South Korean skincare brand Dr. Jart+.
2021	Increase of the stake in Deciem Beauty Group Inc. ("DECIEM") to approximately 76%, better known as "The Abnormal Beauty Company" based in Toronto. The sophisticated portfolio includes The Ordinary and NIOD, a science-based skin care brand.
2022	License agreement with Balmain to develop Balmain Beauty luxury products. Terminating the existing license agreements for Donna Karan New York, DKNY, Michael Kors, Tommy Hilfiger and Ermenegildo Zegna.

Repair. During Decentraland Art week in August 2022, The Estée Lauder POAP (Proof of Attendance Protocol) designed by Dr. Box could be claimed at one of three different stations within Decentraland's Art Week: the Sculpture Garden, CashLabs Gallery and ArtNet location. Claiming the POAP led to exclusive access to upcoming web3 activations from the Estée Lauder brand (Estée Lauder Companies, 2022).

Estée Lauder's executive management and descendants recognize the importance of her legacy and commitment to "bringing out the best to everyone we touch" (Estée Lauder, 2024), and they are working to ensure that no major strategic step of the company strays from this mission.

2.3.4 Compagnie Financière Richemont SA

Another luxury group ranking among the most substantial luxury companies, according to Deloitte (2023), is Richemont, a Swiss group with $19.2 billion in sales in 2022, up by 50.1% compared to the previous year. This was the fourth-highest year-on-year growth among the Top 100 companies, leading to regaining the 3rd place in the Top 10 ranking after dropping to 6th place in the previous report (reflecting less recovery from the pandemic). The majority of the sales and growth was generated by the jewelry *maisons* (Deloitte, 2023).

The group has an equally fascinating history as other conglomerates. It was founded in 1988 by Johann Rupert, originally from South Africa. Much earlier, Johann's father Anton had founded its predecessor, the Rembrandt company, after studying chemistry and doing business in dry cleaning.

The Rembrandt Group later held significant stakes in tobacco, financial services, wine and spirits and gold and diamond mining, as well as luxury goods, which – together with the investment in Rothmans International – formed the basis of the Richemont Group through holding minority stakes in Cartier Monde (Cartier, Piaget and Baume & Mercier) and in Rothmans International, which held shares in Cartier Monde, Dunhill and, through Dunhill, also in Montblanc and Chloé.

Johann Rupert founded Richemont, or Compagnie Financière Richemont SA, by separating the international assets of Rembrandt Group Ltd. (at that time Remgro Limited). The division, originally founded in 1979 as Intercontinental Mining and Resources S.A., was renamed IMR Group S.A. in 1987 and finally Richemont S.A. in August 1988, based in Zug, Switzerland. In the same year, Richemont went public. For reasons of tax optimization, at the time of a major restructuring in 1993, Richemont was split into two publicly traded companies: (1) Rothmans International (merged with British Tobacco in 1999) and (2) the luxury group Vendôme (a subsidiary, fully owned by the Richmont group since 1997) (Som & Blanckaert, 2021).

As of March 2022, Compagnie Financière Rupert was the only major shareholder of the group (3% or more of voting rights), with 5.2 million registered "A" shares and 522 million registered "B" shares, representing 10% of the company's capital and 51% of its voting rights. The main managing partner of Compagnie Financière Rupert is Johann Rupert (Richemont, 2022a). The most important milestones in the history of brands, corporations and most important acquisitions are summarized in chronological order in Table 2.6.
Before the changes related to ownership of Yoox Net-A-Porter (YNAP), the organization of the group was divided into four divisions:

1. **Jewelry** (Buccellati, Cartier and Van Cleef & Arpels);
2. **Watchmaking** (A. Lange & Söhne, Baume & Mercier, IWC Schaffhausen, Jaeger LeCoultre, Panerai, Piaget Roger Dubuis, Vacheron Constantin);
3. **Distribution (later "Discontinued Operations")** (Watchfinder & Co., YNAP, Mr. Porter, The Outnet, Online Flagship Stores); and
4. **Fashion (later "Other")** (Alaïa, AZ Factory, Chloé, Delvaux, Dunhill, Montblanc, Peter Millar, Purdey, Serapian and TimeVallée).

Table 2.6 Key milestones in the history of Compagnie Financière Richemont SA. Authors based on data available at Richemont (2022b), Vogue Business (2024a).

1755	Foundation of the oldest watchmaking manufactory Vacheron Constantin in Geneva, a brand whose watches were also owned by Napoleon Bonaparte.
1814	James Purday founds James Purdey & Sons Limited in London, specializing in sporting shotguns and custom rifles.
1829	Establishment of the leather product brand Delvaux in Brussels, which is the oldest leather product brand that has had uninterrupted production since its establishment.
1830	Foundation of the Swiss brand Baume & Mercier.
1833	Antoine LeCoultre founds the Swiss watch brand Jaeger-LeCoultre, which currently holds more than 430 patents.
1845	Ferdinand Adolph Lange founded a watchmaking manufactory in Dresden, which almost disappeared after the 2nd World War. It was not until 1990 that Walter Lange, Ferdinand's great-grandson, revived it under the brand name A. LANGE & SÖHNE.
1847	Louis-François Cartier (1819–1904) founds the Cartier jewelry brand in Paris.
1860	Foundation of the Italian watchmaking brand Panerai Giovanni Paneraiem in Florence.
1868	American engineer Florentine Ariosto Jones lays the foundations for the IWC Schaffhausen (International Watch Company) brand in Switzerland.
1874	Foundation of the Swiss watchmaking and jewelry brand Piaget.
1893	Alfred Dunhill founds the eponymous brand in London, specializing initially in motoring accessories, later tobacco and today luxury fashion and accessories.
1906	At 22 Place Vendôme in Paris, Alfred Van Cleef founded the Van Cleef & Arpels brand after marrying Estelle Arpels in 1895. Establishment of the German brand Montblanc.
1919	Establishment of the Buccellati brand in Milan.
1928	Establishment of the Milanese brand Serapian, known for custom leather creations.
1952	Gaby Aghion, a Parisian of Egyptian origin, founds the Chloé brand in Paris.
1964	Azzedine Alaïa founds the eponymous brand (Alaïa) haute couture in Paris.
1977	Acquisition of the Montblanc brand (through Alfred Dunhill Ltd., now Richemont).
1985	Acquisition of the Chloé brand (through Alfred Dunhill Ltd., now Richemont).
1988	The Vendôme Group, now Richemont, acquires the Piaget brand.
1994	Acquisition of the British brand Purdey.
1995	Foundation of the Roger Dubuis brand and watchmaking manufactory in Geneva.
2000	Acquisition of IWC Schaffhausen. Fashion journalist Natalie Massenet founds Net-a-Porter in London, becoming the world's leading online luxury retailer, offering more than 800 global designer brands and more than 200 beauty brands. Federico Marchetti founds the online retail brand YOOX in Milan, combining the names of two chromosomes and the infinity symbol, later part of the acquisition of the Yoox-Net-a-Porter Group.

(Continued)

Table 2.6 (Continued)

2001	Founding of the American clothing brand Peter Millar.
2002	Establishment of the retail brand Watchfinder & Co. in London, which specializes in the purchase, sale and partial exchange of used luxury watches, from bestsellers to vintage and limited editions.
2006	Yoox Net-a-Porter Group's Online Flagship Stores division is partnering with leading luxury brands to equip them with their own e-commerce.
2009	Establishment of the London-based retail brand The Outnet, engaged in the sale of post-season collections, later part of the acquisition of the Yoox-Net-a-Porter Group.
2011	Establishment of the men's online platform for the sale of luxury brands MR PORTER, later part of the acquisition of Yoox-Net-a-Porter Group.
2012	Acquisition of the Peter Millar brand, entry into the golf apparel sector.
2014	Richemont founds the TimeVallée brand, a multi-brand retail with luxury watches of the Richemont Group.
2015	Merger of the Net-a-Porter Group with the YOOX Group to form the YOOX Net-a-Porter Group, listed on the Italian Stock Exchange, with Richemont holding 50% of the share capital and 25% of the voting rights.
2017	Acquisition of the Italian brand Serapian.
2018	Acquisition of Watchfinder & Co. Acquisition of 95% of shares in Yoox-Net-a-Porter Group, a global e-commerce player with luxury brands.
2019	Fashion designer Alber Elbaz founds AZ Factory in Paris, the first brand of their own developed within the Richemont Group. Launch of FENGMAO 风茂, a joint venture established between Yoox Net-a-Porter Group and Alibaba Group.
2021	Acquisition of the Belgian leather brand Delvaux.
2023	Acquisition of a controlling stake in privately owned luxury Italian shoemaker Gianvito Rossi.
2024	YNAP to exit the Chinese market altogether – liquidating the Fengmao joint venture with Alibaba

Since 2024, the organization reports four main divisions – Jewelry *Maisons,* Specialist Watchmakers, Other (fashion brands and Watchfinder) and Discontinued Operations (YNAP).

Each of the brands has its own CEO and is managed independently, with its own marketing, development, distribution and so on. The Group provides selected forms of central and regional support (Richemont, 2022b; Som & Blanckaert, 2021). In terms of sales volume, according to data for 2022, the largest division was jewelry (58%), followed by watchmaking (18%), distribution (14%) and fashion (10%) (Richemont, 2022a).

Unlike other large luxury groups, Richemont was more active in e-commerce. By 2010, the group entered an online shopping platform (Net-a-Porter) focused on luxury brands by purchasing a majority stake in it. Five years later, Net-a-Porter merged with another platform, the YOOX Group, to form the YOOX Net-a-Porter (YNAP) group, in which Richemont had a 50% ownership stake with 25% of the voting rights. In addition to the acquisition of the luxury worn watch retail brand Watchfinder & Co., 2018 also saw an increase in its ownership stake in YNAP to 95%.

In November 2020, Richemont and China's Alibaba each invested $300 million in another largely online e-commerce platform, Farfetch, and paid an additional $250 million each for a 25% stake in the joint venture that includes Farfetch's operations in the Chinese market (Reuters, 2020; Richemont, 2022c), allowing the Richemont brands traded on the Farfetch platform and the later Chinese Tmall Luxury Pavilion to build penetration in that market.

Another crucial step towards the digitization of the luxury industry was the collaboration between Richemont and Farfetch, announced in August 2022. The goal of the rather complex operation was to create a global online platform of luxury brands: Richemont planned to sell a 50.7% stake in YNAP to Farfetch and a 3.3% to Alabbar. YNAP thus would become a neutral platform without a majority shareholder. Farfetch would then transform YNAP into Farfetch technology, accelerating YNAP's growth and moving it toward a hybrid business model. Most Richemont brands would adopt Farfetch solutions for their online stores, connecting to existing brick-and-mortar locations. At the same time, they planned to open so-called e-concessions in Farfetch marketplaces.

Furthermore, a future merger of YNAP with Farfetch (with Richemont as shareholder of Farfetch) was envisaged Richemont, 2022c). The combination of Richemont's retail expertise and Farfetch's extensive technological capabilities to jointly develop innovative services and technology solutions was supposed to be an important strategic step for the company's further development, as Farfetch founder and CEO José Neves clarified for *Forbes*: "Our mission is to be a global platform for luxury. one where the boundaries between the different modes of shopping [online, offline, monobrand and multibrand] have been completely dissolved, revolutionizing the shopping experience for consumers globally and elevating the human connection between the creators, curators and the consumers of luxury. We call this vision 'Luxury New Retail' (LNR)." (*Forbes*, 2022b; Richemont, 2022c)

For Johann Rupert, chairman of the Board of Directors of Richemont, the operation was "a dream come true of building an independent, neutral online platform for the luxury industry that would be highly attractive to both luxury brands and their discerning clientele." In this context, he also appreciated the technological prowess and creative thinking of his son Anton (Richemont, 2022c).

In early 2023, however, the deal structure changed due to evolving market conditions. The planned sale of YNAP to Farfetch was modified to reflect a 47.5% stake acquisition by Farfetch, while Symphony Global, affiliated with Mohamed Alabbar, acquired a 3.2% stake in YNAP, reinforcing the platform's neutral stance. The transaction was later in 2023 approved by the European Commission. This deal, involving a share swap of Farfetch Class A shares with Richemont, aligned with Richemont's ambition for an independent luxury online platform. The agreement also encompassed the adoption of Farfetch's platform solutions by YNAP and Richemont *Maisons* and the introduction of e-concessions on Farfetch's marketplace by Richemont's brands, aiming to enhance the online luxury shopping experience (Deloitte, 2023). Despite having the transaction approved by European authorities, as reported by Reuters in October 2023 (Reuters, 2023), the deal was not accomplished due to financial issues on Farfetch's side (more details in Chapter 5 related to distribution.

Dexterity in distribution policy is one of the key success factors of Richemont. Another is its **regional policy**. Asia has been a key growth market in previous years, and the launch of the YNAP-Alibaba Group Fengmao joint venture in 2019 confirmed the strategic focus on developing this market. However, in 2024, Richemont announced the **closure of the Fengmao joint venture due to YNAP's declining performance**, and it focused on more profitable regions. This exit signifies a retreat from what was once considered a key growth market, reflecting the challenges and competitive pressures in China's luxury e-commerce sector (Vogue Business, 2024a).

An equally important factor is the **unique mix of brands** in the Group's portfolio, which includes the most exclusive jewelry brand Van Cleef & Arpels, as well as the oldest watchmaking manufactory in the world, Vacheron Constantin. Skillful management of brands in separate companies with a long-term emphasis on building the value of brands and consideration of their heritage and identity is a natural part of the group's strategic vision.

2.3.5 Other groups of luxury brands

Other important groups in the luxury brand market include the **Swatch Group** with luxury watch brands such as Breguet, Blancpain, Harry Winston, Glashütte, Jaquet-Droz and Omega. With a turnover of $7.5 billion in 2022, it ranks 12th in Deloitte's ranking of luxury companies. With the exception of its own Swatch brand (which is not a luxury brand), all of the Group's brands have been gained through acquisitions. An important success factor for the entire Swiss group led by the Hayek family is considered **vertical integration**, which allows the group to produce high-quality Swiss products at affordable prices in a country where production is extremely expensive. **The management of individual brands is completely independent**, but the coherence in production is significant and the presence in all price segments of the market and the associated economies of scale contribute to the high competitiveness of the group.

L'Oréal's luxury division, with a turnover of $15.4 billion in 2022, with brands such as Lancôme, Helena Rubinstein, Yves Saint Laurent and Giorgio Armani, accounts for about 38% of the company's sales and is a key player in the luxury perfume and cosmetics market. According to Deloitte, the luxury division ranks fifth between Richemont and Chanel. Among the success factors, it is important to mention the impressive **corporate culture** in which the company nurtures the best talent in the FMCG sector, while encouraging competition between divisions and brands. Furthermore, L'Oréal cleverly exploits **synergies between individual brands** and, above all, sales channels. However, the biggest advantage of this corporation is considered its **research and development** and the **resulting innovations** that are used not only by mainstream brands but also by luxury ones (Som & Blanckaert, 2021; Deloitte, 2023). In 2022 and the first half of 2023, L'Oréal Luxe, aiming to become a leader in Beauty Tech, chose not to buy any luxury beauty brands but instead invested in biotech and neurotechnology firms through its BOLD venture capital fund. These investments are part of L'Oréal's vision to innovate within the beauty sector. They partnered with Verily in January 2022 to study the effects of the environment on skin aging and develop new dermatology technologies using AI and sensors. In March 2022, they collaborated with Emotiv to create a unique fragrance selection method using brainwave responses. L'Oréal also invested in Sparty Inc., a Japanese company offering personalized beauty products; Microphyt, a French biotech focusing on "green sciences"; and Debut, a US firm creating innovative cosmetic ingredients. Moreover, alongside Unilever and Kao, L'Oréal invested in Geno in March 2023 to develop sustainable beauty product ingredients, showcasing its commitment to advancing beauty through technology and sustainability (Deloitte, 2023).

PVH Corp, occupying the 10th position in Deloitte's ranking, is the umbrella brand for the Calvin Klein and Tommy Hilfiger brands and has turnover of nearly $8.4 billion. Portfolio brands are considered fashionable but are not luxury brands. However, the company is gradually selling off part of its portfolio (Speedo, IZOD, Van Heusen, Arrow and Geoffrey Beene) in order to focus on building luxury brands (Deloitte, 2021, 2023).

According to Deloitte, the **Italian EssilorLuxottica group** – in 7th position in sales in 2020 – focuses on the luxury sector portion of glasses, lenses and frames portfolio and was formed by the merger of Essilor and Luxottica in 2018. The history of the group's brands in some cases dates back to the 19th and 20th centuries Essilor (1849), Salmoiraghi and Viganò (1865), Persol (1917), Ray-Ban (1937), and Luxottica (1961)." Examples of the brands owned by the group and years when established. The group includes not only brands acquired through their own development or acquisition (Ray-Ban or Alain Mikli) but also licenses about 20 luxury brands such as Chanel, Tiffany & Co., Prada and others (Essilor Luxottica, 2022). As of 2021, the group is not listed in Deloitte's rankings because the data were not available and "no reasonable estimates could be made" (Deloitte, 2022, p. 33).

Chinese group **Chow Tai Fook Jewellery Group Limited**, in 7th place in the Deloitte ranking, reported sales of almost $12.6 billion in 2022, which is 41.1% more compared to the previous year. Chow Tai Fook Jewellery Group Limited's strategy for growth primarily involves expanding its reach through wholesale channels to regional distributors and franchise partners, which significantly increased by 79.5% in 2022, accounting for 45% of the group's luxury revenue. Direct retail sales also rose by 20.2%. The company experienced a robust sales increase of 45.6% in Mainland China thanks to the opening of new franchises and a resurgence in consumer demand. Sales in Hong Kong, Macau and other regions jumped by 63%, particularly with Macau seeing a near doubling of sales, buoyed by a rebound in tourism and stable local demand. Efforts to tap into markets with high retail growth potential led to new openings in countries like Malaysia and Singapore (Deloitte, 2023). The growth in jewelry was fueled by the success of the Chow Tai Fook HUÁ Collection, created based on the essence of heritage and ancient craftsmanship. It contributed to the 52.5% growth in gold jewelry, which accounted for nearly 75% of the group's total sales (Deloitte, 2023; Chow Tai Fook Jewellery Group, 2024).

The Prada brand is often considered an independent brand. In reality, it belongs to the **Prada Group**, with turnover of $4.4 billion (2022) and more than 13,000 employees (Deloitte, 2022). The Group covers the brands Prada, Miu, Church's, Car Shoe, Marchesi 1824 and Luna Rosa (Prada Group, 2022). The Prada brand, founded in 1913, was taken over in 1978 by the granddaughter of founder Miuccia Prada. Since then, she has been involved in the design of the brand and is also the co-executive director of the company together with her husband. According to Forbes magazine (2013), Patrizio and Miuccia Bertelli are one of the world's most influential couples (Forbes, 2013). The group's shares have been traded on the Hong Kong Stock Exchange since 2011, but the family, led by the Bertellis, owns around 80% of the shares (Rambourg, 2020). In March 2023, the Prada Group partnered with Adobe to enhance its personalized online and in-store customer experiences. Using Adobe's digital tools, Prada aims to offer content that's relevant to its customers at their convenience. This includes recognizing customers in stores, understanding their preferences or creating tailored experiences. Additionally, Adobe Creative Cloud is used for crafting marketing initiatives, brand activities and supporting product development. In September 2022, Prada acquired 43.65% of Tuscan calfskin tannery Superior Spa contributing to vertical integration of the Group's supply chain (Deloitte, 2022). Interestingly, Prada, in collaboration with Axiom Space, has unveiled a newly designed spacesuit set for NASA's Artemis III mission, marking the first crewed Moon landing since 1972. The suit was showcased at the International Astronautical Congress in 2024 and represents the result of the collaboration between technology and creativity at Prada Group (Prada Group, 2024). Picture 2.1

shows potential landing areas for the Artemis III mission on the Moon. The brand's innovation in terms of materials they are using has gained a lot of media attention. The Group is expected to expand through acquisitions.

Another group is **Tod's Group**, with its Tod's flagship brand and three others: Hogan, Fay and Roger Vivier. The group was listed on the Milan Stock Exchange but is still controlled by the descendants of the founder of the Tod's brand from the 1920s, the Della Valle family (Rambourg, 2020). A longstanding shareholder in Tod's, LVMH in 2021 raised its stake in the Italian group to 10%, which sources at the time described as "friendly support." After an unsuccessful first attempt to make the group private in 2022, they seem to be succeeding in 2024 with the help of the private equity firm L Catterton, who (with backing from LVMH) has initiated a tender offer for a 36% stake in Tod's Group. This move was part of a long-term plan to strengthen its presence in the luxury fashion sector, leveraging LVMH's extensive experience and resources in the industry. Tod's founding family, Della Valle, tried to take the originally Milan-listed group private to revive its fortunes by managing its diverse brands separately (Reuters, 2024).

For a complete picture of the luxury world of brands, it is necessary to briefly mention two more groups whose importance may grow in the future; there is even talk of space for an American group in the style of LVMH (Rambourg, 2020). The first is the US group **Tapestry**, which generated $6.7 billion in revenue in fiscal year 2022, an increase of more than 15% compared to the previous year and 11% over the pre-pandemic level of 2019 (Tapestry, 2022). The company changed its name from the original Coach Inc. Group to Tapestry in 2017 following the acquisition of the brands Kate Spade New York and Stuart Weitzman. It has ambitions to become a diversified group of so-called democratic luxuries following the example of European groups (Rambourg, 2020). In particular, the Coach brand aspires to appeal globally to Gen Z customers through the message of "courage to be real" (Tapestry, 2022).

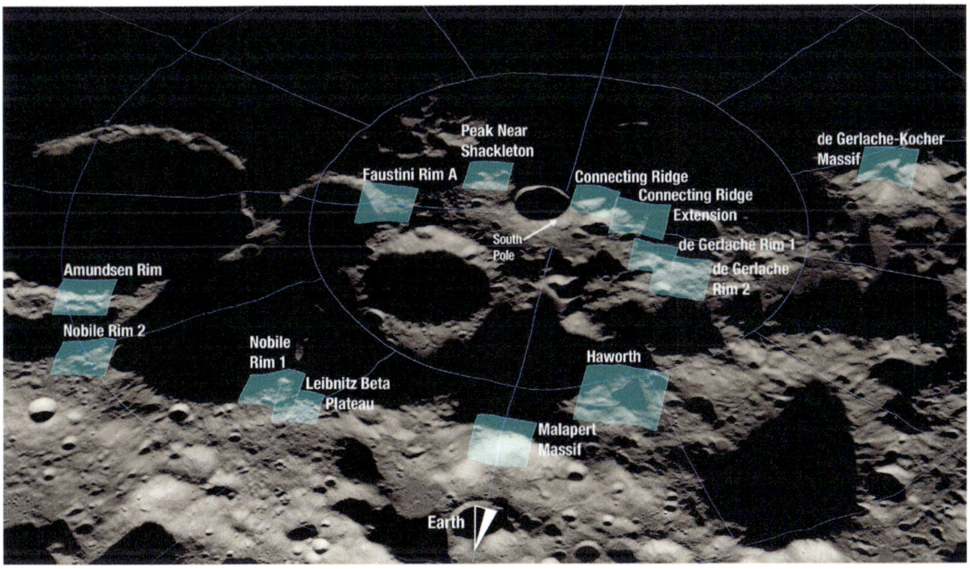

Picture 2.1 Artemis III landing regions on the Moon. By Pline. Available as public domain at (Wikimedia Commons, 2022).

The second group was **Capri Holdings Limited**, headquartered in the British Virgin Islands, renamed from the original name Michael Kors following the acquisition of British brand Jimmy Choo and Italian Versace in 2017–18. According to the 2022 annual report, the majority of the turnover is still sourced from Michael Kors (70%), followed by Versace (19%) and Jimmy Choo (11%). The group's total turnover was $5.65 billion (Capri Holdings Limited, 2022). In the case of Capri Holdings, further investments were expected to stabilize the Versace brand and integrate the brands into the group with a global growth strategy for all three of the Group's brands. In 2023 it was announced that **Tapestry acquired Capri Holding** with the strategic rationale to expand the portfolio reach and diversification across consumer segments, geographies, and product categories (Capri Holdings, 2023).

2.4 Characteristics of independent luxury brands

In Deloitte's ranking, three brands among the top ten luxury brands by sales in 2022 are still family controlled and not yet part of a conglomeration – Chanel, Hermès and Rolex. In the 1990s, at the time of the establishment of LVMH and the Kering group or earlier, the list of independent brands would include others, such as Boucheron, Guerlain, Chaumet, Lanvin, Kenzo, Givenchy, Gucci and many others. These brands were part of the acquisition raids of luxury groups created or regrouped in the 1980s. Families also dominate these groups, but at the same time, they are managed by professional managers. The role of families in these cases shifts from the founders and creative designers of brands at the center of management to an important element in the form of maintaining a legacy in the identity and personality of the brand.

2.4.1 Chanel Limited

Chanel Limited is ranked 5th in the luxury ranking, according to Deloitte, and the first stand-alone brand (Table 2.1) after the groups described in the previous subchapter (LVMH, Kering, Richemont and Estée Lauder). Its sales in 2022 were $17.2 billion, up 10.1% compared to the previous year, with a record profit margin of 26.7%. It makes Chanel the second strongest stand-alone brand after Louis Vuitton, achieving brand double-digit growth across all product categories. The only brand surpassing its profit margin in 2022 was Hermès, with a 29.1% net profit margin. The company is not active in acquisition efforts or expansions in other categories (men's fashion, for example). They focus their strategic efforts on securing the supply chain through integration of small factories and specialists essential to the supply of its luxury products and innovation in sustainable materials (Deloitte, 2023).

Chanel is a private company owned by the Wertheimer family. The history of the company begins in 1910, when Gabrielle "Coco" Chanel founded Chanel Mode in Paris. Her story did not begin at the famous Rue Gambon but rather at the apartment of her friend, Monsieur Balsan. He provided her a place in Paris on Boulevard Malesherbes, while another friend provided her with the finances to start her own business. Gabrielle Chanel started by selling her own self-made hats. She had a sense for fashion, and despite the fact that the hats were not original – made from simple straw hats bought at the Galeries Lafayette department store – she made them chic by trimming them with ribbon. Her business at Malesherbes grew too big for the apartment, and in 1910, she finally opened her own premises at 21 Rue Cambon with "Chanel, modes" on the door (Picardie, 2017).

In 1913, she opened her first store in Deauville, Normandy, where she focused on collections of ready-to-wear sportswear made from jersey, from which only men's underwear had previously been made. The following year, she opened her first salon in the seaside resort of Biarritz, focusing on her own high-fashion collections, where she already employed about 300 people. At the end of WWI, she opened the first large salon on Paris' rue 31 Gambon, near the Ritz Hotel. In addition to the salon, there were also workshops in the house. To facilitate the expansion of the business, she added number 29 in 1923 and number 25 in 1926, followed by Rue Cambon number 27 and 23 in 1927 (Picardie, 2017).

To complement La Maison Chanel's collections with fragrances, Gabrielle Chanel began working with perfumer Ernest Beaux. In 1921, they launched Chanel No. 5, which was revolutionary for its time in terms of composition, name and method of presentation. A year later, Chanel No. 22 and others came to the market (Chanel, 2022a). Pierre Wertheimer provided capital for the further development of Parfums Chanel in exchange for a 60% stake in the company. Another 30% was owned by Théophile Bader, founder of the Paris-based department store Galeries Lafayette, which facilitated the deal. Gabrielle owned the remaining 10% and for a long time tried unsuccessfully to regain a controlling stake at the co-owned company Les Parfums Chanel, established in April 2024. During WWII, the Wertheimers had to leave for New York because of their Jewish origin. However, before they left, they managed to entrust their share of the administration to a French businessman Félix Améliot, who ret urned the company to them after the war. Gérard and Alain Wertheimer, Pierre's great-grandsons, still head what is now Chanel Limited, which employs approximately 28,500 people (Chanel, 2022b).

After Gabrielle Chanel's death in 1971, her legacy stagnated until Karl Lagerfeld took over as the brand's creative director in 1983. He revived the brand and brought it closer to a younger target group. In 2019, Virginia Viard became creative director after working for Lagerfeld since 1987 as Chloé's creative director, emphasizing traditional craftsmanship and quality combined with the practical side of fashion (Vogue, 2020). Virginia worked not only in accordance with the legacy of Gabrielle Chanel herself but also with regard to the legacy of Lagerfeld (Financial Times, 2022).

From the point of view of corporate finances, Chanel Limited was mysterious for a long time, as it did not publish its results; thus, consulting firms had to speculate on the amount of sales or profits. The change came in 2018, when the company restructured under London-based Chanel Limited and published its earnings for the first time at $9.6 billion with a profit of $1.7 billion, officially placing it among the Top 10 luxury companies or groups (Hoover's Company Records, 2022).

One of the key success factors for the Chanel brand is **limited distribution**. The brand operates only 200 fashion boutiques worldwide (excluding Chanel beauty stores). Queues often form in front of stores, further intensifying potential clients' desire to own some of the items in her portfolio. The company is therefore opening a new concept of boutiques for so-called ultra-elite customers, who will not have to stand in line at regular brick-and-mortar stores. According to Chanel CFO Philippe Blondiaux's statement for Business of Fashion, the core of the luxury business is providing the exclusivity of services for selected customers: Chanel's "biggest preoccupation is to protect our customers and in particular our pre-existing customers. We're going to invest in very protected boutiques to service clients in a very exclusive way" (Fashion United, 2022).

Another success factor is **the pricing policy**. Chanel regularly raises prices, and some of the handbags are already at the level of the Birkin and Kelly line from Hermès. The price of the Chanel Medium Classic Flap (a new version of the iconic 2.55 handbag from 1955, designed by Karl Lagerfeld in 1983) increased from $1,150 in 1990 to $8,800 in November 2021 (Figure 2.2) and to $10,200 in 2024. In some boutiques, there are rules restricting one-time purchases of multiple handbags. The restrictions on availability created in this way signal scarcity and contribute to the growth of desire or dreaming about Chanel. And desire is the key to the success of a luxury brand. At the same time, **limited availability and continuous price growth** contribute to the perception of buying a Chanel handbag as a good investment. Prices in the market for worn handbags are also expected to rise. According to Sotheby's, Chanel has increased its prices four times over three years (2020–2022), and being more expensive directly correlates with being more exclusive (Sotheby's, 2022a).

Chanel is one of the few luxury houses that does not sell its products online (except for make-up, perfumes, skincare and eyewear), and this approach is part of a strategy to create experiences for Chanel customers in their limited number of brick-and-mortar boutiques. According to company president Bruno Pavlovsky, customers who don't want to have an **exclusive shopping experience at their boutique** "don't go to Chanel" (Interino, 2020). In the case of Chanel, this approach to e-commerce does not appear to be an old-fashioned preference for brick-and-mortar stores and traditional distribution but rather part of a strategy to offset lost revenue from online sales with future revenue from a brand that maintains an aura of unavailability, as confirmed by the number of Instagram followers. Chanel's official Instagram site has 59.9 million followers; this is more than other prominent luxury brands (Louis Vuitton 55.6 million, Gucci 52.3 million and Hermès 14.3 million) (data as of August, 2024) and demonstrates the considerable brand awareness among Instagram users.

A brand with a legacy of Gabrielle Chanel can afford such a strategy. The way Karl Lagerfeld and his followers continue her style is relevant to contemporary customers, appealing to potential customers, creating an emotional connection with the brand and at the same time not deviating from the original brand identity based on simple and sophisticated elegance, quality craftsmanship and materials.

2.4.2 Hermès

Founded in 1837 by Thierry Hermès, Hermès ranks 8th in Deloitte's comparison of brands, with sales of $12.2 billion (+29% sales growth YOY) and, together with Chanel and Rolex,

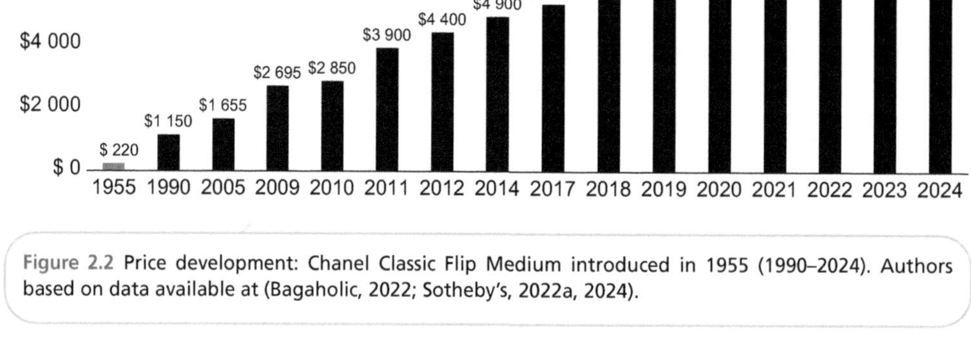

Figure 2.2 Price development: Chanel Classic Flip Medium introduced in 1955 (1990–2024). Authors based on data available at (Bagaholic, 2022; Sotheby's, 2022a, 2024).

forms the only trio of independent brands in the top ten (Table 2.1). It has the industry's highest profit margin in 2022 (29.1%), up by 1.8pp vs. last year (Deloitte, 2023).

The history of the brand began with the opening of a harness workshop in Basse-du-Rempart in Paris. Thierry Hermès, the founder, was awarded for his technical workmanship at the Exposition Universelle in 1867. In 1880, the founder's son moved the workshop to 24 Faubourg Saint-Honoré, where the Hermès boutique still stands today. In the interwar period, Charles-Émile of the third generation of Hermès adapted the portfolio of the family business to the needs of a company in which automobiles largely replaced horses. They were still engaged in saddlery, but at the same time Émile acquired the rights to use the zipper, which changed the direction of the family business. They began to use zippers not only on many bags but also to create clothes. In 1925, they created the first men's ready-to-wear clothing – the golf jacket. The clothing collection was soon followed by jewelry, watches and sandals.

The first silk scarf, *Jeu des omnibus et dames blanches*, was created in 1937 by his son-in-law Robert Dumas, who replaced him with his second son-in-law, Jean René Guearrand, at the head of the company in 1951. Robert Dumas was at the forefront of the development of not only the first silk scarves but also the Kelly handbag (1935) and the *Chaîne d'ancre* bracelet, inspired by a ship's anchor chain. The handbag was named Kelly in 1956, when a photograph of Princess Grace Kelly carrying an Hermès bag with the original name *Sac à dépêches* was published. People spontaneously began to call it Kelly, which the fashion house adopted when they renamed the handbag.

The famous logo with a horse pulling a cart as well as orange paper boxes dates the important brand codes back to the early 1950s. The first women's collection was launched in 1967 under the baton of Catherine Karolyi, a French stylist of Hungarian origin, who designed collections of clothing and accessories, including the now-famous "H" buckle. In 1978, Robert Dumas' son Jean-Louis took over and incorporated watchmaking, shoes (John Lobb), silversmith Puiforcat and crystal manufacturer Saint Louis. The 1984 Birkin handbag was the result of his chance meeting with actress Jane Birkin on a plane from Paris to London; this led to the creation of a bag design sufficiently voluminous and at the same time elegant. In 1993, Hermès went public, but the family retained a majority stake, and the rest of the shares were traded on the stock exchange.

In 2005, a member of the sixth generation of the family, Pierre-Alexis Dumas (son of Jean-Louis) became art director. During his tenure, Hermès complemented the offer with the first collection of high-end jewelry and home accessories in the form of fabrics and wallpaper. In addition, at his initiative, the *Fondation d'entreprise* Hermès was created, which, in keeping with the artistic and craft tradition of the family business, operates in the field of creation, transfer of know-how, protection of the planet and solidarity programs. After Jean-Louis retired in 2006, the company was led for several years by his co-CEO Patrick Thomas, who helped bridge the gap in the family line until the arrival of Axel Dumas, Jean-Louis' nephew, in 2013.

Axel steered the company through a new era of technology, contributing to the restoration of the web and omnichannel distribution and also partnering with Apple to launch the Apple Watch Hermès in 2015 (Hermès, 2022; Hermès International, 2021). At the same time, in 2014, he ended a four-year battle related to the attempt to take over Hermès by LVMH. In October 2010, it came to light that LVMH owned 17% of Hermès, which Bernard Arnault had acquired not on the open market but through equity derivatives. LVMH began buying Hermès shares in 2002 through equity swaps settled in cash, a vehicle used by hedge funds that do not want to disclose their purchases. To protect their heritage and continue the brand's independence, the Hermès family rallied and formed the H51 holding company, in which they locked up 50.2% of the shares for 20 years and agreed to sell shares only among themselves if necessary. Only two owners, members of the fifth generation Bertrand and Nicolas Puech, retained their shares outside the holding but agreed to give the other family members the right of the first refusal if they ever decided to sell. The creation of the holding ended the takeover attempt by LVMH, but the legal battle continued until the agreement, which the president of the French civil court mediated. LVMH has agreed not to purchase any Hermès shares for the next five years, and the current Hermès shares owned by LVMH will be distributed to LVMH shareholders, including the Arnault Groupe. This essentially left Bernard Arnault with an approximately 8.5% stake in Hermès (The Guardian, 2014; Forbes, 2014).

Hermès International, registered in France in 1938, is the parent company of the group and is controlled by the Hermès family. The subsidiary that manages the company's day-to-day activities is Émile Hermès SAS, with Axel Dumas as Group CEO.

The company is divided into divisions, internally called *métiers*. The largest segment by sales in 2021 was leather products and saddlery (46%), followed by ready-to-wear and accessories (22%), fabrics and silks (7%), perfumes (4%), watches (3%) and other (14%). "Other" consists of Hermès jewelry, tableware, housewares and previously mentioned brands from acquisitions such as John Lobb and Puiforcat. Forty-seven percent of sales in 2021 were generated in the Asia-Pacific region, 16% in the Americas, 15% and 9% in Europe and France and 11% in Japan. At the time of writing, the company's latest published results indicate a substantial increase in sales to €8.98 billion (+41% compared to 2020), with the two largest segments (leather and ready-to-wear) recording the largest growth (Hermès International, 2021).

What led Hermès into the top ten luxury houses? As with other companies, it is a combination of various factors. One of the most essential factors is **considered differentiation** from other luxury brands in the **brand's uniqueness** in terms of its DNA and brand codes, which are easily recognizable. Hermès targets the most elite customers of all luxury brands and places enormous emphasis on craftsmanship and valuable materials. Another factor is strong **creativity**, as Axel Dumas pointed out for Forbes: "Our business is about creating desire. It can be fickle because desire is fickle, but we try to have creativity to suspend the momentum" (Adams, 2014). **Family** itself is another success factor. Non-family managers rarely make strategic or branding decisions without the consent of at least one family member (Adams, 2014). This is also related to predominantly organic growth, as the family focuses on building its brand with a significantly limited number of acquisitions compared to other luxury groups. As with Chanel, Hermès has a highly **controlled and limited distribution**, specifically more than 300 stores in 45 countries and e-commerce (Hermès International, 2021). All future store employees must undergo training called "Inside the Orange Box," after the iconic orange box for packaging Hermès products. During the three-day cycle, they receive information about the history of the company and its products and the opportunity to absorb the brand's DNA. **Brand communication** fuels desire and dreaming about the brand. Shop windows are famous for communicating the brand, its style and craftsmanship. There are 136 installations that are repeated at certain intervals in shop windows around the world. They contain art objects designed by Leila Menchari (Hermès designer from 1978 to 2013) that have never been for sale. Last but not least, the emphasis on product innovation is worth mentioning. Som states that the company replaces 50,000 items in its portfolio every six months (Som & Blanckaert, 2021).

Unlike the previously mentioned brands, Hermès is known primarily for its exclusive leather and silk products, which account for more than half of the company's turnover. Strengthening brand value beyond these categories is likely to be a challenge that the company will respond to by strengthening other segments such as luxury watches and cosmetics. Hermès has been able to adapt to changes in consumer needs over time while retaining the original brand identity. It can be assumed that the group will continue to develop and build on the pillars of craftsmanship, exclusive distribution network and creative heritage.

2.4.3 Rolex

In 9th position on the ranking of luxury companies is Rolex (with sales of $10.3 billion in 2022 and an estimated growth rate of 20% – the privately owned company does not publish any data (Deloitte, 2023)). Its history is connected with the entrepreneur and visionary Hans Wilsdorf, originally from Bavaria. In 1905 he began working with a small Swiss watch manufacturer in Bienne, who produced watches with unusually compact movements. He took them to London, where he had them fitted into cases, and in the same year, he was able to start his own watchmaking company. Hans Wilsdorf believed that wristwatches, worn at that time mostly by women as jewelry, could be both elegant and reliable. He thought for a long time about the name of the new watch. He tried to compose different letters of the alphabet to find a short, concise and easy-to-remember name. In 1908, while riding on the upper deck of a horse-drawn carriage in London, the name Rolex came to mind. The word had style and authority, and it looked good on the watch face. Within days, Hans Wilsdorf registered his trademark.

In 1910, he received the first certificate of chronometric accuracy of wristwatches from the Watch Evaluation Centre in Bienne, Switzerland. In 1914, when he was not yet 30 years old, the London Kew Observatory awarded him a Class A certificate of accuracy, which until then had been reserved essentially only for nautical chronometers, the most accurate watches of the time. In 1919, he established a permanent plant in Geneva, where he recruited quality craftsmen and engineers of Swiss watchmaking for Rolex.

Rolex's communications through sports and artistic personalities began with the launch of the world's first waterproof wristwatch, the Rolex Oyster, in 1926. In 1927, when Mercedes Gleitze became the first British woman to swim across the English Channel, she wore a Rolex Oyster watch and also became the first ambassador of the Rolex brand. This tradition has been followed by hundreds of prominent personalities from the world of sports and art (Sir Edmund Hillary, Roger Federer, Tiger Woods and many others). Today, in addition to golf, motorsport and equestrianism, Rolex also supports individuals and organizations that are actively trying to protect the planet and push the boundaries of their field.

In 1931, the five-pointed crown became part of the logo, and the first automatic wristwatch, the Rolex Oyster Perpetual, was launched on the market; its operation depended only on wrist movements. The company celebrated its 40th anniversary in 1945 with the launch of the Rolex Date just with the added date function in the window on the dial. After the death of Hans Wilsdorf's wife in 1944, the childless Hans Wilsdorf decided to find a way to secure a philanthropic future for his business and established the foundation *La Fondation Hans Wilsdorf*, to which he transferred ownership of the entire company in 1960 (Rolex SA, 2022). The foundation operates in the Swiss canton of Geneva, where it supports social institutions, students, schools and culture and, according to available information, remains the sole owner of Rolex (Fondation Hans Wilsdorf, 2022). Rolex is one of the few private companies in the world that dedicates its profits to society. It is estimated that the Hans Wilsdorf Foundation donates up to half a billion dollars a year (Tribune de Genève, 2018).

After Hans Wilsdorf left the management, the Heiniger family managed the company for more than 50 years. André J. Heiniger took over the management in 1962. He contributed to the crucial decision to continue the focus on mechanical watches and to support sporting events and personalities. In 1976, he founded the Rolex Awards to mark the 50th anniversary of the launch of the Rolex Oyster watch. The award was supposed to be the only celebration, but it generated such international interest that Rolex turned it into a long-term program, which has supported many projects over the years. These projects have significantly contributed to improving life around the world and protecting the planet. In 1992, André's son, Patrick Heiniger, took over the management and focused on vertical supply chain integration to achieve full control over the entire production in turbulent times. After leaving in 2008, he remained an advisor to the firm, but CEO positions are filled in-house or by external managers.

Rolex has long maintained its number one position in Swiss watch exports based on sales. The dominant position for 2021 was confirmed by the Morgan Stanley report, which states Rolex's 28.8% share of the Swiss watch market, up 3.9 percentage points compared to the previous year (Professional Watches, 2022).

What is the source of Rolex's long-term success? The first important factor is **brand awareness.** A luxury customer who is not an expert in watches and watch manufacturing is certainly aware of the brand and spontaneously thinks of a Rolex when he thinks of a watch. A professional customer with awareness of other luxury watch brands will appreciate the craftsmanship, the brand's tradition and the delicacies of select editions. For most ordinary customers, Rolex is synonymous with luxury watches. **The long-term emphasis on quality** without fads is another factor in the success of the brand, which gives the brand a certain robustness and reliability. The already mentioned **vertical integration** is another factor and is related to the quality of the product. At Rolex, all components are manufactured in its own manufacturing facilities in Switzerland. The production chain also includes a foundry on the outskirts of Geneva with the production of three different types of gold and its own stainless-steel mold. All components come from its own production, are hand-assembled and undergo final quality control at the Geneva headquarters (Som & Blanckaert, 2021). The long-term **consistency of the design** of the individual series is another success factor. Each product from the new collections is an inspired revival of the original design. As with the previously mentioned Chanel handbags, Rolex is even more visibly perceived as an **investment** whose value has growing potential – especially in the case of the selected pieces. According to Sotheby's, Rolex is king for many watch collectors, especially the Daytona brand, which until 2017 held the record for the most expensive wristwatch ever sold (Sotheby's, 2022b). The **controlled shortage** of some models is another part of a strategy, which supports the desire for the brand. In the case of Rolex, for example, it is the steel Daytona model, popularized in the 60s by Paul Newman's wrist, for which long waiting lists are kept. The list price of model no. 116500LN is around $15,000; the price of the same model on the secondary market is more than double. Rolex keeps the offer within such limits to maintain an aura of unavailability. Paul Newman's personal Daytona was auctioned off in 2017 for a then-record $17.75 million (Chrono24, 2022). Consistent **brand communication in the form of a celebration of success** through the promotion of prestigious sports and athletes is another success factor. The brand's slogans *Crown for every achievement* or *Live for Greatness* associate Rolex with success.

2.4.4 Other independent luxury brands

In addition to the previously mentioned Chanel, Hermès and Rolex brands, independent and privately owned fashion houses still include Italian brands Armani, Dolce & Gabbana, Ermenegildo Zegna, Salvatore Ferragamo or Burberry and many others. The only purely British representative of traditional luxury in fashion is the Burberry brand, founded in

1856, which has managed to diversify its portfolio. In addition to the classic trench coat, it is also active in leather products, accessories and fragrances.

Independent watch and jewelry manufacturers include Audemars Piquet (1875, still owned by members of the founding family) (Audemars Piquet, 2022), Asprey London (with a tradition of supplying the royal palace since 1781) (Asprey, 2022), Chopard (jewelry and watchmaking from 1860, owned by the German Scheufele family) (Chopard, 2022), Graff (jewelry brand founded in London in 1960, managed by the founding family) (Graff, 2022) and Patek Philippe (1851, today a private company in the hands of the Stern family, which invested in the brand as early as 1932, and its members still stand at its head today) (Patek Philippe, 2022).

2.5 Luxury cars: Advanced technology for the demanding Chinese market

According to Bain & Company, luxury car sales, the largest segment of the overall luxury market, reached a new high in 2023, with an estimated value of €635 billion, reflecting a 12% increase from 2022 and a 15% increase compared to 2019. After years of limited growth due to supply chain disruptions, the luxury car sector expanded across all categories. **The fastest growth occurred in the ultra-luxury segment**, driven by heightened demand for highly **customized vehicles** and a growing focus on sustainable powertrain options. Steady growth was also monitored in the **aspirational segment, where electric vehicles have become increasingly popular**. Across the market, brands are focusing on cultivating direct relationships with clients to enhance both the purchasing and after-sales experience, while online platforms have become a more important channel for making purchases (Bain & Company, 2024). In Europe, Asian car producers (especially Chinese brands) are gaining market share. With growing demand for eco-friendly vehicles, premium manufacturers are focusing on larger models to offset the higher costs of electric vehicles. Personalization, digital connectivity and rising service expectations are also key trends, with brands adopting direct-to-consumer models for a more luxurious shopping experience (Bain & Company, 2023). The luxury car market accounts for approximately 20% of the total global market value.

Total global new car registrations account for up to 72.5 million units (2023). Just over a 30% **(30.8%) share of the new registrations comes from China**, followed by the United States (17.0%) and European Union (14.6%). China is the largest world's producer, with a 33.5% market share. Interestingly, in 2023, Indian passenger car sales reached a record high of approximately 4.2 million units, marking an 8.5% increase and exceeding Japan's sales volume. This surge was fueled by a growing demand for personal mobility and the launch of new vehicle models (ACEA, 2024). Chinese and Indian consumers are reported as very loyal in terms of preferring their personal cars to have local origins. For 37% of Indian and 24% of Chinese customers, the **local country of production** of their next car is very important (e.g. compared to 11% of German consumers) (Deloitte, 2024). This is one of the main reasons (together with supply chain development, size of the market, government policies and other factors) various manufacturers are considering moving or expanding their production facilities to China and India. Tesla, as an example, has built a Gigafactory in Shanghai, which is one of its largest production facilities in the world.

According to the analyses of Mordor Intelligence report, the Chinese luxury car market is worth $154.7 billion (vs. the global luxury car market of $738.6 billion) in 2024. It is forecast to climb at a CAGR of 3.35% to $181.5 billion in 2029. This growth is projected to be driven by the rise of SUVs, electric vehicles and Gen Z customers (Mordor Intelligence,

2024). It is worth mentioning that these market estimates include sales of brands like BMW, Audi, Lexus and Mercedes Benz, which are not considered luxury brands within the context of traditional European luxury literature.

In China, luxury cars – traditionally dominated by European legacy brands such as Rolls-Royce, Bentley, Ferrari and Porsche – are being challenged by emerging domestic brands such as Zeekr 001, NIO ET9, HiPhi and Hongqi L5 (Gulf News, 2024). However, there are indications that the further development and maintenance of a Chinese brand in this sector may not be sustainable. In August 2024, it was announced that HiPhi's parent company, Human Horizons, had filed for bankruptcy. This could foreshadow concern for the Chinese automaker, which is known for its innovative electric vehicles (CarNewsChina, 2024).

Compared to their counterparts in major developed automotive markets, Chinese car buyers have a broader perspective on what constitutes as "luxury." While traditional factors like craftsmanship and quality continue to be significant, a McKinsey survey indicated that **Chinese consumers strongly emphasize technology**. They are particularly interested in advancements related to powertrain systems, digital interactions, connectivity and advanced driver-assistance systems (ADAS). In contrast, **European and American luxury car buyers tend to prioritize styling, performance and the driving experience.**

Beyond electrification, which luxury segment customers now expect as a given, Chinese luxury-car buyers also place a high value on the "smartification" of their electric vehicles (EVs). Approximately 40 to 50% of serious EV buyers view the latest ADAS and connectivity features as essential components of their EV purchases. Currently, up to 20% of Chinese car buyers believe that new EV manufacturers are outperforming traditional automakers in terms of smartification – a gap that the established industry needs to address.

Consumers are also looking for **fast-charging stations and battery services** that effectively address concerns about battery life. Today, around 70% of Chinese consumers who are hesitant to consider EVs cite **range and charging issues as the primary deterrents**. Globally, original equipment manufacturers (OEMs), governments and related organizations are working to ensure that sufficient charging stations are available on key routes to meet the growing demand for EVs; nevertheless, these challenges remain a significant obstacle. In response, local OEMs are heavily innovating in these areas. Various factors are contributing to success, including a seamless, technology-enhanced customer experience both within and beyond the vehicle (McKinsey, 2022).

Mini-case 2.1 Maserati and Gen Z: Effective targeting, but challenges due to market dynamics in China

Maserati, founded in 1914 in Bologna, Italy, by the Maserati brothers, has a rich history of innovation and excellence in automotive engineering. Initially focused on motorsports, the brand became known for its high-performance vehicles. Maserati's legacy includes iconic models like the Maserati A6GCS, 3500 G and the Quattroporte, which set standards in both racing and luxury markets. Over the decades, Maserati has evolved, blending its racing heritage with luxury; it continues to be a symbol of Italian craftsmanship and performance (Maserati, 2024).

Nowadays, Maserati is owned by Stell antis N.V., a multinational automotive group formed in 2021 through the merger of Fiat Chrysler Automobiles (FCA) and the French PSA Group. Stellantis oversees a portfolio of well-known automotive brands (Jeep, Alfa Romeo, Lancia, Chrysler, Fiat, Opel and many others), including Maserati, and continues to support Maserati's operations as a luxury vehicle manufacturer within the global automotive market (Maserati Media, 2024). FY 2023 results showed growing Maserati performance with 26,700 cars sold globally, up 8% compared to 2022 (Stellantis, 2024a).

The Gen Z demographic in China constitutes a pivotal consumer base within the luxury goods sector, distinguished by its affinity for digital engagement, personalization and brand authenticity. Gen Z consumers are digital natives and are expected to drive new requirements in various segments of the luxury market. They tend to prefer **unique, customized experiences and seek brands that resonate with their individual values and personal lifestyles**. These customer preferences will require a revision of traditional luxury marketing strategies.

Maserati has skillfully exploited the power of social media to establish and maintain a strong connection with younger consumers in China. The brand's social communication strategy has been rooted in the utilization of **major Chinese social media platforms,** including WeChat, Weibo, Douyin and Xiaohongshu. These platforms served as channels for Maserati to deliver content transcending conventional advertising, focusing instead on creating immersive, experience-oriented stories that resonate with a young audience. Therefore, the content aimed to **establish and cultivate dialogue** with a brand community **of followers with a deep personal connection to the brand**.

In an interview for The Luxury Conversation, Sophia Sun, marketing director for Maserati in China, confirmed that the company pays close attention to the insights related to young Chinese consumers: "the mainland China market now has already become the youngest market for Maserati. Those young elites here not only have diverse preferences, but also are keen on expressing their unique tastes and individuality through personalized luxuries or even customizations" (The Luxury Conversation, 2020). She also named two factors contributing to the successful social strategy in China, namely **sincerity** (accept and understand them, get closer to them and start communication) and **fresh and creative content** powered by digital information and data. It is also vital to attract young talents who understand Gen Z preferences and lifestyle, events, topics and the viral happenings that attract their attention. And finally, she also pointed out the need for traditional integrated marketing communication that reaches consumers at each point of the customer journey (The Luxury Conversation, 2020).

Early on, Maserati recognized and understood the significance of **gaming culture** among Chinese Gen Z; consequently, the company expanded its brand presence into the industry. One significant example is Maserati's collaboration with Tencent Games (Tencent is one of the largest Chinese tech companies (Investopedia, 2023)). **The integration of the Maserati Ghibli model into the widely popular "Game for Peace"** has enabled Maserati to connect with younger audiences in the virtual environment, where they already spend a considerable amount of time. This created a new digital touchpoint on the potential customer journey. The gamification strategy has engaged Gen Z within a context they find appealing; it also enables them to experience the luxury and performance associated with Maserati vehicles in a dynamic and interactive way. This approach effectively bridged the gap between the brand's luxury heritage and the digital preferences of younger consumers, thereby reinforcing Maserati's relevance in the evolving luxury landscape (The Luxury

Conversation, 2020). The Maserati gaming involvement has continued, and another cooperation with Tencent Games was announced in 2023 by Maserati Chinese licensing partner Endeavor China (License Global, 2023).

However, Maserati has experienced a **decline in its sales performance in China** since 2020. Several factors reflecting the broader challenges facing the Chinese luxury automotive have contributed to this deterioration. First, it has become increasingly comp etitive, with many brands vying for market share. Maserati has struggled to keep pace with competitors like Porsche and Lamborghini, both of whom have outperformed Maserati in terms of product innovation and consumer appeal. The "product part" of Maserati's marketing mix has been slow to innovate, with delays in updating key models like the Quattroporte and Ghibli (Stock Dividend Screener, 2024; Stellantis, 2024b). It is important not to underestimate solid brand building or product development. An innovative communication strategy paired with the correct use of social media is still not enough unless balanced with the other Ps of the marketing mix. Product policy and branding must be front and center.

Growing environmental awareness and stimulations provided by governmental policies have contributed to a shift in consumer preferences towards electric vehicles. Maserati, which has only recently begun to introduce electrified models, has responded slower to this trend than some of its competitors. This delay has contributed to a perception that Maserati is not as forward looking as other luxury brands (Stock Dividend Screener, 2024; Italpassion, 2024). Slower economic growth and increased consumer caution have also affe cted consumer demand in the luxury car market. Maserati has been affected by these macroeconomic factors, resulting in reduced sales volumes. For example, in the first half of 2024, Maserati's total sales dec reased by more than 50%. Despite these challenges, Stellantis, the parent company of Maserati, has confirmed its commitment to the brand. However, the future will require substantial efforts to revitalize its product lineup and regain consumer interest in China (Stellantis, 2024b).

In summary, the market segment of luxury cars in China is transforming, and Chinese domestic brands continue to challenge the established European luxury manufacturers by reflecting reshaped consumer expectations, resulting in demand for innovative features, electric vehicles and personalization. Traditional luxury brands like Maserati must adapt their marketing mix to the unique desires of the young demographic, with increased implementation of digital touchpoints along the customer journey. The challenges are significant, but the opportunity for growth remains vast.

2.6 Luxury hospitality and experiential marketing

According to Bain & Company, the luxury hospitality sector rose to €191 billion in 2022, more than doubling from the previous year, but still 7% below 2019 levels. Growth was steady as people fulfilled postponed travel plans, though Chinese lockdowns and reduced Asian tourism limited overall growth. Travelers showed increased interest in both major cities and remote destinations, continuing the trend of seeking rural escapes. Intuitive, technology-enhanced service is becoming crucial, allowing operators to automate predictable tasks and allow employees to focus on meaningful interactions (Bain & Company, 2023).

However, in 2023, the luxury hospitality market reached an estimated €213 billion, finally surpassing pre-pandemic levels, driven by higher occupancy rates and a more stable average daily rate (ADR – the total revenues from occupied rooms divided by the total number of occupied rooms over a given period). The US and Latin American markets grew due to increased regional tourism, while China remained below pre-COVID levels. Room price rates have stabilized at higher-than-usual levels across the globe. There has been an **increase in demand for unique, personalized and transformative experiences,** that is, those that offer a break from everyday life. High-net-worth and ultra-high-net-worth individuals now seek experiences that go beyond traditional luxury, focusing more on authenticity, cultural immersion and sustainability. Younger generations, in particular, are driving this shift towards impact-conscious travel, and rising service expectations are prompting the use of new technology and data-driven solutions (Bain & Company, 2024).

Luxury tourism is a complex and multifaceted concept that a single defining attribute cannot encapsulate. Traditionally, luxury hospitality was associated with attributes such as quality and price, the combination of which created an expectation of luxury as an objective standard. However, contemporary discussions emphasize that luxury within the context of hospitality and tourism is more subjective and therefore shaped by individual consumer perceptions. Luxury tourism goes beyond product features, quality and price. Rather, it **encompasses unique and unconventional experiences that prioritize meaningfulness and preciousness.** The other attributes, such as authenticity, novelty and uniqueness, are relevant but often overlooked (Iloranta, 2022). According to Bain reports, the growth in demand for luxury experiences is driven by a renewed desire for social interaction and travel, reconnected with luxury offerings that go beyond material goods (Bain & Company, 2024).

2.6.1 The experience economy and luxury hospitality

According to Atwal and Williams, *experiential marketing* relates to "taking the essence of a product and amplifying it into a set of tangible, physical and interactive experiences that reinforce the offer" (2009, p. 49).

The *Experience Economy* by Pine and Gilmore (1998) argues that businesses must orchestrate memorable events for their customers, and that the memory itself becomes the product – the "experience" (Pine II & Gilmore, 1998). "Experiences" are strongly linked to all segments in luxury – personal luxury, automotive, luxury dining, private jets, yachts and others. Within the context of luxury hospitality, *experiential marketing* approaches offer **personalized, immersive and memorable experiences that go beyond the standard service to deeply engage guests.** This approach can contribute to building long-term brand loyalty and justify the premium price by making the experience itself a key aspect of the value offered (Pine II & Gilmore, 1998).

In the rapidly evolving landscape of luxury hospitality, the metaverse (more in Chapter 7) as a new space for experiential marketing, is emerging as a transformative approach that leverages new technologies to enable better guest experiences. The metaverse, a virtual reality-based universe, might become a platform where luxury hospitality brands can develop charming, interactive environments. Integration of virtual (VR) and augmented reality (AR) can mirror or even surpass the physical guest experience and provide guests with a sense of presence that was previously unimaginable.

Within the metaverse, guests can personalize their individual avatars and surroundings to deepen the emotional connection with the brand. Additionally, the metaverse can facilitate development **of story-driven, multi-sensory experiences,** which can be continuously updated to keep the guest experience fresh. By implementing these product policy tactics, luxury hospitality brands can offer guests a blend of exclusivity, novelty and immersive luxury, setting new standards across the industry (Vijai & Wisetsri, 2024).

VR and AR technologies enable immersive virtual tours, allowing potential guests to explore hotel properties, rooms and amenities in a realistic manner. The virtual tours can help to make better informed decisions about the luxury hospitality journey. VR technology can create virtual event spaces, enabling remote participation. AR can improve guest experiences by providing virtual concierge services and interactive menus, or assisting with language translation and cultural education (Vijai & Wisetsri, 2024).

To conclude, **combining cutting-edge technology with highly personalized, authentic and immersive experiences** is the approach enabling more immersive experiences for luxury guests. Singh and Kaunert (2024) suggest the following to enhance experiences in luxury hospitality:

- Metaverse integration – leveraging the metaverse to offer immersive and personalized guest experiences. This includes virtual property tours, where guests can explore luxurious accommodations before their stay, and virtual reality (VR) or augmented reality (AR) experiences that allow guests to engage with destinations or customize their environments digitally;
- Customization and personalization – tailoring experiences to individual guest preferences through advanced technologies. VR and AR enable guests to adjust aspects such as lighting, decor, and ambiance in virtual environments, enhancing the personalization aspect of luxury hospitality;
- Immersive storytelling – creating unique narratives and immersive experiences is seen as essential in delivering luxury services. Guests are increasingly looking for transformative and memorable experiences, which can be elevated by blending the virtual and physical worlds; and
- Focus on sustainability and authenticity – the younger generation in particular is increasingly prioritizing sustainability and authentic, culturally immersive experiences, providing luxury brands an opportunity to enhance their uniqueness (Singh & Kaunert, 2024).

2.6.2 Experiential luxury: The intersection of hospitality and iconic brands

Luxury groups and independent brands are entering luxury hospitality to offer unique experiences that are fully aligned with their existing brand identities. Integrating luxury hospitality into a portfolio of established brands allows them to build customer loyalty by creating an environment for them to spend their leisure time. These environments reflect the DNA and existing brand codes. Brands are diversifying revenue sources, capitalizing on the growing demand for luxury experiences, and leveraging synergies between existing brand customers and hospitality businesses.

LVMH, as an example, has strategically partnered with hotel group Accor to develop the Orient-Express brand (this is despite the fact that they already owned Belmond since 2019 – a group with almost 50 luxury hotel properties in 26 countries including Venice Simplon-Orient-Express as well as Eastern & Oriental Express and British Pullman (Belmond, 2024)). While Accor has launched several Orient-Express projects, including luxury trains and hotels, progress has been slower than expected (CPPLUXURY, 2024) (more about the planned expansion of Orient Express into the sea in the next section). Belmond's strategy is, according to its CEO Dan Ruff, based on providing the best experiences for luxury travelers at each point of their journey. They understand how time is valued by their clients and therefore their aim is focused on the **concept of slow luxury**, which should enable their clients to disconnect from the fast-paced world and reconnect to people, places and themselves (Ruff, 2024).

Expansion of luxury brands into the luxury hospitality sector engages HNWIs in exclusive, branded environments in places like beach clubs, hotel pools and yachts. This strategy allows brands to target affluent customers during their leisure time, enhancing brand visibility and driving sales. Successful examples include the Miu or Balmain partnerships with luxury resorts and yachts, which have generated significant media value and sales. Miu Miu's Summer Club in Cannes generated over $2.18 million in earned media value (EMV) in summer 2024 when they started to post on social media directly at the beach (Vogue Business, 2024b). These collaborations succeed by blending exclusivity with high social media engagement, creating unique experiences that resonate with their target audience.

The strategic landscape of LVMH's luxury hospitality ventures, for example, is extremely complex and multi-faceted, exemplified by the operations of BVLGARI Hotels, a brand under LVMH's portfolio, which operates globally in partnership with Marriott International. LVMH does not currently own these properties, and the integration of BVLGARI Hotels into LVMH's wholly owned hospitality ventures could present opportunities for operational synergies within the group. BVLGARI Hotels are continuing to expand, for example into Miami and the Maldives. Therefore, the importance of consistent ownership and sustained investment in maintaining the BVLGARI brand guidelines is becoming increasingly evident. This is particularly relevant when comparing the operational models of other leading luxury hotel groups, such as the Dorchester Collection and Aman, where ownership is critical in delivering a consistent, high-level of service and brand experience. The precedent set by these groups underscores the potential benefits LVMH could realize through a more integrated approach to its hospitality portfolio with better control over the brands' offerings (CPPLUXURY, 2024).

LVMH's excellence in hospitality is further illustrated by its Cheval Blanc and Belmond properties. Both are owned and managed by LVMH and represent the group's ability to harmonize luxury branding with high hospitality standards. The potential integration of BVLGARI Hotels into this model could strengthen LVMH's leadership in luxury hospitality and create a consistent brand experience across its portfolio. Moreover, LVMH's Parfums Christian Dior has been actively expanding its luxury wellness offerings, as evidenced by the launch of the new Dior Spas and the innovative "Dior Spa Cheval Blanc Cruise" on the Seine in Paris, following other pop-up spa locations in Portofino and Taormina (LVMH, 2023a).

The example of LVMH's strategic focus on its luxury hospitality ventures, such as Cheval Blanc, Belmond and potentially BVLGARI Hotels, is a showcase example of experiential marketing. The brands create memorable experiences for clients thereby building a strong emotional connection. The experiences – ranging from the refined elegance of Cheval Blanc properties to innovative Dior Spa offerings – reinforce the exclusivity and prestige associated with the brands.

2.7 Remaining segments in luxury: Experiences from art to adventure and gourmet delights

The remaining segments capture the diverse, high-end experiences and products that go beyond traditional personal luxury goods. **Fine wines and spirits** sales reached €100 billion in 2023, up 5% from 2022. Fine wines experienced modest growth, driven by the return of social interactions and gatherings. However, the growth is limited by aspirational consumers opting for lower-priced alternatives – sparkling and rosé wines exhibit the strongest performance. Spirits overall show positive growth, but there were significant differences between categories. Spirits consumed at home saw a slowdown, while spirits linked to mixology and out-of-home consumption, such as in bars and restaurants, accelerated, confirming the luxury customer need of experiences. Interestingly, agave-based spirits (like tequila) continued to gain popularity, particularly in mixology, taking market share from gin (Bain & Company, 2024).

Gourmet food and fine dining grew 10%, reaching €60 billion in 2023 and fully recovering to pre-pandemic levels. The trend of enjoying gourmet food at home continued from 2022, boosting select retailers and demand for culinary education (Bain & Company, 2023, 2024). The growth in 2023 was driven by the segment referred to as "entertainment-is-the-star," suggesting that fine dining is evolving to focus on creating **unique, immersive experiences that entertain guests**, such as theatrical presentations, interactive elements or live performances. The enjoyment of gourmet food has apparently shifted towards the overall experience, a concept that has become a key driver in the fine dining industry. The Michelin Guide, a synonym for fine dining, has seen a significant boom in 2023, adding new global destinations like Buenos Aires and Hanoi and awarding 930 restaurants with stars. It also introduced the Michelin Key for exceptional hotels and **highlighted sustainability by recognizing 505 establishments with "Green Stars"** (Michelin, 2024). The Michelin Guide was established in 1900 by brothers André and Edouard Michelin to promote car travel in France by offering useful information for motorists, such as maps, tire repair tips and recommendations for places to eat and stay. Initially given out for free, it began selling in 1920, and in 1926, the guide introduced its famous star rating system for fine dining. **Today, the Michelin Guide rates over 30,000 establishments** worldwide and is recognized as a symbol of culinary excellence (Michelin Guide, 2024).

High-end furniture and housewares sales were at €53 billion, stable since 2022 (Bain & Company, 2024). Previous years' growth was driven by the increased importance of home life since the pandemic, with lighting and living/bedroom furnishings seeing the most gains. In commercial spaces, demand for high-end furniture grew as consumers sought refined aesthetics and higher quality (Bain & Company, 2023).

Fine art market sales reached €42 billion. Unlike in previous years, Bain highlights a shift towards Gen Y and female clientele. Growing interest in diversity, equity and inclusion subjects was emphasized (Bain & Company, 2024), with galleries and collectors focusing more on diversity, including female artists and African art. Art itself is increasingly being considered an alternative asset, used to hedge against volatility in the financial markets. The market for nonfungible tokens (NFTs) stabilized, and art-related NFTs still represent a small but growing portion of the market (Bain & Company, 2023; Art Basel & UBS, 2023). From the geographical perspective, the US market is the biggest with 42% of sales by value, followed by China (19%) and the UK (8%). These markets are also the most significant for public auction sales. Sales of **art-related NFTs** on platforms outside the art market reached $2.9 billion in 2021 but have dropped over the last two years, reaching $1.2 billion in 2023. Despite the decline, this market is still much larger than in 2020 when it was only $20 million. Nevertheless, the slowdown indicates that the initial interest of the investors behind art-related NFTs is calming down (Art Basel & UBS, 2023).

The sales of **private yachts and jets** grew by 11%, a sales value of €29 billion in 2023. Orders for luxury yachts have reached record levels thanks to the desire of millionaires for a deeper connection with nature and comfort. Sustainability seems to be increasingly important, evident from greener propulsion systems and recyclable yacht materials. Private jet usage also increased, driven by safety and efficiency concerns, though rising sustainability issues and operational costs have limited this market's growth (Bain & Company, 2023, 2024).

The luxury cruises market, a €4 billion segment (Bain & Company, 2024), includes brands like Orient Express, Paul Gauguin, Ponant and Ritz-Carlton, which are known for their high-end offerings and unique experiences. The market is expected to grow significantly, with at least 97 luxury ships projected by 2028. The focus is on smaller, more intimate vessels that cater to affluent travelers seeking exclusive and personalized experiences. The segment is driven by new ships, new brands and a strong demand for luxury travel experiences (Cruise Industry News, 2024).

Mini-case 2.2 The Orient-Express: The brand's nostalgic heritage in the luxury cruise segment

The Orient Express brand has long been synonymous with luxury and elegance. It now plans to expand its legendary brand from rail to sea. The announced introduction of the *Orient Express Silenseas* indicates a new milestone, promising a unique and luxurious sailing experience that blends the opulence of the past with cutting-edge innovations for the future while respecting the brand identity of the traditional luxury experience provider.

The Orient Express originally began its journey as a luxury train service in 1883, connecting major cities across Europe with elegance and style. Over the decades, the brand has become emblematic of luxurious travel, offering an experience that exceeds ordinary transportation. It has always represented the essence of adventure, opulence, luxury and timeless charm (Orient Express, 2024). Initially part of the Com pagnie Internationale des Wagons-Lits, the Orient Express brand has faced several ownership transitions over the years.

By the 1970s, the original Orient Express trains had made their last journeys, and the wagons were retired. James Sherwood, an American entrepreneur, invested $31 million in the acquisition and restoration of carriages to establish the "Venice Simplon-Orient-Express," which is currently owned by Belmond. To further expand his enterprise, Sherwood incorporated a collection of hotels under the name "Orient-Express Hotels," later rebranding the company as Belmond in 2014 (later acquired by LVMH). Separately, Swiss tour operator Albert Glatt initiated a rail service connecting Zurich and Istanbul, referred to as the "Nostalgie-Istanbul-Orient-Express" (CNBC, 2022). This service was eventually acquired by Accor, a global leader in hospitality, in 2017. Under Accor's ownership, the brand has undergone a revitalization, focusing on expanding its luxury offerings beyond the confines of rail travel to include hotels, trains and sailing yachts. The Orient Express is integrated within Accor's Luxury & Lifestyle Division, alongside with respe cted brands like Raffles and Fairmont. This strategic initiative is aligned with Accor's broader objective of enhancing its luxury portfolio and delivering incomparable, unique and high-end travel experiences across diverse sectors (Accor, 2024).

Challenges related to implementing a luxury business strategy may occur when expanding the Orient Express brand into marine territory. The luxury cruise market is highly competitive, and well-established brands already dominate the market. In order for *Orient Express Silenseas* to succeed, it should offer unique experiences yet at the same time strongly and consistently

Picture 2.2 Orient Express restaurant. By Epistola8. Available under the Creative Commons Attribution-Share Alike 4.0 International license on (Wikimedia Commons, 2015).

respect the distinct identity of the original brand. In addition, the brand should appeal to a new generation of travelers who, while seeking opulent travel experiences, also value sustainability and environmental responsibility.

Central to this maritime venture is the *Orient Express Silenseas*, scheduled to launch in 2026. This vessel, a result of collaboration with Chantiers de l'Atlantique (a shipbuilding company), should represent a step forward in sustainable maritime technology – it is supposed to be equipped with innovative SolidSail rigs, each covering 1,500 square meters, and should feature a hybrid propulsion system that combines sail power with a liquefied natural gas motor, with provisions for future green hydrogen use. The 220 meter ship will have 54 suites averaging 70 square meters, along with two swimming pools, two restaurants and a bar (Accor, 2024; Orient Express, 2024).

This focus on sustainability is in-line with the growing demand among luxury travelers for experiences that are not only indulgent, but also environmentally conscious. As Accor's CEO Sébastien Bazin remarked, "This exceptional sailing yacht, with roots in Orient Express' history, will offer unparalleled service and refined design spaces, reminiscent of the golden age of mythical cruises" (The New Zealand Herald, 2023). The expansion of the Orient Express brand into the sea with the forthcoming launch of the *Silenseas* represents a new chapter in the brand's storied history. The new venture also underscores its commitment to offering sustainable, luxurious journeys.

2.8 Summary: Stories of strong brands, founders and the dynamics of individual luxury segments

The overview of groups and brands in the personal luxury segment shows the consolidation of the sector taking place since the establishment of the LVMH, Richemont and Kering groups in the 1980s to the present, associated with significant acquisitions of brands operating in luxury for several centuries. On the contrary, brands such as Rolex, Chanel or Hermès demonstrate the strength of their identities by their presence among strong groups; they face the managerial challenges of large groups as well as potential acquisition efforts, yet they remain independent. According to predictions, these three brands will maintain their independence, while others will become part of larger groups. This is likely for separate brands, especially from the luxury fashion sector, such as Armani or Burberry and others (Rambourg, 2020).

The strong story, history and heritage of the most valuable brands hint at the foundations of traditional luxury. Gabrielle Chanel's stubbornness, doggedness, independence and courage are still present in the brand's DNA. Nevertheless, a key question remains: how to most effectively face the challenges of today's turbulent times, retain the original brand identity, and yet still appeal to a new generation of consumers, thus ensuring long-term growth?

The last section is dedicated to luxury segments outside of personal luxury. First, it explores how Chinese consumers, particularly the younger generation, are reshaping the luxury car market, both inside China and around the world. Thus, there is an open question regarding how the luxury car segment will adapt to these evolving consumer behaviors, such as the desire for personalization, advanced technology and sustainability. The mini-case on Maserati's engagement with younger Chinese consumers highlights the brand's effort to communicate effectively while simultaneously adapting to rapidly changing market conditions. It also emphasizes the importance of integrating well targeted digital touch points when planning communications

The luxury hospitality sector is viewed through the lens of experiential marketing. It discusses how the experience economy provides a significant opportunity for this sector to differentiate its brands by offering memorable, personalized experiences that go beyond traditional luxury offerings. It investigates the synergies between luxury hospitality and established brands from the personal luxury segment. A mini-case study on Orient-Express discusses the brand's potential growth into the luxury cruise segment. It explores how to expand its legendary heritage into new territories without devaluing the brand's unique and valued heritage.

The last part of the chapter briefly describes the dynamics of the remaining segments within the luxury industry such as art or gourmet cuisine. It points out how these segments are increasingly becoming an integral part of the luxury experience and offer wealthy consumers tailor-made experiences.

Key terms

Brand Independence: A strategic approach within luxury groups where each brand is operated independently, with independent marketing, new product development and distribution as well as other functions, allowing for distinct brand identities.

Concepts of Luxury: A framework that distinguishes between various aspects of luxury, including absolute luxury (exclusive and inaccessible), relative luxury (more accessible, small pleasures), personal luxury (emotionally driven, experiential), luxury as an industrial sector (focused on market analysis and segmentation) and luxury as a business model and strategy (brand management, pricing and distribution strategies). This framework helps to understand the multi-faceted nature of luxury and its application across different contexts within the industry.

Controlled Scarcity: A strategic approach in luxury brand management where the availability of certain products is intentionally limited to increase desirability and maintain exclusivity.

Craftsmanship: The emphasis on superior quality and artisanal skills in the production of luxury goods, often a key differentiator for brands like Hermès and Rolex.

E-Commerce in Luxury: The adaptation of online retail strategies by luxury brands, often carefully balanced with maintaining exclusivity and brand identity, as seen in the cautious approach by brands like Chanel.

***Griffe*:** A term used in luxury brand management to describe the highest level of luxury products, characterized by an artist's unique creative signature and supreme craftsmanship.

Kapferer's Luxury Criteria: A set of six criteria formulated by Jean-Noël Kapferer to distinguish luxury brands from premium brands, focusing on aspects such as hedonistic experience, quality, heritage, limited distribution, specific pricing or personalized accompanying services.

Luxury Automotive Market: Refers to the segment of the automotive industry that produces high-end, luxury vehicles known for superior quality, advanced technology and exclusive features. This market includes traditional luxury brands like Rolls-Royce.

Luxury Conglomerates: Large corporations (groups) that manage multiple luxury brands under a single corporate umbrella (e.g. Kering, LVMH or Richemont). These conglomerates typically operate with a strategy that allows individual brands to maintain their unique identities while benefiting from shared resources.

LVMH (Moët Hennessy-Louis Vuitton SE): A French multinational luxury goods conglomerate that is the largest in the world, setting the benchmark for the luxury industry through strategic management and acquisition.

Operational Synergies: The cost-saving or efficiency benefits gained when different brands within a conglomerate share resources such as research and development, distribution channels or human resources.

Personal Luxury Goods: This segment within the luxury industry includes high-end fashion, accessories and beauty products, that is, brands that are widely recognized and visible to the general public. This segment is often seen as the personification of luxury.

Smartification: A trend where luxury vehicles are equipped with advanced technologies like AI, autonomous driving and connectivity features, highly valued by Chinese consumers.

Vertical Integration: A business strategy where a company controls its supply chain by owning or managing production, distribution and retail processes.

Discussion questions

1. What factors contributed to the consolidation of the personal luxury goods sector in the late 1990s?
2. How does LVMH maintain its leadership position in the luxury market?

3. What are the key differences between absolute luxury and relative luxury?
4. According to Kapferer, what distinguishes luxury brands from premium brands?
5. What distinguishes luxury brands from fashion brands?
6. How does vertical integration contribute to the success of luxury brands like Rolex?
7. What role does e-commerce play in the luxury industry, and how do brands like Chanel approach it?
8. Why is controlled scarcity an effective strategy in luxury brand management?
9. What challenges do family-owned or independent luxury brands face in the modern market?
10. How is the concept of luxury in the automotive market evolving in China?
11. What role does Gen Z play in shaping the luxury car market in China?
12. How does the Chinese luxury car market differ from traditional Western markets?
13. Why is personalization important in the luxury car segment, particularly in China?
14. What are the implications of the shift towards electric vehicles in the luxury segment?

Reference list

Accor. (2024). *2023 Universal Registration Document*. Retrieved August 2024, from group.accor.com: https://group.accor.com/en

ACEA. (2024, March). *Economic and Market Report Global and EU Auto Industry: Full Year 2023*. Retrieved August 2024, from acea.auto: https://www.acea.auto/files/Economic_and_Market_Report-Full_year_2023.pdf

Adams, S. (2014, August 20). *Inside Hermès: Luxury's Secret Empire*. Retrieved October 2022, from Forbes: https://www.forbes.com/sites/susanadams/2014/08/20/inside-hermes-luxury-secret-empire/

Art Basel & UBS. (2023). *The Art Market*. Retrieved August 2024, from theartmarket.artbasel.com: https://theartmarket.artbasel.com/global-market

Asprey. (2022). *By Royal Appointment*. Retrieved October 2022, from asprey.com: https://www.asprey.com/uk/by-royal-appointment

Atwal, G., & Williams, A. (2009). Luxury Brand Marketing – The Experience Is Everything! In *Advances in Luxury Brand Management* (Vol. 16, pp. 338–346). Palgrave Macmillan.

Audemars Piquet. (2022). *Our Savoir-Faire*. Retrieved October 2022, from audemarspiguet.com: https://www.audemarspiguet.com/com/en/about/savoir-faire.html

Bagaholic, B. V. (2022, September). *Chanel Classic Bag US Price List Reference Guide*. Retrieved October 2022, from lvbagaholic.com: https://lvbagaholic.com/blogs/lv_bagaholic/chanel-classic-flap-bag-us-price-list

Bain & Company. (2022). *From Surging Recovery to Elegant Advance: The Evolving Future of Luxury*. Retrieved August 2022, from Bain and Company: https://www.bain.com/insights/from-surging-recovery-to-elegant-advance-the-evolving-future-of-luxury/

Bain & Company. (2023, January 17). *Renaissance in Uncertainty: Luxury Builds on Its Rebound*. Retrieved August 2024, from bain.com: https://www.bain.com/insights/renaissance-in-uncertainty-luxury-builds-on-its-rebound/#

Bain & Company. (2024, January 18). *Long Live Luxury: Converge to Expand through Turbulence*. Retrieved September 2024, from bain.com: https://www.bain.com/insights/long-live-luxury-converge-to-expand-through-turbulence/

Bastien, V., & Kapferer, J.-N. (2013). More on Luxury Anti-Laws of Marketing. In K. P. Wiedmann, & N. Hennigs, *Luxury Marketing* (pp. 19–34). Wiesbaden: Gabler Verlag.

Belmond. (2024). *Trains, by Belmond*. Retrieved November 2024, from belmond.com: https://www.belmond.com/trains

Bengtsson, M., Akenji, L., Toivio, V., Lettenmeier, M., Fawcett, T., Parag, Y., . . . Kenner, D. (2021). *1.5-Degree Lifestyles: Towards a Fair Consumption Space for All*. Retrieved October 2022, from hotorcool.org: https://hotorcool.org/wp-content/uploads/2021/10/Hot_or_Cool_1_5_lifestyles_FULL_REPORT_AND_ANNEX_B.pdf

Berthon, P., Pitt, L., Parent, M., & Berthon, J.-P. (2009). Aesthetics and Ephemerality: Observing and Preserving the Luxury Brand. *California Management Review*, *52*(1), 45–66.

Chanel. (2022a). *Financial Results*. Retrieved September 2022, from chanel.com: https://www.chanel.com/cz/financial-results/

Chanel. (2022b). *The History*. Retrieved September 2022, from Chanel: https://www.chanel.com/cz/about-chanel/the-history/

Capri Holdings Limited. (2022). *2022 Annual Report*. Retrieved October 2022, from Capri Holdings Limited: http://www.capriholdings.com/corporate-overview/default.aspx

Capri Holdings Limited. (2023, August 10). *Tapestry, Inc. Announces Definitive Agreement to Acquire Capri Holdings Limited, Establishing a Powerful Global House of Iconic Luxury and Fashion Brands*. Retrieved March 2024, from capriholdings.com: https://www.capriholdings.com/news-releases/news-releases-details/2023/Tapestry-Inc.-Announces-Definitive-Agreement-to-Acquire-Capri-Holdings-Limited-Establishing-a-Powerful-Global-House-of-Iconic-Luxury-and-Fashion-Brands/default.aspx

CarNewsChina. (2024, August 9). *HiPhi's Parent Company Files for Bankruptcy*. Retrieved August 2024, from carnewschina.com: https://carnewschina.com/2024/08/09/hiphis-parent-company-files-for-bankruptcy/

Cavender, R., & Kincade, D. H. (2014). Management of a Luxury Brand: Dimensions and Sub-Variables from a Case Study of LVMH. *Journal of Fashion Marketing and Management*, *18*(2), 231–248.

Chanel. (2022a). *Financial Results*. Retrieved September 2022, from chanel.com: https://www.chanel.com/cz/financial-results/

Chanel. (2022b). *The History*. Retrieved September 2022, from Chanel: https://www.chanel.com/cz/about-chanel/the-history/

Chopard. (2022). *Family Spirit*. Retrieved October 2022, from chopard.com: https://www.chopard.com/en-intl/our-identity.html

Chow Tai Fook Jewellery Group. (2024). *Chow Tai Fook HUÁ Collection*. Retrieved March 2024, from https://www.chowtaifook.com/en/jewelry/series/info_25269.html

Chrono24. (2022, February 8). *Why Is the Rolex Daytona So Expensive?* Retrieved October 2022, from Chrono24: https://www.chrono24.com/magazine/why-is-the-rolex-daytona-so-expensive-p_97960/

CNBC. (2018). *Louis Vuitton chief Bernard Arnault Says He Regrets Selling His Apple Shares too Early*. Retrieved August 2022, from https://www.cnbc.com/2018/05/01/lvmh-ceo-bernard-arnault-regrets-selling-his-apple-shares-too-early.html

CNBC. (2022, November 22). *Two Companies Have Luxury Trains Called the 'Orient Express.' Here Are the Differences*. Retrieved November 2024, from cnbc.com: https://www.cnbc.com/2022/11/22/tickets-on-the-orient-express-are-sold-by-two-companies.html

Cosmetics Business. (2020, August 14). *Lauder Partners with Biotech Firm on Botanical Senomodulators Research*. Retrieved September 2022, from Cosmetics Business: https://www.cosmeticsbusiness.com/news/article_page/Lauder_partners_with_biotech_firm_on_botanical_senomodulators_research/168926

CPPLUXURY. (2024, June 18). *LVMH Consolidates Luxury Hospitality. Should Bvlgari Hotels Follow Suit?* Retrieved August 2024, from cpp-luxury.com: https://cpp-luxury.com/lvmh-consolidates-luxury-hospitality-should-bvlgari-hotels-follow-suit/

Cruise Industry News. (2024). *2024 Luxury Market Report.* Retrieved August 2024, from cruiseindustrynews.com: https://www.cruiseindustrynews.com/store/product/digital-reports/2024-luxury-market-report/

De Barnier, V., Falcy, S., & Valette-Florence, P. (2012). Do Consumers Perceive Three Levels of Luxury? A Comparison of Accessible, Intermediate and Inaccessible Luxury Brands. *Journal of Brand Management, 19*, 623–636.

Deloitte. (2021). *Global Powers of Luxury Goods 2021.* Retrieved September 2022, from deloitte.com: https://www2.deloitte.com/content/dam/Deloitte/at/Documents/consumer-business/at-global-powers-of-luxury-goods–2021.pdf

Deloitte. (2022). *Global Powers of Luxury Goods 2022.* Retrieved March 2024, from deloitte.com: https://www2.deloitte.com/content/dam/Deloitte/fi/Documents/consumer-business/gx-global-powers-of-luxury-goods-report.pdf

Deloitte. (2023, November 29). *Global Powers of Luxury Goods 2023.* Retrieved February 2024, from deloitte.com: https://www.deloitte.com/global/en/Industries/consumer/analysis/gx-cb-global-powers-of-luxury-goods.html

Deloitte. (2024). *2024 Global Automotive Consumer Study.* Retrieved August 2024, from deloitte.com:https://www.deloitte.com/global/en/Industries/automotive/perspectives/global-automotive-consumer-study.html

Dubois, B., Laurent, G., & Czellar, S. (2001). *Consumer Rapport to Luxury: Analyzing Complex And Ambivalent Attitudes.* Consumer Research Working Article, No. 736, HEC, Jousy-en-Josas.

Essilor Luxottica. (2022). *Our History.* Retrieved October 2022, from Essilor Luxottica: https://www.essilorluxottica.com/our-history

Estée Lauder. (2024). *Sustainability.* Retrieved November 2024, from esteelauder.com: https://www.esteelauder.com/discover/sustainability?srsltid=AfmBOora8j6Ehe0AQgFrcMATGXrVOaKRtokl67GPCtMqnvOzSAPFmdAo

Estée Lauder Companies. (2022). *Who We Are.* Retrieved August 2022, from elcompanies.com: https://www.elcompanies.com/en/who-we-are/the-lauder-family/the-estee-story

Estée Lauder Companies, Inc. (2021). *Annual Report Pursuant to Section 13 or 15(d) of the Securities Exchange Act of 1934 For the fiscal year ended June 30, 2021.* Retrieved August 2022, from Estée Lauder: https://media.elcompanies.com/files/e/estee-lauder-companies/universal/investors/investor-resources/toolkit/form-10k–2021.pdf?_ga=2.204061778.31195780.1661954849-584224008.1661954849&_gl=1*115okuo*_ga*NTg0MjI0MDA4LjE2NjE5NTQ4NDk.*_ga_V9QZ4PSDRY*MTY2MTk1ND

Estée Lauder Companies, Inc. (2022). *Annual Report 2022.* Retrieved September 2022, from Estée Lauder Companies: https://media.elcompanies.com/files/e/estee-lauder-companies/universal/investors/investor-resources/toolkit/form-10k–08242022.pdf?_ga=2.203183825.13546936.1662376410-584224008.1661954849&_gl=1*zelbq3*_ga*NTg0MjI0MDA4LjE2NjE5NTQ4NDk.*_ga_V9QZ4PSDRY*MTY2MjM

The Fashion Law. (2021). *LVMH: A Timeline Behind the Building of the World's Most Valuable Luxury Goods Conglomerate.* Retrieved August 2022, from https://www.thefashionlaw.com/lvmh-a-timeline-behind-the-building-of-a-conglomerate/

Fashion United . (2022, May 25). *Chanel to Open Private Boutiques for Its Top Clients.* Retrieved October 2022, from fashionunited.uk: https://fashionunited.uk/news/retail/chanel-to-open-private-boutiques-for-its-top-clients/2022052563271

Financial Times. (2022, May 18). *All the World's a Stage: Gucci, Louis Vuitton and Chanel Go Global for Cruise*. Retrieved October 2022, from ft.com: https://www.ft.com/content/1ce50c53–0e61–4deb-a63e-244a9bb273db

Fondation Hans Wilsdorf. (2022). *Fondation Hans Wildorf*. Retrieved October 2022, from hanswilsdorf.ch: https://hanswilsdorf.ch/home.html

Forbes. (2013, May 22). *Partners In Power: The World's Most Influential Couples*. Retrieved October 2022, from Forbes: https://www.forbes.com/sites/katepierce/2013/05/22/partners-in-power-the-worlds-most-influential-couples/?sh=71233f044b41

Forbes. (2014, September 11). *Hermès and LVMH Make Peace*. Retrieved September 2022, from forbes.com: https://www.forbes.com/sites/susanadams/2014/09/11/hermes-and-lvmh-make-peace/

Forbes. (2021, January 7). *Bottega Veneta Shutting down Its Social Media Accounts Might Signal a Trend*. Retrieved August 2022, from forbes.com: https://www.forbes.com/sites/pamdanziger/2021/01/07/bottega-veneta-cancels-its-social-media-accounts-it-may-signal-a-trend/?sh=5fc40d7164fe

Forbes. (2022a, September 14). *Estée Lauder Careful Investment Selections Pay Off as a Growth Strategy*. Retrieved September 2022, from Forbes: https://www.forbes.com/sites/walterloeb/2022/02/14/este-lauder-careful-investment-selections-pay-off-as-a-growth-strategy/?sh=8a975d411906

Forbes. (2022b, August 28). *Richemont-YNAP Deal Puts Farfetch Closer to Being the Global Platform for Luxury*. Retrieved September 2022, from forbes.com: https://www.forbes.com/sites/pamdanziger/2022/08/28/richemont-ynap-deal-puts-farfetch-closer-to-being-the-global-platform-for-luxury/

Forbes. (2023). *Forbes*. Retrieved February 2024, from Bernard Arnault with Family: https://forbes.cz/lists/nejbohatsi-lide-sveta-2023/bernard-arnault-s-rodinou/

Graff. (2022). *This Is Graff*. Retrieved October 2022, from graff.com: https://www.graff.com/eu-en/house/graff.html

The Guardian. (2014, September 3). *LVMH and Hermès Settle Long-Running Dispute over Ownership Stake*. Retrieved October 2022, from The Guardian: https://www.theguardian.com/business/2014/sep/03/french-brands-lvmh-hermes-settle-long-running-dispute-ownership-stake

Gulf News. (2024, April 2). *Dynasties on Wheels: China's Top 5 Luxury Cars*. Retrieved August 2024, from gulfnews.com: https://gulfnews.com/kurator/luxury/dynasties-on-wheels-chinas-top-5-luxury-cars-1.1712060045944

Harvard Business Review. (2001). *The Perfect Paradox of Star Brands: An Interview with Bernard Arnault of LVMH*. Retrieved August 2022, from https://hbr.org/2001/10/the-perfect-paradox-of-star-brands-an-interview-with-bernard-arnault-of-lvmh

Harvard Business Review. (2014, March). *Kering's CEO on Finding the Elusive Formula for Growing Acquired Brands by François-Henri Pinault*. Retrieved November 2024, from hbr.org: https://hbr.org/2014/03/kerings-ceo-on-finding-the-elusive-formula-for-growing-acquired-brands

Hermès. (2022). *Six Generations of Artisans*. Retrieved October 2022, from www.hermes.com: https://www.hermes.com/us/en/story/271366-six-generations-of-artisans/

Hermès International. (2021). *2021 Universal Registration Document*. Retrieved October 2022, from www.finance.hermes.com: https://labrador.cld.bz/Hermes-2021-Universal-Registration-Document/10/

Hoover's Company Records. (2022, July 1). *Chanel Profile*. Retrieved October 2022, from Proquest: https://www.proquest.com/docview/1860789437/fulltextPDF/E5CFDDB209534B93PQ/1?accountid=17203

Ijaouane, V., & Kapferer, J.-N. (2012). Developing Luxury Brands Within Luxury Groups – Synergies Without Dilution? *Marketing Review St Gallen*, *29*(1), 24–29.

Iloranta, R. (2022). Luxury Tourism – A Review of the Literature. *European Journal of Tourism Research*, *30*, 1–32.

Interino, M. (2020, July 26). *Chanel's Digital Strategy: Old Habits Die Hard*. Retrieved October 2022, from fashionabledata.com: https://www.fashionabledata.com/blog/chanels-digital-strategy-old-habits-die-hard

Investopedia. (2023, July 19). *How Tencent Makes Money*. Retrieved December 2024, from investopedia.com: https://www.investopedia.com/articles/insights/113016/what-tencent-baba-bidu.asp

Italpassion. (2024). *Maserati Reports Lower Sales and Blames China*. Retrieved August 2024, from italpassion.fr: https://www.italpassion.fr/en/maserati/maserati-sales-decrease-and-accuse-china/

Kapferer, J.-N. (1997). Managing Luxury Brands. *Journal of Brand Management*, *4*, 251–259.

Kapferer, J. N., & Bastien, V. (2009). *The Luxury Strategy: Break the Rules of Marketing to Build Luxury Brands*. London, New York: Kogan Page.

Kapferer, J.-N., & Bastien, V. (2012). *The Luxury Strategy: Break the Rules of Marketing to Build Luxury Brands* (2nd edition). Kogan Page Limited.

Keller, K. L. (2017). Managing the Growth Tradeoff: Challenges and Opportunities in Luxury Branding. In J.-N. Kapferer, J. Kernstock, T. O. Brexendorf, & S. M. Powell, *Advances in Luxury Brand Management*. Journal of Brand Management Advanced Collection.

Kering, S. A. (2021). *Kering 2020 Integrated Report*. Retrieved August 2022, from Kering SA:https://keringcorporate.dam.kering.com/m/2b2606c1186fa9ed/original/Kering-Integrated-Report–2020.pdf

Kering, S. A. (2022). *Group History*. Retrieved August 2022, from kering.com: https://www.kering.com/en/group/culture-and-heritage/group-history/?page=3

Kering, S. A. (2023). *Kering Beauté*. Retrieved February 2024, from https://www.kering.com/en/houses/others/kering-beaute/

License Global. (2023, January 6). *Pubg Mobile Partners with Maserati*. Retrieved August 2024, from licenseglobal.com: https://www.licenseglobal.com/video-games/pubg-mobile-partners-with-maserati

The Luxury Conversation. (2020, August 5). *How Maserati in China Gives Gen Z Gamification, Personalisation and Innovation – With Sophia Sun, Director of Marketing*. Retrieved August 2024, from luxuryconversation.com: https://luxuryconversation.com/maserati-china-personalisation-marketing-collaboration-sophia-sun/

LVMH. (2022a). *LVMH 2021 ANNUAL REPORT Passionate about Creativity*. Retrieved August2022,fromhttps://r.lvmh-static.com/uploads/2022/03/lvmh_rapport-annuel-2021-va.pdf

LVMH. (2022b). *The LVMH Model*. Retrieved August 2022, from https://www.lvmh.com/group/

LVMH. (2023a). *LVMH: Translation of the French Financial Documents Fiscal Year Ended December 31, 2023*. Retrieved August 2024, from lvmh.com: https://lvmh-com.cdn.prismic.io/lvmh-com/ZmMq-pm069VX1j0w_financial-documents-lvmh-december-31–2023.pdf

LVMH. (2023b, November 10). *LVMH Exhibits the Best of Its Know-How for Its 4th Participation at the CIIE*. Retrieved February 2024, from https://www.lvmh.com/news-documents/news/lvmh-exhibits-the-best-of-its-know-how-for-its-4th-participation-at-the-ciie/

LVMH Group. (2022). *Milestones – LVMH*. Retrieved August 2022, from https://www.lvmh.com/group/milestones-lvmh/1593-to-the-present/

Manlow, V., & Nobbs, K. (2013). Form and Function of Luxury Flagships: An International Exploratory Study of the Meaning of the Flagship Store for Managers and Customers. *Journal of Fashion Marketing and Management*, *17*(1), 49–64.

Maserati. (2024). *1910: The Foundations Are Laid*. Retrieved August 2024, from maserati.com: https://www.maserati.com/global/en/brand/history

Maserati Media. (2024). *Maserti Company Profile*. Retrieved August 2024, from media.maserati.com: https://www.media.maserati.com/contents/us

McKinsey. (2022, July 8). *Five Trends Shaping Tomorrow's Luxury-Car Market*. Retrieved August 2024, from mckinsey.com: https://www.mckinsey.com/industries/automotive-and-assembly/our-insights/five-trends-shaping-tomorrows-luxury-car-market

Michelin. (2024, January 26). *2023 Was a Key Year for the Michelin Guide*. Retrieved September 2024, from michelin.com: https://www.michelin.com/en/publications/products-and-services/le-guide-michelin-2023-un-millesime-clef-2024-s-annonce-resolument-tournee-vers-l-art-de-vivre

Michelin Guide. (2024). *About Us*. Retrieved September 2024, from guide.michelin.com: https://guide.michelin.com/en/about-us

Miller, K. W., & Mills, M. K. (2012). Probing Brand Luxury: A Multiple Lens Approach. *Journal of Brand Management*, *20*(1), 41–51.

Mordor Intelligence. (2024). *China Luxury Car Market Size & Share Analysis – Growth Trends & Forecasts (2024–2029)*. Source: https://www.mordorintelligence.com/industry-reports/china-luxury-car-market. Retrieved August 2024, from mordorintelligence.com: https://www.mordorintelligence.com/industry-reports/china-luxury-car-market

The New York Times Magazine. (1989). *A Luxury Fight to the Finish*. Retrieved August 2022, from https://www.nytimes.com/1989/12/17/magazine/a-luxury-fight-to-the-finish.html

The New Zealand Herald. (2023, January 23). *Orient Express Goes to Sea in World's Largest Sailing Ship in Cruise Venture*. Retrieved August 2024, from nzherald.co.nz: https://www.nzherald.co.nz/travel/orient-express-goes-to-sea-in-worlds-largest-sailing-ship-in-cruise-venture/BYTHLATYIRHDRLRTCVKZ6YWMQ4/

Okonkwo-Pézard, U. (2017). The Luxury Brand Strategy Challenge. In J.-N. Kapferer, J. Kernstock, T. O. Brexendorf, & S. M. Powell, *Advances in Luxury Brand Management*. Journal of Brand Management Advanced Collections.

Online Etymology Dictionary. (2022). *Luxury (n)*. Retrieved September 2022, from Online Etymology Dictionary: https://www.etymonline.com/word/luxurious

Orient Express. (2024). *Orient Express Sillenseas: The Legendary Train Heads Out to Sea as the World's Largest Sailing Ship Is Unveiled*. Retrieved August 2024, from orient-express.com:https://www.orient-express.com/high-life/orient-express-silenseas-the-legendary-train-heads-out-to-sea-as-the-worlds-largest-sailing-ship-is-unveiled/

Patek Philippe. (2022). *The History of Patek Philippe from 1839 until Today*. Retrieved October 2022, from patek.com: https://www.patek.com/en/company/history#1989-2019

Picardie, J. (2017). *Coco Chanel: The Legend and the Life*. London: HarperCollinsPublishers.

Pine II, B. J., & Gilmore, J. H. (1998, July–August). *Welcome to the Experience Economy*. Retrieved August 2024, from *Harvard Business Review*: https://hbr.org/1998/07/welcome-to-the-experience-economy

Plug and Play. (2021). *Estee Lauder and Plug and Play Seek to Power the Next Generation of Beauty*. Retrieved September 2022, from Plug and Play: https://www.plugandplaytechcenter.com/press/estee-lauder-and-plug-and-play-seek-power-next-generation-beauty/

Prada Group. (2022). *Prada Group: Who We Are*. Retrieved October 2022, from Prada Group: https://www.pradagroup.com/en/group/group-profile.html

Prada Group. (2024, October 16). *Prada and Axiom Space Unveil the Spacesuit Design for Moon Return*. Retrieved November 2024, from pradagrouup.com: https://www.pradagroup.com/en/news-media/news-section/24-10-16-prada-axiom-space.html

Professional Watches. (2022, March 9). *Morgan Stanley's Top 20 Swiss Watch Company Ranking for 2022*. Retrieved October 2022, from Professional Watches: https://professionalwatches.com/morgan-stanleys-top-20-swiss-watch-company-ranking-for-2022/

Rambourg, E. (2020). *Future Luxe: What's Ahead for the Business of Luxury*. Vancouver: Figure 1 Publishing, Inc.

Reuters. (2020, November 5). *Alibaba, Richemont to Invest $1.1 Billion in Farfetch with Focus on China*. Retrieved September 2022, from reuters.com: https://www.reuters.com/article/uk-farfetch-investment-alibaba-idUKKBN27L2Z7

Reuters. (2023, October 23). *European Regulator Approves Farfetch Deal for YNAP, Richemont Says*. Retrieved March 2024, from https://www.reuters.com/markets/deals/european-regulator-approves-farfetch-deal-ynap-richemont-says-2023-10-23/

Reuters. (2024, February 11). *Tod's Owner Gets Help from L Catterton to Take the Company Private*. Retrieved March 2024, from https://www.reuters.com/markets/deals/lvmh-backed-l-catterton-launch-tender-offer-36-tods-2024-02-11/

Richemont. (2022a). *Investor Presentation*. Retrieved September 2022, from Richemont: https://www.richemont.com/en/home/investors/results-reports-presentations/

Richemont. (2022b). *Our Maisons*. Retrieved Septembeer 2022, from Richemont: https://www.richemont.com/en/home/our-maisons

Richemont. (2022c, August 24). *Richemont, FARFETCH and Alabbar Cement Partnership to Advance the Digitalisation of the Luxury Industry*. Retrieved September 2022, from Press Releases: https://www.richemont.com/en/home/media/press-releases-and-news/richemont-farfetch-and-alabbar-cement-partnership-to-advance-the-digitalisation-of-the-luxury-industry/

Rolex, S. A. (2022). *The Man Behind the Crown Hans Wilsdorf*. Retrieved October 2022, from rolex.org: https://www.rolex.org/perpetual/the-man-behind-the-crown

Ruff, D. (2024, November 20). In Conversation With Dan Ruff, CEO of Belmond. *Inside LVMH*. Retrieved from https://www.insidelvmh.com/blog/47/post/view/294

Singh, B., & Kaunert, C. (2024). Convergence of the Metaverse and Luxury Hospitality as Avenues for Future Investigation. In P. Thaichon, P. K. Dutta, P. R. Chelliah, & S. Gupta, *Technology and Luxury Hospitality* (pp. 65–79). Routledge.

Solca, L. (2007). *PPR: Value-Creation Through Luxury Focus* (pp. 1–131). Black Book – PPR.

Som, A., & Blanckaert, C. (2021). *The Road to Luxury: The New Frontiers in Luxury Brand Management* (2nd edition). Wiley.

Sotheby's. (2022a, March 14). *The Luxury Price Boom: Why You Should Invest in Chanel Handbags Today*. Retrieved October 2022, from sothebys.com: https://www.sothebys.com/en/articles/the-luxury-price-boom-why-you-should-invest-in-chanel-handbags-today

Sotheby's. (2022b, October 7). *G.O.A.T: The Rolex Daytona*. Retrieved October 2022, from sothebys.com: https://www.sothebys.com/en/articles/g-o-a-t-the-rolex-daytona?locale=en

Sotheby's. (2024, March 21). *Understanding the Latest 2024 Chanel Bag Price Hikes and the Resale Market*. Retrieved July 2024, from Sotheby's: https://www.sothebys.com/en/articles/understanding-the-latest-2024-chanel-bag-price-hikes-and-the-resale-market

Stellantis. (2024a, February 15). *FY 2023 Results*. Retrieved August 2024, from stellantis.com: https://www.stellantis.com/content/dam/stellantis-corporate/investors/events-and-presentations/presentations/Stellantis-FY2023-Results-Presentation.pdf

Stellantis. (2024b, June 13). *Stellantis Investor Day*. Retrieved August 2024, from Stellantis.com: https://www.stellantis.com/en/investors/events/stellantis-investor-day-2024

Stock Dividend Screener. (2024, February 29). *Maserati Global Vehicle Sales and Sales By Country*. Retrieved August 2024, from stockdividendscreener.com: https://stockdividendscreener.com/auto-manufacturers/maserati-global-sales-statistics/

Tapestry. (2022). *Investor Relations*. Retrieved October 2022, from tapestry.com: https://www.tapestry.com/investors/

Tribune de Genève. (2018, February 2). *Wilsdorf, More than a Patron, a Real Cash Machine*. Retrieved October 2022, from tdg.ch: https://www-tdg-ch.translate.goog/wilsdorf-plus-quun-mecene-une-vraie-machine-a-cash-797828901292?_x_tr_sl=fr&_x_tr_tl=en&_x_tr_hl=en

Tynan, C., McKechnie, S., & Chhuon, C. (1964). Co-Creating Value for Luxury Brands. *Journal of Business Research*, *63*(11), 1156–1163.

Vigneron, F., & Johnson, L. W. (1999). A Review and Conceptual Framework of Prestige Seeking Consumer Behavior. *Academy of Marketing Science Review*, *1*, 1–15.

Vigneron, F., & Johnson, L. W. (2004). Measuring Perceptions of Brand Luxury. *Journal of Brand Management*, *11*(6), 484–506.

Vijai, C., & Wisetsri, W. (2024). Digital Trends in the Hospitality Industry. In P. Thaichon, P. K. Dutta, & P. R. Che, *Technology and Luxury Hospitality AI, Blockchain and the Metaverse*. Routledge.

Vogue. (2020, November 24). *Virginie Viard, the Woman Behind Chanel's New Chapter*. Retrieved October 2022, from vogue.com: https://www.vogue.com/article/virginie-viard-chanel-new-chapter

Vogue Business. (2024a, June 19). *Why Yoox Net-a-Porter Quit China*. Retrieved September 2024, from voguebusiness.com: https://www.voguebusiness.com/story/companies/why-yoox-net-a-porter-quit-china

Vogue Business. (2024b, August 27). *Brands Took over Europe's Luxury Beach Clubs This Summer: Are They Here to Say?* Retrieved August 2024, from voguebusiness.com: https://www.voguebusiness.com/story/fashion/brands-took-over-europes-luxury-beach-clubs-this-summer-are-they-here-to-say?uID=fa44d56a3421e1bd59eeaa0b01a60e5912e32f35339c1ca98294907eebb5d5c0&utm_campaign=VB_NEWS_Kirsty_TUES_270824&utm_source=newsletter&utm

Wikimedia Commons. (2015, August 30). *File:Orient Express, Restaurant car.jpg*. Retrieved February 2025, from commons.wikimedia.org: https://commons.wikimedia.org/wiki/File:Orient_Express,_Restaurant_car.jpg

Wikimedia Commons. (2022, August 19). *File:Artemis-iii-Landing-Regions Space mission.jpg*. Retrieved February 2025, from commons.wikimedia.org: https://commons.wikimedia.org/wiki/File:Artemis-iii-landing-regions_space_mission.jpg

Chapter 3

Luxury geography and demographics

Understanding the basics of "who" and "where"

The first section delves into traditional segmentation by wealth and, consequently, into examining the conventional and emerging methods of segmenting luxury customers based on alternative market segmentation approaches. The subsequent sections focus on luxury consumers' demographic and geographic aspects and the impact of the country of origin effect.

3.1 Luxury customers and how to segment them?

From a global perspective, the number of luxury consumers with increasing wealth has continued to grow over the last decade, with a decline only in some markets in 2022. There are multiple views on the identification of customers of luxury brands, and it is not always just about income or the amount of assets. In addition to basic segmentation according to investable assets, there are several other methods that may be used: segmentation based on lifestyle and attitudes towards cultural changes, segmentation according to wealth and the need to signal status and, last but not least, a conceptual model of segmentation of luxury customers according to their knowledge of luxury or wealth.

3.1.1 Total investible assets

Capgemini's World Health Report 2023 quantifies the most promising luxury clients, so-called **high net worth individuals (HNWIs)**, whose investable assets are estimated at more than $1 million (excluding private residences and non-durable and short-term items). It further divides HNWIs into ultra-HNWIs (with assets of more than $30 million), medium HNWIs ($5–30 million) and smaller millionaires ($1–5 million) (Table 3.1).

In total, according to Capgemini's survey, there were more than 22.8 million people with investable assets above $1 million in 2023 (+4.8% vs. the previous year). In 2005, there were 8.7 million of them (5.5% compound annual growth rate 2005–23). The population of all three HNWIs segments by wealth grew year-on-year in 2022/23 by 5% on average. The total wealth of the HNWIs is estimated to be $86.8 trillion, and 1% of the ultra-rich HNWIs own more than one-third of this wealth.

DOI: 10.4324/9781003593706-3

Table 3.1 Distribution of HNWIs and development of their assets.

	Number of individual HNWIs by group	Segments' share of HNWIs wealth	% change in the number of HNWIs	% change in the size of HNWIs wealth
	2023	**2023**	**2022–23**	**2022–23**
$30 million	220K 1% of total	34%	5.0%	3.9%
$5–30 million	2,075K 9.1% of total	23%	5.0%	4.9%
$ 1–5 million	20,533K 89.9% of total	43%	5.2%	5.2%

Source: Authors based on data available at (Capgemini Research Institute, 2024).

The highest number of HNWIs is in North America (7.9 million, 35%), followed by the Asia-Pacific region (7.4 million, 32%), Europe (5.8 million, 25%), the Middle East (0.9 million, 4%), Latin America (0.6 million, 2.6%) and Africa (0.2 million, 0.9%) (Capgemini Research Institute, 2024). In terms of individual countries, almost 2/3 of all HNWIs come from the United States, Japan, Germany or China. The top ten countries with the highest number of HNWIs also include France, UK, Switzerland, Canada, the Netherlands and Italy (Capgemini Research Institute, 2022).

In addition to the previously mentioned millionaires and multimillionaires, the mass segment of so-called *mass affluents* is also important for the future of the luxury sector. Their resources, in the form of investable assets, range from $250,000 to $1 million. Their number is estimated at 11% of the world's population (Capgemini Research Institute, 2022). Affluent clients may be temporarily present in the luxury sector as *the excursionists* who buy the cheapest items of luxury brands (Kapferer & Bastien, 2012, p. 115).

3.1.2 Lifestyle and income

Luxury goods are expensive in both relative and absolute terms, and they are usually without a functional advantage over conventional products. Therefore, a luxury sector customer is typically defined in terms of income as the best indicator of measuring demand. In 1899, Thorstein Veblen developed a theory according to which consumers use the prices of products as a means of ostentatious expression of their wealth. Income is a major contributor to wealth, and the Veblen effect is particularly striking in the luxury sector. Income should therefore play a dominant role in market segmentation (Veblen, 1899/2003).

At the same time, it is clear that the purchase of luxury goods, given the emotions associated with it, is not guided only by economic factors. The symbolic and social values of a luxury brand have a significant influence on customer behavior stemming from their cultural identity. For example, one might buy a product in an attempt to differentiate oneself from others (snobbish effect) or in an attempt to be associated with a particular reference group (bandwagon effect), both of which will be discussed in more detail later. With regard to the associated cultural identities, Dubois and Duquesne (1993) shaped **attitudes toward cultural change** as another variable (in addition to income) for the segmentation of luxury customers. From a total sample of 7,600 European luxury sector customers, the respondents were examined in terms of their attitudes towards cultural change (their cultural profile) using the methodology of the Swiss International Research Institute for Social Change (RISC), whose specific expertise is monitoring socio-cultural changes. The most important dimension, called the "attitude to cultural change," summarizes the degree of compliance of respondents with the global development trends of society, and the result of its analysis is the characteristics of *trendy* people who:

- Are in favor of risk-taking;
- Do not trust hierarchical and formal structures and prefer to take control of their own destiny, making the most of their physical, mental and affective (attitudinal) potential;
- Appreciate spontaneity and try to preserve their ability to adapt to the outside world.

Conversely, people labeled as *off-trend* are more attached to their roots and their own safety. They appreciate a close relationship with their immediate surroundings, but they feel insecure when confronted with social trends. Respondents were divided into four levels according to attitudes towards cultural change with corresponding percentages: 14%, 26%, 24%, 36% (from most to least *trendy*) (Table 3.2). The results show that **both *on trend* and *off-trend* come from both higher and lower income segments**, and thus attitudes to cultural change cannot be predicted based only on income position and vice versa.

The penetration of luxury goods within the individual segments, defined here through income size and attitudes towards cultural change, is shown in Table 3.3. For the purposes of this study, a consumer of luxury goods was defined as any person who purchased at least three "affordable" luxury products (such as jewelry or a watch below $400) and two "extraordinary" luxury products (one garment over $500 or a jewel over $400) during the period considered. In each cell, the number of luxury consumers is displayed as a percentage of the cell's population. In other words, the 22% in the upper-right corner have the highest income and are also the trendiest, indicating they have the most open minds towards cultural change and consumption of luxury goods. In the lower-left corner, we see a demographic that has a low income and who are not trendy; thus, only 2% of this population consume luxury goods.

The overall penetration rates of luxury products in the left-hand column show a large difference between the highest income segment (13%) and the lowest (3%). But culture has an equal role, as consumption of luxury goods triples when we shift to the trendiest consumers, regardless of income level.

Table 3.2 Distribution of the European population by cultural profile; authors based on (Dubois & Duquesne, 1993).

Monthly income (%)	*Completely out of trend*	*Out of trend*	*On trend*	*Significantly on trend*	Total
Very high (over $3k)	5	4	4	2	**15**
High ($2–3k)	8	6	6	4	**24**
Low ($1–2k)	13	9	10	5	**37**
Very low (less than $1k)	10	5	6	3	**24**
Total	**36**	**24**	**26**	**14**	

Attitude towards cultural change (%)

Table 3.3 Penetration of luxury products into segments according to income and attitude to cultural change; authors based on (Dubois & Duquesne, 1993).

Income (%)				
13	7	12	16	22
6	3	5	8	9
4	2	3	5	8
3	2	1	4	5
	3	5	7	10
	Attitude towards cultural change (%)			

This kind of segmentation has revealed additional possibilities for managing luxury brands in addition to the traditional approach of premium pricing and selective distribution for ostentatious display of wealth. The link between a positive attitude towards cultural change and the consumption of luxury goods suggests that many people buy such goods for what they symbolize, as an extreme form of expression of self-values, where the level of income plays only one role. Thus, the luxury market may appear to be divided into two segments: (1) traditional customers who appreciate **authentic luxury, the search for absolute quality, and the brand as a standard of excellence,** and consumption is linked to ostentatious display of wealth and (2) **the brand as a symbol** – when customers buy the product because of what it symbolizes, that is, as an expression of one's values.

The highest penetration of luxury purchases in these patterns is still evident in situations where the consumers' attitudes towards cultural change meet with higher income. But brands at the intersection of the two segments can alternatively use the authenticity and legitimacy of the brand to fascinate the other segment with its brand symbolism (Dubois & Duquesne, 1993).

Kapferer and Bastien (2012) add to this segmentation the need to look not only at personal income but above all at the disposable income of a luxury customer. An example is the boom in the luxury sector in Japan dating back to the late 1970s, when single working women, still living with their parents, could invest a large part of their income in luxury. Buying a recognizable and visible Louis Vuitton, Chanel or Hermès handbag was motivated by a desire to distinguish themselves from their stay-at-home mothers and show themselves as modern, working women. This was possible even though their income would not typically have afforded the prices of the purchased luxury items.

3.1.3 Signaling status through luxury brand selection

The symbolic use of luxury products is significantly associated with the status of their wearer. Leibenstein (1950) provides a view of this type of consumer behavior using economic terms and emphasizes the importance of external influences on utility (e.g. the total satisfaction or benefit derived from consuming a good or service) derived from factors other than the qualities inherent in the product. Through mathematical explanation, he suggests that the value that consumers receive from certain products increases or decreases according to the price level of the good or when other consumers reduce or increase their consumption. He considers the results of such behavior types of dysfunctional demand with external effects on utility and distinguishes them into Veblen, snobbish and bandwagon effects.

He defines the **bandwagon effect** as the extent to which demand for a commodity increases because others also consume the same commodity. It represents the desire of people to buy goods to be more like the people with whom they want to be connected, that is, to be fashionable or stylish or to look like one of them. The effect could be illustrated by a group of trendy individuals all eagerly purchasing the same type of luxury handbag, driven by its popularity and trendiness rather than its intrinsic value.

The **snobbish effect** refers to the extent to which the demand for consumer goods is reduced since others also consume the same commodity (or increase its consumption). Or conversely, the demand for the item increases when fewer people consume it. This effect represents people's desire to be exclusive, to be different or to separate themselves from herd consumption. In other words, an individual would express clear disinterest and disappointment by turning away from a luxury handbag that has become too common.

The **Veblen effect** refers to the phenomenon of conspicuous consumption, that is, the effect of an increase in demand when the price of a good is higher. The difference between the snobbish and Veblen effects is that the Veblen is a function of price, while the snobbish is a function of others' consumption patterns (Leibenstein, 1950). The effect could be illustrated by a luxurious handbag with an increasing price tag, surrounded by affluent individuals whose interest grows as the price rises, symbolizing the allure of prestige.

In the context of luxury consumption, the bandwagon effect as a social function of luxury consumption was examined by Kastanakis and Balabanis (2011) to identify the psychological factors of customers that have an impact on such behavior. They concluded that this effect is positively associated with a person's self-concept. If a person perceives him/herself independently of others (independent self-concept), then the fear of missing out ("FOMO") does not apply. On the contrary, the effect is strong in the case of people who have a so-called interdependent self-concept, that is, those who seek social approval for the luxury type of consumption. For consumers under the influence of the bandwagon effect, the reward or social advantage is the symbolism of a luxury product that is also used by other individuals important to them. At the same time, they avoid the punishment of being considered members of lower social strata by using a luxury brand.

On the contrary, the need for the uniqueness of the consumer in the sense of striving to be different from others through the acquisition and use of consumer goods to enhance one's self-image and social image has a negative relationship with the bandwagon effect. This means that if the need for consumer uniqueness is higher than average, it has a negative impact on the bandwagon effect (Kastanakis & Balabanis, 2011).

Signaling one's status through luxury brand selection is another possible segmentation criterion for segmenting luxury customers. Han et al. (2010) introduced a brand notability concept that reflects the prominence of a brand or brand logo on a luxury product and proposed a classification, dividing consumers into one of four groups according to their wealth and need for status (Table 3.4). The individual quadrants demonstrate how each group's preference for conspicuously or inconspicuously branded luxury goods corresponds to their need to belong to or distance themselves from a particular group.

Wealthy consumers (**Patricians**), with little need to help themselves, brand in order to reference their status, want to associate with their own kind, and are willing to pay a premium for silent branding that only they or other Patricians can recognize. In principle, Patricians are more interested in associating with other Patricians than in distancing themselves from other classes of consumers. They use subtle signals because only other Patricians

Table 3.4 Segmentation by wealth and the need to signal status, authors based on (Han et al., 2010).

Wealth		
Haves	**Patricians** signal to each other through silent branding, quiet signals.	**Parvenus** associate with other "haves" but want to distance themselves from "have-nots" through loud signals, loud branding.
Have-nots	**Proletarians** are not involved in signaling at all.	**Poseurs** imitate parvenus, trying to look like they belong to the "haves."

The need to signal a prestigious status

can interpret them. They have the financial means, a low need to consume for prestige, and like to associate with other patricians.

Wealthy consumers who need to emphasize their status (**Parvenus**) are relatively new members of the upper socioeconomic class. They use loud luxury branding to signal to the less affluent that they are not one of them. They possess considerable wealth but not the expertise necessary to interpret the silent signals of brands. Synonymous with luxury is the distinctive monogram "LV" or the well-known Damier canvas pattern from Louis Vuitton, as the brand's price transparently proves that it is beyond the reach of the lower classes. However, they are unlikely to recognize the fine details of a quietly branded Hermès bag or appreciate the delicate properties of a Vacheron Constantin watch. Parvenus are wealthy and can afford brands with less signaling. However, they are primarily concerned with separating or distancing themselves from the "have-nots" and at the same time, associating with other "haves," both Patricians and other upstarts.

Those who are in great need of status but cannot afford real luxuries (**Poseurs**) pretend to be who they are not. They use loud counterfeits to imitate those to whom their wealth is trusted. Like Parvenus, they are highly motivated towards luxury consumption because of their need to signal status. However, they do not have the financial means to readily afford authentic luxury goods. Still, they want to distance themselves from other less affluent people. Thus, they are particularly prone to buying counterfeit luxury goods as cheaper substitutes for originals. Luxury handbag counterfeiters usually choose items with loud branding – those that would appeal to upstarts, who in turn impress Poseurs.

Proletarians refer to less affluent consumers who are less aware of status. For the purposes of this model, they are not driven to consume for status and either cannot or do not want to engage in status goods signaling. They do not seek to associate with the upper class or distance themselves from others.

The status signaling model using brand prominence or volume was supported by field experiments along with analysis of market data (including fake products). This segmentation of luxury consumers slightly distances itself from Veblen's theory of the motivation of luxury purchases, which is based on the predominance of status as the main motivator for the acquisition of luxury items. The democratization of luxury, supported by the efforts of large luxury brands to offer cheaper designer items that deliver the aura of the brand at an affordable price into the hands of ordinary consumers, adds another dimension to the traditional segmentation of haves and have-nots. In a simplified way, the authors of this study suggest that manufacturers of luxury goods produce similar products within the same line, distinguished only by distinctive (loud) or inconspicuous (silent) branding. In contrast, **a silent logo could be significantly more expensive**, according to the results of this study.

Based on the results of this study, the authors recommend several implications for the management of luxury brands. First of all, it returns to the term brand *griffe* (Chapter 2) as a unique designer signature that satisfies the needs of Patricians not only with its low availability but also with very quiet branding, recognizable and appreciated only by this group of customers. Second, in luxury, you need to resist opportunities to over-popularize your brand consistently. Introducing a cheaper line or expanding the brand into other product categories increases short-term sales, but a brand can lose the ability to signal the status of its wearer by expanding too much among mass audiences, and thus lose at least wealthy upstarts. A delicate balance needs to be struck between the need for short-term brand growth and its ability to signal the wearer's status. Third, in accordance with the #10 anti-law of luxury (Chapter 4) and contrary to traditional marketing, luxury goods manufacturers should create and target advertising to all consumers, as even an upstart needs to trust that proletarians and posers will recognize the brand, and this will help them signal their social status (Han et al., 2010).

3.1.4 Status signaling through the acquisition of knowledge about luxury

In an effort to understand the contemporary luxury customer, another approach integrates an established view of luxury based on wealth with a focus on the luxury competencies of the consumer, including expertise, aesthetic taste and sensitivity to luxury symbolism. These aspects are developed through education and enjoyment of unique luxury elements related to design and craftsmanship, sensory attraction and socio-cultural stories. Wang's (2022) concept study examines the relationship between wealth and the capabilities of consumers of luxury brands. It takes into account the previous segmentation, emphasizing the need for status signaling, and does not condemn the criterion of wealth, which is still the most important for entering luxury, but it adds the perspective of luxury clients' knowledge.

Wang believes that luxury consumption can be positioned at different points along a continuum in terms of wealth and competence, as shown in the conceptual framework (Figure 3.1). Luxury consumption based on wealth and competence differs according to this concept in terms of (1) consumption targets; (2) consideration, selection and use; and (3) consumption outcomes related to consumer-brand relations and social influence. This model does not suggest that consumption based on wealth and competence occurs only in this pure form. Some consumers (e.g. Parvenus or Poseurs) may be more inclined towards wealth-based consumption, while others (e.g. Patricians) may be more involved in competency-based consumption (Han et al., 2010).

Competency-based luxury consumption is likely to provide **intrinsic benefits to consumers through the learning** and enjoyment processes resulting from dealing with the unique characteristics of luxury. Consumers can aspire to become sophisticated luxury experts and aesthetic taste experts.

Model of luxury customer segmentation according to knowledge of luxury and wealth. Characteristics of the wealth-based consumption on the left, competencies-based consumption on the right, moderating factors at the bottom.

Wang (2022) builds on the assumption based on previous publications that **wealth-based luxury consumption** is largely driven **by the pursuit of external benefits**, that is, the pursuit of social rewards or the avoidance of social punishments. The main characteristics of luxury based on wealth are high price and exclusivity, which can be used to seek social benefits in

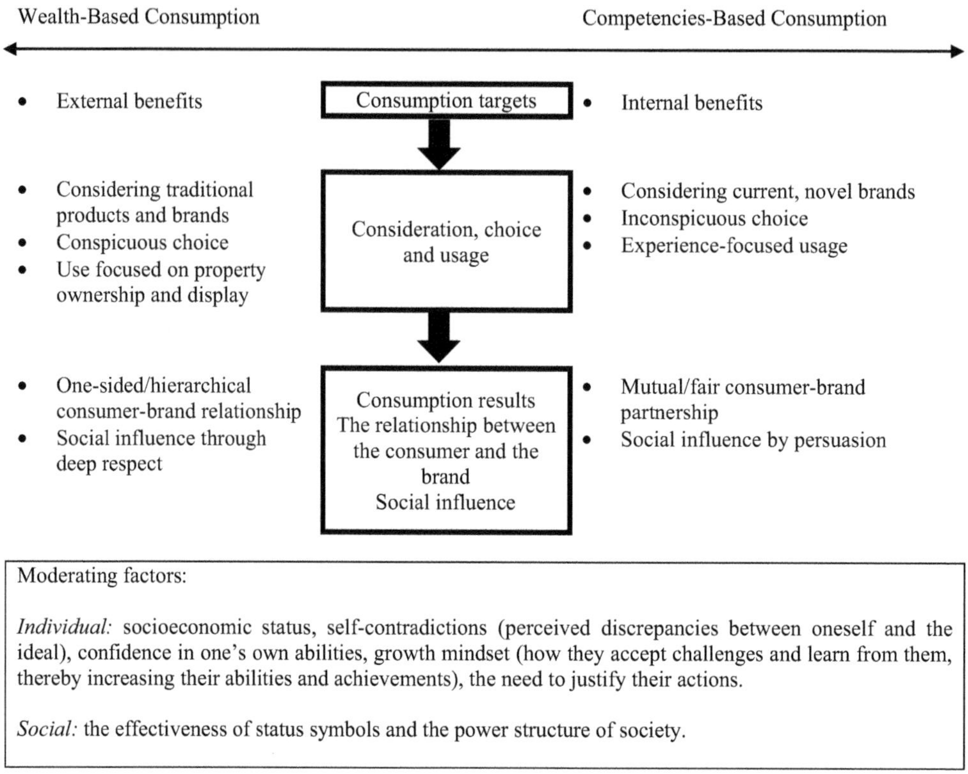

Figure 3.1 Conceptual model of luxury customer segmentation according to knowledge of luxury and wealth, adapted from Wang (2022).

the form of, for example, differentiation from others or, conversely, the manifestation of belonging to a certain social class. Consumers show a greater interest in luxury goods when they are trying to either differentiate themselves from lower-class consumers or facilitate their connection with other rich or wealthy ones.

Lee and Shrum (2012) have even shown conspicuous purchases when a person is ignored or excluded in certain social situations. In addition, consumer interest in luxury property increases when socio-economic status is generally valued in society, which can be a tool for improving social status (Lee & Shrum, 2012).

In contrast, **in competency-based consumption**, consumers become interested in unique luxury traits related to design and craftsmanship, sensory appeal and socio-cultural stories. In other words, they **look for intrinsic benefits and rewards**. People who seek to consume luxury for intrinsic advantages and have the ambition to acquire deeper knowledge and skills can become quite sophisticated experts in luxury and aesthetics, investing time and energy to achieve their aspirations.

Wang (2022) also suggests that different types of products and brands should be part of the model. **In wealth-based consumption, these are generally traditional or classic products and brands**, as these iconic representatives of luxury can be easily recognized as symbols of wealth-based status (e.g. Hermès Birkin handbag or the Panthère de Cartier collection). Conversely, in **competency-based consumption, consumers are more open to consider current, novel brands** (e.g. Virgil Abloh's creative design, innovative materials from Stella McCartney's work). These brands represent innovations in design, aesthetics and cultural references and can therefore set new trends, requiring a deeper knowledge of consumers to understand that they can be as valuable as traditional luxury.

Some brands are considered more striking in luxury than others because of their design, appearance, impression and brand identity (Han et al., 2010). **Consumption based on wealth is closely tied to the choice of brands considered very striking.** Highly visible and easily recognizable logos, designs and symbols are unambiguous, and they function as loud signals that express wealth and economic power (Vigneron & Johnson, 2004). **However, competencies-based luxury choices tend to be unobtrusive** as a reward to competent customers in a more refined way (that is, it requires specialized knowledge and skills). Consumers with more fashion knowledge may avoid luxury products with easily identifiable logos or designs.

The model further assumes that the **use of a luxury product** has a different character when consumers engage in wealth-based consumption compared to competency-based luxury consumption. Ownership of a luxury item offers psychological benefits, including a sense of control and personal identification. The basis of the wealth-based view is the assumption that the utility that the consumer derives focuses on the expensive nature of the property that is publicly displayed to others. The use of a luxury product here is based on its **exposure**. In contrast, consumers engaged in competency-based consumption focus on their **experience** when using luxury products.

The experiential dimensions of brands have been conceptualized in the form of four dimensions: sensory (strong effect of the brand on visual or other senses), affective (influence on emotions, on feelings), intellectual (stimulates curiosity, thinking) and behavioral (physical experience, involvement in physical activity). Competent consumers focus on experience because they are more deeply interested in the brand and have knowledge of the unique characteristics of the product and the brands they have acquired. Post-purchase, these consumers are likely to continue being interested in further education, participating in brand-related events or doing their own exploration online. They may even join brand communities where they can influence other likeminded brand users. To put it simply, the model suggests that wealth-based consumption choices for luxury products and brands are mostly focused on striking products and brands, and use is focused on product ownership and display, while competency-based consumption selection is more subtle and use is experience oriented (Schmitt et al., 2009; Muniz & O'Guinn, 2001).

In consumption based on wealth, the **relationship between consumer and brand is rather one sided and hierarchical**, with a luxury brand playing a dominant role. Consumers are often passive recipients of luxury brand marketing and follow the example of the brand. Sales assistants educate customers on what to buy and how to use it to signal their wealth, and customers appreciate this hierarchical relationship. The brand dominates the client, in accordance with luxury anti-law #6 (Chapter 4) – for a brand to maintain its status, it must always dominate the client. In competency-based consumption, the consumer-brand relationship is reciprocal and fair; that is, it is a partnership. The brand is co-created by the company and the consumer. On social networks, they can influence other members of their community with their knowledge and connect them with the brand. Consumers are actively engaged in communicating luxury brands and sharing their stories.

Another result of luxury consumption is social influence, as people seek approval or appreciation of their consumption from others. Wealth-based consumption signals class and social position, influencing the interactions between those who indulge in such products and others who don't. In particular, it affects how others recognize and show respect for the status of these consumers. This **respectful social influence in the consumption of luxury based on wealth** is replaced by a consumption based on competence by **persuasive influence.** Consumers with competence in luxury show expertise, taste and sensitivity to the symbolism of luxury in that area and are therefore trusted sources for others. They can become opinion leaders through word of mouth or influencers on social media.

The last part of the model is the influencing, moderating factors of both types of behavior, divided into individual and social. **Individual factors** include the consumer's **socio-economic** status and social class, assuming that the status acquired through one's own work over the course of a consumer's life tends to lead to consumption based on wealth, while high status or class acquired by birth will lead to consumption based on competences. Formal and family education of consumers born with a higher social status cultivates the appreciation of beautiful things, the aesthetics of the individual and thus his/her behavior in luxury. Another individual influencing factor is the way in which consumers **deal with their own self-discrepancies,** that is, differences between themselves and the ideal, which can influence their link to luxury consumption.

Wang relies on empirical research by Sivanathan and Pettit (2010), which showed that consumers signal the luxury of wealth to protect themselves from negative beliefs or experiences such as self-threat, low self-esteem and a sense of powerlessness, simply put, as a means of repairing their ego. The desire for luxury, on the contrary, decreases if these inner fears are overcome. On the other hand, confidence in one's own abilities should lead to a desire to acquire greater knowledge and competences leading to a sense of personal excellence, control over one's abilities and **overcoming external challenges** (Sivanathan & Pettit, 2010).

Finally, the individual moderation factor here takes into account the way consumers are able to **justify their luxury purchases**, which are generally considered extravagant and lead to waste. Those who feel ashamed about it may resort to deepening their knowledge of luxury, since demonstrating such competence in luxury shopping may be considered more socially acceptable. Such consumption will provide the necessary rationalization of its decision, since its aim is not to show off but to develop knowledge and skills specific to this area. If, on the other hand, the need to justify their luxury purchases is low, consumers can freely engage in wealth-based consumption (Khan et al., 2010).

The model ranks the effectiveness of status symbols among the social factors influencing the way luxury is consumed. Consumers use luxury to differentiate themselves from the lower classes and consolidate their position on the social ladder. The extent to which these status symbols are effective in signaling social status and providing social benefits affects consumers' involvement in wealth-based luxury consumption. The symbolic value of luxury may be reduced through its democratization (where a larger proportion of consumers access the luxury brand through lower-priced items such as accessories or perfumes) or, for example, by lending or reselling. Given these trends, consumers may signal their status through luxury competence rather than their own wealth.

The **power structure of society** is the last social factor moderating the type of consumption in luxury. The way power is distributed in society can change consumption based on wealth into consumption based on competence. Power distance is an intercultural factor that shows the extent to which members of society believe it is acceptable for power to be shared unequally, "showing the degree of inequality in power between the less powerful individual and the more powerful" (Hofstede & Xu, 2001, p. 83). If an unequal distribution of power is generally accepted in society, the consumption of luxury based on wealth may prevail, as well as if society approves of the legitimacy of social hierarchies based on power and elitism. As the power gap in society is narrowed, elites are seen as less legitimate, society is structured more evenly, and consumers will engage more in competency-based consumption that allows expertise and taste to be expressed.

The conceptual model of segmentation of luxury customers according to knowledge of luxury and wealth has implications for the management of luxury brands. Identifying consumers with their competence-based behavior in the luxury sector should lead to adapting communication targeted to these segments, such as on social networks, where their knowledge can be cultivated through the right content. At the same time, thanks to their knowledge and presence in the online space, the consumer becomes an actor in the market of luxury brands, where his/her knowledge and example can influence other luxury customers without the control of the brand management (Wang, 2022).

3.2 Generations Z and Alpha: The challenge for luxury brand management

According to generational cohort theory, groups of individuals (cohorts) who were born during the same time frame and experienced similar distinguishable external events during the early period of their adulthood (17–23 years) share similar values, attitudes, preferences and consumption behavior throughout their lives (Ryder, 1965). The specifics of today's strongest shopping group – *Generation* Y (millennials born between 1986 and 1999) – are important for the strategies of luxury brands, but *Generation* Z (born between 2000 and 2010) and *Generation Alpha* (including those born from 2011 onward) are key to shaping the long-term vision (Table 3.5). Understanding the differences between the older *Generations* X (1965–1985) *and* Y, which have long been the key to success in luxury, seems a challenging task for luxury business management. According to consultants' forecasts, in 2025 the share of Gen Z and Y in the luxury market was supposed to be more than 20% and 50%, respectively (D'Arpizio & Levato, 2021). Newer forecasts predict an even higher proportion, such as that by 2030, Gen Z will account for 25% to 30% of luxury market purchases, while

Table 3.5 Comparison of generation cohorts X, Y, Z and Alpha, authors based on (Bielińska-Dusza, 2022; Schneider & Lee, 2022).

Generation X **1965–1985** **Post-boomers**	**Generation Y** **1986–1999** **Millennials**	**Generation Z** **2000–2010** **Digital natives**	**Generation Alpha** **2011+** **Digital natives**
Carefulness, diligence and perseverance	Creativity	Entrepreneurship	High demands
Communicability	Impatience	The need for feedback	Social isolation
Fidelity	Average fidelity	The decision "here and now"	
Skepticism	Indecision	Pragmatism	Realism
Monotasking	Multitasking	Multitasking, multiscreening	Multiscreening
Independence	Technological competencies	Ability to connect the real and virtual worlds	Virtual Proficiency

millennials will account for 50% to 55%, which means that younger generations (Generations Y, Z and Alpha) will become the biggest buyers of luxury by far, representing nearly 85% of global purchases (Claudia D'Arpizio et al., 2024).

Generation Z represents 25% of the world's population, and a large number of them are entering the luxury brand market. Their formative period has been fundamentally different from that of previous generations thanks to technology, making it difficult to understand their behavior and creating a wider gap between them. Social networks allow them to socialize without having to meet, which sometimes leads to social isolation. Gen-Z is more pragmatic than previous generations, growing up with technology and maturing in a period of worsening climate crisis, global movements such as "Me Too," "Black Lives Matter" and the COVID-19 pandemic.

Climate change has brought about an emerging psychological phenomenon called *climate anxiety* or *eco-anxiety*, which has been described as a chronic fear of environmental destruction (Albrecht, 2011). Some people are deeply affected by feelings of loss, helplessness and frustration due to their inability to contribute to stopping climate change (Clayton et al., 2017). A study of respondents aged 18 to 26 showed a significant link between climate anxiety and the mental health of this generation (Reyes et al., 2021), who often blame previous generations for the state of the environment. This sets them apart even more significantly as they place greater emphasis on sustainability and social responsibility.

For Generation Z, another important characteristic is the need to belong, that is, to **be accepted by their peers**. The group to which a person belongs is a decisive factor in relation to his/her own self-concept and attitudes towards themselves. In key areas where Gen Z members influence each other – such as music, fashion, cosmetics and video games – fitting in is important. Social networks are the usual platform for creating online communities or groups of friends (Williams et al., 2010).

According to research agency Archival, which conducted an extensive study on the sample of U.S. Generation Z, **Influencers** are an essential part of the inspiration journey. More than half (51%) of Gen Z believe social media influencers create new trends (versus 36% of millennials), and 21% of Gen Z and millennials credited celebrities with creating new trends, compared to 15% who said brands do. The most powerful social media where Gen Z gets its inspiration are YouTube (57%), TikTok (53%) and Instagram (44%). Nevertheless, most of the Gen Z US sample prefer making a purchase in-store while shopping (73%), and only 27% prefer making a purchase on social media (Vogue Business, 2024a). It should be noted, however, that social commerce is significantly more important to Gen Z in the Asia-Pacific (APAC) region.

In the luxury industry, as in other sectors, Generation Z will make up the bulk of consumption. According to current research, the university student generation shows that some traditional characteristics of a luxury product, such as rarity, honest craftsmanship, uniqueness and limited distribution, are less important for the perception of a product as a luxury one than, for example, **higher price, design and recognized style, social differentiation**, brand **country of origin**, indulgence, top quality or brand heritage. When choosing a luxury product, young people are significantly influenced both by the role of family and that of the celebrities when they select a particular item. In terms of motivation for luxury purchases, the effect of "**being seen**" was the strongest among respondents, **ahead of the snobbish effect** (that is, reducing demand for a luxury product if others own it) and the **bandwagon effect** (increased demand for a luxury item if it is owned by others). This suggests that Gen Z consumers do not necessarily see the consumption of luxury as something reserved for elites but rather as a tool to express their identity in the context of everyday life or consumption simply for their own enjoyment and entertainment. The possibility of adapting a product design to express one's own identity and individual uniqueness is one of the implications for product management of luxury brands (Shin et al., 2021).

Young Generation Z doesn't want to irritate or irk others with their luxury. They show their status, but discreetly, because they don't want others to think negatively about them. They don't want to look like they're showing off or trying too hard. They prefer to **express in subtle codes rather than loud logos** because they are more tasteful. Luxury fashion, for example, is driven by the need to fit into their communities (i.e., the bandwagon effect) and not to stand out (i.e., the Veblen or snobbish effect) (Eastman et al., 2018).

People from Generation Z often logically assign sports brands such as Nike or Adidas to luxury, as they have more personal experience and thus a closer relationship with them. It is therefore no coincidence that Gucci has launched limited collections under collaboration with the Adidas brand with the iconic Gucci canvas, marked with an emblem that combines the Adidas and Gucci logos (Gucci, 2024).

In fashion, young people are described as those who do not look for trends or status confirmation but perceive it as important for their **own identity and self-esteem.** They often tend to adapt fashion trends to their own personal styles. The October 2022 US Gen-Z Consumer Survey of 947 respondents aged 13–25 shows that luxury brands are still underrepresented in the minds of this generation. The only exception is the Gucci brand, which was ranked among the three most important fashion brands by 12% of the respondents (according to spontaneous brand knowledge). Gucci's Roblox, metaverse and NFT activities are likely to have some impact on brand awareness among young consumers, as do social media communications and product innovations. Another spontaneously mentioned brand is Louis Vuitton (3%). The most known are mass and sports fashion brands: Nike (22%), Adidas (11%), H&M (10%) and Zara (9%). At the same time, the panel indicated the interest of young consumers to pay over time (with increasing income) for more luxury items (Schneider & Lee, 2022).

The generational difference is well demonstrated by the so-called **meme culture**, that is, shared content – usually humorous – in the form of a picture or video. Memes are such an obvious and omnipresent means of communication between Gen Z individuals that they are usually unable to explain to an older person what the meme means or even why the "funny picture" is called a meme (example picture 3.1) The most viral memes are usually related to animals, (typically cats, dogs and others) or food.

Picture 3.1 Example of cat meme. By PantheraLeo1359531, licensed under the Creative Commons Attribution 4.0 International license. Available on (Wikimedia Commons, 2020).

Generations react differently to brand communication. For example, Roth-Cohen et al.'s (2021) team empirically demonstrated differences in the perception of mobile advertising by generations X, Y and Z. A Gen X customer positively receives informative and trustworthy messages, including entertainment. If an ad contains more detailed product data, it doesn't irritate this group. Gen Y also responds well to informative and reliable messages as part of their multitasking, and as multitaskers, they don't find mobile advertising irritating or intrusive. Gen Z responds positively to simple, informative and trustworthy messages that are entertaining. However, they get annoyed when mobile ads interrupt their personal activity on a mobile device. Ads targeting Gen Z should therefore be designed to be consistent with their natural consumption of mobile content (Roth-Cohen et al., 2021).

Research on the **Alpha Generation** (born after 2010) does not yet have enough information regarding purchasing behavior. However, some characteristics are already available. Gen Alpha includes **intellectually strong individuals** who were born into the digital era and were raised in the presence of modern technology. They are hyperactive and quickly learn new things. Despite their young age, their family members involve them in the purchase decision-making process due to their digital prowess, often relying on their advice on technology purchases or the use of various apps. Due to their **ability to collect and combine information** from different sources, **they are not easily persuaded** to purchase goods or services. They are active on social networks at an early age but are not particularly aware of the importance of the security of shared data (Raja et al., 2021). Gen Alpha's parents believe in democracy and let their children freely express their opinions when making purchasing decisions. So, Alpha becomes, directly or indirectly, one of **the dominant influencers of purchasing decisions** (Williams et al., 2010). The Alpha consumer uses platforms based on artificial intelligence and virtual reality – Siri, Google, Alexa – to engage in a relationship with the brand. Thus, it will be necessary for brands to use state-of-the-art technologies, including virtual or augmented reality, gamification and illustrative visualization without long descriptions (Thomas & George, 2021).

Today's luxury brand management needs to understand, above all, the culture that surrounds Gen Z consumers and their values, as brand communications should resonate. As Gen Z ages, its income should grow, making them an increasingly attractive cohort for luxury brands. It is essential to figure out how to build a relationship between the brand and Gen Z consumers at the current stage of their life cycle; this relates to all aspects that differentiate them from previous generations and their associations with traditional luxury brands. This same process will also be necessary in the future with regard to the Alpha generation. Significantly different behaviors are expected from younger cohorts compared to today's traditional luxury customers, particularly at the point of purchase or in distribution channels like e-commerce and social commerce. There is a greater emphasis on the social responsibility of both the brand and company, increased online communication and new technologies applied to brand management.

For luxury brands, entering the world of technology is one of the paradoxes or contradictions of luxury, which is called "The Phygital Dilemma" (Som & Blanckaert, 2021, p. 132), where the management of luxury must balance the timelessness, legitimacy and exclusivity of the brand with modernity, democracy and innovation. A well-thought-out **balance in online and offline** brand strategies can reach young and affluent consumers around the world in a highly competitive global environment.

Given the context of younger cohorts and their characteristics, the strategy of luxury brands will need to address challenges that are not yet a priority for current generations of luxury customers. These relate to trends in distribution, in establishing the strategy of corporate social responsibility (and how to communicate these activities), online communication, building online communities of brands and new technologies in brand management and communication.

3.3 New demographic challenge for online communication of luxury brands

The reasons for luxury brands' concerns about being too involved in online communication can be summed up by explaining the **paradoxes between luxury and digitalization.** First, luxury brands worship tradition, while digitization is a contemporary phenomenon. The communication of luxury brands is constant, unchanging and based on the brand identity and its DNA, while digital communication is dynamic and constantly changing. Further, luxury brands are selective and designed for elites, while the internet and social media are extremely democratic. Finally, luxury brands seek total control over all aspects of their communications, while the internet and social media are too flexible in terms of follower engagement and luxury brands' communications can spiral out of control (Som & Blanckaert, 2021).

The decision to engage in the digital environment is challenging for luxury brands due to the aspect of maintaining exclusivity, but it is essential because **online strategies have the potential to strengthen the brand, especially among a younger target group**. The refusal to embrace the internet as a complement to offline retail and the inability to innovate could become a threat to the future of luxury brands. With the opportunity to reach billions of people internationally, the digital landscape gives luxury brands the opportunity to build their image and mythology online. This is despite concerns about the loss of exclusivity stemming from the internet's main characteristic, which is ubiquity. The online communication of luxury brands will allow the interested community to become part of their dream (Hennings et al., 2012). Building a brand community, which is defined as "specialized, non-geographically bound community, based on a structured set of social relationships among admirers of a brand. It is specialized because at its centre is a branded good or service" (Muniz & O'Guinn, 2001, p. 412), which is an integral part of the luxury brand's communication strategy.

Online communities of brands communicate in a virtual internet environment and differ from traditional online communities not only by their commercial nature, but mainly by the common interest of their members, admiration, sympathy and even love for a particular brand. Love for the brand has, according to Albert et al. (2006), a total of 11 dimensions: passion for the brand, the long-term duration of the relationship between the customer and the brand, consistency between your own image and the image of the product, satisfaction of the consumer's dreams, memories evoked by the brand, the pleasure that the brand provides, brand attraction, the uniqueness of the brand and of the customer's relationship to the brand, brand beauty, embedded trust that the brand has never failed and brand influence. Brand functional values such as quality and price are not among the leading dimensions of brand love (Albert et al., 2006).

The fundamental peculiarity of a brand's online community lies in the **ability of its members to interact with each other**, exchange information and knowledge about the brand or simply express their passion for it, thus influencing each other's relationship with the brand. Research among the online community of brands (e.g. Louis Vuitton, Burberry, Gucci, Prada, etc.) has shown that community dynamics (active participation in the community, community-generated content, members' perception of brand quality) positively influence brand value. In particular, the level of participation of community members and the production of shared content directly affects brand loyalty. Following the spontaneous dynamics of the community with respect to members' ideas and suggestions is an essential aspect of brand management for gaining awareness of consumer response to brand activities (Brogi et al., 2013).

Further research (Brogi et al., 2013) among customers of luxury brands confirmed that there is a positive and significant relationship between the number of famous followers or fans of a luxury brand on social networking sites and the customer's purchase intent towards this luxury brand. The positive role of celebrities and prominent personalities has been proven in their activities on social networks and their visibly paid promotions, that is, advertising campaigns for the brand. On social networking sites, it is impossible to get a tangible experience about the quality of a luxury product, and the customer instead relies on the positive comments of others, that is, so-called **electronic word-of-mouth**. Furthermore, there is a positive and significant relationship between the form of a luxury brand's marketing post on a social network in terms of its aesthetics and the purchase intent, and finally, between the content of the post, which takes into account the symbolic meaning of the brand in the sense of remembering the cultural heritage of the brand (MajlesiRad & Shoushtari, 2020).

Social networks are important for luxury brands not only from the internal point of view of marketing communication management, but also from the point of view of the number of so-called hashtags (#, the number of user mentions with the brand name), which signals the number of mentions of the brand and shows the emotional connection and relationship of the user with the brand. According to Luxe Digital, the brands listed in Table 3.6 are among **the top ten most digitally active luxury brands**, as they are the focus of network users. Each of them conducts extensive online conversations across social media channels and is in the spotlight of modern consumers (LUXE DIGITAL, 2024).

With a total of 52.3 million active followers on social media, **Gucci remains a digital powerhouse** despite a decline in the number of followers in the past couple of years. Its focus on innovation, particularly in digital spaces like the metaverse, keeps it relevant. The brand also continues to engage audiences through creative campaigns and strong online content. They entered the virtual worlds of web3 relatively early with the unmistakable tokens SuperGucci or Gucci Town on Roblox (more in the Welcome to Gucci Town mini-case). Gucci Ancora and related mini-games later replaced Gucci Town. In addition to digital innovations, Gucci also actively and visibly promotes gender balance and a sustainable supply chain – two important values for the emerging younger generation of luxury customers.

Chanel maintains a strong digital presence, especially on social media, where it commands significant attention (almost 60 million followers on Instagram as in table 3.6). However, the brand is selective about e-commerce, limiting online availability for some products. Chanel's strategy emphasizes exclusivity and high-end appeal. Chanel's position with the most user mentions demonstrates the strength of a brand that occupies a prominent position in the minds of network users. Chanel still resists e-commerce collections of clothing and handbags.

Table 3.6 Numbers of followers, posts and # of selected brands on Instagram, authors using data from Instagram August 2024 (main brand pages only, no divisions).

	Chanel	Gucci	Louis Vuitton	Dior	Rolex	Hermès
Number of followers	**59.9 mil.**	52.3 mil.	55.6 mil.	46.4 mil.	16.6 mil.	14.3 mil.
Number of branded # *	**38.4 mil.**	37.9 mil.	18.2 mil.	28.2 mil.	20.6 mil.	18.0 mil.
Number of brand posts	6,357	448	8,163	**12,500**	1,558	2,969

• For example, hashtagged phrase associated with a specific brand used typically on Instagram.

Louis Vuitton focuses on artistic collaborations and high-profile **fashion shows** to foster online community engagement. Their website and social media channels attract significant traffic, reflecting its strong presence in the luxury market. **The Dior brand works well in digital marketing,** using social media and e-commerce, and according to Luxe Digital, it has exceptional online engagement. Its diverse product lines, including fashion, beauty and jewelry, contribute to its dominance. This is evidenced by the number of contributions, which far exceeds all other top players (Table 3.6).

The presence of brands on the internet through their own websites is already a matter of course; with regard to luxury strategy, it is necessary to mention the following rules of good practice that luxury websites should take into account:

1. In luxury, even more than in other industries, having **no website is better** than having an average one;
2. Understanding the importance of **customer communities** in sharing a passion for the brand and the value of their feedback and customer interaction;
3. The content of brand communication **tells stories** in the context of brand depth, personality and history, in the context of the entire brand identity; and
4. Maintaining a luxury perspective in creating **consumer experiences** in the online environment (Kapferer & Bastien, 2012).

3.4 The impact of geography on luxury brand building: Country of origin effect

The effects of a country of origin on specific brands are driven by the image of the nation, which is an external factor that cannot be controlled by brand management. Roth & Romeo (1992) defined the image of a country of origin in relation to the perception of a product as "the overall perception of a country that consumers of products from certain countries form based on their previous perception of production in that country and the strengths and weaknesses of that country's marketing" (Roth & Romeo, 1992, p. 480). What the consumer knows or thinks about a country, in particular with regard to the production possibilities of different product categories and the country's capacity for innovation, has a major impact on the way a country is perceived as a product's country of origin. Consistency between a product type and a consumer's perception of a country's production in a given product sector can be an indicator of consumer willingness to purchase products with that country of origin (Roth & Romeo, 1992).

To distinguish between domestic and international brands, the definition refers to **domestic ones as brands that exist in one country or in a limited geographical area** and are owned by a local, international or global firm (Schuiling & Kapferer, 2004; Wolfe, 1991), while **global brands are those that use a standardized marketing strategy** and mix in all markets, assuming the existence of homogeneous consumer segments (Levitt, 1983). Another approach defines global brands based on consumer perception, that is, those that consumers themselves perceive as global, confirming the positive relationship between the perceived globality of a brand and its perceived quality and prestige. As a result, the quality and prestige of the brand have a positive relationship with the purchase intent of consumers (Steenkamp et al., 2003; Llonch-Andreu et al., 2016).

Ger (1999) emphasized in his conceptual model of local brand competitiveness the importance of **using domestic cultural capital** "to build sustainable, unique value and to offer symbolism of authenticity and prestige" (Ger, 1999, p. 70). Businesses that build domestic brands as "local culture icons can create more brand value" (Steenkamp et al., 2003, p. 62).

In the luxury industry, the question of the influence of a brand's country of origin on consumer perception is obvious at first glance. French and Italian brands are among the most valuable, and their connection to local culture adds additional value to their perception. Is there room for the successful development of domestic luxury brands outside these traditional countries of origin? Kapferer and Bastien suggested that one of the strongest sources of scarcity and rarity associated with luxury brands stems from their ability to be ambassadors of the virtues or advantages of individual nation countries (Kapferer & Bastien, 2009). Other research in the field of luxury goods analyzed the perception of the country of origin of the brand and its influence on the purchase intention of consumers. The findings pointed to the crucial importance of the brand, which had a greater influence on product evaluation and purchasing decisions than the country of origin effect. Other influential factors playing a role in the purchase decision, after the brand itself, include the following: design, warranties, the country of the brand's design, and brand country of origin (where the product is produced) (Aiello et al., 2009).

Prior to the COVID-19 pandemic, studies on domestic luxury brands focused primarily on the Chinese market, and the possibility of building new domestic luxury brands that would be able to compete with established global luxury brands in China. These studies usually concluded that, despite the huge potential of luxury customers in China, the chances of new luxury brands emerging there were relatively small, as Chinese luxury consumers doubted domestic brands and believed that only Western-origin products could be called luxuries. This was reflected in the marketing strategies of the world's leading luxury brands, which referred to the brand's country of origin, its affinity with Western countries and Western origins on their websites, significantly more often than references to the brand's global nature or affinity with non-Western developed countries (Strebinger & Rusetski, 2016).

During the pandemic, consumers became aware of the importance of regional (local) products and environmentally friendly products; and these factors are starting to influence consumers' selection criteria. For example, it has already been confirmed that a higher degree of global identity in food purchasing (where consumers believe in the positive effects of globalization and recognize commonalities rather than differences between people) leads to higher levels of **consumer xenocentrism** (i.e., a consistent preference for foreign products despite higher prices and lower quality). Conversely, a higher degree of local identity (where consumers believe more in local traditions, customs and local communities, respect them and are interested in local events) leads to lower levels of consumer xenocentrism (Zhang et al., 2022).

In the post-pandemic era, **consumer ethnocentrism** (a tendency of consumers to prefer products and brands from their own country over those from other countries; their preference is often driven by nationalistic or patriotic feelings and the belief that purchasing domestic products supports the local economy and employment) is expected to increase, which may contribute to the preference of local brands, including in the luxury sector, where opportunities for previously limited domestic luxury options may grow.

In order to understand whether buyers of luxury products perceive any significant differences in the values of foreign and domestic luxury brands, to what extent buyers of luxury goods know domestic luxury brands, as well as whether the local country of origin of the brand has an impact on the purchasing process of luxury items, research using a sample of Czech luxury customers was conducted in 2019. The team of authors also examined product categories with the potential of domestic luxury and demographic factors for potential targeting of local luxury brands (Olšanová et al., 2020). Respondents first identified the country of origin of selected brands that they themselves purchased during the past year.

Figure 3.2 shows a group of French brands with strong correct identification (Dior, Chanel, Lancôme) and a group of American brands where the correct identification of the

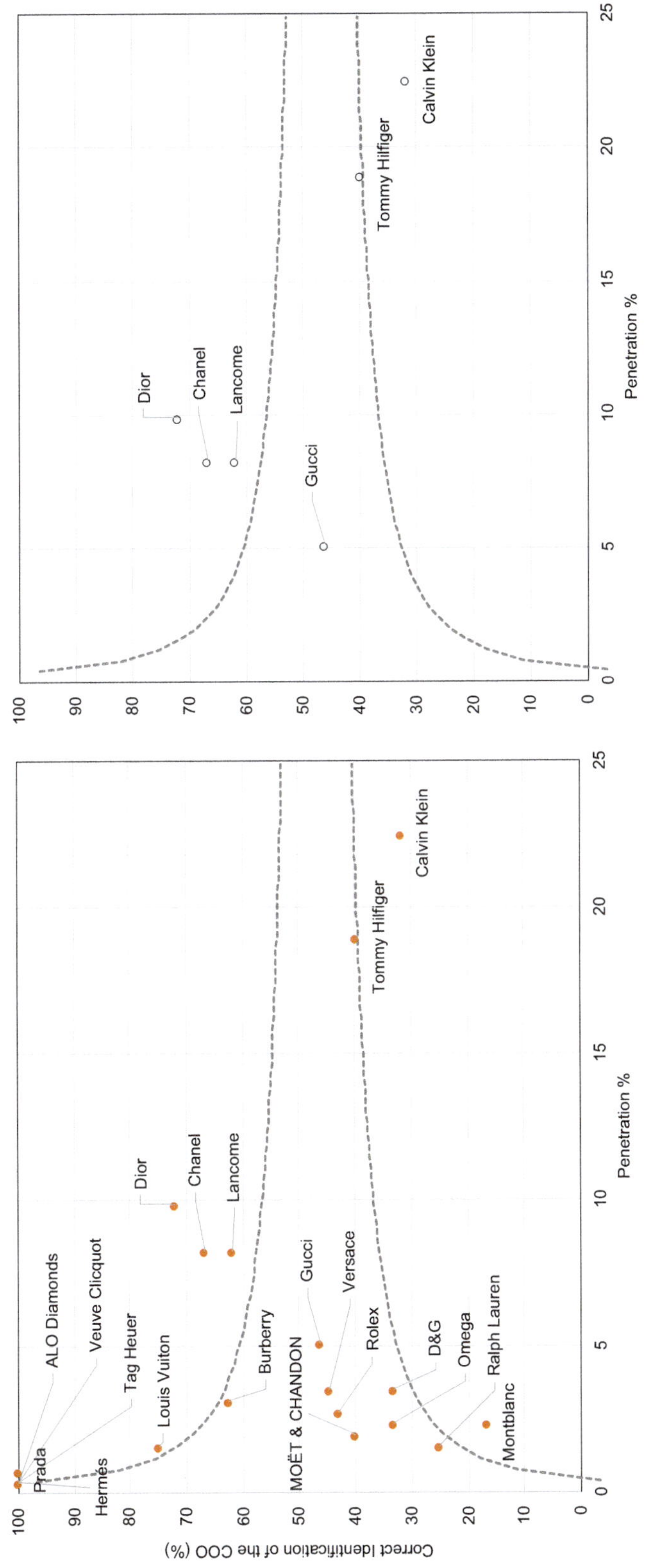

Figure 3.2 Percent expression of identification of the correct country of origin of the luxury brand (Olšanová et al., 2020).

country of origin is lower despite the high penetration of purchases in the last year. Dotted lines distinguish between three segments: (1) upper, with significantly higher identification of the correct country of origin; (2) medium with significantly lower identification; and (3) bottom, where no identification was identified. The left side of the middle segment, between the dotted lines, shows low-penetration marks in the sample; therefore, even a high identification of the country of origin is not important (at the level of 5% significance). The results confirmed the findings of earlier research that consumers' overall ability to identify the brand's country of origin is limited (Balabanis & Diamantopoulos, 2008).

A comparison of the perception of traditional luxury values between domestic and international brands showed that **domestic luxury brands are perceived as: rare, unique, produced in small collections (not mass), available and owned or worn by only a small group of people.** On the other hand, the traditional values of luxury (very expensive, dreamy and the brand as a symbol of luxury) are less associated with the domestic luxury brand, according to respondents.

A comparison of perceived luxury dimensions between Czech luxury brands and traditional luxury (Figure 3.3) suggests that there are similarities in perception in terms of hedonistic dimensions (top in quality of workmanship, aesthetic (beautiful), a sign of good taste), qualitative (sophisticated, top in quality of execution) and dimensions of uniqueness (selected (exclusive), exceptional). For domestic luxury brands, **the perception of elitism** (available only to a small number of people, owned or worn by only a small number of people, produced in small collections) and **specific items of uniqueness and design** (top quality in workmanship and rare) is **higher than that of traditional luxury brands.** On the contrary, domestic brands are not perceived as dreamy, very expensive or a symbol of luxury.

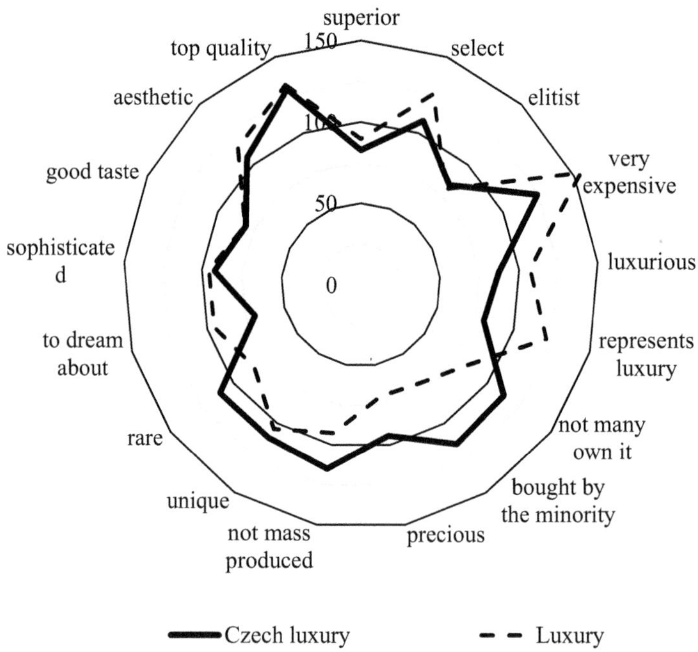

Figure 3.3 Perception of luxury values in international and domestic luxury brands (Olšanová et al., 2020).

The highest spontaneous knowledge of domestic luxury brands was recorded in the category of watches (Prim brand 8.3%) and design glass (Moser 7.9%). The highest aided brand awareness belongs to the glass sector (Bohemia Crystal 66.4%, Moser 37.9% and Lasvit (6.3%), followed by fashion brands (Kara 65.2%; Liběna Rochová 20.6%; TATIANA 13.6% and Ivana Mentlová 5.1%) and watches/jewelry (Prim 41.5%, Zorya 3.6%). In the knowledge of domestic luxury brands, there are similarities in the demographics of respondents with the highest awareness of home luxury: on average, respondents identified 2.7 brands they knew on the list, but the results showed significantly **higher awareness existed amongst older respondents, respondents with a university education** and those with older children or children in college.

Almost three-quarters of respondents agreed that "the Czech origin of a luxury brand is a reason to consider buying it," and almost two-thirds would prefer to buy Czech luxury when it comes to glass and crystal home accessories. However, for a large proportion of respondents, brand origin has no impact on their purchases (an average of 43% of all categories). Respondents of higher age and education prefer Czech brands in more categories, but the difference is significant only for the 61+ age group. These findings are in line with López-Lomelí (2019), their conclusions defined **the group of domestic brand lovers as significantly older compared to other identified segments** (López-Lomelí et al., 2019).

The findings of this research (Olšanová et al., 2020) suggest that domestic luxury brands have the potential to attract a target group that buys mainly established international luxury brands. Specifically, for more than 70% of the sample, the domestic origin of the luxury brand was a reason to buy. **The purchase intent strongly depends on the product category,** and it is also influenced by the age and education of the respondent. **The importance of domestic origin increases with the age and education of the buyer.** Given the differences in consumer perceptions of luxury values between domestic and international brands, domestic luxury brands should focus on their uniqueness and some attributes of elitism, as these values could potentially differentiate domestic luxury from traditional, foreign brands (which is supported by the creation of sustainable unique value based on local culture and offering symbolism of authenticity and prestige (Ger, 1999)). The older target group 65+ will play a growing role for domestic luxury, which, according to the forecasts of the Czech Statistical Office, will grow from the current approximately 20% of the total population to 31% by 2050 (Czech Statistical Office, 2004). This same trend applies across Central and Eastern Europe (CEE). A timely response to this emerging demographic challenge in CEE is recommended and could also contribute towards having a competitive advantage (Perlitz et al., 2010).

Moser is a local (Czech) brand for which this target group can be useful. More than other industries, the glass industry is energy intensive; thus, it must overcome the uncertainties of expensive energy. This is especially important given that it follows other recent crises related to COVID lockdowns, restrictions on traditional Asian export markets and the loss of Russian customers (due to sanctions). The history of the company and the current challenges it faces are covered in the following case study.

Mini-case 3.1 Moser: More than 160 years of Czech design

Moser is a traditional brand of designer glass with Czech origins; it represents specific aspects of luxury as well as respecting the anti-laws of luxury. It is the only brand in the region that is a member of Comité Colbert (currently associating 92 leading French brands, 17 cultural institutions and 6 other European brands), where more than half of the brands are among the world's leading luxury groups. Comité introduces Moser on its website with the slogan *"The king of glass, the glass of kings"* and as a company specializing in crystal and glass work, which has weathered many storms – from Austria-Hungary to the establishment of Czechoslovakia, today's Czech Republic and transformation into a joint-stock company (Comité Colbert, 2022).

Glassmaking is one of the sectors that is positively associated with the Czech country of origin, which can be an indicator of consumer willingness to buy products from the given nation and, in the case of Moser Glassworks, one of the positive factors of domestic and international demand.

Historically, the brand's creations have been appreciated by imperial and royal families in Austria, Britain and Spain, as well as the Vatican and the Turkish sultanate. Since 1863, Moser has used exclusively lead-free crystal. No other material requires more from its glassmakers in terms of skills and knowledge. Lead-free crystal limits the glassmaker's time to shape it, and, at the same time, it is difficult to grind. The craftsmanship of the product is more demanding but with a much better final effect. The glassworks is still located in Karlovy Vary, where there is also a sales gallery and a museum mapping the history of the company (Moser, 2017). In 2020, master engraver Moser Tomáš Lesser received the knighthood of the Order of Arts and Letter in France for his masterful work, in recognition of his efforts to elevate the glass craft and a model for other traditional crafts (IDNES, 2020).

The history of the brand dates back to 1857, when glass engraver Ludwig Moser opened a workshop in Karlovy Vary at the age of 24 after completing an apprenticeship in the workshops of the renowned engravers Mattoni and Hoffmann. In 1873, after the success at the World Exhibition in Vienna, Emperor Franz Joseph I granted Ludwig Moser the privilege of supplying his products to the imperial Viennese court. In 1900, Moser successfully presented himself at the World Exhibition in Paris. Soon thereafter, the Persian Shah Mozaffar-ed-Din visited the glassworks in Karlovy Vary during his travels around Europe; the glassworks subsequently received the honorary title of court supplier. The house also won at an International Exhibition in Milan in 1906, thanks to the unique combination of engraved floral motifs with the colorful inlaying of Ludwig Moser's collection of vases. Two years later, Moser became a supplier to the court of King Edward VII of England (Moser, 2017).

Ludwig Moser died in 1916, and the company was taken over by his sons, Leo, Richard and Gustav Moser. Leo Moser became a pioneer of new types of colored glass, created experimentally by adding oxides of precious metals. This became an inspiration for future generations of designers and a symbol of progress. In memory of his progressive thinking, a bell – which was ceremonially christened in Karlovy Vary in 2022 – bears his name. The Leo Bell is intended to commemorate the 165-year history of the brand and symbolizes hope for the future of the organization. The company's employees also contributed significantly to the purchase of the bell, which previously announced to glassmakers living near the glassworks that the furnaces were sufficiently hot and it was time to blow glass. The decoration of the bell is inspired by the technique of *oroplastic* (etched and gilded décor) typical for Moser products, which was patented by Leo Moser in 1911 (Moser, 2017; IDNES, 2022b).

The economic problems of the 1920s and 1930s also affected Moser. The time was not favorable to the sale of artistic, craft-intensive glass, and French competition for luxury glass in particular grew. As a result of declining sales, only one of the two furnaces in Dvory near Karlovy Vary was in operation from 1926. Leo Moser, in cooperation with well-known designers, put much effort into developing competitive types of glass in order to try and reverse the unfavorable situation; nevertheless, the company continued to deteriorate. In 1932, he ended his work at the glassworks. According to available sources, he was motivated to do so not only by the company's difficulties but also by his fear of nationalism associated with the Sudeten German movement (a movement among ethnic Germans in Czechoslovakia advocating for greater autonomy or annexation by Germany in the 1930s, which was later exploited by Nazi Germany to justify intervention into the country). Richard Moser lost his membership in the Board of Directors the following year, and both brothers sold their shares to the financial house Česká Unionbanka. The last brother, Gustav, had his mandate expire in 1934 (The Jewish Community Karlovy Vary, 2022).

In 1936, Egon Ritter was appointed director of the Moser joint-stock company, and sculptor Arnold Zadikow became the chief artist. At the end of the 1930s, he influenced the political development and history of the Moser Glassworks. Karlovy Vary became part of the German Reich and the glassworks factory was assigned to the administration of the State Porcelain Manufactory in Berlin. Production continued during the war, and the company cooperated with the designers of the time. Thanks to being world renowned, the glassworks retained its name Ludwig Moser & Söhne, Karlsbader Kristallglasfabriken AG, and employed around 300 workers (Moser, 2017).

In 1946, the process of nationalization was completed. The successor of the company, a national enterprise called České sklo (Czech glass), continued to employ almost 300 people. After 1948 and the nationalization of Czech industry due to the new communist regime, the company's international activities were transferred to the foreign trade enterprise Skloexport. The only remaining company store was located in Prague, and in 1950, the company was given a new name again – Karlovy Vary Glass, National Enterprise. The Prague store Na Příkopech was restored to the traditional name Bohemia–Moser and soon became a privileged place for diplomats and government circles. Credit for the development of the store is attributed to its manager, the artist František Chocholatý, who – through his diplomatic skills – brought many important contacts to the glassworks. On his initiative, the Giant Snifters Club was founded at the end of the 1950s, when he himself designed a new collection of glasses called *Physiognomic Bar*. Each of the six giant glasses represents a different type of person. Membership in the club is not subject to any fees or obligations, but it is hereditary, which is why the company states that it is probably the largest club in the world. Those interested in membership must hit one of the spinning giant goblets with at least a few drops of drink. The ritual typically takes place within the Karlovy Vary Film Festival (for which they traditionally produce festival statuettes) or in company stores or at the company's headquarters. Members have included the Spanish King Juan Carlos I, the Japanese Princess Sayako, Louis Armstrong, Robert Redford and Gina Lollobrigida, as well as Václav Havel, Madeleine Albright, Yuri Gagarin and many others (Moser, 2017).

Between 1960 and 2000, many renowned personalities of Czechoslovak design worked for the glassworks – Ludvika Smrčková, René Roubíček, Luboš Metelák,

Vratislav Šotola, Vladimír Jelínek, František Vízner, Jiří Šuhájek, engravers Vladimír Skála, Milan Holubek and many others who have won prestigious international awards.

In the 1960s, a long reconstruction of the obsolete glassworks took place. At that time, it was already one of the 50 plants associated with the branch company Industrial Utility Glass based in Nový Bor, renamed Crystalex in 1974. Moser Glassworks was part of it until 1988, when it was able to become independent thanks to its export prowess. It became an independent state enterprise (that is, independent of Crystalex) and was renamed back to Moser. At that time, 410 employees worked for the company and 60% of sales consisted of export to 70 countries around the world, still mediated by Skloexport. At the turn of the millennium, the privatization of state property led to the establishment of the private joint-stock company Moser, a.s. (Moser, 2022). Two years later, the newly created joint-stock company took over its foreign trade from Skloexport and returned to the possibility of direct contact with foreign customers, which had been typical for it until 1949. The glassworks opened new sales galleries (Karlovy Vary, Prague, Old Town) and continued to develop. In 1997, at the request of President Václav Havel, on the occasion of the visit of Pope John Paul II, they produced a crystal cross as a presidential gift designed by artist Karel Bečvár as well as a decanter with the family emblem as a personal gift of the president to Prince Charles in 1999 (Moser, 2017).

The brand has also cooperated with global luxury manufacturers, such as Marc Jacobs and Tiffany. René Roubíček, a renowned Czech designer, started working with the glassworks in 2007, Rony Plesl in 2011. In the same year, the French Comité Colbert accepted non-French manufacturers as members for the first time in its history, and Moser was one of them. At that time, the Moser company established a competition called the "Ludwig Moser Award" for students of specialized glass and art schools. The winning creations of young designers and craftsmen were presented at design shows in Paris, Frankfurt, New York and Milan, along with Moser collections. The most distinctive ones could become part of the glassworks' portfolio. In 2012, the Pear vase by artist Lukáš Jabůrek was created and won the Czech Grand Design Audience Award, awarded by the Academy of Design of the Czech Republic. The highlight of the collection for the 160th anniversary of the company's foundation was the Ludwig Chandelier with 133 gold-colored hand-cut trimmings with *oroplastic* designed by Filip Houdek and Lukáš Jabůrek, created in honor of the founder of the company (Moser, 2017; Moser, 2022).

The art of the masters of the Moser Glassworks is unique and irreplaceable, as evidenced by the story of the large *Pear* vase, the production of which ended when glass master Zdeněk Drobný retired. He had been working for the company since 1971, and none of his successors were capable of comparable performance. The master, who participated in the creation of the design, managed to scoop up to 30 kg of glowing mass on the pipe and further process it into the creation (IDNES, 2022a). Nevertheless, this is good news for a luxury strategy. Limiting supply can contribute to price increases as well as activate collectors. A smaller Pear vase, shown in Picture 3.2, is based on the heritage of the collection and introduces some new colors with warm, natural tones and was designed by the creative director Jan Plecháč in 2024.

Picture 3.2 Pear Vase, © Moser, reprinted with company permission. Available at (Moser, 2024).

In 2016, there was a change in the main shareholders of the company. Previous minority owners Josef Brož and Jiří Zapletal became the main owners. "We take over Moser with dignity and respect and we want to further develop it so that we, its employees and the entire Czech Republic can be proud of it. Moser is certainly one of the businesses called family silver, and we will treat it as such," said co-owner and chairman of the board Jiří Zapletal as he outlined the management strategy for the Czech Press Agency (CTK, 2016). According to the 2020 annual report, the company employed 254 employees, which was 64 fewer than the previous pre-pandemic year, and the number remained unchanged until release of the 2022 annual report. Total sales decreased to just under 146 million CZK (from the previous almost 286 million) and the operating loss increased from 73 million to 109 million CZK. In the 2022 financial year, total sales returned to growth and reached 203 million CZK and the operating result returned to a positive 7 million CZK (Justice, 2021, 2024).

The Moser brand overcame the crisis of the 1930s, survived the period of communism and then the privatization of state property in the 1990s. However, due to the high volume of exports to markets such as the USA, Great Britain, Taiwan, China and the Middle East – which is close to 50% of the glassworks' production – the situation during the COVID-19 pandemic was very difficult; some of these markets closed, and others were restricted. However, domestic luxury customers have remained loyal to the glassworks. Company priorities reflected the energy crisis, and they implemented measures to reduce energy intensity and optimize the use of resources. Examples include the introduction of 24/7 shift operations at the steelworks for maximum use of energy resources, the implementation of a solar power plant project, the modernization of glass furnaces and also digital transformation through the introduction of new systems for better functioning of the entire company and business (Justice, 2024).

At present, there is an effort to revive brand communication, combining an emphasis on the brand's identity and the legacy of its founder. From a demographic point of view, the target group in the domestic market includes young millionaires around age 40, who are skilled not only economically but also technologically, with their own opinions (often outside the majority opinion), whose behavior can be characterized by advanced simplicity, speed and efficiency. The second key group are successful women in their 50s, proficient in their field, with the need for a long-term intimate relationship with a brand. According to the NeedScope research tool, which combines qualitative and quantitative data to understand consumers on an emotional level, it identifies the general characteristics of Moser's target group as self-confident (successful, individual, ambitious, status-oriented) and responsible (educated, intelligent, longing for deeper knowledge, seeking meaning and order).

In the brand's communication strategy, emphasis is placed on social networks and e-commerce, which includes a newly introduced configurator through which existing and new customers (who are primarily targeted by the platform) can customize the design and get a unique piece. The configurator is connected to an international e-shop, and the customer can create his/her own work or adapt the color scheme of an existing product according to his/her own taste. With regard to the characteristics of the brand's target groups, it is clear that the new technological challenges of luxury communication are being carefully considered, whether it is the potential of metaverse, NFTs, live shopping via social networks or involvement in luxury platforms of global luxury e-commerce.

Despite fluctuations in demand caused by the pandemic situation and the increase in costs related to the energy crisis, investments in communication are still considered a priority in order to maintain a satisfactory awareness of the Moser brand among Czech luxury clientele and to build the awareness of foreign clientele. In terms of product policy and luxury strategy, there is an element of rarity – the portfolio includes, for example, a limited collection of *Pineapple* vases by designer Lukáš Jabůrek or the *Era* vase. Each Era vase bears its own number (the amount is limited to 77 pieces) and is signed by its creators on the bottom (the glassmaking master and Knight of the

Ordre des Arts et des Lettres Sir Zdeněk Drobný and winner of the Czech Grand Design Awards 2023 Jan Plecháč).

Managing the scarcity (lack of availability) of select products has the potential to increase the customers' desire to own an extraordinary piece, one whose value increases over time. The designers of Moser Glassworks, as well as other traditional luxury brands, are constantly faced with the challenge of continuing the fascinating history of the company and combining the best of it with contemporary design and art. An example of facing the challenge is one of the newest collections called *Soul of the Forest* – designed by art director Jan Plecháč – which was awarded first place in Czech Grand Design 2023 (Picture 3.3).

Picture 3.3 *Pinea* vase from the *Soul of the Forest* collection, ©Moser, reprinted with company permission. Available at (Moser, 2024).

An example of a Czech domestic luxury fashion brand is TATIANA. A brand with an international-sounding name is often one of the strategies that companies use to disguise their country of origin if the sector in which they do business is not positively influenced by the image of the country of origin. There are other strategies to avoid the adverse effect of the country of origin, such as building a strong brand without any connection to the country of origin, various international certifications, the so-called false country of origin (through a name evoking a positive connection with a sector in another country) and others. In some cases, the image of the country of origin is so unfavorable to the sector that an international-sounding brand name is one of the easier ways to avoid the negative effect of the country of origin. TATIANA is a domestic luxury fashion brand with the potential for international development, which even reformatted the first name of its founder from the original Taťána to Tatiana.

Mini-case 3.2 TATIANA: Emotion and style

The TATIANA fashion brand was founded in 1995 by fashion designer Tatiana Kováříková, and her salon in Prague's Dušní Street in the Old Town is a popular place for Czech celebrities and others. She was the first Czech designer whose model was worn by a member of the British royal family, the Countess of Wessex, for a Swedish royal wedding. She has designed dresses for the very popular Czech version of StarDance several times and is also known for her film costumes (TATIANA, 2022).

TATIANA models are easily recognizable. They are characterized by simplicity, refinement, emphasis on femininity and precision in processing. They differ from other products in terms of nice cuts and the use of imported, quality materials from Spain, Italy or France. The purity of the lines and precision contribute to the timelessness of the models to the extent that clients consider a purchase from Tatiana to be a good investment despite the high price. The personality of the brand – based on femininity, elegance and comfort – is the basis of an identity incomparable with other brands of the local fashion scene such as Liběna Rochová or traditional luxury fashion brands Dior, Prada or Chanel.

How did the Czech fashion designer gain favor with her customers? Tatiana knows most of her regular high-fashion customers personally and approaches the creation of designs very individually with regard to their personal needs. The salon is not far from the workshop where the models are sewn, and clothing accessories can be adjusted according to the client's needs in just a few hours. Famous personalities of Czech cultural life and their make-up artists are bound to the brand by many years of cooperation and friendship with both the founder and the manager of the boutique.

The clients of Tatiana's collections are different from the customers of the boutiques on the famous Pařížská Street. International customers account for only 20% of sales; thus, most purchases are made by domestic clients. Typically, these are women who do not need to line their world with brands from Pařížská, but this does not mean that they will not go there for a quality handbag. The TATIANA model underlines and develops their personality but does not overwhelm it. The personal approach in the boutique and warm friendly emotions make buying a T-shirt or dress an experience that they do not get at Dior or Chanel. In the words of the designer, fashion is "about emotion, beauty and style, which we women like to be absorbed in" (Moda.cz, 2022). The clientele are often independent women, with their own careers and visions. Women who

Picture 3.4 Tatiana Collection Spring/Summer 2023, ©TATIANA, reprinted with company permission. Available at (TATIANA, 2023).

appreciate art, the world of design, film, dance – fields with which the TATIANA brand is intertwined. For them, the Czech origin of the brand is an extra bonus, part of its DNA, inextricably linked to the brand and its identity.

The TATIANA ATELIER collections are only available in the Prague boutique in the Old Town. According to the designer, an e-shop cannot replace the personal approach to each client, the possibility of tailoring clothes and the feeling that each client leaves the salon with a piece that suits her and develops her personality. Nevertheless, the designer perceives e-commerce as an integral part of the company's business and has worked on her own online platform for ready-to-wear collections for many years. The online shop of selected items was finally launched in 2024.

The brand is present on social networks through sharing new additions to the boutique or videos from fashion shows. S-commerce as a form of selling directly on networks is not yet considered and communication on social networks, especially on Instagram and Facebook, is perceived primarily as an important brand and sales support. Tatiana considers the most effective way of communication a well-balanced mix of communication on social networks, in lifestyle magazines and above all through word of mouth, that is, recommendations from clients.

The brand maintains relationships with loyal clients throughout the year via many events. These include, for example, seasonal fashion shows of new collections in the most prestigious locations in Prague (e.g. Prague Castle, Four Seasons near Charles Bridge, Žofín Palace) and Christmas get-togethers in the salon but also off-season shows associated with a charity or a vernissage of a selected artist in Prague's Leica Gallery (TATIANA, 2023). The issue of long-term growth is not a major challenge for a brand. The descendants or daughters of loyal customers represent the younger generation. The question of succession and further development remains open in all directions, including international expansion through traditional sales or selected luxury e-commerce platforms.

3.5 Highlights of "where" personal luxury is most purchased

In luxury, there are significant differences between the countries where the product is produced and customers' nationalities. Before the pandemic, as visible from Figure 3.4, Asian markets were the most significant in terms of luxury consumer nationality. In other words, in 2019, Chinese customers were responsible for 32% of the global luxury purchases, while only 11% of the global luxury shopping was actually made in China. This shifted towards domestic purchases during the pandemic (18% purchases by Chinese, 17% in China), but industry expects a return to the pre-COVID split within the upcoming years (Bain & Company, 2023). Chinese domestic purchases are additionally divided into duty-free channels (the Chinese duty free to be explained later) and pure domestic (Daxue Consulting,

According to Bain & Company, in 2023, the global ranking of luxury sales by region lifted, with Europe reclaiming the top spot for personal luxury goods sales, followed by America which moved to second place, and China in third (Figure 3.5). Despite the current domination of European and American markets, it is important to highlight that the compound annual growth rate **(CAGR) between 2010 and 2023 (estimate) is the most significant for China** (15%), followed by the rest of Asia (8%), America (5%) and Europe with Japan growth of just 4% (Bain & Company, 2024a).

The personal luxury goods market demonstrated significant growth across various regions in 2023 (Figure 3.5). Europe faced robust luxury sales, fueled by strong domestic demand and the return of tourists, particularly from the US and the Middle East. Italy and France led the growth, while spending by Chinese tourists has not yet recovered. The Russian market, however, remained largely inactive due to war-related business suspensions. In the Americas, the market slightly declined and reached an estimated €101 billion (Bain & Company, 2024a).

Asia (excluding mainland China and Japan) faced 8% growth in 2023, with Southeast Asia showing strong progress due to a rising local customer base, robust tourism and foreign

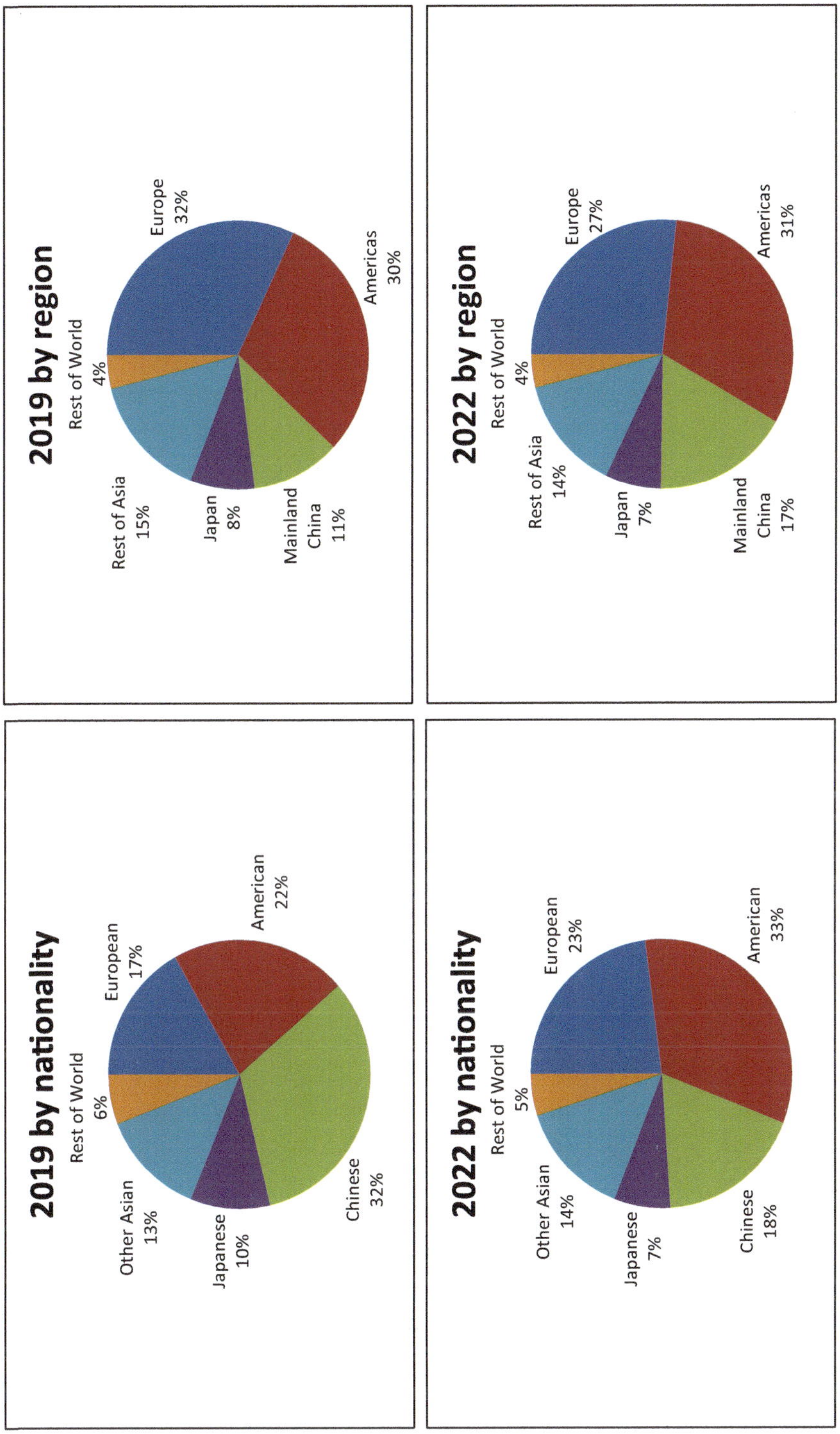

Figure 3.4 Regional highlights: Difference between luxury consumption by nationalities and by regions. Authors based on data available at (Bain & Company, 2023).

investments. Thailand led this growth, while Hong Kong and Macao surged in the first half of the year before slowing due to reduced tourism. In South Korea, local consumption weakened due to adverse macroeconomic factors and a strong currency, which diverted tourists to other destinations. Nevertheless, South Korea remains a key cultural and economic influencer in the region.

Mainland China achieved 9% growth in 2023, starting strong but slowing later due to macroeconomic concerns. Economic stimulus from the third quarter is expected to boost local consumption and foster investments in new Tier 1 megacities. Hainan, in particular, is set to become a prominent luxury hub as China plans to transform it into a fully duty-free island with a special tax regime by 2025, positioning it as a key player in the country's luxury market.

Japan's luxury market grew significantly, reaching €24 billion in 2022 and €29 billion in 2023, and finally returned to pre-COVID levels, supported by strong local consumption and the resumption of tourism. Growth was driven by renewed local consumer interest and a weak yen that attracted tourists, particularly from China. Luxury brands enhanced cultural relevance through exclusive partnerships with local artisans. The Middle East faced robust growth, with Dubai as the regional hub, but the war has introduced uncertainty. Saudi Arabia and Australia are showing significant potential, attracting luxury brand investments (Bain & Company, 2024a).

Currently, no market is expected to replicate China's contribution to the growth of the luxury industry. However, India and the emerging markets in Southeast Asia and Africa have considerable potential. In particular, India stands out with its luxury market potentially growing to 3.5 times its current size by 2030. This growth will be fueled by a younger demographic and a growing upper and middle class (Bain & Company, 2023).

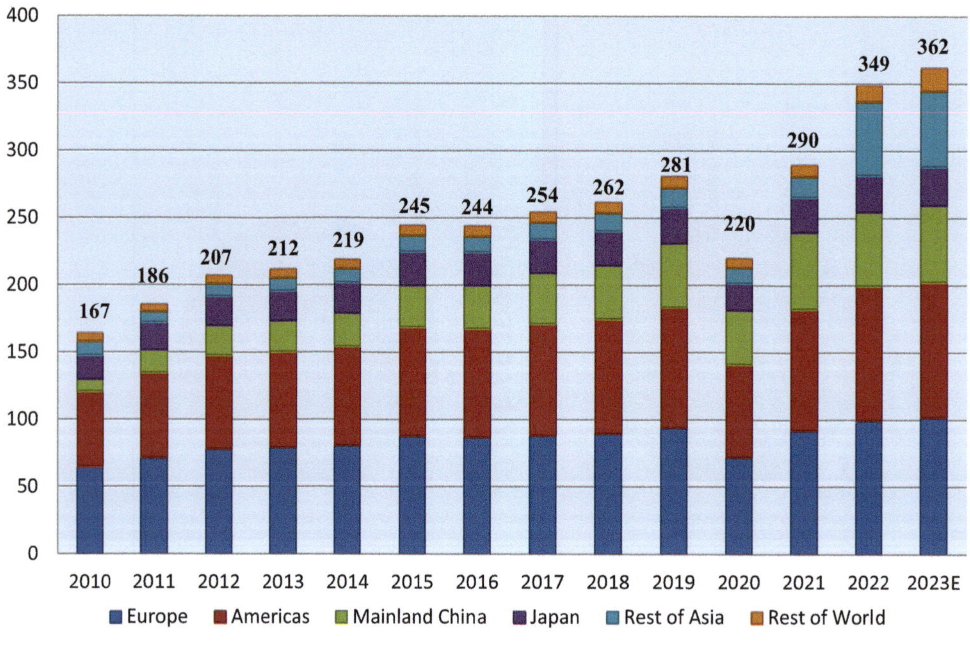

Figure 3.5 Regions' importance in luxury business (EUR billions); authors based on data available at (Bain & Company, 2023).

According to the analysts from Bain & Company, by 2030 Chinese consumers should regain their status as the dominant nationality for luxury as it was before the pandemic, growing to represent 38%–40% of global purchases. Mainland China will become the biggest luxury market globally (25%–27% of global purchases), before America and Europe (Bain & Company, 2024b).

To demonstrate the importance of non-European regions in the business of the largest luxury groups, Tables 3.7, 3.8 and 3.9 show the geographical split of the 2023 revenues of selected groups, confirming stable or growing European and Asian (except for Richemont) sales.

Regarding LVMH, the breakdown is, according to its annual report, a well-balanced geographic split, where most of the revenues come from its leather and fashion business group, followed by selective retailing and watches and jewelry. Half of the Group's revenue comes from the United States and Europe, followed by Asia, Japan and other markets (Table 3.7). Regarding profitability, the top three categories do not include selective retailing but wines and spirits. There was strong performance by the Fashion and Leather Goods business group, and the following brands – Louis Vuitton, Christian Dior, Celine, Fendi, Loro Piana, Loewe and Marc Jacobs – gained market share worldwide, and achieved record levels of revenue and profits (LVMH, 2023).

The strongest proportion of Kering's revenues and profitability comes consistently from the brands Gucci, Saint Laurent and Bottega Venetta. Kering reported 2023 results as a year of mixed results when the performances fell short of expectations. The most significant was,

Table 3.7 LVMH revenue breakdown by region (LVMH, 2023).

LVMH, 2023		
	% of total	**Change vs previous year**
United States	25%	–2pp
Europe	25%	+1pp
Asia (excl. Japan)	31%	+1pp
Japan	7%	+0pp
Other markets	12%	+0%

Table 3.8 Kering revenue breakdown by regions.

Kering 2024		
	% of total	**Change vs previous year**
North America	23%	–4pp
Europe	28%	+0pp
Asia-Pacific (excl. Japan)	35%	+3pp
Japan	7%	+1pp
Other markets	7%	+0%

Source: (Kering, 2024).

Table 3.9 Richemont revenue breakdown by regions.

Richemont, 2023		
	% of total	Change vs previous year
Americas	22%	+1pp
Europe	22%	+2pp
Asia-Pacific	40%	–5pp
Japan	8%	+1%
Middle East and Africa	8%	+1%

Source: (Richemont, 2023).

according to the full year results, a 6% decline in Gucci revenues (Kering, 2024). Similar to LVMH, more than half of the Group's revenues come from North America and Europe (Table 3.8).

Compared to the previously mentioned groups, Richemont's revenues from the Americas and Europe are lower, while Asia-Pacific represents 40%. However, Europe experienced a 31% year-on-year sales increase, which was driven primarily by local solid demand (in France, Italy, and Switzerland) and increased tourism from the US and Middle East. Overall, Europe's contribution to Group revenues rose from 20% to 22%. Besides sales recovery in mainland China, Hong Kong and Macau, the Group is significantly growing in South Korea and South East Asia (mainly in Australia, Singapore and Thailand). Middle East sales are driven primarily by Dubai and Qatar. More than two-thirds (67%) of Richemont's sales come from the jewelry brands (Buccellati, Cartier and Van Cleef & Arpels), followed by the watchmaker brands (20%) represented by A. Lange & Söhne, Baume & Mercier, IWC Schaffhausen, Jaeger-LeCoultre, Panerai, Piaget, Roger Dubuis and Vacheron Constantin (Richemont, 2023).

3.6 Chinese consumers: Major driver in luxury spending

In 2023, China's luxury market recovered with 12% growth, convalescing from the significant downturn experienced in 2022 due to COVID-19 disruptions. While this recovery was significant, the market has not yet returned to its 2021 peak levels. The first half of 2023 showed robust growth due to a low comparison base, but the second half was marked by weaker consumer confidence and economic challenges, leading to a more tempered performance (Bain & Company, 2024b).

The Chinese luxury market is heavily influenced by **very important customers** (**VICs**), who are the primary drivers of sales. Shopping malls are significant for both VIC and non-VIC traffic, but VICs maintain higher conversion rates and spending levels. However, spending patterns among non-VICs showed recent signs of decline, indicating a cautious approach to luxury spending among the broader consumer base.

A critical region in the Chinese luxury market is Hainan, known for its **duty-free shopping**. Duty-free in the Chinese context refers to a government-sanctioned initiative allowing domestic tourists to purchase luxury goods without paying import taxes, provided these items are used within China. In 2023, Hainan's duty-free sales increased by 25%, a significant recovery from the sharp decline in 2022, although still below the peak levels of 2021. This rebound was supported by the return of domestic tourists and various government stimulus measures aimed at boosting consumption in the region (Bain & Company, 2024b), and as mentioned in the previous part, 20% of total domestic luxury purchases in China in 2023 were made in duty-free channels (Daxue Consulting, 2024a).

Luxury customers in **higher-tier cities, accounting for 53% of total spending, are more open to niche or emerging labels** and are less price-sensitive compared to their counterparts in lower-tier cities; therefore, these cities are a primary target for luxury brands. On the contrary, lower-tier city consumers have stronger preferences for domestic brands (Daxue Consulting 2024a; Daxue Consulting, 2024b). The Chinese city-tier system ranks cities into different levels, with Tier 1 being the highest. Some classifications have four tiers, while others have five, and Tier 1 can be split into "first tier" and "new first tier." Factors like GDP, income, administrative status and population determine a city's tier. Although there is no official government list, this system is commonly used by international media for purposes like business, transportation, tourism and education. Lower-tier cities are usually Tier 3 and below (Daxue Consulting, 2024b).

Looking ahead, China's luxury market is expected to return to growth, although at a more moderate pace. The current projections indicate single-digit growth. Despite uncertainties surrounding the pace of economic recovery and the potential rebound of Chinese consumer shopping abroad, the long-term outlook for luxury consumption in China remains positive.

3.6.1 Luxury brands and Chinese consumers

According to Chadha and Paul (2006), the following were suggested as key success factors for establishing and building a luxury brand for Chinese customers:

1. **Leverage the show-off factor** (the importance of visibility and prestige in the Chinese luxury market) – In China, luxury consumption is often about displaying status and wealth, and brands must create products and experiences that cater to this desire. Brands should focus on creating **exclusive, high-profile events, limited edition products and prominent advertising campaigns that allow consumers to "show off"** their luxury purchases. The ability to be seen and recognized as a luxury consumer is a crucial driver of purchasing decisions in China.
2. **Maintain global prestige** (not diluting the international credentials and authenticity of the brand) – Chinese consumers are drawn to Western luxury brands because of their global reputation and heritage. Therefore, it is crucial for brands to **preserve their core identity** and not dilute their international appeal by making too many concessions to local tastes. Brands should balance localization with maintaining the essence of what makes them globally recognized and respected.
3. **Appeal to younger demographics** – With China's younger generations becoming increasingly affluent, luxury brands must adapt their strategies to appeal to younger consumers. Luxury brands must target millennials and Gen Z with products, marketing, and experiences that resonate with their values and lifestyles. Younger Chinese consumers are more digitally savvy, trend-conscious and interested in experiences rather than just products. Brands should, therefore, focus on digital engagement, sustainability and personalization to attract this demographic.

4. **Focus on wealth concentration** – Focus on regions and cities in China where wealth is concentrated. While major cities like Beijing and Shanghai are obvious choices, there is also significant opportunity in Tier 2 and Tier 3 cities where the luxury market is growing rapidly. Brands should tailor their distribution and marketing efforts to target these affluent areas, ensuring they are present where the wealthiest consumers are.
5. **Cultivate style leadership** – Brands should not only sell products, but also inspire and educate consumers about luxury, style and trends. By positioning themselves as tastemakers and influencers in the luxury market, brands can build a deeper connection with their customers, who look to these brands for guidance on what is stylish and desirable (Chadha & Paul, 2006).

Examples of brands with massive demand on the Chinese market are Gucci, Saint Laurent or Balenciaga. These brands' high-end handbags are among the best sellers on Tmall (the biggest B2C e-commerce platform) (Daxue Consulting, 2024b).

Brands that have succeeded in the Chinese luxury market share several key common characteristics as reported by Bain & Company:

1. **Iconic Offerings:** Brands with timeless, iconic products outperform those that depend on cyclical fashion trends. Chinese luxury consumers tend to value items as long-term investments, and favor branded products that maintain their value over time;
2. **VIC-Centric Strategies:** A strong focus on VICs, that is, high spenders who are more resilient during economic downturns and thus drive a significant portion of sales;
3. **Brand Strength:** Larger, well-established brands generally perform better; they have been able to navigate the challenges of the past few years more effectively, reinforcing their dominance in the market (Bain & Company, 2024b).

The advice related to "what it takes to win in China" was historically centered around showing off ("Play to the Show Off Stage" (Chadha & Paul, 2006)) because the Chinese have a strong symbol memory that creates the link of the symbolic elements with the brand. This is being questioned by the growing interest of Chinese consumers in ***quiet luxury***, that is, brands that do not significantly express their logo on the products. With the economy slowing and growing unemployment rates among young people, those who can afford luxury no longer need to be "Gucci from head to toe"; they have passed the point of showing off with very loud luxury branding. The factors of the economic downturn and a maturing luxury market are steering consumers away from conspicuous consumption towards more subtle and refined expressions of wealth (Daxue Consulting, 2024a).

The move above reflects a broader shift in Chinese consumer preferences, especially in higher-tier cities, towards quiet luxury. This shift is characterized by an appreciation for high-quality, logo-free luxury that communicates sophistication through understated elegance rather than ostentation.

Higher-tier cities (Beijing, Shanghai, Guangzhou, Shenzhen) represent approximately 33% of the luxury consumption; together with the new first tier, it adds up to 53%. Customers value the culture and heritage of the brands and are more willing to pay a premium for uniqueness and for brands that align with their values. Additionally, they are more open to niche or emerging labels and are less price-sensitive compared to lower-tier cities. Second-tier city customers use luxury items to demonstrate their social status and wealth and, therefore, prefer traditional and well-recognizable brands (Daxue Consulting, 2024a).

The luxury market in China is highly competitive. **Collaborations** are one of the tools that allow brands to stand out by offering unique, limited-edition products. Co-branding and collaborations typically include fresh, innovative designs that resonate with these demographics. Some examples include Louis Vuitton's collaboration with Fotografiska Shanghai Museum to promote the brand as a cultural and lifestyle curator linked to local culture or Valentino's cross-category collaboration with Italian legacy brands Cova (pastry shop owned by LVMH) and Venchi (chocolate manufacture) to promote its iconic Pink PP color in their products like Venchi's pink gelato (Daxue Consulting, 2024a; JingDaily, 2023b). Both examples demonstrate **balance between the exclusivity** of the Louis Vuitton and Valentino brands **and the aim to produce buzz** with a relatively high reach of luxury customers.

Mini-case 3.3 Fendi and Pokémon: Balancing luxury's aura with mass-market appeal in China

In China's fast-paced luxury market, a collaboration between luxury brands and widespread cultural phenomena is, for some demographics, a key to staying relevant. These partnerships not only boost brand visibility but also create unique value propositions that resonate with younger, digitally savvy consumers.

Fendi, an iconic Italian luxury fashion house, was founded in Rome in 1925. Known for its craftsmanship, innovation, and signature "double F" logo, Fendi has built a legacy around luxury, creativity and avant-garde design. The third and fourth generations of the family are still involved as artistic directors of the brand (Fendi, 2024). The brand is currently owned by the LVMH (Moët Hennessy Louis Vuitton) conglomerate, one of the largest luxury goods companies in the world. Fendi's solid global performance significantly contributes to LVMH's overall success, particularly in their main revenue stream, that is, the fashion and leather goods sector, along with the Louis Vuitton and Dior brands.

Fendi entered the Chinese market in the early 2000s, recognizing the flourishing demand for luxury goods. The brand quickly established a strong presence, with flagship stores in major cities like Beijing, Shanghai and others (up to 44 stores in 2024 (Fendi, 2024)). Fendi has performed well in China, leveraging the country's growing luxury market, and regularly engages in collaborations and exclusive collections to appeal to Chinese consumers.

In 2023, Fendi collaborated with a leading Chinese tea brand Heytea. The promotion objective was to engage with younger, trend-conscious consumers. Limited-edition products and pop-up experiences that combined Fendi with Heytea's popular beverages were the most visible part of the partnership. Fendi demonstrated efforts to strengthen its brand presence in China by **tapping into local consumer culture and aligning with influential Chinese brands**. The case showed its adaptability and innovative marketing approach in the region. The limited-edition products featuring Fendi's signature design elements on the plastic cups with passion fruit and mango drink sold out quickly, and the collaboration generated widespread social media engagement. The hashtag #喜茶fendi联名# has been read by 32.6 million people on Weibo, with 8,662 organic posts on the platform in two days after launch (JingDaily, 2023a). This success demonstrated Fendi's ability to blend luxury with local cultural trends, solidifying its brand presence and appeal in the Chinese market using only **delicate compromises related to luxury business strategy**.

Pokémon GO is the augmented reality mobile game that leverages GPS technology to create an immersive science fiction narrative that unfolds across a global landscape. It was launched in 2016 by Niantic, Inc. in collaboration with Nintendo Co. Ltd. and The Pokémon Company. Thanks to its innovative AR use and the Pokémon franchise's enduring popularity, the game became an international phenomenon with millions of players worldwide. Pokémon GO continues to engage a vast player base, with approximately 70 million active users monthly. Many companies like Starbucks or McDonalds have cooperated with Pokémon Go by building virtual Pokéstops or Gyms on their premises (Pokémon Go Wiki, 2024).

The collaboration between Fendi, Pokémon GO and the well-known Japanese designer Hiroshi Fujiwara – known for the streetwear design and his streetwear label Fragment (FRGMT) – was launched in January 2024, to celebrate the Chinese Year of the Dragon. This partnership introduced **virtual fashion avatar items** featuring dragon-type Pokémons like Dragonite, Dratini or Dragonair in Pokémon GO (e.g. hoodie, hat and T-shirt). The collaboration included FENDI x FRGMT x POKÉMON **physical items** designed by Hiroshi Fujiwara, such as the Baguette and Peekaboo Iseeu, along with accessories and limited-edition clothing (L'Officiel, 2023; FASHIONUNITED, 2023). There is also an opportunity to get other virtual items (useful for playing the game) at special Fendi-sponsored PokéStops. Spinning the Fendi-sponsored PokéStops allowed the trainers to get two unique FENDI x FRGMT x POKÉMON avatar items: a hat and a T-shirt.

The Fendi x Pokémon collaboration was accepted by younger consumers who appreciate the blend of high fashion and gaming. The partnership increased Fendi's engagement and demonstrated the brand's ability to include gaming as a customer touchpoint along the purchase journey. The collaboration was an example of how Fendi aimed to stay relevant for the new demographic segments where digital and cultural trends significantly influence consumer behavior.

However, the Fendi x Pokémon GO collaboration **may create tension within the brand strategy**. Luxury business strategy principles advocate for maintaining exclusivity and distance from the mainstream, mass-market associations that Pokémon GO typically generates. Therefore, this collaboration may risk dilution of the brand's aura of exclusivity by aligning it with a widely accessible and popular game.

3.6.2 Domestic luxury groups and brands in China

The Chinese affinity for Western brands is deeply rooted in a combination of historical, social and cultural factors. The transition from a period of isolation to rapid modernization created a fertile ground for Western brands to be perceived as symbols of progress, status and quality. Social standing in Chinese society is closely tied to the goods one consumes. Western brands offer local consumers a means to express their success and sophistication. The perceived superior quality and rich heritage of these brands solidify their appeal and make them highly sought after in the Chinese luxury market. It may change with time, especially after the isolation caused by the pandemic.

Despite low awareness of them in Europe, domestic luxury brands in China are evolving. Deloitte reports one Chinese group as part of the Top 10 global luxury companies (Table 2.1), namely **Chow Tai Fook Jewellery Group**, founded in 1929 by Chow Chi Yuen in Guangzhou, China. The company relocated to Hong Kong in 1946 due to the Chinese Civil War. Under the stewardship of Cheng Yu-Tung, who married into the founding family and assumed leadership in 1956, the company significantly grew and was transformed into a dominant force in the Chinese jewelry market.

One of the most remarkable milestones in the history of Chow Tai Fook was its acquisition of the "Heritage Diamond" in 1989. This unusual 255.61-carat rough diamond was purchased for a then-record $10 million, the highest price ever paid for a rough diamond. This acquisition was not just a business transaction. Rather, it should be understood as a strategic move underscoring Chow Tai Fook's ambition and its capacity to play at the highest levels of the global jewelry market. The "Heritage Diamond" represents the commitment to securing and showcasing one of the world's most prestigious and valuable gemstones. Today, Chow Tai Fook continues to build on its rich heritage, blending time-honored techniques with innovative practices to maintain its position as a leading luxury brand worldwide (Chow Tai Fook Jewellery Group, 2022). The company is a subsidiary of Chow Tai Fook (Holding) Limited, which itself is part of a broader conglomerate controlled by the Cheng family. This conglomerate includes Chow Tai Fook Enterprises Limited, which has diverse interests across several industries, including real estate, transportation, energy, telecommunications and hospitality.

The remaining groups listed in Deloitte's report of top luxury brands or groups include: Chow Tai Seng, Luk Fook, Lanvin Group China National Gold Group, Chow Tai Seng, Guangdong CHJ, DR Corporation and Zhejiang Ming (Deloitte, 2023).

These companies dominate the luxury sector in China due to their extensive retail networks, significant market capitalization and longstanding presence in the industry. However, it is also true that there are several standalone luxury brands in China that are noteworthy. In a paper published in 2018, Heine and Gusatz analyzed eight Chinese luxury brands using a multiple case study method. This approach was chosen for its explanatory power in understanding real-life organizational phenomena, particularly in the emerging and underexplored context of Chinese luxury brands. The study was based on 18 semi-structured interviews with representatives of Chinese luxury startups, industry professionals and luxury consultants in China. The authors also visited ten stores of Chinese luxury brands in Shanghai, observing store culture and speaking with salespeople to understand product and brand philosophies.

The authors discuss a notable paradox within the Chinese luxury market. While China is recognized as the world's most important luxury market, **it has not yet established itself as a significant country of origin for luxury brands.** This paradox is mainly due to the dominance of established Western luxury brands and the relatively recent emergence of Chinese luxury brands. However, the authors' analysis reveals that there are over 100 potential Chinese luxury brands, though many of these are still small, new and not widely recognized, even among experts within China. This indicates that while the Chinese luxury market is growing rapidly, the development of globally recognized Chinese luxury brands is still in its early stages. Many of these brands are still building their reputations and gaining market traction, which is why they are not yet well-known. This situation underscores the emerging nature of Chinese luxury brands and the potential for growth and recognition on a global scale as these brands continue to develop and establish themselves (Heine & Gutsatz, 2015).

Creation of a luxury brand in China involves different strategies including creating new brands, reviving historical ones, partnering with Western companies and leveraging existing distribution networks. Heine and Gutsatz (2015) presented cases with different entries into the Chinese luxury market, each representing unique strategies and market approaches. **SHANG XIA** is the brand created by Hermès in 2008, and it represents a Western luxury corporation's effort to establish a China-specific luxury brand (Heine & Gutsatz, 2015). The brand focuses on merging traditional Chinese craftsmanship with modern design, aiming to redefine "Made in China" as synonymous with luxury. Over the years, SHANG XIA has expanded its global presence with stores in Shanghai, Beijing, Shenzhen, Paris and more. In

2020, Exor, an Italian investment firm (the large investor in Ferrari and Stellantis), invested €80 million into a deal with Hermès to become the majority shareholder, helping the brand reach new levels of global prominence. SHANG XIA's founder, Jiang Qiong Er, attributed this success to the unwavering support from Hermès and expressed belief that with the addition of Exor as a partner, the brand will be more empowered to realize its ambitions (Exor, 2020).

The brand focuses on creating high-quality products that embody Chinese cultural heritage while catering to modern, global tastes (Picture 3.5). Their offerings include a range of items from fashion and accessories to furniture and homeware, all crafted with an emphasis on fine materials and meticulous craftsmanship. SHANG XIA aims to present a lifestyle that bridges the past and the present, **bringing the elegance of Chinese culture to the international luxury market** (SHANG XIA, 2024a).

Another example of a similar strategy Western luxury brands use to enter and establish themselves in the Chinese luxury market includes acquiring existing Chinese luxury ventures

Picture 3.5 SHANG XIA travel tea set in round leather case. © SHANG XIA, reprinted with company permission. Available at (SHANG XIA, 2024c).

or premium brands and transforming them into higher-end luxury labels. For instance, in 1998, Richemont acquired **Shanghai Tang,** one of the first modern Chinese luxury brands. This strategy allowed Richemont to capitalize on the growing Chinese luxury market by leveraging an already established brand with local cultural significance (Heine & Gutsatz, 2015; Shanghai Tang, 2024). Although Richemont eventually sold Shanghai Tang in 2017, the initial acquisition reflects a similar approach to the one Hermès took with SHANG XIA, emphasizing the importance of local relevance and cultural integration in luxury brand building in China.

Seagull, also known as Tianjin Seagull Watch Group, is a state-owned enterprise in China. It was founded in 1955 as a government-backed initiative to develop China's watchmaking industry. The Seagull brand was formally introduced in 1973 as China's first export-oriented wristwatch brand. In the mid-1990s, the company strategically shifted its focus towards the niche market of mechanical movements and high-end watches. This transition enabled Seagull to become the largest producer of automatic movements worldwide and a major supplier to the Western watch industry (Heine & Gutsatz, 2015; Seagull, 2024).

Seagull began producing luxury watches under its own label in 2002, despite its mass market origins and original equipment manufacturer (OEM) status. At first, it was difficult to overcome production problems related to the lack of skilled and experienced craftsmen. However, the company gradually succeeded; in 2012, it celebrated the assembly of the first high-end mechanical watch in mainland China. This timepiece, priced at over €150,000, featured a tourbillon, minute repeater and calendar function, and it became the most expensive domestic watch in Chinese history (Heine & Gutsatz, 2015).

Seagull's entry into a product category traditionally dominated by Swiss brands signifies a unique achievement. However, the brand's extensive industry experience, pioneering achievements and strong heritage position it well for success. Like other brands that have transitioned from mass production into luxury, Seagull has the potential to leverage its historical narrative, including the production of China's first wristwatch and successful international intellectual property disputes, to build symbolic and emotional value as a luxury brand. The brand's history and authentic stories are elements that can be transformed into significant competitive advantages in the luxury market. From the perspective of the luxury business strategy and Seagull's product and pricing policy, it can be argued that its portfolio (from value to super premium watches) does not support the perception of the brand being a luxury one.

The key findings of the Heine and Gutsatz (2015) study highlighted several criteria for defining Chinese luxury brands. These criteria include the location of the brand's headquarters, the nationality of key personnel, the country where their iconic products are manufactured, and the alignment between the brand's history, identity and its country of origin image. Additionally, the perception of the brand by consumers as authentically Chinese is also an important factor. The study categorizes the major players in the Chinese luxury market into several groups:

- Western luxury corporations: The companies establishing Chinese luxury brands by creating new brands tailored specifically for the Chinese market or by acquiring and transforming existing Chinese brands into luxury labels;
- Western entrepreneurs: Individual entrepreneurs from the West sometimes establish luxury brands in China, often in collaboration with local designers and utilizing their knowledge of both Western and Chinese markets;
- Chinese state-controlled corporations: These are large corporations, often with government backing, that either create new luxury brands or elevate existing brands to the

luxury segment. Their strategies are often aligned with national policies to promote Chinese cultural and creative industries;

- Chinese entrepreneurs: Independent Chinese business owners who establish luxury brands, typically drawing on Chinese culture and craftsmanship to appeal to both domestic and international markets;
- Chinese luxury distributors: These companies initially acted as distributors for foreign luxury brands in China but have increasingly started to create or acquire their own luxury brands, leveraging their market knowledge and distribution networks;
- Chinese designers: Designers in China who have created luxury brands that combine traditional Chinese elements with modern design, positioning themselves within the luxury market through their unique creative visions (Heine & Gutsatz, 2015).

The study suggests that these different players employ strategies that can guide market entries into the Chinese luxury market.

3.7 India as the new China?

India's economic growth is driven by its young population, urbanization and growing incomes. The market is projected to become the third-largest global economy by 2027. The rise of digital adoption and innovation, coupled with expanding job opportunities, are other drivers of this growth. As disposable income grows, so does demand for premium and luxury goods, making India a highly promising market for luxury brands (McKinsey, 2024).

The Knight Frank wealth sizing model predicts that **the Ultra HNWI population in India (with investable assets above $30 million) will double by 2028 (compared to 2023) to 19.9 thousand** people, similar to Australia or Italy. India's predicted growth of UHNWIs is the biggest of all monitored markets. Comparing the UHNWI populations of India with China is still disproportionate, but India's growth is notably higher. In 2023, China had 98,551 UHNWIs, projected to grow by 47.0% to 144,897 by 2028. India, starting with 13,263 UHNWIs in 2023, is expected to grow by 50.1% to 19,908 by 2028. Despite China's larger base, India's higher growth rate reflects its emerging economic influence, though it remains far behind in absolute numbers. Globally, UHNWI growth is predicted to be 28.1% (Knight Frank, 2024).

India is the **second-largest gold jewelry market after China**, with more than half of its sales tied to **weddings** (Deloitte, 2023). Moreover, there are a lot of other festive occasions when people celebrate and buy presents, often golden jewelry. During the Festival of Lights, as an example, people light oil lamps and candles to symbolize the victory of light over darkness and good over evil (Picture 3.6). Before the festive day, people buy gold, silver or even new metal accessories or utensils, as it is believed to bring wealth and good luck into the household (BBC, 2024).

Economic growth, demographic shifts and urbanization fuel demand, especially among the middle class. Jewelry retail in India is rapidly modernizing, with organized luxury jewelry chains replacing traditional retailers. By 2020, organized retailers made up one-third of the market, compared to just 5% in 2000. In FY2022, Indian luxury jewelers saw sales growth exceeding 20%, driven by major players like Malabar and Titan, who rebounded strongly from pandemic-related declines. Despite strong sales growth, Indian companies reported a relatively low composite net profit margin of 6% (Deloitte, 2023).

To illustrate the importance of weddings and jewelry, consider the example of the wedding of Anant Ambani and Radhika Merchant. Mukesh Ambani (father of the groom), the

Picture 3.6 Woman lighting the candles for the Festival of Lights in India. By Aristes, made available under the Creative Commons Attribution-Share Alike 4.0 International license. Available at (Wikimedia Commons, 2023).

head of Reliance Industries, is India's richest person and ranks 9th on the 2024 Forbes Billionaire List with a net worth of $116 billion. His wealth stems from transforming Reliance Industries into a diversified conglomerate, with interests spanning telecommunications, petrochemicals, retail and energy. The Ambani family has recently expanded its business activities into other green energy and digital services sectors. The founder's smart decisions strengthened the family's position as one of the most influential in India. For example, Anant Ambani's recent wedding – including worldwide media coverage – exposed their substantial financial resources and cultural influence to a global audience. The family's continued investment into new industries, such as green technology, indicates a focus on future growth and dominance in the Indian market (Forbes, 2024).

Vogue India said the wedding celebrations were comparable to a Met Gala event at the Metropolitan Museum of Art in New York, including the global celebrities on the invite list. The jewelry worn at the wedding played an indispensable role in the ceremony, symbolizing wealth, cultural and emotional significance. From Radhika Merchant's *polki jadau* necklace made from Jaipur Jewels to Nita Ambani's 100-carat diamond necklace, the jewelry highlighted both tradition and personalization. In Indian society, such jewelry is deeply connected to identity, status, heritage and matrimonial rituals. Western brands were also included – for the wedding reception, Radhika Merchant, the bride, wore a metallic gold corset top from

Dolce & Gabbana's Alta Moda Sardegna 2024 collection, paired with a couture sari by Anamika Khanna. The Alta Moda line is known for its exclusive, high-end designs, tailored for elite clients. These custom-made pieces are so intricate and rare that designers often personally oversee fittings (Vogue India, 2024b).

One of the challenges luxury brands face in India is the tendency of affluent Indian consumers to **shop for luxury products abroad,** often in destinations like Dubai and Paris, where they find better pricing and a wider range of products. This trend challenges luxury brands trying to grow their presence in the Indian market. **Dior was among the early entrants,** successfully mapping out a blueprint for luxury brands in India. They hosted a **major fashion show in Gateway of India in 2023** (a monument built at the beginning of the 20th century on the waterfront of Mumbai, Picture 3.7), demonstrating their commitment to the Indian market. Chanel launched its e-commerce platform in India in August 2024, making luxury more accessible to Indian consumers (Vogue Business, 2024).

A Dior fashion show was held in Mumbai the same weekend as the launch of the Nita Mukesh Ambani Cultural Center by the Reliance Foundation (the philanthropic initiative of Reliance Industries Limited established by Nita Ambani in 2010). The event attracted international celebrities and influencers to Mumbai, including Gigi Hadid, Zendaya and many others (Vogue Business, 2024b).

Similar to the situation in China, **Gen Z** is the target segment attracting attention from luxury brands in India; this group is considered to be a game changer. There are over 100 million consumers born between 1996 and 2010. Gen Z in India is characterized by its focus on personal development, self-development and mindful consumption. In other words, potential future Indian luxury customers tend to be digital natives who seek **meaningful**

Picture 3.7 The Gateway of India. By Ajenkya.shinde, made available under the Creative Commons Attribution-Share Alike 3.0 Unported license. Available at (Wikimedia Commons, 2013).

interactions and brands that align with their values (such as **sustainability) and social causes.** Many prioritize investing in self-improvement through online learning and new experiences. They value products with purpose, and are open to challenging traditional norms. Moreover, **they show pride in India's growth, supporting home-grown brands that reflect their ideals of personalization,** self-expression and dynamic engagement with the world (NIQ, 2024).

Managerial implications based on an empirical study of Indian Gen Z by Ghosh and Bhattacharya (2022) further support the previous characteristics by suggesting **how luxury brands can enhance loyalty among Indian Gen Z consumers:** (1) brands need to focus on creating strong brand attachment and trust by emphasizing luxury brand attributes, product attributes and social media presence; (2) corporate social responsibility (CSR) and sustainability efforts should be aligned with the brand's core business to appeal to environmentally conscious consumers; and (3) effective communication of these values can build trust, ensuring long-term brand loyalty within this demographic (Ghosh & Bhattacharya, 2022).

Gen Z's potentially higher affinity towards domestic brands signals the need for adaptation of the main global luxury players. Bulgari launched its B.zero1 Kada, inspired by the traditional Indian Kada bracelet, after previously introducing a *mangalsutra* (traditional necklace worn by married women in India) in 2021 with Priyanka Chopra Jonas as ambassador (Indian actress, singer and film producer who gained international fame through her work in both Bollywood and Hollywood). Cartier is also planning a collaboration with Indian designer Rimzim Dadu (Vogue Business, 2024).

While India currently faces a **shortage of luxury retail outlets**, significant developments are underway to address this. In November 2023, Mukesh Ambani, chairman of Reliance Industries Limited, inaugurated the luxury mall Jio World Plaza in Mumbai featuring prominent brands such as Balenciaga, Gucci and Louis Vuitton. In addition, the French parent company of Sandro and Maje (SMCP) has partnered with Reliance to expand its presence in India, which may further boost the influx of European luxury brands into the Indian market (Vogue India, 2024a).

3.8 Summary: Demographic and geographical challenges

The first section studies the segmentation of luxury consumers. While wealth remains a primary segmentation criterion, luxury consumers might also be segmented based on lifestyle, their attitudes toward cultural change or the need to signal status. In 2022, the number of HNWIs in North America and Europe declined slightly, while their numbers increased in regions like Latin America and Africa. Additionally, the "mass affluent" segment, with investable assets between $250,000 and $1 million, has great potential for luxury brands.

Beyond income, consumer segmentation incorporates lifestyle factors. Veblen's theory of conspicuous consumption links luxury goods to wealth display, but attitudes toward cultural change also influence buying behaviors. A European study found that both trend-conscious and less trendy consumers engage in luxury consumption, with cultural attitudes sometimes outweighing income. Status signaling is a significant factor in luxury consumption. Consumers use luxury brands to communicate social standing, with behavior divided into four categories: patricians (subtle signals), parvenus (loud signals), poseurs (counterfeit users) and proletarians (indifferent to status). This segmentation reveals how different consumer groups use luxury to either distinguish themselves or blend in. Last, the first section introduces a model that segments consumers based on both wealth and knowledge of luxury. While wealth-driven consumers seek external recognition, competency-based consumers focus on craftsmanship, design and personal fulfillment. Therefore, the growing importance of expertise and intrinsic value in luxury consumption suggests that brands should cater to both wealth and competency-focused consumers.

Generations Z and Alpha constitute a unique challenge for luxury brand management. Their consumption behaviors, shaped by technological advancements and global social movements, seem to differ significantly from those of previous generations. While millennials currently dominate the luxury market, by 2030, Generations Z and Alpha will account for the majority of luxury purchases, with Gen Z alone predicted to make up 25–30% of the market. Gen Z is distinct for its digital nativity, pragmatism and increased awareness of issues such as climate change and social justice. This contributes to their emphasis on sustainability and social responsibility in consumption. They rely heavily on social media influencers for trend discovery but prefer in-store purchases over online platforms, particularly in the U.S., although social commerce is more prevalent in the Asia-Pacific region.

Luxury consumption for **Generation Z is less about exclusivity and more about self-expression, identity and community**. Traditional markers of luxury, such as rarity and craftsmanship, are less significant to Gen Z than price, design or brand heritage. This generation values subtle displays of status, favoring understated luxury over ostentatious logos and tends to adapt trends to their personal style rather than seeking status confirmation. Influencers and digital platforms like YouTube, TikTok and Instagram play a crucial role in shaping their preferences. As Generation Alpha emerges, they are expected to drive further changes in luxury consumption, with an even **deeper integration of technology, artificial intelligence and virtual reality into the shopping experience**. To engage these younger cohorts effectively, luxury brands must **embrace new digital strategies, prioritize sustainability and balance the timelessness of luxury with the demands of modernity and innovation.**

The influence of a **brand's country of origin (COO)** is a significant factor in consumer perception, particularly in luxury markets. According to Roth and Romeo (1992), a country's reputation for producing certain goods affects how consumers perceive brands from that country (Roth & Romeo, 1992). Global luxury brands, typically from France and Italy, benefit from strong associations with craftsmanship and tradition, while domestic luxury brands from less established countries often struggle to achieve the same status. Research indicates that, while the country of origin has a role in shaping luxury brand perceptions, factors such as design, brand prestige and quality often outweigh the COO effect in purchasing decisions. Studies show that the perception of domestic luxury brands is improving, especially as consumers grow more conscious of sustainability and local products, an effect amplified by the COVID-19 pandemic. The pandemic led to a **shift in consumer preferences towards local products**, with predictions that post-pandemic, ethnocentric tendencies may further increase. In markets like China, domestic luxury brands have long been overshadowed by Western competitors, although the potential for local luxury growth is becoming more apparent. Additionally, research conducted in the Czech Republic also highlights differences in the perception of local versus international luxury brands. Local brands are seen as unique and rare, but less associated with traditional luxury values such as high prices and prestige. This finding suggests that local brands can create their space by emphasizing authenticity and cultural heritage. In particular, the study indicated that older, more educated consumers are more likely to prefer domestic brands.

The geographical distribution of luxury consumption reveals **significant regional differences**. Before the pandemic, Chinese consumers were responsible for over 30% of global luxury purchases, although most occurred abroad. During the pandemic, domestic luxury purchases in China increased enormously. This trend is expected to persist despite the gradual recovery of international travel. In 2023, Europe regained its position as the largest market for personal luxury goods, supported by local demand as well as tourism from the U.S. and Middle East. The Chinese luxury market is expected to grow, but it faces economic headwinds slowing the post-pandemic recovery. Meanwhile, emerging markets like India seem to be ready for significant growth. In short, the future of luxury brands is likely to be influenced by growing demand from regions outside the traditional markets of Europe and the U.S. Specifically, India is seen as the region with the most significant growth potential.

Key terms

Bandwagon Effect: Demand for a luxury product increases as more people purchase it. This behavior is common for consumers who seek social validation and aspire to be part of a group associated with a particular luxury brand or lifestyle.

Consumer Ethnocentrism: A concept describing consumers' preference for goods from their own country over foreign-made products, often motivated by national pride or the belief that purchasing local goods supports the domestic economy.

Consumer Xenocentrism: The tendency of consumers to prefer foreign products over domestic ones because they perceive them as being of higher quality or more prestigious. This is common in emerging markets where Western luxury brands dominate consumer preferences.

Country of Origin Effect (COO): Refers to the influence that a product's country of origin has on consumer perceptions of its quality and desirability. Strong associations between certain countries and specific products can affect consumer preferences.

Domestic Luxury Brands: Brands that operate within a specific country or region and often emphasize local culture, craftsmanship and authenticity.

Gen Z and Alpha in Luxury Consumption: Generational cohorts, born after 2000. They represent a growing opportunity for luxury brands. Their brand preferences are shaped by digital nativity, a focus on sustainability and social responsibility, as well as a need for self-expression through luxury goods.

Global Luxury Brands: Luxury brands with a standardized marketing strategy across multiple international markets. These brands are often associated with a high level of prestige and are perceived as status symbols across different cultures.

High Net Worth Individuals (HNWIs): A segment of consumers with investable assets exceeding $1 million. Due to their significant purchasing power, HNWIs are a primary target for luxury brands.

Luxury Brand Collaborations: Strategic partnerships between luxury brands and other entities (such as popular cultural figures or mass-market brands) to create limited-edition products that generate buzz and attract new consumer segments, especially younger audiences.

Luxury Democratization: The process through which luxury brands broaden their consumer base by offering more affordable, entry-level products, such as accessories or perfumes. This allows more consumers to access the brand, though it risks diluting the brand's exclusivity.

Mass Affluents: Consumers with investable assets ranging from $250,000 to $1 million. While they do not belong to the ultra-wealthy class, mass affluents represent an important segment for luxury brands, as they often purchase entry-level luxury goods, providing brands with a broader customer base.

Phygital Dilemma: The challenge luxury brands face in balancing the timeless, exclusive appeal of their products with the need to engage digitally with younger, tech-savvy consumers who expect innovation and modernity in brand experiences.

Quiet Luxury: A trend characterized by luxury products that emphasize subtlety and craftsmanship over bold branding or logos.

Snobbish Effect: A consumer behavior in which demand for a luxury good decreases as the good becomes more widely owned. In luxury segmentation, this behavior is observed in consumers who seek exclusivity and avoid products that become too common or accessible to the broader market.

Status Signaling: Segmentation approach that divides consumers into segments based on their need for visible status symbols. Some segments prefer loud branding, while others opt for subtle, silent branding regardless of the income.

Discussion questions

1. Why is it important to segment luxury customers by factors other than wealth or income? What are some examples of alternative segmentation strategies?
2. What are the key characteristics of Chinese very important customers (VICs), and why are they critical to luxury brands?
3. How does the *country of origin effect* influence consumer perceptions of luxury brands, particularly from countries like France and Italy?
4. Why do some domestic luxury brands struggle to gain the same level of prestige as their international counterparts?
5. What role does the COVID-19 pandemic potentially play in shifting consumer preferences toward domestic luxury brands?
6. How did the geographical distribution of luxury purchases shift during and after the COVID-19 pandemic?
7. Why has China become a key player in the global luxury market, and how is this expected to evolve by 2030?
8. How does the trend toward *quiet luxury* influence Chinese luxury consumers, particularly in higher-tier cities?

Reference list

Aiello, G., Donvito, R., Godey, B., Pederzoli, D., Wiedmann, K.-P., Hennings, N., . . . Singh, R. (2009). An International Perspective on Luxury Brand and Country-of-Origin Effect. *Journal of Brand Management*, *16*(5/6), 323–337.

Albert, N., Merunka, D., & Valette-Florence, P. (2006). When Consumers Love Their Brands: Exploring the Concept and Its Dimensions. *Journal of Business Research*, *61*, 1062–1075.

Albrecht, G. (2011). Chronic Environmental Change: Emerging 'Psychoterratic Syndromes. In I. Weissbecker, *Climate Change and Human Well-Being: Global Challenges and Opportunities* (pp. 43–56). Springer Science + Business Media.

Bain & Company. (2023, January 17). *Renaissance in Uncertainty: Luxury Builds on Its Rebound.* Retrieved August 2024, from bain.com: https://www.bain.com/insights/renaissance-in-uncertainty-luxury-builds-on-its-rebound/#

Bain & Company. (2024a, January 18). *Long Live Luxury: Converge to Expand through Turbulence.* Retrieved September 2024, from bain.com: https://www.bain.com/insights/long-live-luxury-converge-to-expand-through-turbulence/

Bain & Company. (2024b, March 8). *2023 China Luxury Goods Market: A Year of Recovery and Transition.* Retrieved August 2024, from bain.com: https://www.bain.com/insights/2023-china-luxury-goods-market/

Balabanis, G., & Diamantopoulos, A. (2008). Brand Origin Identification by Consumers: A Classification Perspective. *Journal of International Marketing*, *16*(1), 39–71.

BBC. (2024, October 31). *India Celebrates Diwali, the Festival of Lights*. Retrieved November 2024, from bbc.com: https://www.bbc.com/news/articles/c99rx7nyypgo

Bielińska-Dusza, E. (2022). The Motivation of Generations: What Drives Generation X, Y, Z? *Journal of Human Resources Management Research*, *2022*.

Brogi, S., Calabrese, A., Campisi, C., Capece, G., Costa, R., & Di Pillo, F. (2013). The Effects of Online Brand Communities on Brand Equity in the Luxury Fashion Industry. *International Journal of Engineering Business Management*, *5*(Special Issue), 1–9.

Capgemini Research Institute. (2022). *World Report Series Wealth Management 2022*. Retrieved November 2022, from Capgemini Research Institute: https://worldwealthreport.com/pdf/Capgemini_WWR_2022_VFinal_Digital.pdf

Capgemini Research Institute. (2024). https://www.capgemini.com/wp-content/uploads/2024/05/WWR_2024_web.pdf. Retrieved September 2024, from capgemini.com: https://www.capgemini.com/wp-content/uploads/2024/05/WWR_2024_web.pdf

Chadha, R., & Paul, H. (2006). *The Cult of the Luxury Brand*. London: Nicholas Brealey International.

Chow Tai Fook Jewellery Group. (2022). *The Early Days of Chow Tai Fook Jewellery*. Retrieved September 2022, from Chow Tai Fook Jewellery Group: https://www.ctfjewellerygroup.com/en/group/history/story-1.html

Claudia D'Arpizio, C., Levato, F., Steiner, A., & de Montgolfier, J. (2024, January 18). *Long Live Luxury: Converge to Expand through Turbulence*. Retrieved March 2024, from bain.com: https://www.bain.com/insights/long-live-luxury-converge-to-expand-through-turbulence/

Clayton, S., Manning, C., Krygsman, K., & Speiser, M. (2017, March). *Mental Health and Our Changing Climate: Impacts, Implications, and Guidence*. Retrieved November 2022, from American Psychological Association: https://www.apa.org/news/press/releases/2017/03/mental-health-climate.pdf

Comité Colbert. (2022). *Members*. Retrieved September 2022, from Comité Colbert: https://www.comitecolbert.com/en/members

CTK. (2016, December 5). *Luxusní sklárna Moser má nové vlastníky. Majiteli jsou bývalí manažeři Škody Plzeň*. Retrieved December 2022, from zpravy.aktualne.cz: https://zpravy.aktualne.cz/ekonomika/ceska-ekonomika/luxusni-sklarna-moser-ma-nove-vlastniky-majiteli-jsou-jiri-z/r~dcce9366babc11e68cd20025900fea04/

Czech Statistical Office. (2004). *Populační prognóza ČR do r. 2050*. Retrieved November 2024, from https://csu.gov.cz/docs/107508/ee2328ee-a356-c96a-c85a-c71fc20c3527/4025rra.pdf?version=1.0

D'Arpizio, C., & Levato, F. (2021, November 11). *Luxury Is Back . . . To the Future*. Retrieved November 2022, from Altagamma & Bain and Company: https://altagamma.it/media/source/Altagamma%20-%20Bain%20Luxury%20Market%20Monitor%202021.pdf

Daxue Consulting. (2024a). *China's Luxury Market in 2024: VICs, Omnichannel & CRM Strategies China's Luxury Market in 2024: VICs, Omnichannel & CRM Strategies*. Retrieved August 2024, from daxueconsulting.com: https://daxueconsulting.com/wp-content/uploads/2024/07/Luxury-CRM-2024-final.pdf

Daxue Consulting. (2024b, March 29). *Capturing the Neglected Market: Strategies to Connect with Lower-Tier City Consumers in China*. Retrieved August 2024, from daxueconsulting.com: https://daxueconsulting.com/lower-tier-city-consumers-in-china/

Deloitte. (2023, November 29). *Global Powers of Luxury Goods 2023*. Retrieved February 2024, from Deloitte: https://www.deloitte.com/global/en/Industries/consumer/analysis/gx-cb-global-powers-of-luxury-goods.html

Dubois, B., & Duquesne, P. (1993). The Market for Luxury Goods: Income versus Culture. *European Journal of Marketing*, *27*(1), 35–44.

Eastman, J. K., Iyer, R., Shepherd, C. D., Heugel, A., & Faulk, D. (2018). Do they shop to stand out or fit in? The luxury fashion purchase intentions of young adults. *Psychology and Marketing*, *35*, 220–236.

Exor. (2020, December 9). *Exor Invests in Shang XIA Partnering with Hermès to Take the Chinese Luxury Company to the Next Stage of Its Development*. Retrieved September 2024, from exor.com: https://www.exor.com/press-releases/2020-12-09/exor-invests-shang-xia-partnering-hermes-take-chinese-luxury-company-next

FASHIONUNITED. (2023, December 18). *Fendi Unveils Collaboration with Fragment and Pokémon*. Retrieved November 2024, from fashionunited.uk: https://fashionunited.uk/news/fashion/fendi-unveils-collaboration-with-fragment-and-pokemon/2023121873193

Fendi. (2024). *History of Fendi*. Retrieved August 2024, from fendi.com: https://www.fendi.com/cz-en/cm/inside-fendi/about-fendi/the-history-of-fendi

Forbes. (2024, September 30). *Mukesh Ambani*. Retrieved September 2024, from forbes.com: https://www.forbes.com/profile/mukesh-ambani/

Ger, G. (1999). Localizing in the Global Village. *California Management Review*, *41*(4), 64–83.

Ghosh, K., & Bhattacharya, S. (2022). Investigating the Antecedents of Luxury Brand Loyalty for Gen Z Consumers in India: A PLS-SEM Approach. *Young Consumers*, *23*(4), 603–626.

Gucci. (2024). *The Latest Chapter on Adidas x Gucci*. Retrieved October 2024, from Gucci: https://www.gucci.com/us/en/st/stories/article/adidas-x-gucci-the-latest-chapter?srsltid=AfmBOoopXv4WjSI42ln6pL1t61bkoTjgpSImpEu_vUKyjF4QVUcbNqpI

Han, Y. J., Nunes, J. C., & Drèze, X. (2010). Signaling Status with Luxury Goods: The Role of Brand Prominence. *Journal of Marketing*, *74*, 15–30.

Heine, K., & Gutsatz, M. (2015). Luxury Brand Building in China: Eight Case Studies and Eight Lessons Learned. *Journal of Brand Management*, *22*(3), 229–245.

Hennings, N., Wiedmann, K.-P., & Klarmann, C. (2012). Luxury Brands in the Digital Age-Exclusivity versus Ubiquity. *Marketing Review St. Gallen*, *29*, 30–35.

Hofstede, G. H., & Xu, L. (2001). *Culture's Consequences: Comparing Values, Behaviors, Institutions, and Organizations across Nations* (2nd edition). Thousand Oaks, CA: SAGE.

IDNES. (2020, March 15). *Měl jsem jen štěstí, říká rytec z Moseru, který se stal rytířem umění*. Retrieved December 2022, from iDNES.cz: https://www.idnes.cz/karlovy-vary/zpravy/rozhovor-tomas-lesser-rytec-sklarna-moser-oceneni-rad-umeni-rytir.A200309_538025_vary-zpravy_ba

IDNES. (2022a, January 20). *Mistr sklář jde do důchodu a spolu s ním v Moseru končí i ikonická váza Zdroj*. https://www.idnes.cz/karlovy-vary/zpravy/sklarsky-mistr-zdenek-drobny-sklarna-moser-vaza-hruska.A220118_646392_vary-zpravy_ba. Retrieved December 2022, from iDNES.cz: https://www.idnes.cz/karlovy-vary/zpravy/sklarsky-mistr-zdenek-drobny-sklarna-moser-vaza-hruska.A220118_646392_vary-zpravy_ba

IDNES. (2022b, June 16). *Ve sklárně Moser se rozezní zvon Leo, přispěli na něj i zaměstnanci Zdroj*. https://www.idnes.cz/karlovy-vary/zpravy/sklarna-moser-zvon-leo-krest.A220616_669726_vary-zpravy_ba. Retrieved December 2022, from iDNES.cz: https://www.idnes.cz/karlovy-vary/zpravy/sklarna-moser-zvon-leo-krest.A220616_669726_vary-zpravy_ba

The Jewish Community Karlovy Vary. (2022). *Rodina a Firma Moser*. Retrieved December 2022, from kehilakv.cz: http://www.kehilakv.cz/Moser.htm

JingDaily. (2023a, May 19). *From Heytea To Hand In Hand: Fendi Bets Big On China.* Retrieved August 2024, from jingdaily.com: https://jingdaily.com/posts/from-heytea-to-hand-in-hand-fendi-bets-big-on-china

JingDaily. (2023b, August 10). *Valentino Bets on the Pink Cult in China via Food Collaboration.* Retrieved August 2024, from jingdaily.com: https://jingdaily.com/posts/valentino-bets-on-the-pink-cult-in-china-via-food-collaboration

Justice. (2021, December 25). *Sbírka listin Moser, a.s.: Výroční zpráva 2020.* Retrieved December 2023, from or.justice.cz: https://or.justice.cz/ias/ui/vypis-sl-detail?dokument=69874934&subjektId=176399&spis=473468

Justice. (2024). *Sbírka listin Moser, a.s.: Výroční zpráva 2022.* Retrieved November 2024, from or.justice.cz: https://or.justice.cz/ias/ui/vypis-sl-detail?dokument=80409722&subjektId=176399&spis=473468

Kapferer, J. N., & Bastien, V. (2009). *The Luxury Strategy: Break the Rules of Marketing to Build Luxury Brands.* London, NY: Kogan Page.

Kapferer, J.-N., & Bastien, V. (2012). *The Luxury Strategy: Break the Rules of Marketing to Build Luxury Brands* (2nd edition). Kogan Page Limited.

Kastanakis, M. N., & Balabanis, B. (2011). Between the Mass and the Class: Antecedents of the "Bandwagon" Luxury Consumption Behavior. *Journal of Business Research, 65*, 1399–1407.

Kering. (2024, February 8). *2023 Full-Year Results.* Retrieved August 2024, from kering.com: https://www.kering.com/api/download-file/?path=Kering_Presentation_2023_Full_year_results_b0719c3b13.pdf

Khan, U., Dhar, R., & Schmidt, S. (2010). Giving Consumers License to Enjoy Luxury. *MIT Sloan Management Review, 51*(13), 12–13.

Knight Frank. (2024). *The Wealth Report.* Retrieved September 2024, from content.knightfrank.com: https://content.knightfrank.com/resources/knightfrank.com/wealthreport/the-wealth-report-2024.pdf

Lee, J., & Shrum, L. J. (2012). Conspicuous Consumption versus Charitable Behavior in Response to Social Exclusion: A Differential Needs Explanation. *Journal of Consumer Research, 39*(3), 530–544.

Leibenstein, H. (1950). Bandwagon, Snob, And Veblen Effects in the Theory of Consumers' Demand. *Quarterly Journal of Economics, 64*(2), 183–207.

Levitt, T. (1983). The Globalization of Markets. *Harvard Business Review, 61*(3), 92–102.

Llonch-Andreu, J., Lopez-Lomelí, M. A., & Gomez-Villanueva, J. E. (2016). How Local/Global Is Your Brand? A Technique to Assess Brand Categorisation. *International Journal of Market Research, 58*(6), 795–813.

L'Officiel. (2023, December 18). *Our First Look at FENDI x FRGMT x POKÉMON Collab Celebrating the Year of the Dragon.* Retrieved August 2024, from lofficielsingapore.com: https://www.lofficielsingapore.com/fashion/fendi-pokemon-fragment-fashion-collaboration-collection-bags-details-2024

López-Lomelí, M. Á., Alarcón-del-Amo, M.-d.-C., & Llonch-Andreu, J. (2019). Segmenting Consumers Based on Their Evaluation of Local, Global and Glocal Brands. *Journal of International Consumer Marketing, 31*(5), 395–407.

LUXE DIGITAL. (2024, August 26). *The 15 Most Popular Luxury Brands Online.* Retrieved August 2024, from luxe.digital: https://luxe.digital/business/ranking/most-popular-luxury-brands/

LVMH. (2023). *LVMH: Translation of the French Financial Documents Fiscal Year Ended December 31, 2023.* Retrieved August 2024, from lvmh.com: https://lvmh-com.cdn.prismic.io/lvmh-com/ZmMq-pm069VX1j0w_financial-documents-lvmh-december-31–2023.pdf

MajlesiRad, Z., & Shoushtari, A. H. (2020). Analysis of the Impact of Social Network Sites and eWOM Marketing, Considering the Reinforcing Dimensions of the Concept of Luxury, on Tendency toward Luxury Brand. *Future Business Journal*, 1–19.

McKinsey. (2024, July 3). *What Does the Future Hold for India?* Retrieved September 2024, from mckinsey.com: https://www.mckinsey.com/featured-insights/mckinsey-explainers/what-does-the-future-hold-for-india

Moda.cz. (2022, May 18). *Tatiana Kovaříková představila letní kolekci vystihující unikátnost každé ženy*. Retrieved June 2022, from moda.cz: https://www.moda.cz/a/tatiana-kovarikova-predstavila-letni-kolekci-vystihujici-unikatnost-kazde-zeny--24342

Moser. (2017). *Moser 160 Let*. Retrieved December 2022, from Moser: https://www.moser.com/file/edee/downloads/moser_book_cz.pdf

Moser. (2022). *The Story of Moser*. Retrieved October 2022, from Moser: https://www.moser.com/en/about-moser/the-story-of-moser

Moser. (2024). *Pear Vase*. Retrieved September 2024, from moser.com: https://www.moser.com/en/pear

Muniz, A. M., & O'Guinn, T. C. (2001). Brand Community. *Journal of Consumer Research*, 27(4), 412–432.

NIQ. (2024, March 18). *Decoding GenZ & New India*. Retrieved September 2024, from nielseniq.com: https://nielseniq.com/wp-content/uploads/sites/4/2024/03/decode-genz-and-new-india.pdf

Olšanová, K., Cook, G., Král, P., Vilikus, O., & Zlatić, M. (2020). Exploration of Opportunities for Development of CEE Domestic Luxury Brands: Case of the Czech Republic. *Central European Business Review*, 9(4), 59–72.

Perlitz, M., Schulze, L., & Wilke, C. B. (2010). The Demographic and Economic Transition in Central and Eastern Europe – Management Implications. *Journal for East European Management Studies*, 2, 149–176.

Pokémon Go Wiki. (2024). *Development and Release*. Retrieved August 2024, from pokemongo.fandom.com: https://pokemongo.fandom.com/wiki/Pokémon_GO#Development_and_release

Raja, A. M., Gurung, D. J., & Vincent, T. N. (2021). Market Segmentation Framework for Generation Alpha Cohorts. *Productivity*, 62(3), 248–254.

Reyes, M. S., Carmen, B. B., Luminarias, M. P., Mangulabnan, S. N., & Ogunbode, C. (2021). An investigation into the Relationship between Climate Change Anxiety and Mental Health among Gen Z Filipinos. *Current Psychology*.

Richemont. (2023). *Richemont Annual Report and Accounts 2023*. Retrieved August 2024, from richemont.com: https://www.richemont.com/media/vjjclruw/richemont-fy23-annual-report-en.pdf

Roth, M. S., & Romeo, J. B. (1992). Matching Product Category and Country Image Perceptions: A Framework for Managing Country-of-Origin Effects. *Journal of International Business Studies*, *23*(3), 477–497.

Roth-Cohen, O., Rosenberg, H., & Lissitsa, S. (2021). Are You Talking to Me? Generation X, Y, Z Responses to Mobile Advertising. *Convergence*, *28*(5), 1–20.

Ryder, N. B. (1965). The Cohort as a Concept in the Study of Social Change. *American Sociological Review*, *30*(6), 843–861.

Schmitt, B., Zarantonello, L., & Brakus, J. (2009). Brand Experience: What Is It? How Is It Measured? Does It Affect Loyalty? *Journal of Marketing*, *73*(3), 52–68.

Schneider, B., & Lee, D. (2022, October). *Gen-Z and Fashion in the Age of Realism*. Retrieved November 2022, from BoF: https://www.businessoffashion.com/reports/retail/

gen-z-fashion-in-the-age-of-realism-bof-insights-social-media-report/?cid=other-eml-mtg-mip-mck&hlkid=aa79c6e776d64e09a4fec235487de61c&hctky=1711743&hdpid=2aca0cfa-6346-40c1-93d6-48680a8382a4

Schuiling, I., & Kapferer, J.-N. (2004). Executive Insights: Real Differences Between Local and International Brands: Strategic Implications for International Marketers. *Journal of International Marketing*, *12*(4), 97–112.

Seagull. (2024). *About Us*. Retrieved September 2024, from seagullwatches.com: https://seagullwatches.com/pages/about-us

SHANG XIA. (2024a). *About Us*. Retrieved September 2024, from shangxia.com: https://www.shangxia.com/en/pages/about-us

SHANG XIA. (2024c). *Travel Tea Set in Round Leather Case*. Retrieved September 2024, from shangxia.com: https://www.shangxia.com/en/pages/新品-new-products

Shanghai Tang. (2024). *Our History*. Retrieved September 2024, from shanghaitang.com: https://www.shanghaitang.com/our-story?srsltid=AfmBOoq-NaBuLFZOQ-uUTsUowioXldgFc8KKKCAbeR0AAIs0hFWs_2uh

Shin, H., Eastman, J. K., & Li, Y. (2021). Is It Love or Just Like? Generation Z's Brand Relationship with Luxury. *Journal of Product & Brand Management*, *31*(3), 394–414.

Sivanathan, N., & Pettit, N. C. (2010). Protecting the Self Through Consumption: Status Goods as Affirmational Commodities. *Journal of Experimental Social Psychology*, *46*(3), 564–570.

Som, A., & Blanckaert, C. (2021). *The Road to Luxury: The New Frontiers in Luxury Brand Management* (2nd edition). Wiley.

Steenkamp, J.-B., Batra, R., & Alden, D. L. (2003). How Perceived Brand Globalness Creates Brand Value. *Journal of International Business Studies*, *34*(1), 53–65.

Strebinger, A., & Rusetski, A. (2016). Prioritizing Geo-References: A Content Analysis of the Websites of Leading Global Luxury Fashion Brands. *Journal of Global Marketing*, *29*(5), 282–297.

TATIANA. (2022). *O Tatianě*. Retrieved June 2022, from https://www.tatiana.cz/cs/o-tatiane

TATIANA. (2023). *Spring/Summer 2023*. Retrieved May 2024, from https://tatiana.cz/pages/ss-23

Thomas, M. R., & George, G. (2021). Segmenting, Targeting, and Positioning (STP) of Generational Cohorts Y, Z and Alpha. *IIMS Journal of Management Science*, *12*(2), 115–129.

Veblen, T. (1899/2003). *The Theory of the Leisure Class* (E. C. Series, Ed.). Pennsylvania State University/Electronic Classics Series.

Vigneron, F., & Johnson, L. W. (2004). Measuring Perceptions of Brand Luxury. *Journal of Brand Management*, *11*(6), 484–506.

Vogue Business. (2024a). *Gen Z Broke the Marketing Funnel*. Retrieved March 2024, from https://www.voguebusiness.com/story/consumers/gen-z-broke-the-marketing-funnel?uID=fa44d56a3421e1bd59eeaa0b01a60e5912e32f35339c1ca98294907eebb5d-5c0&utm_campaign=newsletter_weekly&utm_source=newsletter&utm_brand=vb&utm_mailing=VB_NEWS_Kirsty_FRI_080324&utm

Vogue Business. (2024b, February 22). *Can Luxury in India Build on Last Year's Landmark Moments?* Retrieved September 2024, from voguebusiness.com: https://www.voguebusiness.com/story/fashion/can-luxury-in-india-build-on-last-years-landmark-moments

Vogue India. (2024a, January 7). *Luxury Will See India as a Prime Market in 2024*. Retrieved September 2024, from vogue.in: https://www.vogue.in/content/the-regions-luxury-will-be-heading-to-in-2024

Vogue India. (2024b, July 15). *The Most Spectacular Jewellery from Anant Ambani and Radhika Merchant's Wedding*. Retrieved September 2024, from vogue.in: https://www.vogue.in/content/the-most-unique-jewellery-from-anant-ambani-and-radhika-merchants-wedding

Wang, Y. (2022). A Conceptual Framework of Contemporary Luxury Consumption. *International Journal of Research in Marketing*, *39*(3), 788–803.

Wikimedia Commons. (2013, February 15). *File: The Gateway of India at Night 01.JPG*. Retrieved November 2024, from commons.wikimedia.org: https://commons.wikimedia.org/wiki/File:The_Gateway_Of_India_At_Night_01.JPG

Wikimedia Commons. (2020, November 4). *File:MONDAY-Meme Dsc5436.png*. Retrieved January 2025, from commons.wikimedia.org: https://commons.wikimedia.org/wiki/File:MONDAY-Meme_Dsc5436.png

Wikimedia Commons. (2023, June 20). *File:Woman Lighting the Candles for the Festival of Lights in India (cropped).jpg*. Retrieved November 2024, from commons.wikimedia.org: https://commons.wikimedia.org/wiki/File:Woman_lighting_the_candles_for_the_Festival_of_Lights_in_India_(cropped).jpg

Williams, K. C., Page, R. A., Petrosky, A., & Hernandez, E. H. (2010). Multi-Generational Marketing: Descriptions, Characteristics, Lifestyles, and Attitudes. *Journal of Applied Business and Economics*, *11*(2).

Wolfe, A. (1991). The Single European Market: National or Euro-Brands? *International Journal of Advertising*, *10*(1), 49–58.

Zhang, T., Chen, J., & Grunert, K. G. (2022). Impact of Consumer Global–Local Identity on Attitude Towards and Intention to Buy Local Foods. *Food Quality and Preference*, *96*.

Chapter 4

The enduring principles specific to luxury brand management

This chapter explores the principles of luxury brand management that have proven effective over time and should not change. While luxury brand management must innovate to stay relevant, it also relies on timeless principles that are distinctive to luxury brands and different from traditional marketing.

The marketing management of luxury brands requires specific tools, different from those used in the mass market. The basic principles of traditional marketing do not apply here. Luxury brands are built; ordinary brands are marketed. The strategies used are often completely the opposite of marketing strategy applied in the FMCG market. To understand the luxury strategy, it is first necessary to characterize the individual aspects or basic building blocks of luxury brands and to distinguish them from the traditional marketing strategy, to understand the so-called *anti-laws* of luxury marketing and to characterize the typical segments of luxury brand clients.

4.1 Aspects of contemporary luxury

From simply observing the rankings of luxury brands or walking on the most expensive streets of the world's metropolises, it may seem that the world of luxury brands is closed, made up of a few large groups controlling it, and that the space for new luxury brands is very limited or even non-existent. The structured overview of aspects of contemporary luxury in the following section is intended to contribute to an understanding of how these fears can be overcome and how to, under specific circumstances and by following certain rules, create, regenerate or maintain a luxury brand that may not have the backing of a large existing group of luxury brands.

4.1.1 Luxury products and brands: The need for emotions

What qualifies a brand as "luxury"? Luxury is part of the process of creating and maintaining social distancing in society. At the same time, it implies an intimate, intense **satisfaction** associated with the **product itself,** which has its own imagery and beauty and which was

DOI: 10.4324/9781003593706-4

purchased on the basis of its qualities. This satisfaction distinguishes between those who can appreciate the product and deeply enjoy it, and those who can afford it but are simply followers of the tastes of others: good taste is what money cannot buy. Gabrielle Chanel's famous saying distinguishes between "those who have money and those who are actually rich" (Virgin Money, 2014).

Luxury is not clinically pure perfectionism in design or quality. That's enough for a premium brand but not a luxury one. Luxury needs **emotions** – feelings that will lead to the desire for a brand, which will turn into a dream of owning a specific product of a luxury brand. In addition to emotions, traditional luxury brands have a connection with the elite of their time, and current or newer brands have particular links to the elite of our time (Kapferer & Bastien, 2012).

Cartier is known for his creations for the nobility and high society. In 1856, Emperor Napoleon III's cousin, Princess Mathilde, introduced the Cartier House to Parisian high society with her first order and thus to the international elite of her time (Cartier, 2022a). The artistic and craft mastery of the glass engraver Ludwig Moser and his glass workshop, founded in 1857, was appreciated by Emperor Franz Joseph I, who, after his success at the World Exhibition in Vienna, granted him the privilege of becoming a distinguished supplier to the imperial court (Moser, 2022).

Today's **elites** – CEOs of large corporations with families, cultural celebrities, appropriately chosen influencers or sports personalities – can demonstrate a luxury brand's introduction to high society. Founded in 2013 by American designer Virgil Abloh, himself a skilled influencer, Off-White became part of the LVMH Group in 2021. Virgil was also the creative director of Louis Vuitton. The Off-White brand is based on the identity of its founder, hailed as a creative genius who managed to combine streetwear with luxury fashion and bring millennials to the LVMH Group. The Milan-based brand skillfully uses "Made in Italy" as a stamp of quality, on which it places great emphasis. The brand is active on social networks with very creative posts from the process of creating new collections. Working with Nike, Virgil created studded shoes in his signature orange color, which Kylian Mbappé first wore in the French league final. Over the years, the brand has collaborated with designers from other brands including IKEA, Jimmy Choo, Timberland, KITH and Takashi Murakami. Virgil himself created for Kanye West, with whom he had long been friends (Industries Academy, 2021; Off-White, 2022). After Virgil Abloh's untimely death in 2021, LVMH continued to manage the brand. However, recent reports confirm that LVMH has sold Off-White to Bluestar Alliance (an American brand management company that owns multiple other fashion brands), citing strategic reasons, to focus on its core luxury portfolio and optimize its brand management efforts (Euronews, 2024).

The luxury of the object is also demonstrated through the fame and taste of the people who appreciate, buy or are otherwise associated with it. By including these supporters, we assign the object of their passion to a brand, and it is the brand that further benefits from their aura.

4.1.2 Incomparability of luxury brands

From the marketing point of view at companies such as P&G, Unilever or Mondelez, the aspect of luxury's incomparability is probably the one that is most different from traditional consumer goods brands. This is because their marketing is based on a certain product frame of reference, including the widest possible set of brand substitutes, against which they define themselves and seek a competitive advantage – formulated as a brand promise. Positioning then defines what makes a brand unique within a given product category and which benefit, whether functional or emotional, it wants to inscribe in the minds of consumers. In luxury, we do not talk about positioning, nor do we look for a frame of reference or compare with others. Each piece is unique. It's impossible to compare Louis Vuitton and Chanel handbags. Each of them is associated with different concepts and ideas related to their history, heritage, loyalty to their values and craftsmanship. Walking through the Louvre, we do not compare the works of Paul Rubens with those of Rembrandt. We enjoy them separately; we feel the emotions of their creators, and just like in luxury – we do not compare the incomparable.

Kapferer cites the example of Lexus, which in its first advertisement in the US, defined itself against the Mercedes E-Class, claiming that only by purchasing the Lexus will customers get a better car than the Mercedes E-Class at a cheaper price. This example illustrates two major mistakes of luxury business strategy – defining against competitors and promoting cheaper prices. Lexus, despite its luxurious name, is not even a luxury car today (Kapferer & Bastien, 2012).

The dimension of a luxury brand's incomparability should not be underestimated, even in distribution or communication. In the case of exclusive distribution, which is easier, the brand controls the distribution channels and conducts the customer experience at the point of sale. In the case of selective distribution, emphasis should be placed on ensuring that comparable brands are not in close proximity. Furthermore, the brand's origin, materials and design form part of the brand's heritage in a way that is also not comparable to a similar product of the same category. Here, in luxury, as in other categories, it is not beneficial to communicate right next to a similar category of products.

4.1.3 History and culture

History gives brands depth and makes their products timeless (Kapferer & Bastien, 2012). The most valuable luxury brands in the world – such as Dior, Hermès, Cartier, or Louis Vuitton – are those with over a century of history, where tradition and heritage have become integral to their brand identity. Traditional luxury literature emphasizes the significance of history as a cornerstone of luxury. However, even young luxury brands, while adhering to other key principles of luxury brand strategy, can create their own legacy by developing compelling stories and narratives, building their own heritage through storytelling and emotional connection with their audience.

If a brand is missing a strong history, it must try to invent it. Contemporary luxury brands without strong history can create their own story by, as an example, finding inspiration in a certain time, historical period or event. Others may use a name which evokes a rich history, like the champagne Dom Pérignon, invented in 1950. The brand name links the brand many centuries back when the French Benedictine monk Dom (Pierre) Pérignon made several important contributions to the production of sparkling wine.

Carlo Crocco, who founded Hublot in 1980, is another example of a man who created history via storytelling. At the time of the brand's creation, Hublot was an unusual combination of natural rubber strap and luxury materials like gold, which elevated the watch business. In contrast to conventional watch manufacturers with a far longer history, Hublot's brand was established on the idea of *The Art of Fusion*, which refers to the fusion of cutting-edge materials like titanium, carbon fiber, and ceramic with traditional Swiss workmanship. Hublot was positioned as a pioneer in modern luxury thanks to this audacious combination of materials and design, which was further cemented in 2005 with the introduction of the "Big Bang" series in 2005 (Hodinkee, 2018).

Not every luxury brand prides itself on the history of being "Founded in 1847" like Cartier (more in the next mini-case), yet much younger luxury brands perform comparatively well.

The year is only a number showing age. The brand itself, if well managed, carries a deep heritage and continuity. At Cartier, every product has a hidden story based on its unique brand identity. The Panthère or Trinity collections, more than a century old, are still cherished, and designers are creating new lines based on their heritage. None of today's fashion icons, boasting a panther on their wrist or three braided rings on their fingers, consider these jewels old or, worse, old-fashioned (Kapferer & Bastien, 2012). Luxury brands originating in Europe owe their history to the long and enduring existence of the wealthy middle or business class that demanded them.

The Asian representative of luxury groups ranking, according to Deloitte, is the Chow Tai Fook Jewellery Group based in Hong Kong. The group operates individually its flagship brand (Chow Tai Fook, founded in 1929) and other brands from the acquisitions within the past decades (Enzo, Hearts on Fire, SoInLove, Monologue) to address different segments of consumers. By 2023, it had opened more than seven thousand points of sale in mainland China, and its organic and acquisition growth potential is enormous. To emphasize the history and roots of the brand, the Group purchased the 507-carat Cullinan Heritage diamond, which forms the basis of the jewelry masterpiece unveiled in 2015. The $200 million artwork is titled *Heritage in Bloom* and points the way to building historic brand milestones along the lines of European companies (Chow Tai Fook Jewellery Group, 2022). Another approach to encompassing history into the identity of an Asian luxury brand is SHANG XIA. The brand, founded by Chinese designer Jiang Qiong Er in 2009 in Shanghai as a joint venture with Hermès Group, was designed to revive and promote China's 5,000-year-old cultural heritage and leverage almost forgotten Chinese craftsmanship to design contemporary products (Harvard Business Publishing, 2017).

European luxury brands draw on their long history of self-confidence, stemming from uniqueness, from inherited values transformed into products or objects that respect these values with almost religious respect. However, it is not enough just to add "Founded in 1834" to the packaging. An old brand doesn't create a luxury product or support a brand; it takes a story to do that (Kapferer & Bastien, 2012).

Another aspect in the management of luxury brands is culture. Luxury brands can only exist because they hire masters of their fields – in art, design and craftsmanship – to carry on the founder's legacy. History and tradition, accompanied by the story of the brand, including the stories of previous owners or creators, are then able to evoke a dream of the brand, which brings customers to luxury stores (Kapferer & Valette-Florence, 2016).

Mini-case 4.1 *Panthère du Cartier*: Continuity and integrity in the *Maison*'s collection

Cartier was founded in Paris by Louis-François Cartier (1819–1904) in 1847 and was ruled by his descendants until 1964. Today, it is sold in more than 267 stores on the most prestigious streets of the world's largest cities, and its brand value is estimated at more than $9.9 billion, according to Interbrand (2023).

The history of the now-iconic panther began in 1914, when the grandson of founder Louis Cartier, used a drawing by George Barbier with an illustration of a black panther lying at the feet of a woman adorned with jewelry (Picture 4.1) that was used on an invitation to a jewelry exhibition. At that time, panthers were very popular in Parisian society. In the same year, the panther appeared on Cartier women's wristwatches with black onyx and diamonds, and thus 1914 is considered the birth of the *Panthère du Cartier* collection (Cartier, 2022b).

In 1917, Louis Cartier created a cigarette case made of diamonds, onyx, and platinum, with a black panther reproduction on it, as a gift for his friend Jeanne Toussaint. Madame Toussaint became part of a jewelry company in the early 1920s. She headed the accessories and handbag department but did not become the creative director of jewelry until 1933. She was a well-known lover of panthers, as demonstrated in Video 4.1. Her Parisian apartment was full of furs and items from the Orient, and she herself wore a long coat of panther fur. Louis Cartier called her *Ma petite panthère* (Sotheby's, 2019; Cartier, 2022b).

In 1948, she managed to revive the panther, changing Cartier and the animal symbol. At the top of a brooch for the Duchess of Windsor, Wallis Simpson, Jeanne Touissant placed a 116-carat emerald and a 3D statuette of a roaring panther. The Duchess was considered one of the most stylish women of the times, and the following year she bought another Panthère

Picture 4.1 Drawing of George Barbier with a panther. By MassiveEartha available as public domain at (Wikimedia Commons, 1914).

brooch with a 152-carat sapphire, which she wore perched on her shoulder.

Madame Toussaint was formally active at Cartier until 1970, when she stepped down from her position, but Cartier designers continue to utilize the panther collection (Sotheby's, 2019).

In 2014, to commemorate the 100th anniversary of the first panther jewelry, the jewelry house launched a new collection of 56 items ranging from bracelets and necklaces to rings and earrings. Fierce, shy, or triumphant-looking panthers with green emeralds instead of eyes appear in the form of a $23,000 pendant or a $291,000 ring with aquamarine, beryl, emerald, onyx and diamond (Forbes, 2014). The brand still honors Madame Toussaint and its founders and honestly follows the original historical collections with modern design.

Video 4.1 Odyssée de Cartier: Jeanne Toussaint, (Cartier, 2019).
https://www.youtube.com/watch?v=Kws1Vlw7oyM

4.1.4 Time and tradition: Celebrated aspects

Luxury brands need time, tradition and long-lasting visions. The time necessary for luxury is less relevant for fashion brands, which have a shorter, more or less seasonal lifespan, while the value of luxury brands increases over time (Kapferer & Valette-Florence, 2016).

The time aspect has several characteristics in luxury: (1) time is **part of the development of a luxury product.** Growing the best ingredients, maturing, finding and producing the best material, as well as acquiring the competence and expertise of the best craftsmen, all need enough time to produce a luxury product; (2) contemporary **designers of brands** such as Chanel, Christian Dior and Cartier **must spend a lot of time** penetrating the souls and creative thinking of the founders so that their collections do not lose any of their heritage, but at the same time do not look old-fashioned. Furthermore, nowadays, with the need to enter the web3 environment, it takes enormous time for digital developers to create virtual or digital identities of the brands that reflect the same physical identity of the brand in the digital environment; (3) customers are willing to wait a long time in order to obtain the product, since it fulfils a dream (e.g. the waiting time for a Hermès Kelly handbag is up to six years); and finally, (4) **time devoted to the consumption** of a luxury product. Louis XIII is a Rémy Martin's brand of cognac with a tradition since 1874. Its unique tasting ritual refers to the expression of its taste complexity because it has been created for years, and its sensory qualities have developed over decades. The tasting experience should evoke a tangible connection with the past (Rémy Martin, 2021). The time factor is celebrated and valued in luxury; the original collections of the founders are refreshed with little added creativity, and we do not talk about bestsellers but about "long-sellers" (Kapferer & Bastien, 2012).

The emphasis on tradition and timelessness is often at odds with market trends, which is one of the most important paradoxes of the luxury world. Timelessness and trendiness go together, at least through special collections or various limited editions. Tradition must be handled very carefully, because tradition is a small step away from "old-fashioned," and it must be avoided even in a luxurious environment. Therefore, for a brand to build on its tradition, it must take into account the current trends with regard to its brand identity but avoid "mummification" of the brand by too much settling into the past. De Beers of 1888 combines tradition with the future (with the slogan *A Diamond Is Forever*), Patek Philippe with the next generation and family *(Begin Your Own Tradition)*, and IWC with masculinity (*IWC. Since 1868. And for as long as there are men*). What is important is the way in which the brand communicates in the context of its tradition without giving up the values that its own tradition means.

4.1.5 Handicraft production: Proof of top craftsmanship

A luxury product does not always have to be entirely handmade to prove top craftsmanship. A luxury product lies on the border of art and craft, so it can be assumed that artists participate in its design and the best craftsmen participate in its production. Nowadays, however, it is expected that at least some part of a luxury product is made by hand. Yet some brands communicate handmade, such as Louis Vuitton or Hermès: "Authentic Louis Vuitton bags are handmade by experienced craftsmen who pride themselves on making perfect products from only the finest and highest quality materials" (Louis Vuitton, 2022b). Hermès hand-produces bags, glassware and leather saddles for horse riding in its French factory. In one month, for example, they produce 15 bags of different styles and textures costing from $10,000 to $150,000, depending on the size and material used (Business Insider, 2012). The luxury literature suggests that at least a part, however small, of a luxury product should be handmade to distinguish it from flawless mass production and to give the impression of rarity and preciousness (Kapferer & Bastien, 2012).

Another example is from Moser producing crystal glassware. The handmade production of the Moser *Pear* vase is a physically demanding process where artisans hand-blow 25 kg of lead-free crystal, reducing it to 15 kg through cutting. The vase is then precisely hand-cut and polished to achieve a high-gloss finish. Its unique design refracts light, creating an extraordinary visual effect, making it one of Moser's most celebrated crystal works (Moser, 2024).

Handcrafting of the *Pear* vase gives it **immense value and uniqueness**, from hand-blowing the crystal to complex cutting and polishing processes. Each vase is one of a kind, **a rare collector's item** that gains value over time as a testament to the artisan's skill.

4.1.6 The value of rarity: The balance between volume and scarcity

Luxury lies in the rarity or unavailability of ingredients, materials, artists, designers, know-how of processing and products as such. In connection with the luxury industry, we distinguish between five types of rarity (Catry, 2003). The first is **the natural scarcity of ingredients,** the scarcity which is a clear obstacle to sales ambitions driven by demand from a globally growing luxury middle class. It is difficult to find enough diamonds with a reasonable price to meet demand and maintain quality levels. If the shortage affects the quality of a luxury product, it can damage the brand image. Naturally, human expertise is also rare, which is related to the manual production of luxury items or their parts. This may also be related to the interruption of the production of an authentic product due to the loss of a top craftsman, as in the case of the Moser glassworks and the large size of the *Pear* vase upon the retirement of the glass master (more in the Moser case study in Chapter 3).

Natural rarity has little compatibility with the volume of production. Today, luxury manufacturers must also ask tough questions and carefully consider how their business model affects aspects like energy, climate, natural resources and supply chain sustainability. The second type of rarity is **technical rarity** in the form of innovation and research and development, which, on the contrary, has a higher compatibility with volume but is financially demanding, and if it is not protected by a patent, it can soon be imitated by competitors. A third way to introduce the aspect of scarcity into brand management is **limited offers**, where the brand designer authorizes only a limited amount of an extraordinary collection to sell. In 2012, Louis Vuitton designer Marc Jacobs collaborated with artist Yayoi Kusama on a range of handbags, accessories, shoes and clothing in bold colors with polka dots. Among the most popular handbags from this partnership are the "Pumpkin Dot Neverfull and Speedy," which are sold at Sotheby's for multiples of the original retail price if they are in excellent condition (Sotheby's, 2021).

Limited offers are common for luxury watches. In 2022, to celebrate the 20th anniversary of Tambour watches, Louis Vuitton launched a limited series of 200 pieces called Tambour Twenty Limited Edition at a cost of just under $18,000 (Hodinkee, 2022). The fourth option is to **restrict distribution**. A limited number of Chanel boutiques (around 300 worldwide) located only in the best locations of the largest cities and e-commerce selling only Chanel cosmetics are part of the company's strategy to limit distribution. The last type of rarity is the so-called **informational** one, which restricts information not only about the brand's items but also about famous people who represent them in some way. It is a rarity of official information about celebrities, ambassadors, and designers associated with the brand. Conversely, public relations departments or agencies feed the press and virtual networks with fake news or fake gossip to which a luxury brand is neutral. In many luxury companies, there is a culture of confidentiality and even censorship built around a set of sacrosanct portfolio items or information about them. It is very difficult to get information about the number of Louis Vuitton handbags sold, as information about relatively high volumes could reduce the perception of the brand's exclusivity in the eyes of customers.

Rarity is one of the measures of luxury, yet its importance in this sector is on the wane. The demand for luxury is growing, as is the number of customers who can afford it. It is not in the interest of the large groups controlling most luxuries to keep rarity at the top of the long-term strategy rankings. The reason is the need for long-term growth and responsibility towards shareholders or investors of large groups. Conversely, independent brands such as Chanel or Hermès could increase store capacity and produce more Birkin handbags for volume growth or loosen up strictly controlled distribution, but they are not doing so to preserve rarity.

To maintain the appearance of rarity and unavailability of selected items, the following procedures can be used:

1. Unique collections in limited quantities, allowing the brand's clients to compete with each other to obtain the selected item;
2. Adding value to limited collections by using well-known avant-garde artists. The value of such items on the secondary market may immediately increase when the last piece is sold;
3. A company may decide to put select, unique items not available on the primary market in the auction and donate the proceeds to charitable or socially sustainable projects;
4. Limiting distribution, as perceived unavailability increases customer eagerness;
5. Maintaining the level of dreaming about the brand so that the penetration of the brand is less than the awareness of it;

6. Connecting with elite customers through social media and communicating from various brand events to disperse the image of ordinary, unknown customers in the queue in front of the store;
7. Implementing a pricing policy that differentiates the brand by signaling that it is not accessible to everyone and that by purchasing it, the luxury customer had to invest significant resources (Kapferer, 2017).

The **principle of scarcity** in the strategy of luxury brands with the gradual democratization of luxury does not play such a fundamental role, especially for large groups covering most of the top luxury brands. More and more rich people can afford to invest in luxury, and large new markets and opportunities are opening, which gradually limits the principle of scarcity in the interest of increasing volume.

Mini-case 4.2 Ferrari: "Being on the waiting list is itself a status symbol"

Founded by Enzo Ferrari in 1939, Ferrari has evolved into one of the most iconic luxury car brands in the world. What began as a racing division within Alfa Romeo quickly developed into a standalone company by 1947, when the first Ferrari-badged car, the 125 S (photo of a museum exhibit in Picture 4.2), was unveiled. Ferrari's deep motorsport roots and commitment to performance, innovation and exclusivity have cemented its reputation as the pinnacle of the automotive luxury (Ferrari, 2024b).

The concept of scarcity is central to the brand's philosophy – Ferrari has never intended to be a mass-market brand. On the contrary, it has systematically cultivated a sense of product rarity and this consistent approach has helped Ferrari build an aura

Picture 4.2 Ferrari 125 S – Exhibit at the Museo Enzo Ferrari, Modena, Italy, By Cloverleaf II., licensed under the Creative Commons Attribution 2.0 Generic license. Available at (Wikimedia Commons, 2014b).

of dreaming about the brand, ensuring that ownership is a privilege reserved for a select few customers. The strong and unique market position and desirability were supported by **limiting the production volumes** to around 7,000 to 10,000 cars annually until 2022. The iconic prancing horse logo symbolizes a legacy of craftsmanship, innovation and exclusivity that spans over eight decades (prancing horse on Picture 4.3).

In 2022, Ferrari made a significant yet carefully considered expansion of its lineup with the introduction of its first SUV, the Purosangue, at approximately €390,000. Entering the lucrative and popular SUV market did not mean the brand's rarity was reduced. Ferrari launched the Purosangue as a highly exclusive model and limited production to prevent it from becoming a mass-market product. The amount of produced SUVs should not exceed 20% of the total volume to remain exclusive and avoid the trap of large volume at the expense of the core products (Pitt, 2022). So, production has increased from the previously mentioned 7,000 to 10,000 cars to approximately 12,000 to 14,000.

Combining the performance in Ferrari's DNA with the versatility and comfort expected of an SUV, the Purosangue appeals to a new segment of luxury car buyers while maintaining a degree of the brand's inaccessibility. This strategic move allows Ferrari to tap into the growing demand for luxury SUVs without diluting its core values of exclusivity and rarity. It is the first ever four-door, four-seater car in Ferrari's history. The name *Purosangue* is an Italian expression for *thoroughbred*, which is also an additional link to the brand's DNA (Ferrari, 2024a).

Picture 4.3 A prancing horse in Maranello. By SurfAst. Available under the Creative Commons Attribution-Share Alike 3.0 Unported license. (Wikimedia Commons, 2011).

As the global luxury market evolves, Ferrari faces the challenge of staying relevant to younger, affluent consumers who may have different expectations and values than previous generations. This demographic tends to value sustainability and responsibility, technological innovation and personalization more than the traditional luxury values like heritage and exclusivity. The rise of electric vehicles (EVs) and a growing focus on environmental responsibility put pressure on traditional luxury brands, including Ferrari, to adapt without losing their core identity.

To maintain its status as a symbol of rarity even amongst luxury cars, Ferrari has implemented several strategies, one of which is limiting production to keep demand high and supply low. A recent and notable step is Ferrari's approach to launching its first fully electric vehicle, scheduled for 2025. According to a report by Reuters, Ferrari's EV is expected to cost over $500,000. The extremely high price guarantees that it remains rare and accessible only to the brand's wealthiest clientele. The high price point is part of Ferrari's broader strategy to maintain its exclusive image even as it ventures into the increasingly competitive EV market. This is a demonstration of the Veblen effect in practice – in contradiction with the traditional economic laws of supply and demand, the Veblen goods are more desirable when more expensive, as they are a demonstration and symbol of the owner's status. Moreover, Ferrari's strict vetting process for potential buyers adds another layer of **exclusivity**. Not everyone who can afford a Ferrari can buy one; the brand often prioritizes loyal customers or those with a history of Ferrari ownership. "There is an increasing demand out there for Ferraris, and they have room to meet part of it without compromising exclusivity," commented Fabio Caldato, a portfolio manager at AcomeA SGR (which holds Ferrari shares) for Reuters (2024). Despite the investment into the factory in Maranello, the limitation in terms of volume will remain and so will the wait times for the new cars, which may take up to two years. "That is not getting any shorter. Being on the waiting list is in itself a status symbol," said Fabio Caldato and confirmed expectations of a demand increase from potential wealthy customers in emerging markets, such as India and the Middle East. This practice ensures that the brand's community remains exclusive and that its vehicles are owned by individuals who truly appreciate Ferrari's legacy and values (Reuters, 2024). Ferrari also engages in limited editions and personalized bespoke services. By offering highly customized vehicles that reflect the personal tastes of their owners, Ferrari reinforces its position as a brand that provides not just a car, but a unique, rare and personalized experience.

For the future, Ferrari will likely continue to accentuate its core values of exclusivity, performance, rarity and innovation, while gradually adding **electrification and sustainability**. The brand's ability to adapt while sustaining its feeling of rarity will be crucial to its success. It is very likely the EV models will remain niche in Ferrari's product line as for most of the current customers, the roaring engine is one of the core parts of the brand identity. By combining cutting-edge technology with its storied heritage, Ferrari is likely to continue attracting both its traditional clientele and a new generation of wealthy, younger consumers who value both luxury and innovation. As long as Ferrari continues to evolve while staying true to its roots and DNA, it will remain a symbol of ultimate luxury for decades to come.

4.1.7 Exclusivity: Expression of hierarchy

Another aspect of a luxury brand is its exclusivity, which is associated with the Veblen effect, which describes an increase in demand when the price of certain goods increases (see Chapter 3 for more detail). Veblen attributes the consumer's willingness to pay a higher price for a product with the same functional value (e.g. another product that has a lower price point) to an effort to point out his or her wealth and social status (Veblen, 1899/2003). According to the Cambridge Dictionary, exclusivity means "the right to have or do something that is limited to only one person or organization" or "the quality of being available only to a small number of people who are rich enough or considered good enough" or "the state of being expensive and of a high quality, and therefore only for people who are rich or of a high social class" (Cambridge Dictionary, 2023). However, the brand of the handbag not only refers to the income of its wearer but also expresses her cultural and professional orientation and creates and expresses a hierarchical difference from others. For men, a similar role is often played by watch brand. The exclusivity of brands hierarchically divides wearers into "clubs," as luxury is the enemy of equality, according to Kapferer and Bastien (2012).

Luxury brand strategies must work hard to maintain and build a semblance of exclusivity. However, it is difficult for new brands in the luxury field to **draw the line between the level of exclusivity and the sales volume that would lead them to profitability**. Even before expanding the exclusive club of the brand, it is necessary to work on building a certain degree of unavailability, which is the source of desire.

Limited availability and scarcity are the cornerstones of luxury and are aspects that help justify their price premium. The feeling of exclusivity should be maintained at all customer points of contact, which requires a specific location, excellent product presentation and qualified sales staff. Maintaining the exclusivity of luxury brands is challenging in terms of how to deal with the internet, which is based on the principles of democracy and accessibility and is ubiquitous. How can luxury brands combine a sense of exclusivity with the potential of the internet? Real luxury is available to few people, but many want it, and all marketing communication of luxury brands is by definition in the spectrum between affordability and exclusivity.

Luxury brands should use the internet to spread the brand dream and attract new consumers but still maintain a sense of exclusivity by offering selective online content and services to the brand's traditional customers. In a brick-and-mortar store, the high aesthetics of luxury products are presented in an exclusive shopping atmosphere full of multisensory experiences that appeal to people's emotions. Combining the traditional image of a luxury brand with the use of innovative technologies is indeed a key challenge (Hennigs et al., 2012), as discussed in the subchapter devoted to online communication of luxury brands.

4.1.8 Art in luxury: We are setting the taste of the future

The connection of luxury with art comes from history, from sacred art. Religious temples were full of art, and religious rituals were accompanied by the use of art objects created by the best artists of the time. The sacred dimension of art, through the uplifting of souls with which it was associated, remains to this day. The church and the nobility supported artists for the construction and decoration of churches, temples and palaces, where art could be admired by the privileged as well as reached by the general population. Thanks to the support of the nobility and the church, valuable works have been preserved to this day. The accumulation of material wealth was to encourage and offer elevation through intangible possessions – here art – to all (Kapferer & Bastien, 2012).

Art, in its essence, tends towards eternity: the work will outlive its creator and, in time, his or her epoch. Luxury thus tries to signal that it is not a simple product and lightens the commercial character of the luxury business. Luxury brands are often associated with innovation, exclusivity and trendsetting. Modern art, with its emphasis on new ideas, experimental approaches and cutting-edge techniques, aligns well with these values. Supporting modern art allows these brands to project an image of being at the forefront of cultural and artistic movements.

Luxury brands hold exhibitions of modern art worldwide, and some of their works – such as jewelry pieces or watches – are themselves objects of art. In 2014, the LVMH Group opened the Fondation Louis Vuitton in Paris, designed by architect Frank Gehry, which, in addition to large exhibitions of modern art, also presents exhibitions dedicated to great art personalities and contemporary scenes in France and around the world. No less important is the Fondation pour l'Art Contemporain by Cartier, Gucci Foundation and others.

Local culture is important when, for example, designing the new stores. Louis Vuitton's flagship store design in Osaka, Japan, incorporating curved glass sails designed by architects Jun Aoki & Associates and Peter Marino, is based on the sails of old Japanese merchant ships (Picture 4.4) to celebrate the city's history as an essential port (Astbury, 2020). The architecture delicately connects the brand DNA linked to traveling with the local culture.

The democratization of the luxury market through mass production, or cheaper entry into the sector through less expensive accessories, requires keeping the myth of handicrafts, respectful of tradition. Associations with artists in the galleries of LVMH Richemont and others is a way to reinforce the aura of exclusivity associated with each brand (Fondation Louis Vuitton, 2022). Additionally, modern artworks have shown significant investment potential with increasing value over time. Luxury brands may also view their support of modern art as a strategic investment. Luxury customers may see the purchase of some luxury items as an investment too.

Picture 4.4 Cotton Transport Ships Racing to Edo Set Sail from the Mouth of Aji River in Osaka, by Gansuitei-Yoshitoyo, circa 1855. By Artanisen. Public domain, available at (Wikimedia Commons, 2021)

Mini-case 4.3 Van Cleef & Arpels: Ballet as part of the luxury brand's identity

Part of the identity of the Van Cleef & Arpels, a jewelry brand of the Richemont Group, with a history since 1906, has been ballet. The founder of the brand and an avid ballet fan, Louis Arpels, used to take his nephew to the Paris Opera. Ballet dancers became the inspiration for the first collection of brooches depicting ballerinas from the 1940s; this has become a distinctive creation of the Van Cleef & Arpels workshop (Richemont, 2022; Van Cleef & Arpels, 2022). The silhouette of Anna Pavlova, famous ballerina, was one of the many inspirations for the design of the brooches (The Adventurine, 2024) (Picture 4.5). The contemporary elite still honor the *Maison's* heritage. For example, Queen Camilla added a Van Cleef & Arpels glittering ballerina brooch to her dress when she visited the English National Ballet at the Mulryan Centre for Dance in London in 2024 (WWD, 2024).

Figures of ballerinas with pink diamond faces complemented by a precious headband are depicted with pointed shoes and a tutu skirt of diamonds or colored stones, which seem to flow and reflect the dancers' movements, and attract collectors to this day. In 1961, Claude Arpels met New York City Ballet co-founder choreographer George Balanchine, and their shared passion

Picture 4.5 Anna Pavlova. By Mr.Nostalgic, public domain. Available at (Wikimedia Commons, 2024a).

for gemstones gave rise to the ballet named *Jewels* in 1967. The ballet triptych is inspired by emeralds, rubies and diamonds; each of the gems takes center stage during one act, and each part contains music by a different composer: Gabriel Fauré for Emeralds, Igor Stravinsky for Rubies and Pyotr Ilyich Tchaikovsky for Diamonds (Van Cleef & Arpels, 2022).

Today, ballet is still part of the brand's identity. In 2020, the brand launched the "Dance Reflections by Van Cleef & Arpels" initiative, which supports artists and institutions with choreographic repertoire and also aims to promote new productions and contemporary dance.

Since 2012, the brand has supported the L'École School of Jewelry Arts at Place Vendôme in Paris, which presents the world of jewelry, its history and role in different civilizations and cultures, to the general public in Paris, Tokyo, New York, Dubai and Hong Kong through lectures, exhibitions and courses related to jewelry production (L'ÉCOLE School of Jewelry Arts, 2022).

The Van Cleef & Arpels jewelry house has important milestones in the history of jewelry; in other words, it has something to show and build on. For example, in 1967, the crown by Van Cleef & Arpels was part of the coronation ceremony of the Shah of Iran (Picture 4.6). The Shah and the monarchy were then presented as revolutionaries and reformists but also as defenders of tradition. The ceremony was inspired by the coronation of Queen Elizabeth II in 1953. However, European influence was nowhere as noticeable as in the role and appearance of Queen Farah, for whom a new crown had to be created. The organizers chose from 50 designs of the greatest jewelers of the time and decided on a design by Van Cleef & Arpels. The imposing crown was set with 36 emeralds, 34 rubies, 2 spinels, 105 pearls and 1,469 diamonds from the royal treasury and weighed almost 1.5 kilograms (Steele, 2021).

Since 2019, L'École School of Jewelry Arts has had a physical permanent branch in Hong Kong under the name L'École Asia-Pacific. According to Nicolas Bose, the

Picture 4.6 Imperial Empress Crown. By Kei, public domain. Available at (Wikimedia Commons, 2014a).

brand's president at the time, the school's main purpose is to educate consumers about jewelry, even if they cannot afford to buy gemstones: "L'École's primary role is to provide access to knowledge and education. It is an opportunity to become an expert and learn. You appreciate what you know and understand more." Because just like in art, if you know what to look at, you will appreciate it more (L'ÉCOLE School of Jewelry Arts, 2022; La Torre, 2019).

4.1.9 Charity and cause related marketing in luxury

It is already an established rule that luxury brands contribute to charity and do it publicly. At present, brand altruism is part of a social responsibility strategy, which has other sustainability pillars in addition to charity or donation. These are discussed further in the chapter related to sustainability. Purely philanthropic projects are usually not communicated by individual luxury brands at the point of sale but are carried out within the umbrella group. Even purely philanthropic projects have a broader subtext of social responsibility. Dior creative director Maria Grazia Chiuri, for example, involved a young South African designer Thebe Maguga, who won the LVMH Young Designers Award in 2019, to create a limited collection of contemporary interpretations of the original New Look collection from the 1940s. On behalf of Dior, LVMH also contributed to the projects of long-time Dior brand ambassador Charlize Theron in the Africa Outreach Project (CTAOP). The aim is not only to financially support the organization for the benefit of young people in the region on behalf of the Dior brand, but it also has an artistic component in that it provides an opportunity for young artists (LVMH, 2022).

Cause-related marketing (CRM), a strategy consisting of cooperation between the brand and a non-profit organization, where it is not only about philanthropy but also about supporting brand sales, is also applied in the luxury sector. Luxury brands have started to cooperate with well-known non-profit organizations in recent decades, but the pioneers in this area are FMCG manufacturers – typically Unilever, Coca Cola, P&G and so on. By partnering with an established, credible organization, they avoid the risk of bringing social issues into the very identity of a luxury brand, while at the same time giving them the necessary scope to produce special collections of clothing or jewelry in a value that can really contribute to improvement in the selected projects. Communication usually occurs only at the point of sale, on the web and through public relations.

Research suggests that with regard to the identity of the luxury brand itself, two types of campaigns can be successfully applied in cause-related marketing (Kim et al., 2022):

1. **Campaigns characterized by direct donations,** where the customer pays a contribution to the charitable cause at the point of sale and that is included in the price of the product. This is how Louis Vuitton started working with UNICEF in 2016. Among the initiatives taken under the partnership, Louis Vuitton has listed a collection of specially designed Silver Lockit jewelry, and donates up to $200 to UNICEF for each Silver Lockit pendant or bracelet purchased. Every year, a new version of the bracelet is introduced, which is inspired by the mansion invented by Georges Vuitton in 1890, chosen as a symbol to seal the brand's promise to help children in need. The design of the 2022 collection was created by (at that time) LVMH designer Virgil Abloh. From the beginning of the cooperation through 2023, the company raised $20 million, donated to UNICEF (Louis Vuitton, 2022a; UNICEF, 2022).
2. **Product campaigns associated with limited editions of the partner organization.** These types of campaigns are often very successful in generating positive publicity for luxury brands,

and they work better for materialistic clients who are more willing to engage in product-related projects than directly with charity. Products usually have a visible brand (logo, slogan) that associates the product with a charitable cause. These limited editions allow consumers not only to signal status through the luxury product itself but also to make their socially beneficial behavior visible through a highly visible link to a well-known partner organization. Since 2009, Bulgari has partnered with the charity Save the Children to raise money to expand educational programs by selling a limited collection of partner jewelry. More than half a million people have already bought a ring, bracelet or pendant from the collection. By wearing jewelry and spreading the campaign slogan *Stop, Think, Give* via social media, about 250 celebrities supported the program's communication. From the start of the collaboration to the end of 2022, Bulgari has raised over $100 million through jewelry sales. These funds have been invested in approximately 120 projects to help more than 2 million vulnerable children and youth through programs to support education, emergency assistance, poverty reduction and youth empowerment (Save the Children, 2022).

In summary, limited-edition luxury products in product-linked campaigns usually feature a visible marker that connects them to a charitable cause. These products enable consumers to display both their status and their prosocial behavior. This marketing strategy appeals to luxury consumers' self-enhancement motives by showing they spend money in a socially valued way (Sukhyun et al., 2022).

4.2 The anti-laws of luxury: Proven over time

The previous section outlines how the strategy of luxury brands differs from that of premium brands. For premium brands, manufacturers promise better product performance at higher prices, but at the end of the day, these brands chase customers through special offers or discounts to meet business and, above all, volume targets. However, a luxury strategy requires customers to chase a brand that has a very strong and artistic nature of the offering. And, like art, luxury has a timeless quality because its value far exceeds its performance and functional values. The goal of a luxury strategy is to create incomparability. Just as it is impossible to compare the landscape paintings of Camille Pissarro and Alfred Sisley, the client does not compare Tiffany and Cartier jewelry, nor Patek Philippe and Vacheron Constantin watches. The reason for the incomparability is the roots of the brands, their history, heritage, art, know-how and creativity, which in any case are so different that the comparison does not make sense to a luxury customer (Bastien & Kapferer, 2013).

Building a luxury brand is about creating and staying in the dream of the target consumer. It is also about maintaining a symbolic gap between brands that copy luxury brands while following a different business model – premium, mass brands. The anti-laws of luxury (Table 4.1) contain 24 management principles proven over time by the most valuable luxury brands (Kapferer & Bastien, 2012):

4.2.1 Incomparability: Luxury is superlative, not comparative

The anti-laws #1, #2 and #17 exclude comparisons from luxury brand management. Traditional brand positioning defining a key brand promise to differentiate it from the competitors does not apply in luxury. It is impossible to compare the cultures and heritage of individual brands. Brands work with their identity and either have it or they don't, but they don't define themselves against the competition. In premium brands, as opposed to luxury

Table 4.1 24 Anti-laws of luxury, adapted from (Kapferer & Bastien, 2012, pp. 65–84).

1	Luxury is incomparable; forget about positioning.	Positioning, in terms of defining key brand promises, does not apply to a given target group in luxury. It is impossible to compare the cultures and heritage of individual brands. Brands work with their identity and either have it or they don't, but they don't define themselves against the competition. Luxury is superlative, not comparative.
2	The luxury product is defective.	The perfect product is serial and belongs in the FMCG market. A luxury brand is not necessarily the top in practicality or functional values, and their error rate, usually stemming from manual production, is a source of emotions for clients. However, artificially introducing errors into a premium product does not make it a luxury product.
3	Don't pander to customers.	In direct contrast to the "customer is king" rule in FMCG marketing, where listening to customers creates new products, a luxury brand is built with the long-term vision of the creators and its identity with extreme care for the product, but it goes its own way regardless of the wishes of customers.
4	Keep your distance from customers who are not passionate about the brand.	FMCG brands grow by penetrating customer segments in which there is a stronger competitive brand. Luxury brands grow by penetrating new geographic markets, since "poaching" among customers of other luxury brands would only dilute their values.
5	Do not respond to growing demand.	Traditional marketing driven by meeting volume targets responds promptly to growing demand, the failure of which to satisfy would affect the customer experience with the brand. In luxury, rarity or inaccessibility is not a sign of poor planning. When a new product sells too much, production and availability must be reduced. In the event of extremely high demand for a product, respond by discontinuing it.
6	Dominate the client.	Luxury stratifies society – previously according to who was born to whom, today according to abilities (aristocracy vs. meritocracy). A luxury brand must dominate the client as a parent is dominant over their child. Brand = advisor, educator and social guide.
7	Make it difficult for the client to make a purchase.	A luxury product needs to be earned. Longer waiting times increase the desire for the brand. Immediate availability through intensive distribution of FMCG products is the opposite of the rarity that limited distribution creates for a luxury brand.
8	Separate clients from non-clients.	Separate loyal, privileged customers from others. Separate lounges in stores, selective invitations to events with designers or perfumers and so on. Parallel to the separation of first and economy class in travel, where airlines ensure that passengers do not meet at all during the journey, including during their stay at the airport.
9	The goal of advertising is not to sell.	Creativity in advertising creates the dream of a brand. Just as a brand does not have positioning, it does not have key benefits for interpretation in advertising. Advertising creates a dream in accordance with the brand identity. A brand's cultural heritage can be interpreted in advertising in a surprising, distracting way so as not to come across as old-fashioned.

(Continued)

Table 4.1 (Continued)

10	Communicate with those you're not targeting.	There are fundamentally more customers who never buy a luxury brand than clients. Luxury brand awareness has a much wider consumer base than potential or actual users of the brand. If someone does not recognize the brand on the bearer, it is a loss of part of the value of the purchase of the brand bearer. That's why brands build a wide awareness beyond the target group.
11	The presumed price is always higher than the real one.	In luxury, the price is talked about in the last place. Brands should not communicate prices even as part of the photo stories of luxury magazines (better = "price information in the boutique"). The aura of a luxury brand causes people to expect a higher price for a product than the real one, which further increases the value of the brand in the eyes of both clients and non-clients.
12	Luxury is the creator of price, but prices do not create luxury.	Fast-moving marketing is looking for a gap in the market for a new product or a place on the price map to locate the product most advantageously with regard to competing products. A luxury product is designed, manufactured, and the more it is demanded by clients, the higher its price should be.
13	To increase demand, increase the price.	There is no reasonableness of prices in luxury, because there is no analogy or comparability. Proportionality would lead to the reduction of the product to a tangible item, but in luxury the intangible dimension is more valuable. See Chanel's pricing policy mentioned earlier. A price increase may force some customers to leave, but it will reassure others, who might not come, to make the right choice.
14	Constantly increase the average price of the entire assortment.	Traditional brands usually skim the cream of the market through a pricing strategy until competitors enter and force them to decrease prices in order to increase volumes. In luxury, it's the opposite. The growth in volume is related to the growth of world wealth and the search for new wealthy clients in different regions who are looking for a way to reward themselves and for a symbol to show their wealth.
15	Do not sell.	By its very nature, a luxury brand should be so attractive that it doesn't need any of the aggressive sales techniques known from FMCG. The customer's experience of the brand story submitted by the sales assistant at the store point is sufficient, without sales pressure. True luxury brands never give discounts.
16	Leave the stars out of your ad.	A star celebrity who has no brand affiliation can disrupt our brand dominance (anti-law #6), as they too are potential customers. Moreover, it may suggest that a brand needs to benefit from celebrity status because it doesn't have one.
17	Cultivate closeness to art for the initiated.	Traditional marketing follows people's tastes, but luxury brands create it, just like art. That is why they are looking for and supporting young artists and designers who have potential but who are not in line with the current majority taste. Large luxury groups often exhibit modern art or collaborate with young artists.
18	Do not relocate your factories.	Part of the identity of a luxury brand is often the culture of the country from which it comes. Moving production to countries with cheaper labor erodes the identity of the brand,

(Continued)

Table 4.1 (Continued)

		interrupting the close contact of designers and artists with production, with materials or with craftsmen (unless it is a matter of access to limited processing, like wool from Kashmir, for example).
19	Do not hire consultants.	Drawing on best practice examples of brand and corporate management, consultants can damage the specific characteristics of a luxury brand. The added value of primary data is generally lower in luxury because brands are building a dream, and this is not a question that is answered by respondents of the best samples in a way that is useful for the brand.
20	Do not test.	If a luxury brand were to test new products on consumers, for example, it would mean that their product corresponds to consumers' tastes. But the luxury brand itself is an educator of the tastes of clients. Another obstacle to luxury testing is the selection of a sample of respondents, respectively the criteria for their selection and the willingness of luxury customers to participate in surveys.
21	Don't seek consensus.	Testing would imply a search for consensus. In luxury, for example, campaigns or products that are originally considered provocative and that would not see the light of day due to the search for consensus are successful (e.g. Angel, the most successful perfume of the previous 20 years). Testing and consensus only dilute the process of building a luxury brand.
22	Don't look for group synergies.	Groups such as LVMH and Richemont maintain their independence in managing brands, which is the only way not to erode their identities. On the contrary, synergies in planning, purchasing raw materials or media are a strategic advantage of groups.
23	No to cost reduction.	In the luxury industry, value creation is a watchword, but it must not be balanced by finding ways to reduce costs. Dialogue between the workshop, craftsmen, artists and designers as well as sales staff and brand managers can lead to cost optimization. The process is different from traditional marketing, where the CFO determines the size of the reduction and R&D looks for recipes, tests them and replaces the product with a cheaper one.
24	Careful with e-commerce.	Luxury needs time, interaction between the brand representative and the client, the feeling of being part of an exclusive brand club. Some brands are still cautious, but most of the luxury brands are already active in the online shopping space. Caution in maintaining brand identity is appropriate, but seizing e-commerce as an opportunity to offer additional services to existing customers or as a form of entry into the brand for new clients is part of the distribution strategy of most brands.

brands, the more you pay, the more you get. And you get products without flaws, unlike in luxury. The luxury product is defective. The perfect product is serial and belongs to the FMCG or premium market. A luxury brand is not necessarily the top in practicality or functional values, and the **error rate, usually stemming from manual production, is a source of emotions, charm and a guarantee of authenticity** for clients. For example, luxury mechanical watches with many complications will never be as accurate as a plastic Swatch. Ferrari was built for speed, power and design, not comfort. However, artificially introducing errors into a premium product does not make it a luxury product.

Traditional marketing follows people's tastes, but luxury brands create it, just like art. That is why they are looking for and supporting young artists and designers who have potential but who are not in line with the current majority taste. Large luxury groups often exhibit modern art or collaborate with young artists. Premium or mass brands tend to support pop art or artists that are admired and known by a majority of consumers. They search for a match between tastes, while luxury brands search for extravagance to show their visions.

One of the most known collaborations is with renowned artists Louis Vuitton and Yayoi Kusama. Kusama helped shape the vibrant and diverse art scene of the 1990s, redefining artistic norms with her pioneering techniques and daring expressions (Art in Context, 2024). Renowned for her immersive installations and signature polka-dot patterns, Kusama's art delves into themes of infinity, identity and the human experience – qualities that make her collaboration with Louis Vuitton a seamless fusion of high fashion and avant-garde art (Picture 4.7).

The initial collaboration from 2012 was followed by a second collection in 2023. She is known for her immersive works originating from personal obsessions and hallucinations, expressed by otherworldly sculptures, paintings and public art. Louis Vuitton's Cruise 2023 show featured bags, leather goods and limited-edition perfumes, all with the artist's signature flowers, pumpkins and dot art. Louis Vuitton's vitrines in the leading global shopping streets were decorated with Kusama's artwork. Harrods in London, for example, introduced Kusama's interactive dot and mirror art out to high street, and the store has been reimagined as an experiential art playground (Harrods, 2023).

Picture 4.7 Public art of Yayoi Kusama – Pumpkin with polka dot pattern installed by the Round Pond, in Kensington Gardens in Autumn 2024. Source: authors' photo.

4.2.2 Chasing the dream: How to remain at a close distance but not widely accessible?

In luxury marketing, maintaining a sense of exclusivity and distance from the customers is crucial (anti-laws #3–10 and #15–16). Luxury brands should prioritize their creators' long-term vision over responding to customer demands, carefully curating their identity. The premium or mass brands tend to prefer short-term vision and sales targets. Luxury should avoid pandering to non-passionate customers and prefer to grow by exploring new geographic or demographic markets rather than competing with other luxury brands, which could dilute their values. Just like the sixth-generation member of the family who founded Hermès, Axel Dumas, said: "We are Hermès, and we create desire for our clients" (Style, 2014).

Luxury brands tend to limit product availability to maintain an aura of rarity and exclusivity (anti-law #5) and are advised to reduce production or discontinue it if a product becomes too popular. This contrasts sharply with the traditional marketing approach, which always aims to meet growing demand.

Additionally, luxury brands position themselves as dominant figures in their customers' lives, much like a parent guides a child, offering advice, education and social cues. The purchasing process is made intentionally tricky, as the challenge increases the perceived value and desire for the product. Exclusive experiences and privileges are reserved for loyal customers, creating a clear distinction between clients and non-clients. Some brands, including Chanel (Picture 4.8), for example, create separate lounges for loyal customers to protect them from the queues outside the stores.

Picture 4.8 Gabrielle Chanel. By Maitane Azurmendi. Available under the Creative Commons Attribution-Share Alike 4.0 International license at (Wikimedia Commons, 2023).

Advertising for luxury brands focuses on **creating an aspirational dream** rather than direct sales, using creativity to convey the brand's cultural heritage in surprising and engaging ways. Advertising typically feeds on sustained myths, mystery and art. Advertising is perceived rather as an education, far away from the sales promotion which is typical for mainstream or premium brands. Furthermore, luxury brands communicate broadly to ensure wide recognition, even among those who may never purchase their products. Building broad brand awareness enhances the brand's value for actual buyers, as the recognition of the brand by others adds to the prestige of owning a luxury item.

The star of a luxury advertisement is the brand itself. A star celebrity who has no brand affiliation can disrupt the brand dominance. Moreover, it may suggest that a brand needs to benefit from celebrity status because it doesn't have one. Selected celebrities should be used carefully as symbols in symbiosis with the brand.

By its very nature, a luxury brand should be so attractive that it doesn't need any aggressive sales techniques known from FMCG. The customer's experience of the brand story submitted by the sales assistant at the store point is sufficient, without sales pressure. And finally, it should be evident that luxury brands with properly implemented luxury business strategies never give visible discounts.

4.2.3 Pricing: Continuous price increases of luxury items

In the luxury market, pricing follows distinct anti-laws (#11–14) that diverge from traditional marketing strategies. There is no reasonableness of prices in luxury because there is no analogy or comparability. A luxury brand's aura leads consumers to presume higher prices than the actual ones, thereby enhancing the brand's perceived value. Prices are discussed last (or not at all) and are usually displayed only in boutiques. Contrary to mainstream marketing practices, luxury products define their value. The price of the product is far above its functional value. This pricing strategy underscores the intangible value of luxury, focusing on exclusivity and brand prestige rather than comparability.

Constant price increases of the whole portfolio reassure high-end consumers of the product's worth, supporting their earlier purchase decisions. Unlike conventional brands that lower prices to boost volume or achieve given monthly/yearly sales targets, luxury brands continuously raise prices. They capitalize on global wealth growth and the desire of affluent clients to display their success and reward themselves. These anti-laws ensure that luxury brands maintain their exclusivity and allure amongst their customers.

FMCG marketing looks for a gap in the market for a new product or a place on the price map to locate the product most advantageously with regard to competing products. A luxury product is designed, adequately crafted and manufactured – and the more it is demanded by clients, the higher its price should be. This is why luxury customers pay €5,000 for the Hermès bag and €700 for a Coach bag. And even though €700 is still expensive, luxury exists because not everyone can afford it. Price is explained by **sharing mystery, spirit and the time** invested in producing legendary items. A price increase may force some customers to leave, but it will reassure others that they made the right choice. Companies that can increase the pricing of their lines continuously anchor the brand in roots and legend.

4.2.4 Art directors' brilliance stands above consultants and research

Luxury brands should **avoid relocating factories,** as this disrupts the brand's cultural identity and the vital connection between designers, materials and craftsmen. The country of origin

(COO) of luxury brands, despite slowly deteriorating by lower-tier luxury brands, remains vital for consumers from developed and luxury-aspiring countries. The COO builds trust, symbolizes specific values, gives the feeling of prestige and uniqueness and provides information about product quality. European heritage countries like France, Italy and Switzerland are essential for many global luxury customers who are willing to pay more for the traditional authenticity of the products.

Hiring consultants can damage the unique characteristics of a luxury brand, as luxury thrives on creating dreams, not following standard corporate practices. And this is what the consultants do. They rely on producers' best practices in different product categories and benchmark brand performance to suggest forward strategies.

Testing products on consumers contradicts the role of luxury brands in educating client tastes, and the search for consensus can dilute brand identity, preventing innovative or provocative products from succeeding. Moreover, establishing a meaningful sample of respondents amongst luxury customers is almost impossible. Customers with investable assets above $1 million will hardly spend time filling out a questionnaire or answering questions during a research interview. Luxury brands invent the dreams of the elite and for the elite, not asking what they wish their dream to be about.

Luxury groups like LVMH and Richemont maintain brand independence of the brands in their portfolios to preserve identity, even while **leveraging strategic synergies in planning and procurement.** Cost reduction is not a priority in luxury; instead, value creation through collaboration among craftsmen, designers and brand managers is essential.

And finally, the last anti-law (#24) suggests that luxury brands should be **cautious with e-commerce.** Nowadays, brands recognize it as an opportunity to enhance services for existing clients and introduce the brand to new customers, ensuring it complements the exclusive luxury experience at brick-and-mortar boutiques or flagship stores. Luxury needs time, interaction between the brand representative and the client and the feeling of being part of an exclusive brand club. Some brands are still cautious about selling their entire portfolios online, but most luxury brands are already active in the online shopping space. **Caution in maintaining brand identity is appropriate,** but seizing e-commerce as an opportunity to offer additional services to existing customers or a form of entry into the brand for new clients is part of the distribution strategy of most brands. The internet should be handled as a complementary service for existing customers to initiate the brand story, mainly because the advantages of internet sales in terms of easy accessibility are disadvantages for luxury and exclusivity of the brands' offers.

4.2.5 Luxury brand legends: The intersection with art and religion

True luxury is (and has always been) a way to escape the ordinary and become extraordinary in a world built on pleasure, craftsmanship, art, beauty and culture. The anti-laws of luxury must be considered in management, like crossing a red light at an intersection. It is better to stop and think, but sometimes, we get through it unscathed and with considerable risk.

The management of luxury brands has many intersections with art and religion. Parallel to religion, luxury brands develop:

- Their myths and legends (stories, brand legacy, brand history, perhaps in a disruptive way);
- Brand heroes (often the founder or creative designer);
- Mysteries, magic and avoidance of rational explanations;

- Icons, symbols;
- Celebrations (opportunities for organizing important events);
- Temples (flagship stores); and
- Community management to promote faith (that's why social media is important).

(Bastien & Kapferer, 2013)

Similarly, in parallel to art, luxury brands are looking for uniqueness, exclusivity and creativity so that, like art, their value and the price of individual products grow. Luxury designers, heroes of the brand, must be celebrated as artists whose touch turns every piece of clothing into a piece of art.

The Dior brand myth, as an example, was celebrated during Paris Fashion Week – Dior's Autumn Winter 2023 show was directed by the visionary art director Maria Grazia Chiuri, featuring a striking 24-meter-long installation by Portuguese artist Joana Vasconcelos. The artwork, entitled *Valkyrie Miss Dior*, showcased Chiuri's refined taste for integrating art with fashion, using intricate textile structures that complemented the runway with fabrics from the collection. The collection was inspired by and paid homage to Christian Dior's sister Catherine, who was collaborating with the French Resistance during World War II. After her return from the concentration camp, she dedicated a lot of time to gardening flowers – the brand code of the Dior brand since then ("Christian Dior" Rose as an example in Picture 4.9). This collaboration highlighted the seamless blend between haute couture and visual arts, celebrating both fashion and craftsmanship (Dezeen, 2023) as illustrated by the extravagant floral motives.

Luxury clients can appreciate art and understand the value of beauty, although there are differences between them and especially between their motivations in the luxury sector; these are outlined in the next section.

4.2.6 Brand identity prism: The key to branding in luxury is linked to the anti-laws

An important part of branding in luxury is the brand identity prism. Luxury brands are incomparable; therefore, there is no relevant brand management tool, such as brand

Picture 4.9 Rose "Christian Dior." By Nerve net under the Creative Commons Attribution-Share Alike 4.0 International license. Available at (Wikimedia Commons, 2024b).

positioning, to help assign the brand a clear competitive advantage. For a luxury brand, it is a unique identity that embraces the style and taste of the brand's founder and passes it on to future generations or followers in the event of an interruption in artistic management. A comprehensive view of brand identity is provided by Kapferer's prism, which depicts the six edges (or facets) of the physical and personality traits of the brand, illustrated in Figure 4.1 using the example of Chanel brand.

The brand's identity includes its history, know-how and mysticism; it contains everything that makes it unique. Like positioning for mass brands, brand identity should have long-term durability, as it summarizes all the internal factors of the brand. When combined, they express a brand that is valuable, unique, rare and without the possibility of simply being imitated.

The prism of Chanel's brand identity (Figure 4.1) carries many of Gabrielle Chanel's personal characteristics, such as style, heritage and the identity and image of the customer who buys the brand. Gabrielle was a strong woman who climbed the social ladder thanks to her diligence and talent; her career was unimaginable for many women at that time. Wide, white staircases usually connect the floors of Chanel boutiques worldwide, symbolizing Chanel's climb up the social ladder. Gabrielle freed women from corsets; dressed them in comfortable, stylish clothes; and completely changed the way women dressed. This became comfortable and Parisian chic at the same time, and such clothes are still produced today.

A well-known and visible physical symbol of Chanel is black and white – symbols of masculinity and femininity, which she masterfully combined in her collections. Chanel's clients are usually women who identify with her symbol of independence, strength and success. They are successful and powerful or aspire to be. In advertising campaigns, Chanel models

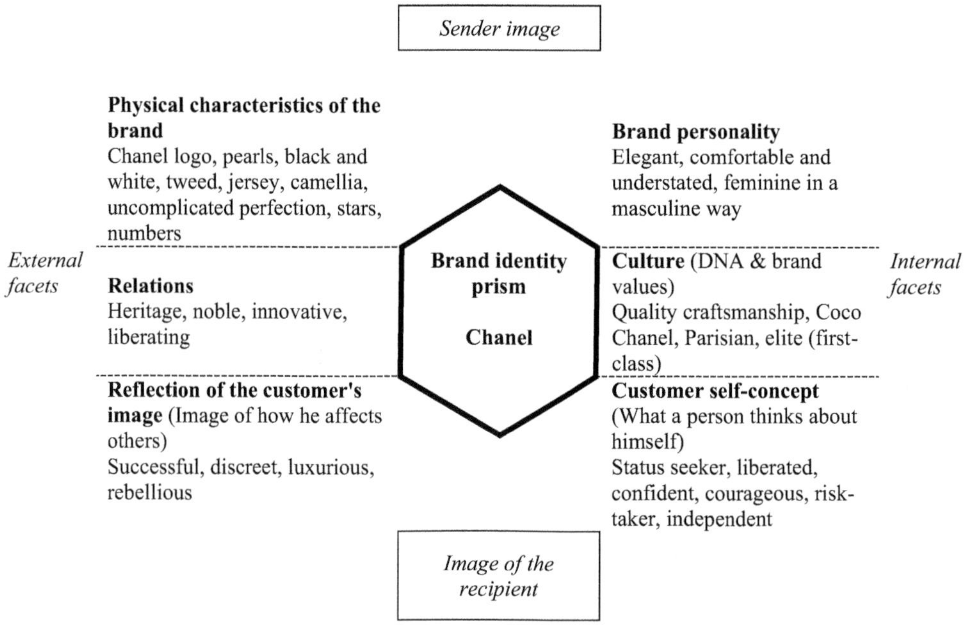

Figure 4.1 Identity prism using the example of the Chanel brand; authors' adaptation based on (Som & Blanckaert, 2021, p. 141; Kapferer & Bastien, 2012).

look like women who know who they are and are ready to achieve their goals (Som & Blanckaert, 2021).

A set of attributes within the **facet of physical brand characteristics** allows customers to recognize the brand without seeing the logo. It's a set of codes, artistic signatures, gestures, colors or properties that connect a customer to a brand. At the Chanel fashion show, the brand can be identified even without a double C on the label through touches of classic design, fabric quality, the use of jersey, pearls, black and white combinations, white camellias and so forth. In other words, **brand codes visually represents the DNA of the brand.**

A brand's personality is usually based on the **personality of its founder** and his/her character traits, which the brand inherits or completes. Thus, the personality of the brand expresses the qualities of a natural person. At Chanel, it's about subtle elegance and comfort. Yves Saint Laurent gave his brand an impertinent, provocative, seductive and unapproachable character. The brand's personality simply describes the brand as if it were an existing person.

The following two facets relate to the created image of the recipient. **The image of the customer** is reflected in the view of the consumer through the external mirror – how do others see the woman with a Chanel handbag? As a successful, luxurious and discreet woman. Yves Saint Laurent is perceived as a femme fatale. The facet **of the customer's self-concept** can be understood as an inner mirror (as opposed to the outer mirror in the facet of the reflection of the customer's image). In some sources, this facet is called brand mentalization. How does a brand consumer see him- or herself? Chanel customers see and feel like a free woman, who is confident, courageous and risk-taking. A customer of Yves Saint Lauren sees herself as a seductive, sexy and provocative woman.

The cultural facet or DNA of a brand is an essential part of its identity, as it creates a kind of cult around the brand and its values with its followers. What is the essence of a brand that feeds its values and its inspiration? Chanel is based on quality craftsmanship, Gabrielle Chanel's personality, first-class Parisian chic and elite fashion. Traditional luxury brands usually stem from their creators, the founders. Louis Vuitton's DNA is based on the traditional luggage with the monogram LV, although the brand has expanded over time into

Picture 4.10 White camelia – Chanel's brand code. By Rennett Stowe. Available under the Creative Commons Attribution 2.0 Generic license at (Wikimedia Commons, 2009).

various accessories, clothing and shoes. Rolex's DNA encompasses three core values: timelessness, sport and adventure and reliability. The successors of founder Hans Wildorf, the Heininger family, maintain the relevance of his brand's heritage in a way that is relevant to today's society. **The relationship facet** defines the relationship between a brand and its consumers. Chanel freed women from corsets, and her legacy still gives them confidence (Kapferer & Bastien, 2012; Som & Blanckaert, 2021).

Figure 4.2 illustrates how each facet of the prism can be linked to specific anti-laws in luxury marketing, showcasing the strategic alignment between brand exclusivity and

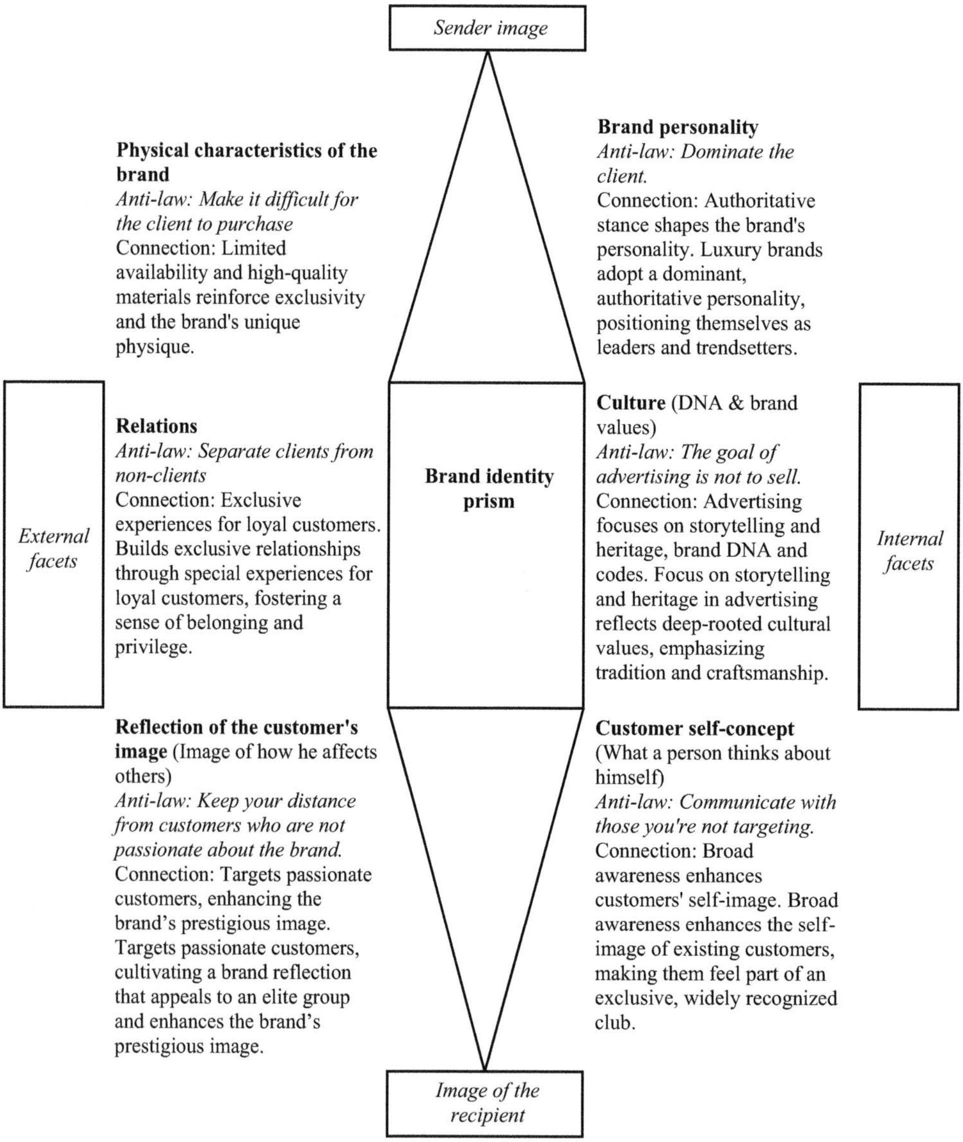

Figure 4.2 Brand identity prism linked to the anti-laws; authors.

identity. The connection between the prism and the anti-laws in luxury marketing is significant because both frameworks focus on defining and maintaining a luxury brand's identity and exclusivity. Understanding this connection helps luxury brands align their marketing strategies with their brand identity to create a cohesive and compelling brand image. Therefore, Figure 4.2 provides a deeper look into the logic and relevance.

The fundamental challenge for luxury brands is to nurture an identity that has been maintained for decades or even centuries while remaining relevant, inspiring and desirable in the face of societal socio-economic and cultural changes and challenges. The combination of all six facets of the brand identity prism is an essential tool for creating or revising the unique identity of a luxury brand. However, it is only a managerial tool, and the content must be made with regard to the other specifics of luxury brand management.

4.3 Summary: Specifics of luxury brand management – Don't ruin the dream

Just as the individual facets of a brand's identity prism must harmonize with each other, a successful luxury brand must also take care of other aspects. Of those that need to be mentioned in the conclusion, there is undoubtedly quality, which is absolutely necessary to meet customer expectations. Any innovation based on traditional craftsmanship must match the culture and DNA of the brand. This does not mean that everyone can be satisfied. There is no need for this in the luxury sector, as the anti-law of luxury #3 says – do not pander to clients. The customer here is not the king; the brand is the queen, and it is necessary to take care of her with royal attention.

Communication in the luxury sector aims to make the brand the object of customers' dreams. The number of luxury customers is growing and there are different perspectives on segmentation, but regardless of consumer diversity, the main goal remains to build dreams. A dream may trigger buying behavior, but too much shopping will ruin the dream – no one will dream of something everyone else has. In the event of a large increase in demand, it is necessary to limit supply in accordance with anti-law #5 and maintain the level of dreaming so that the percentage of brand awareness moves as far away as possible from the percentage of brand penetration – or increase prices. As in other sectors, luxury is all about striking the right balance between different aspects of managing it.

In a nutshell, **the essentials of luxury business strategy** consist of: (1) **total control of the value chain** by luxury houses, preferably with no relocation of the factories unless it is totally impossible due to some rare circumstances associated with transportation issues; (2) absolute **control of distribution** with preferably directly owned and operated points of purchase; (3) **unique *savoir-faire*** or craftmanship is what makes luxury products unique and hard to replicate; (4) a **personal relationship** with the customers and unique experience, which is offered to them by the brand when shopping; (5) a luxury product should be at least partially **handmade**; (6) luxury brands should be **careful with brand extensions or licensing** the brand's credentials to products that are relatively more affordable; (7) **brand heritage** is what makes the brand incomparable, and it should be cultivated and communicated; and finally, (8) a luxury brand should be able to continuously, year on year, **increase its pricing**. The combination of this strategic guidance will sustain the incomparability of the brand.

Key terms

Artistic Collaboration: Partnerships between luxury brands and artists to enhance brand perception, emphasize creativity and position the brand as a cultural and taste trendsetter.

Anti-Laws of Luxury: Specific managerial tenets that luxury firms adhere to, such as exclusivity, scarcity, incomparability. These are counter to conventional marketing strategies.

Brand Codes: Visual interpretation of the brand's DNA.

Brand DNA: The core values, culture and history that shape a luxury brand's identity. DNA makes each brand unique, relates to brand stories and the founder's personality and is often related to the period when the brand was established.

Brand Identity Prism: A model that outlines a brand's physical characteristics, personality, relationship with customers and cultural values, especially relevant in luxury branding for capturing the brand's entire identity.

Craftsmanship/*Savoir-faire*: A crucial aspect of luxury brands, emphasizing the high-quality and often handmade production process that differentiate luxury goods from mass-market items.

Emotional Appeal: The powerful feelings luxury brands evoke in their consumers, such as desire, status and satisfaction. The emotional benefit that goes beyond the functionality of the product.

Exclusivity: A sense of privilege created by limited access to luxury products or experiences, enhancing a brand's desirability.

Heritage and Tradition in Luxury: Luxury value refers to the rich history and cultural significance of the brand including the founder's personality and *savoir-faire*, adding to their perceived value and prestige.

Incomparability: Luxury brands often avoid direct comparisons with other brands due to incomparable brand identities resulting from their heritage and stories, positioning themselves as unique and incomparable to reinforce exclusivity.

Luxury Business Strategy: Refers to the unique strategies required to maintain and grow luxury brands, which differ from those used in mass marketing.

Rarity: A critical factor in luxury, where products are scarce by nature, design or components, thus adding value due to their limited availability.

Social Distancing: Refers to how luxury brands help establish social hierarchies, differentiating between those who can afford luxury items from those who cannot.

Discussion questions

1. What distinguishes luxury brand management from traditional marketing?
2. Why is craftsmanship important in luxury branding, and how does it contribute to a brand's value?
3. What does *incomparability* mean in luxury brand strategy?
4. What are the *anti-laws of luxury*, and why are they important for luxury brand management?
5. Why is heritage important to luxury brands, and how can newer luxury brands compensate for a lack of historical background?
6. What role does exclusivity play in the marketing strategy of luxury brands?
7. How do luxury brands leverage art and culture in their branding, and what benefits does this bring?

8. Why might a luxury brand avoid relocating its factories, and how does this decision affect its brand identity?
9. How do luxury brands balance tradition with the need to stay relevant in a rapidly changing market?

Reference list

The Adventurine. (2024). *The Story of Van Cleef & Arpels Ballerinas*. Retrieved Novembeer 2024, from theadventurine.com: https://theadventurine.com/culture/jewelry-history/the-story-of-van-cleef-arpels-ballerinas/

Art in Context. (2024, February 21). *1990s Art – A Vibrant and Eclectic Decade*. Retrieved October 2024, from artincontext.org: https://artincontext.org/1990s-art/

Astbury, J. (2020, February 21). *Dezeen*. Retrieved June 2024, from Louis Vuitton's flagship Osaka store covered in curving glass sails: https://www.dezeen.com/2020/02/21/louis-vuittons-flagship-osaka-store-covered-in-curving-glass-sails/

Bastien, V., & Kapferer, J.-N. (2013). More on Luxury Anti-Laws of Marketing. In K. P. Wiedmann, & N. Hennigs, *Luxury Marketing* (pp. 19–34). Wiesbaden: Gabler Verlag.

Business Insider. (2012, July 25). *Go Inside the Factory Where $10,000 Hermès Purses Are Crafted By Hand*. Retrieved October 2022, from businessinsider.com: https://www.businessinsider.com/how-herms-bags-are-made-2012-7

Cambridge Dictionary. (2023). *Exclusivity*. Retrieved November 2023, from Cambridge Dictionary: https://dictionary.cambridge.org/dictionary/english/exclusivity

Cartier. (2019). *YouTube*. Retrieved October 2022, from Odyssée de Cartier: Chapter 1 – Jeanne Toussaint: https://www.youtube.com/watch?v=Kws1VIw7oyM

Cartier. (2022a). *The Maison Story & Heritage*. Retrieved October 2022, from cartier.com: https://www.cartier.com/en-cz/maison/the-story/story-and-heritage

Cartier. (2022b). *The Panther in Motion*. Retrieved September 2022, from cartier.com: https://www.cartier.com/en-us/clp-LaMasion_KnowHow.html

Catry, B. (2003). The Great Pretenders: The Magic of Luxury Goods. *Business Strategy Review*, *14*(3), 10–17.

Chow Tai Fook Jewellery Group. (2022). *The Early Days of Chow Tai Fook Jewellery*. Retrieved September 2022, from Chow Tai Fook Jewellery Group: https://www.ctfjewellerygroup.com/en/group/history/story-1.html

Dezeen. (2023, March 2). *Dior Catwalk Features 24-Metre-Long "Tentacular" Installation by Joana Vasconcelos*. Retrieved June 2024, from Dezeen: https://www.dezeen.com/2023/03/02/dior-joana-vasconcelos-paris-fashion-week-catwalk/

Euronews. (2024, October 2). *LVMH Sells Off-White: Is This the End for Virgil Abloh's Brand?* Retrieved October 2024, from euronews.com: https://www.euronews.com/culture/2024/10/02/lvmh-sells-off-white-is-this-the-end-for-virgil-ablohs-brand

Ferrari. (2024a). *Ferrari Purosangue*. Retrieved August 2024, from ferrari.com: https://www.ferrari.com/en-EN/auto/ferrari-purosangue

Ferrari. (2024b). *The Foundation of the Ferrari Brand*. Retrieved August 2024, from ferrari.com: https://www.ferrari.com/en-EN/corporate/about-us

Fondation Louis Vuitton. (2022). *A Place Dedicated to Creation*. Retrieved November 2022, from fondationlouisvuitton.fr: https://www.fondationlouisvuitton.fr/fr/fondation

Forbes. (2014, September 22). *Cartier Celebrates the 100th Anniversary of the Panther with New Collection*. Retrieved September 2022, from forbes.com: https://www.forbes.com/sites/rachelhennessey/2014/09/22/cartier-panther-new-collection-jewelry-anniversary/

Harrods. (2023). *Louis Vuitton X Yayoi Kusama: Infinite Possibility*. Retrieved June 2024, from Harrods: https://www.harrods.com/en-gb/stories/louis-vuitton-yayoi-kusama-collaboration

Harvard Business Publishing. (2017). *SHANG XIA: The Creation of a Chinese Luxury Lifestyle Brand*. Retrieved October 2023, from hbsp.harvard.edu: https://hbsp.harvard.edu/product/517032-PDF-ENG?Ntt=chinese%20luxury%20brand

Hennigs, N., Wiedmann, K.-P., & Klarmann, C. (2012). Luxury Brands in the Digital Age – Exclusivity versus Ubiquity. *Marketing Review St. Gallen*, *29*, 30–35.

Hodinkee. (2018, October 25). *Jean-Claude Biver and the Making of the Modern Watch Industry*. Retrieved October 2024, from hodinkee.com: https://www.hodinkee.com/articles/jean-claude-biver-making-the-modern-watch-industry

Hodinkee. (2022, September 3). *Louis Vuitton's Tambour Collection Turns 20 and Celebrates With a New, Limited Edition Chronograph*. Retrieved 2022 October, from Hodinkee: https://www.hodinkee.com/articles/louis-vuitton-tambour-twenty-anniversary-limited-edition-2022

Industries Academy. (2021, December 7). *Off White Advertising – Inside Virgil Abloh's Strategies*. Retrieved October 2022, from www.academy.440industries.com: https://440industries.com/off-white-advertising-inside-virgil-ablohs-strategies/

Interbrand. (2023). *Best Global Brans 2023*. Retrieved October 2024, from interbrand.com: https://interbrand.com/best-global-brands/cartier/

Kapferer, J.-N. (2017). The End of Luxury as We Knew It? In J. Kapferer, J. Kernstock, T. Brexendorf, & S. Powell, *Advances in Luxury Brand Management, Journal of Brand Management: Advanced Collections*. Cham: Palgrave Macmillan.

Kapferer, J.-N., & Bastien, V. (2012). *The Luxury Strategy: Break the Rules of Marketing to Build Luxury Brands* (2nd edition). Kogan Page Limited.

Kapferer, J.-N., & Valette-Florence, P. (2016). Is Luxury Sufficient to Create Brand Desirability? A Cross-Cultural Analysis of the Relationship between Luxury and Dreams. *Luxury Research Journal*, *1*, 110–127.

Kim, S., Park, K., & Shrum, L. J. (2022). Cause-Related Marketing of Luxury Brands: Nudging Materialists to Act Prosocially. *Psychology & Marketing*, *39*(6), 1204–1217.

La Torre, V. (2019, November 21). *Informing and Educating: How French Luxury Company Van Cleef & Arpels Plans to keep up with the Ever-Changing Retail Scene: Van Cleef & Arpels Opens School in City to Teach Consumers about Jewellery*. Retrieved November 2022, from Proquest: https://www.proquest.com/docview/2316042783/2AEA0B3B4A7641BEPQ/4?accountid=17203

L'ÉCOLE School of Jewelry Arts. (2022). *Program & Booking*. Retrieved November 2022, from L'ÉCOLE School of Jewelry Arts: https://www.lecolevancleefarpels.com/fr/en/sign-up/list?parent_category=44

Louis Vuitton. (2022a). *Silver Lockit By Virgil Abloh*. Retrieved November 2022, from eu.louisvuitton.com: https://eu.louisvuitton.com/eng-e1/stories/lv-for-unicef

Louis Vuitton. (2022b). *What Makes an Authentic Louis Vuitton Bag So Special?* Retrieved October 2022, from ap.louisvuitton.com: https://ap.louisvuitton.com/eng-sg/what-makes-an-authentic-louis-vuitton-bag-so-special

LVMH. (2022, October 31). *Dior teams with Thebe Magugu for an Exclusive Capsule Collection Supporting the Charlize Theron Africa Outreach Project*. Retrieved November 2022, from LVMH: https://www.lvmh.com/news-documents/news/dior-teams-with-thebe-magugu-for-exclusive-capsule-collection-supporting-the-charlize-theron-africa-outreach-project/

Moser. (2022). *The Story of Moser*. Retrieved October 2022, from moser.com: https://www.moser.com/en/about-moser/the-story-of-moser

Moser. (2024). *Pear*. Retrieved October 2024, from moser.com: https://www.moser.com/en/pear

Off-White. (2022). *Brand Story*. Retrieved October 2022, from Off-White: https://www.off---white.com/en-cz/collections-editorial/virgil-is-here

Pitt, T. (2022, September 14). *Ferrari Unveils Its First SUV, the Purosangue*. Retrieved August 2024, from robbreport.com.au: https://robbreport.com.au/motors/automotive/ferrari-unveils-its-first-suv-the-purosangue/

Rémy Martin. (2021). *The Art of Celebrating*. Retrieved October 2022, from Louis XIII: https://www.louisxiii-cognac.com/blogs/news/the-art-of-celebrating

Reuters. (2024, June 19). *Exclusive: Ferrari's First Electric Car to Cost over $500,000*. Retrieved August 2024, from reuters.com: https://www.reuters.com/business/autos-transportation/ferraris-first-electric-car-cost-over-500000-source-says-2024-06-19/

Richemont. (2022). *Our Maisons*. Retrieved September 2022, from Richemont: https://www.richemont.com/en/home/our-maisons

Save the Children. (2022). *Bvlgari and Save the Children*. Retrieved November 2022, from Save the Children: https://www.savethechildren.org/us/about-us/become-a-partner/corporations/bulgari

Som, A., & Blanckaert, C. (2021). *The Road to Luxury: The New Frontiers in Luxury Brand Management* (2nd edition). Wiley.

Sotheby's. (2019, August 29). *How Cartier's Jeanne Toussaint Inspired and Popularised Its Iconic "Panthère"*. Retrieved September 2022, from sothebys.com: https://www.sothebys.com/en/articles/how-cartiers-jeanne-toussaint-inspired-and-popularised-its-iconic-panthere

Sotheby's. (2021, August 13). *The Best Limited Edition Louis Vuitton Handbags*. Retrieved October 2022, from sothebys.com: https://www.sothebys.com/en/articles/the-best-limited-edition-louis-vuitton-handbags

Steele, R. (2021). Crowning the "Sun of the Aryans": Mohammad Reza Shah's Coronation and Monarchical Spectacle in Pahlavi Iran. *International Journal of Middle East Studies*, *53*(2), 175–193.

Style. (2014, September 4). *Axel Dumas, CEO of Hermès, Says True Luxury Does Not always Have to Depend on Marketing*. Retrieved June 2024, from https://www.scmp.com/magazines/style/article/1581182/axel-dumas-ceo-hermes-says-true-luxury-does-not-always-have-depend

Sukhyun, K., Kiwan, P., & Shrum, L. J. (2022). Cause-Related Marketing of Luxury Brands: Nudging Materialists to Act Prosocially. *Psychology and Marketing*, *39*(6), 1204–1217.

UNICEF. (2022). *Louis Vuitton: A UNICEF Corporate Partner since 2016*. Retrieved November 2022, from unicef.org: https://www.unicef.org/partnerships/louis-vuitton

Van Cleef & Arpels. (2022). *Van Cleef & Arpels and Dance: A pas de deux*. Retrieved November 2022, from Van Cleef & Arpels: https://www.vancleefarpels.com/fr/en/the-maison/articles/van-cleef---arpels-and-dance--a-pas-de-deux.html

Veblen, T. (1899/2003). *The Theory of the Leisure Class* (E. C. Series, Ed.). Pennsylvania State University/Electronic Classics Series.

Virgin Money. (2014, August 18). *6 Great Quotes That Show Being Rich Is Not Just about Having Money*. Retrieved December 2024, from virginmoney.com: https://virginmoney.com.au/blog/news/6-great-quotes-that-show-being-rich-is-not-just-about-having-money

Wikimedia Commons. (1914). *File:'Lady with Panther' by George Barbier for Cartier, 1914. jpg*. Retrieved October 2024, from commons.wikimedia.org: https://commons.wikimedia.org/wiki/File:'Lady_with_Panther'_by_George_Barbier_for_Cartier,_1914.jpg

Wikimedia Commons. (2009, March 26). *File:White camelia (3388506807).jpg*. Retrieved October 2024, from commons.wikimedia.org: https://commons.wikimedia.org/wiki/File:White_camelia_(3388506807).jpg

Wikimedia Commons. (2011, October 17). *File:FerrariCavallinoMaranello.jpg*. Retrieved February 2025, from commons.wikimedia.org: https://commons.wikimedia.org/wiki/File:FerrariCavallinoMaranello.jpg

Wikimedia Commons. (2014a, June 24). *File:Imperial Empress Crown 2.png*. Retrieved November 2024, from commons.wikimedia.org: https://commons.wikimedia.org/wiki/File:Imperial_Empress_Crown_2.png

Wikimedia Commons. (2014b, October 11). *File:Ferrari 125 S – Museo Enzo Ferrari.jpg*. Retrieved October 2024, from commons.wikimedia.org: https://commons.wikimedia.org/wiki/File:Ferrari_125_S_-_Museo_Enzo_Ferrari.jpg

Wikimedia Commons. (2021, December 13). *File:Cotton-Transport-Ships-Racing-to-Edo-from-Aji-River-Osaka-by-Gansuitei-Yoshitoyo-c1855.png*. Retrieved February 2025, from commons.wikimedia.org: https://commons.wikimedia.org/wiki/File:Cotton-Transport-Ships-Racing-to-Edo-from-Aji-River-Osaka-by-Gansuitei-Yoshitoyo-c1855.png

Wikimedia Commons. (2023, August 27). *File:Coco Chanel.jpg*. Retrieved February 2025, from commons.wikimedia.org: https://commons.wikimedia.org/wiki/File:Coco_Chanel.jpg

Wikimedia Commons. (2024a, March 20). *File:Balletdanseres Anna Pavlova, staand op een voet in een sprookjesjurk en op spitzen, circa 1920.jpg*. Retrieved November 2024, from commons.wikimedia.org: https://commons.wikimedia.org/wiki/File:Balletdanseres_Anna_Pavlova,_staand_op_een_voet_in_een_sprookjesjurk_en_op_spitzen,_circa_1920,_SFA003003111.jpg

Wikimedia Commons. (2024b, September 28). *File:Christian Dior – Rosaleda Parque del Oeste – Madrid 02.jpg*. Retrieved February 2025, from commons.wikimedia.org: https://commons.wikimedia.org/wiki/File:Christian_Dior_-_Rosaleda_Parque_del_Oeste_-_Madrid_02.jpg

WWD. (2024, September 5). *Queen Camilla Makes a Pointe in Anna Valentine Dress and Ballerina Brooch Celebrating the English National Ballet's 75th Season*. Retrieved November 2024, from wwd.com: https://wwd.com/pop-culture/celebrity-news/queen-camilla-ballerina-brooch-english-national-ballet-1236572736/

Chapter 5

Distribution

Balancing traditional channels and e-commerce

In his book on the future of luxury, Erwan Rambourg predicts, based on interviews with CEOs of luxury brands that physical brick-and-mortar stores will continue to dominate online channels in the world of luxury. His estimated proportion of **online volume** for the 2020s was a maximum of 20% (Rambourg, 2020). Two years after publishing this forecast, Kering SA published a 15% share of sales in online stores (Kering SA, 2022) and Richemont announced an even higher proportion of online sales (19%) (Richemont, 2022c). At the same time, the year-on-year increase of online channels was more than double (+55%) at Kering (Kering SA, 2022). The extreme increase is explained by the COVID-19 pandemic and the increased share of millennials and Gen Z in luxury purchases (Deloitte, 2021).

Besides growth of total sales in luxury e-commerce, there has been a double-digit increase in purchases made on social media. Even with new technological solutions and innovations, and luxury retail channels becoming increasingly digitized, offline retail is still predicted to generate over 70% of luxury companies' revenues in 2025 (Deloitte, 2023).

According to a Bain and Company's (2022) analysis, luxury brands continue to **increase control over their distribution** with the growth of directly operated retail channels, which account for nearly half of the market (49% for 2021, 50% in 2022, and 52% in 2023) (D'Arpizio et al., 2024). The key channels for the market's recovery after the 2021 pandemic crisis were online and mono-brand brick-and-mortar stores. After a 50% increase between 2019 and 2020, online sales of luxury brands continued to grow by 27% in 2021. On the contrary, outlets and department stores have lagged behind the pre-COVID level of 2019, and so far there are no signs or significant recovery (D'Arpizio & Levato, 2022; D'Arpizio et al., 2024).

After COVID, the mono-brand stores gained significant importance, while growth rates online decelerated. Mono-brands' portion of luxury sales grew to 36% of total personal luxury sales because customers returned to in-person shopping. Customer journeys are increasingly mixing physical and digital touchpoints, and the brands aim to adapt their stores to make space for more experiential shopping journeys (D'Arpizio et al., 2024).

E-commerce has evolved from its original definition of online buying and selling into a **comprehensive lifestyle** that integrates advanced technologies like live streaming, 3D demonstrations, augmented reality (AR), virtual reality (VR) and artificial intelligence (AI) to

DOI: 10.4324/9781003593706-5

enhance customers' experiences. It has surpassed traditional point-to-point transactions and evolved into seamless, borderless activity deeply intertwined with social media, giving rise to the concept of *social e-commerce*, where shopping occurs anytime, anywhere, completing the online journey in a continuous 360° loop.

5.1 Luxury e-commerce: The most important groups and business models

The increase in the volume of luxury brand online stores was accelerated by the COVID pandemic, which severely impacted most brick-and-mortar stores. The reluctance of luxury groups and individual brands to engage in more online sales was due to an understandable desire to maintain control over the defining elements of their brands' luxury identity – exclusivity, craftsmanship, authenticity, customer service, distribution control and a consistent in-store consumer experience. In addition, the industry did not have the skills or experience in online stores and did not need to invest in the virtual environment due to long-term growth. The events of 2020 pushed luxury e-commerce past the tipping point, and it has become an essential part of the omnichannel distribution strategy for most global luxury businesses, despite the decrease in luxury online volumes reported in 2023.

The standout luxury e-commerce players in Western markets are Farfetch and Yoox Net-a-Porter Group (YNAP), while Alibaba's Tmall Luxury Pavilion is a leading player in China and other Asian markets. These companies have unrivaled expertise in offering so-called multi-brand marketplaces and hosting single-brand e-commerce sites. Table 5.1 shows the individual business models of contemporary luxury e-commerce with examples of individual platforms.

With nearly $2.3 billion in 2021 revenue (up 26% from the previous year) and 3.7 million active customers, Farfetch Limited ranked among the largest e-fashion retailers (Farfetch, 2022a). Farfetch was founded in 2007 by José Neves as an online marketplace for luxury boutiques around the world. Its mission is to be a global platform for luxury fashion, connecting creators, brand managers and consumers. It operates in approximately 190 countries, selling over 1,400 brands through digital and physical platforms (Table 5.2), including New Guards' brick-and-mortar and e-commerce stores from the 2018 acquisition.

An important part of the company's innovative endeavors is the Luxury New Retail (LNR) initiative, including **Farfetch Platform Solutions (FPS)**, which provides e-commerce and technology services to enterprise clients, and in-store innovations such as the Farfetch Connected Retail suite of technology products (Farfetch, 2022a). Smaller brands or companies can have the same sophisticated and effective online store through FPS as Farfetch itself or its brands. The company offers large luxury brands such as Gucci and Versace, as well as luxury fashion and jewelry from many smaller boutiques worldwide. Other FPS brands include Chanel and Salvatore Ferragamo, which hope to reach younger customers from the partnership with Farfetch (Milnes, 2022).

For retail brands, the platform charges a commission on sales, and if they want to outsource Farfetch's order fulfillment as well, they charge an additional fee. The amount of the commission is around 25% plus another 8% if the platform also delivers goods to the customer (Som & Blanckaert, 2021).

LNR is an initiative that was mentioned in the first chapter in connection with the foreseen complex operation between Richemont, YNAP and Farfetch. It focuses on creating the luxury customer experience of the future. It develops and implements technology

Table 5.1 Luxury e-commerce models; authors based on (Deloitte 2021).

Commercial model		Example
Purely multi-brand online shops, marketplaces, online wholesalers, online shopping centers	• A wide range of luxury brands can be purchased • Providers of technology, logistics, payments, customer analytics and other services	Farfetch Net-a-Porter Tmall Luxury Pavilion JD.com Luxury Amazon Luxury Stores
Purely specialized multi-brand online shops	• Niche stores targeting specific luxury product categories, consumers and/or geographies • Discount sites • Formerly owned luxury goods retailer/secondary market with growth potential as companies respond to growing consumer demand for sustainability • Lease	Sephora (LVMH) VeePee Rue La La/Gilt The RealReal SSENSE Watchfinder (Richemont) RenttheRunway
Single-brand e-shops	• Owned and operated by the owners of a luxury brand	www.louisvuitton.com www.gucci.com www.prada.com (and others)
Multi-brand e-shops	• Owned and operated by a group of luxury brands	www.24S.com (LVMH)
Online stores of luxury multi-brand stores	• E-commerce luxury department stores	www.bergdorfgoodman.com www.selfridges.com
Luxury division of large retailers		eBay Luxury Amazon Luxury Stores

solutions to support the vision of luxury retailers to create new cutting-edge retail experiences for customers by connecting the digital, physical and virtual spheres (Farfetch, 2022a). LNR uses Farfetch and Alibaba's omnichannel retail technology and a suite of enterprise e-commerce solutions driven by the Farfetch technology solution for the needs of luxury brands. In addition to representatives of Farfetch and Alibaba, the LNR steering group also includes Richemont Chairman Johann Rupert and Artemis Chairman François-Henri Pinault, Chairman. Farfetch was launched into the Tmall Luxury Pavilion in 2020 thanks to a $1.15 billion investment from Alibaba, Richemont and Artémis (Kering's majority shareholder).

In this context, José Neves, announcing the cooperation of the aforementioned groups, stated in a press release that "the investment of $1.15 billion in Farfetch from Alibaba Group, Richemont and Artemis is a strong confirmation of our position as a global platform for luxury," while on the same occasion Daniel Zhang, chairman and CEO of Alibaba Group, added that "China's luxury goods market – which is expected to account for half of global luxury sales by 2025 – is made up of hundreds of millions of young, digitally native consumers. By partnering with Farfetch and expanding our existing relationship with Richemont, we will accelerate the digitalization of the global luxury retail industry and turn it into a luxury shopping experience for consumers" (Farfetch, 2020).

Table 5.2 Division of Farfetch Limited; authors based on Farfetch Annual Report 2021 (Farfetch, 2022b).

	Digital division	Physical division	
Segments	**Digital platform (76% of turnover 2021)** The segment includes all online sales channels operated by the Group, including the respective websites of brands in the New Guards portfolio. The division's revenue comes from transactions between vendors and customers on Farfetch's technology platforms, based primarily on a revenue sharing model, where Farfetch retains a commission on these transactions. The segment also includes sales of custom brands from the New Guards portfolio through the Farfetch Marketplace and brand websites.	**Brick-and-mortar stores (3% of turnover 2021)** The segment covers the activities of stores that Farfetch operates, including Browns, Stadium Goods and certain brands in the New Guards portfolio. The division's revenues are made up of the turnover of individual brick-and-mortar stores.	**Brand platform (21% of turnover 2021)** The segment consists of the production and wholesale distribution of brands owned and licensed by New Guards, including the operation of franchise stores.
Shops	Farfetch Browns (e-commerce) Stadium Goods (e-commerce) Farfetch Future Retails NGG_NEWGUARDSGROUP_ Farfetch Platform Solution	Browns Stadium Goods NGG_ NEWGUARDSGROUP_ (operated by NGG stores)	NGG_ NEWGUARDSGROUP_

One of the new consumer experiences connecting the online and offline worlds is the newly refurbished Farfetch flagship store in London (Browns on Brook Street), which connects the history and tradition of the boutique with the present and provides customers with novel experiences such as the Immersive Room, offering 15 minutes of sound escape, reflection and relaxation. For the company, it is the first experimental store of the future and a tangible result of the work of the New Luxury Retail Initiative (LNR).

In addition to its early entry into e-commerce, Farfetch's success factors include four important competencies:

1. A primary focus on the development of **logistics technologies** that enable it to track its inventory worldwide in the early stages of online commerce development;
2. **Self-moderation** of the selection of brands for the portfolio and their individual products for online stores, based on predictive analytics based on the analysis of movements on their sites. This achieves approximately 4% overlap with stores like Net-a-Porter;
3. **Continuous portfolio innovation** – The approximately 1,000 new items per week means always a fresh offer for loyal customers and contributes to repeat purchases by those who come to the site frequently;

4. **Acquisition strategy** – For example, the acquisitions of London boutique retailer Browns, the Stadium Goods store, the New Guards Group with luxury brands such as Off-White or Palm Angels and a joint venture with Tmall Luxury Pavilion invested by Alibaba, Richemont and Artemis (Som & Blanckaert, 2021).

The transaction announced in 2022 between Farfetch, Richemont and Yoox Net-a-Porter allowed Farfetch to acquire a 47.5% stake in rival Yoox Net-a-Porter, previously owned by Richemont. The agreement was seen as a major milestone for the luxury industry, consolidating two key players in e-commerce. Farfetch might have eventually acquired the remaining stakes in loss-making YNAP under the deal, and YNAP would take over the FPS technology platform. Farfetch would be joined by Richemont brands, including Cartier, Chloé and IWC and Vacheron Constantin. This would allow Farfetch to increase the number of shoppers using its platform in the highly competitive luxury e-commerce sector.

Despite having the transaction approved by European authorities, as reported by Reuters in October 2023 (Reuters, 2023), the deal was not completed due to financial issues on Farfetch's side. In December 2023, Richemont announced that it has terminated the agreements for the sale of a majority stake in YNAP to Farfetch and Symphony Global, the adoption of Farfetch Platform Solutions by most Richemont *Maisons* and YNAP as well as the opening of e-concessions on the Farfetch marketplace by several Richemont *Maisons*. They have also highlighted that they "will consider alternative options to pursue the realization of their Luxury New Retail (LNR) vision and are confident that their *Maisons* will benefit from cutting-edge platform technology to best serve the growing omni-channel needs of their discerning clientele" (Richemont, 2023). The reason behind this is related to Farfetch's financing issues which escalated in late 2023 and resulted in South Korean e-commerce giant Coupang's acquisition of the luxury e-tailer, after which it injected $500 million into the company (Vogue Business, 2023). The new deal announced by Richemont in October 2024 involves Mytheresa (multi-brand digital platform founded in 1987) acquiring YNAP from the Group, which will hold a 33% stake in Mytheresa after the transaction is completed. Richemont will provide €555 million in cash and a €100 million credit facility to support YNAP. Mytheresa plans to integrate YNAP's luxury division, separate its off-price brands and discontinue white-label operations (a white-label operation is an e-commerce business practice where platforms provide e-commerce services under other brands' names). The transaction aims to create a global, multi-brand luxury group and is expected to close in the first half of 2025, pending regulatory approvals (Richemont, 2024).

YNAP was formed in 2018 by the merger of Net-a-Porter Group and YOOX before being acquired by Richemont. According to Richemont's 2021 annual report, it had a turnover comparable to that of the Farfetch Group (€2.2 billion), but it showed a long-term loss, which it reduced from €241 million to €223 million in 2021. The 2022 annual report (financial year ends in March) shows an increase in turnover to €2.8 billion and a reduction in loss to €210 million (Richemont, 2022c). As reported by Richemont, in 2023, it had 5.3 million customers in 180 countries. It has a localized approach to serving its clientele around the globe through its network of offices and operations across the U.S., Europe, APAC, joint ventures with Alibaba in China and Symphony Investments in the Middle East (Richemont, 2023).

YNAP is made up of four separate platforms: the flagship online store YNAP, Net-a-Porter, Mr. Porter and The Outnet. **The YNAP flagship store** essentially covers selected standalone online stores of the Richemont Group brands (Alaïa, Armani, Armani Exchange,

Cartier, Chloé, Dunhill, Missoni, Montblanc and others), for which it provides B2B services through the development of online and mobile stores, omnichannel logistics, customer care, digital marketing and global strategy development (YNAP, 2022). **Net-a-Porter** is a multi-brand online store focused on luxury brands of various groups and designers and a female target group, known for exceptional service and iconic packaging, which sells to approximately 170 countries worldwide (Net-a-Porter, 2022). Mr. Porter, an online store founded in 2011, is similar to Net-a-Porter but aimed at men. It represents a vision of men's style through the brands of well-known designers, including Mr P.'s own brand (Mr. Porter, 2022). Finally, **The Outnet** was founded in 2009 as part of Net-a-Porter and is also focused on luxury fashion, but the fundamental difference from previous platforms is the focus on luxury fashion on sale (The Outnet, 2022). What distinguishes YNAP is its ability to create user-friendly pages for each individual brand. Their technological innovations have helped reduce the barrier between the online and offline shopping experience. At the same time, as a technology-oriented company, it invests in artificial intelligence, augmented reality, as well as voice and visual search.

Due to complexities in the e-commerce mergers and acquisitions in the early 2000s, Table 5.3 aims to chronologically sort Richemont's e-commerce activities that resulted in selling YNAP to Mytheresa in 2024.

Tmall Luxury Pavilion has been Alibaba's exclusive e-commerce platform for luxury goods in China since 2017. The luxury pavilion has more than 779 million Chinese customers, almost half under 29. As in the case of Farfetch, it is a comprehensive platform that allows brands to offer personalized experiences and services, such as exclusive VIP bonuses, virtual and augmented reality, tailor-made product recommendations and so on.

Tmall does not disclose data for Luxury Pavilion, only stating that sales of the Luxury Pavilion platform increased by 130–140% in 2020 compared to 2019 and in the first quarter of 2021 even by 159% compared to the same period in 2020. Some brands, such as Estée Lauder, Burberry and Cartier, run e-commerce exclusively on Tmall (Deloitte, 2021). Due to the cooperation between Farfetch, Richemont and Kering, we can expect a significant increase in the presence of traditional luxury brands. The platform charges companies an annual fee and sales commission for a presence in Pavilion, depending on the product category (Som & Blanckaert, 2021). Pavilion provides traditional luxury brands with a safe environment for further development and access to innovations that are known, used and popular to China's Gen Z. Cartier and Burberry use video calls and live streams. Gucci and Dior have taken the opportunity to host virtual fashion shows here. The company is also investing in activities in the metaverse or NFTs, as they expect great competition in this area in the near future (Jing Daily, 2022). The immersive experience of luxury shopping in Tmall Luxury Pavilion is shown in Video 5.1.

In 2019, Net-a-Porter, including Richemont brands such as Cartier, Piaget, Montblanc and Van Cleef & Arpels, was introduced to Pavilion through a joint venture between Alibaba (49%) and YNAP (51%). Alibaba was responsible for the marketing, payments and technology infrastructure services part of the partnership, while Richemont contributed not only to the launch of its brands to Pavilion but also to other non-Richemont brands within YNAP. Farfetch opened its "shop window" in the Luxury Pavilion in March 2021, with visible merchandising – for example, it occupies one of the five main navigation buttons and has a permanent premium banner there (Deloitte, 2021). LVMH brands Tiffany and Chaumet also entered Pavilion in 2024 as part of the luxury hub introduced as La Place Vendôme. Both brands' launch to Pavilion was accompanied by the online debut of a limited-edition Tiffany

Table 5.3 Development of Richemont's e-commerce presence.

2000	**Net-a-Porter,** founded by Natalie Massenet, was launched as an innovative online retailer with **selection of luxury brands.** **Yoox,** founded by Federico Marchetti, starts to build its online luxury model, focusing on **discounted luxury items.**
2010	Richemont acquired a majority stake in Net-a-Porter.
2015	Merger of Yoox and Net-a-Porter, **establishment of the Yoox Net-a-Porter Group (YNAP).** Richemont becomes the majority shareholder at YNAP, marking a major move into luxury e-commerce.
2018	**Richemont acquires full ownership of YNAP,** aiming to develop its e-commerce capabilities. **Richemont partners with Alibaba Group** to bring YNAP's offerings to Chinese consumers through Alibaba's Tmall Luxury Pavilion.
2019	The **Net-a-Porter flagship store was launched on the key position of Alibaba's Tmall Luxury Pavilion.** The partnership was facilitated through a joint venture, Feng Mao.
2020	**Richemont, Alibaba and Farfetch announce a strategic partnership.** Together Alibaba and Richemont invested $1.1 billion in Farfetch. This investment enabled Farfetch to establish a stronger presence in China, allowing the Richemont brands traded on the Farfetch platform and the Chinese Tmall Luxury Pavilion to build penetration in that market.
2022	A complex operation announced to create a global online platform of luxury brands: Richemont **planned to sell a 50.7% stake in YNAP to Farfetch** and a 3.3% to Mohamed Alabbar (Symphony Global). YNAP thus would become a neutral platform without a majority shareholder. Furthermore, a future merger of YNAP with Farfetch (with Richemont as shareholder of Farfetch) was envisaged.
2023	**The deal was terminated** due to financial issues on Farfetch's side. Farfetch had financing issues, which escalated in late 2023, and resulted in South Korean e-commerce giant Coupang's acquisition of the luxury e-tailer, after which it injected $500 million into the company.
2024	Richemont announced the **closure of the Fengmao joint venture,** marking its exit from the Chinese market due to YNAP's declining performance and strategic shifts to focus on more profitable regions. Richemont confirms **the sale of YNAP to Mytheresa** in a €555 million deal. The transaction includes restructuring plans to streamline YNAP, separating its off-price segments (Yoox and The Outnet) from luxury brands like Net-a-Porter and Mr. Porter. This deal, expected to close by mid-2025, underscores Richemont's strategy to concentrate on its core luxury businesses while benefiting from Mytheresa's digital retail expertise.

Source: Authors based on Reuters (2020), Alibaba Group (2019), Richemont (2022a, 2022b, 2024), Forbes (2022), Vogue Business (2023).

rose gold pendant shaped like a key with pink sapphires and Chaumet rose gold Bee My Love necklace (Alizila, 2024).

JD.com is another Chinese e-commerce platform that, according to Deloitte's (2021) report, has lagged behind Tmall Luxury in the battle for the Chinese luxury consumer. The Group has grown into online commerce in the consumer electronics, computers and telecommunications sectors. In June 2017, it invested $397 million in Farfetch, making it one of Farfetch's largest shareholders at the time. In 2017 JD.com sold the firm's luxury platform,

Video 5.1 Tmall Luxury Pavilion: A Guide to Immersive Shopping (Alibaba Group, 2023).

called Toplife, to Farfetch China for $50 million, and the company opened its store on JD.com. However, the strategic partnership was not successful, and in 2019, Farfetch moved its China luxury partnership efforts to Alibaba's Tmall Luxury Pavilion, as mentioned. The Farfetch shop on JD.com closed at the end of 2020, but according to available data, JD.com retained its stake in Farfetch.

The current strategy at JD.com, to scale up its luxury business, is to partner with selected brands and redirect consumers to WeChat's mini-brand programs (Deloitte, 2021). WeChat is a multifunctional messaging, social media and mobile payment app widely used in China. It offers a feature called "mini programs," which are sub-applications within the WeChat ecosystem. Brands can create these mini programs to offer services, sell products or engage with customers within the WeChat app. Tencent, the tech giant behind WeChat, is also a significant shareholder in JD.com, which further facilitates close cooperation between the two platforms (Tencent, 2024).

The availability of increasingly sophisticated systems and partnership options in e-commerce allows many luxury companies to maintain control over digital marketing and client relationships at an affordable price. Many brands enter this market through their own directly operated mono-branded e-commerce sites with their own control and/or through established luxury e-commerce platforms. Both require large investments and multiplying their presence on different e-commerce platforms is multiplying the investments. Some brands like Hermès or Chanel couture have not been convinced by e-commerce to replace the brick-and-mortar experience and remain offline with most highly demanded items.

5.2 S-commerce

S-commerce (or social commerce) is a subset of e-commerce that uses social media to facilitate social interactions between consumers and brands in order to facilitate buying and selling of products and services (Abdelsalam et al., 2020). Simply put, it is shopping through social networks, which is the main shopping channel for many young consumers. In essence, this is interaction between the consumer and the brand at a place where younger consumers are often found. TikTok is an example of such a platform. It is not an advertisement found on social networks but rather about sharing brand stories or an influencer inviting consumers into her wardrobe. It is a place where followers can virtually buy the promoted product directly within the platform at the touch of a finger.

Social media shopping is particularly significant in China, but other important regions are also growing. McKinsey predicts that by 2025, s-commerce's share of total online commerce in the United States will be around 5.2% (McKinsey & Company, 2022). A key factor in the growth of s-commerce is the strength of the social network's influencers and community. Chinese influencers have built communities of fans based on being perceived as experts on a given topic in a particular product category. In industries such as cosmetics and fashion, these social celebrities can sell millions of dollars' worth of products in minutes.

In addition to prominent celebrities, ordinary consumers also have an influence on the networks by sharing recommendations or reviews of purchased products. For example, a simple hashtag, "#TikTok made me buy it," includes posts from regular consumers and their recommendations for specific purchases through this network. TikTok is a strong voice for Generation Z (and those who are younger) and their shopping. It is a place where they can rely on community recommendations instead of relying on the content of sponsored posts or paid influencers.

Custom content, the use of paid influencers, paid promotions or TikTok challenges (#challenge), where a brand can sponsor a selected hashtag and TikTok then invites users to use it to create content, are all tools that can be used on this social network. The goal is to get closer to key Generation Z or Alpha users and build brand awareness for future purchases.

5.2.1 Live stream shopping as a form of s-commerce

Live streaming is a more advanced form of s-commerce and is based on real-time communication, which builds an instant relationship between streamers and viewers. It was established in 2016 with the launch of Alibaba TaoBao Live (McKinsey, 2023). Live streaming is mostly used by Generation Z, who are primary users of social networks and whose purchasing power is growing. The difference is that you can make a purchase with your fingertip while communicating with the brand's extensive community. Gen Z uses this method of shopping extensively; thus far, this is primarily done on the social network TikTok.

Live stream commerce is driven by engaging product demonstrations hosted by influencers or key opinion leaders (KOLs) who bring entertainment and authenticity to the experience. In a typical live stream-commerce event, the consumer watches product demonstrations presented by influencers (also called hosts or creators and in China referred to as KOLs) who are typically chosen for their combination of personality, influence or knowledge, and they help to make the experience entertaining for participants. The product showcases resemble how infomercials (i.e. teleshopping) worked for older generations. The ability of **video to generate higher engagement** than static content has made this format especially appealing to younger generations, who find traditional e-commerce boring. The widespread use of smartphones and social media, particularly TikTok, further fuels live stream shopping's popularity. Unlike solitary online shopping, live stream commerce amplifies a **sense of community**, allowing consumers to **interact and share in real-time events. Influencers** play a predominant role by leveraging their large followings to drive sales through personal connections and social validation (Robertson, 2022).

According to McKinsey (2021), live stream shopping is not just an extension of online shopping. It brings excitement, encourages spontaneous purchases and strengthens the customer's sense of connection to the brand. Traditional online retail cannot offer that. In China, this way of purchasing has transformed the retail industry and has established itself as a major sales channel in less than five years. Data from 2020 confirms that two-thirds of Chinese consumers purchased products via live broadcast in the previous year. Consumers and businesses in European and U.S. markets are lagging behind, but McKinsey estimates that by 2026, sales launched by live streaming could account for 10 to 20% of all e-commerce (McKinsey Digital, 2021).

China is the most developed of all live-commerce markets. McKinsey found that 57% of live-commerce users in China have used live stream shopping for over three years, compared with just 5 to 7% of users in Europe, Latin America and the United States. **The average age globally was, according to McKinsey research, between 33 and 36 years old,** with those aged 25 to 34 years old representing the largest share of frequent live-commerce users. There were some geographical differences, i.e. the US customers were relatively evenly distributed across age brackets, while most European and Chinese customers were younger, 18 to 34 years old (McKinsey, 2023).

The main benefits include (1) **speeding up the buying process**, which is entertaining and immersive and attracts viewers' attention to the live broadcast; viewers watch streaming longer than a regular online store offering, realize the need to buy faster, and retailers report conversions approaching 30%, which is up to ten times more than in traditional online sales, and (2) a well-executed live broadcast **increases** the **brand appeal and differentiation of the brand** and increases traffic to its website. It can strengthen the position among existing customers and attract new ones, especially young people who are interested in innovative shopping formats and experiences. Some companies are seeing an increase in younger audience share of up to 20%.

In 2023, McKinsey noted both the growth of live stream shopping in China, and the fact that the European and American markets were still behind Chinese revenues from live streaming. The **barriers for live stream shopping** outside of China were suggested as **convenience** (mainly due to the timing of live shows for European, American and Latin American customers), **value for money** and **difficulties in making a choice.** Another concern was the **dullness of the content** and its too-apparent **sales-oriented tone.** European and U.S. customers also found shows, in general, **to be too long** (McKinsey, 2023).

In terms of demographics, Gen Z and millennials dominate live stream shopping, predominantly in Asia. By March 2020, nearly 30% of Chinese internet users were using live trading, with Taobao being the largest streaming player with a 35% market share. Streaming event formats are diverse; for example: **tutorials** presenting makeup samples focused on the application of a particular product or possible combinations with other products; these are usually presented by personalities from modeling or influencers. Others include **interviews** with a personality or influencer from a relevant segment that is more personal and authentic than a regular product video; or **behind-the-scenes videos** that invite consumers behind the curtain of the brand by offering a unique and rare experience (McKinsey Digital, 2021).

In s-commerce, consumers can only collect information through text and images, and it is difficult to perceive the quality of luxury goods. When buying luxury goods live stream, consumers can see more detailed information about the goods in real time and thus perceive their quality more realistically. Given the specificities of luxury brands, there have been concerns about the perceived value of luxury brands when shopping via live streaming. Yu and Zheng's (2021) research focused on consumer behavior on China's live luxury shopping platform Taobao Live, the platform with the highest usage and consumer loyalty in China. Research found that **the perceived values of luxury (functional, experiential and symbolic) have a significant positive impact on shopping intent** in the context of live luxury shopping, that is, the same behavior as offline luxury purchases. Furthermore, the perceived values of luxury had a significant positive impact on customer engagement in live streaming, while the level of customer engagement in live streaming had an intermediary effect on the consumers' purchasing intentions. The results eased luxury brands' concerns about selling via live streaming on China's Taobao platform, where live sales are widespread. The results further imply that when launching live streams of luxury brands, individual streamers should emphasize the traditional presentation of luxury brands with weight on their values, culture, design and uniqueness. **Put simply, consumers can perceive the values of a luxury brand in the social media live room**, which further influences customer engagement with live broadcasting. To create an emotional connection between consumers and a luxury brand, they should consider using relevant influencers or provide the luxury customer with multiple platforms to communicate and build a virtual brand community (Yu & Zheng, 2021).

Brands will also face major challenges in penetrating this new business paradigm. In traditional e-commerce, brands route consumers to their own channels, where they can build a direct relationship with them, collect data on customer behavior, and get a higher share of customer spend with additional product offerings shown on the page. Both social media shopping and streaming shopping events are changing this consumer shopping journey, creating **an environment that, in some cases, bypasses brand-owned channels.** For example, a consumer follows one of his/her influencers on Instagram and a brand appears in a post that catches his/her eye. The consumer then goes to the brand's Instagram page, views products or tries out Instagram's shopping feature. At the same time, in the Instagram environment, the consumer then receives additional personalized ads or reads posts in feeds that have been selected by Instagram's algorithm. The brand itself has no influence on this process, which thus affects or even jeopardizes the status of the brand's direct relations with its consumers (McKinsey & Company, 2022).

To conclude, companies may be turning to live stream commerce to accomplish the following key goals: **driving immediate sales, expanding their customer base, launching new products, educating buyers and generating buzz.** Immediate sales often come from showcasing accessible, usually mainstream products. Reaching new demographics, especially Gen Z and young millennials, is essential for luxury brands. Ferragamo, for example, uses TikTok influencers to engage younger audiences authentically, and Jimmy Choo has successfully introduced limited sneakers on Tmall, emphasizing scarcity for exclusivity. New products (or the newness of the offer) are highly correlated with the sales success of the event. Live streaming is also a great educational tool, with companies demonstrating product use and driving online sales. Buzz is created when events are dynamic and community driven, with luxury brands like Gucci benefiting from the high social value of their products (Robertson, 2022).

The Smartzer case study highlights the possibility of combining e-commerce with s-commerce as well as live sales events, through the starting points offered by Smartzer, which develops technology solutions for companies entering these shopping alternatives, including luxury ones.

Mini-case 5.1 Smartzer: Live shopping

Karoline Gross, CEO of London-based British Smartzer, founded in 2014, received the award for best NFT/Metaverse/Live Shopping project at the Luxury Venture Group's innovation conference in October 2022. Other finalists were Exclusible (a premium NFT market for luxury brands and a provider of digital experience in the e-virtual world, thanks to its strong presence in the e-trailer) and Origyn Luxury (a paperless digital certification technology that formally guarantees the authenticity of a luxury item through its own biometric characteristics).

The battle with NFT and metaverse projects was won by a pragmatic application company that understood the potential of linking e-commerce with video. The younger generation is characterized by watching videos, starting with game tutorials, educational videos and popular youtubers. Luxury fashion brands supply social networks with videos from shows, the creation of collections, the life of brands and so on. Smartzer used the shopping potential of video and developed an application that allows you to mark items in a video and then connect them to an online store. The second product closely linked to video is live shopping technology (LVG, 2022).

One of the occasions the company is showcasing on the web is Valentino's Instagram video of a fashion show on Rome's "Spanish steps." Followers can click on the models coming down the 136 steps to learn more about each look, and get information about the designer and craftsmanship of the pieces. Smartzer reports at least a 25% click-through rate and a 55% follower engagement rate. As a result, they were able to confirm that adding an extra layer of click-ability to video content succeeded in drawing in the audience for luxury fashion with a 69% engagement rate and 37,000 clicks on the video (Video 5.2) (Smartzer, 2024b).

Bloomingdale partnered with Dior Beauty to create an interactive live shopping event using Smartzer technology where a make-up artist applied Dior products step by step and explained to the viewers each step he was taking. The event was part of Bloomingdale's series of masterclasses, prompting the customers to learn more about the new expert tips. Interestingly, the event was done in both English and Arabic, resulting in an 18% engagement rate and a 30% add-to-cart rate (Smartzer, 2024a).

Video 5.2 Click to Discover the Look: Valentino Case (Smartzer, 2024b).

Smartzer's pricing policy is based on providing an annual subscription to various service packages prepared based on the required level of services and the needs of internal company systems' integration with Smartzer technologies.

In addition to videos with buyable items, Smartzer is also a technology provider for live shopping streams, which have emerged as a new shopping format from China, led by the success of sites like Taobao. With the gradual global expansion of this format, the live shopping systems have developed into three main channels:

1. **Dedicated mobile apps for live shopping** (NTWRK, OOOOO, YES and Whatnot) where you can watch various live shopping events organized by brands or influencers. The advantage is the concentration of live events in one place. The disadvantage is the need to download new applications and create an account on them, a significant obstacle for consumers. A business needs to redirect its customers to new platforms, and new shoppers don't necessarily trust new platforms enough to want to shop;
2. **Live shopping on major social media platforms** such as Instagram, TikTok and YouTube, which allow brands and influencers to launch live broadcasts and tag products selected for sale in their live streams. The advantage of these formats is the ability to reach a new audience for existing followers during a live shopping event. The disadvantage is the need to enter payment information directly into social platforms, which consumers do

not consider safe. They often prefer to buy directly on the brand's website. In addition, tags have limited access to event data;

3. **Live shopping within a traditional e-commerce brand.** This channel grew more slowly in the early stages of the rollout of live shopping, as it requires more investment. It also needs to involve more elements: technology enabling live shopping on e-commerce brands; moderators and creation of unique content; and targeted marketing communications to attract audiences to live streams. Amazon and Walmart, for example, have added a new section to their websites with live shopping streams, where you can also watch the footage of some past performances. The average watch time is 20 times longer than social media, and consumers can buy directly from a brand they know and trust, using the brand's own e-shop. Another plus is that brands have access to the customer data for further analysis. The disadvantage is the absence of an audience that is present on both of the other channels (social media and apps). A brand must have a strategy to bring its audience to its website through social networks and other marketing communications or to an organized live shopping event on its website.

The decision on an s-commerce strategy and whether to sell via live broadcast depends on communication and business goals. Smartzer states that live streaming on major social channels is best suited for brand awareness purposes. To increase conversions, they recommend hosting live shopping events on the brand's own website and e-shops in the live stream section. Through social networks, one can direct follower traffic to the live section of a brand's own website (Smartzer, 2022, 2024b).

5.3 Personalized luxury shopping experience in omnichannel digital worlds

In the contemporary luxury retail landscape, omnichannel strategies have revolutionized how brands engage with their clientele. Omnichannel retailing refers to a seamless and integrated shopping experience that unites various channels into a **cohesive customer journey**, such as physical stores, e-commerce platforms and social media. This shift is particularly significant in the luxury sector, where personalized experiences are perceived as added value expected by discerning customers. Personalization in this context involves tailoring interactions, products and services to meet each customer's unique preferences and needs. The experiences provided to customers at any stage along the purchase journey support long-term brand loyalty.

Especially in Southeast Asian markets, digital platforms (social media and messaging apps in particular) play a central role in delivering personalized luxury shopping experiences. **WeChat**, China's most popular social platform, exemplifies this trend by offering a comprehensive suite of services **that integrates social media, e-commerce and customer relationship management (CRM) functionalities.** As an all-in-one platform, WeChat enables luxury brands to reach customers through tailored communications, unique content and personalized shopping experiences across multiple touchpoints. WeChat's versatility is further enhanced by its mini programs – apps within the WeChat ecosystem provide users with extensive services delivered instantly, and without leaving the app. They are key for offering personalized shopping experiences, but also for managing customer data and making communication between the company and customers more efficient (Daxue Consulting, 2024).

WeChat mini programs serve as a cornerstone for building and nurturing the communities that foster a sense of belonging and exclusivity – critical components of the luxury shopping experience. For instance, Burberry has leveraged WeChat's mini-program to create a dedicated digital community where customers can **engage with the brand through social sharing, exclusive content and personalized interactions.** This initiative is particularly **targeted at younger, digitally native luxury consumers who appreciate social communication and authenticity of the brand** (Daxue Consulting, 2024; Liu et al., 2019).

Creating digital communities provides brands with **valuable insights into customer behavior and preferences** because the brands can better understand their clientele and tailor their offerings by fostering stronger relationships through these communities.

Customer relationship management systems are fundamental to maintaining and enhancing customer relationships in the luxury sector. CRM systems enable brands to collect, analyze and actually use customer data to deliver highly personalized experiences (Figure 5.1). Key CRM features contributing to customer retention include personalized recommendations, private consultations and loyalty programs. The omni-CRM, as visualized in Figure 5.1, represents a comprehensive management of customer relationships across all touchpoints, involving data collection, personalized marketing, loyalty programs and more.

Figure 5.1 provides visualization of comprehensive management of customer relationships across all touchpoints, involving data collection, personalized marketing and loyalty

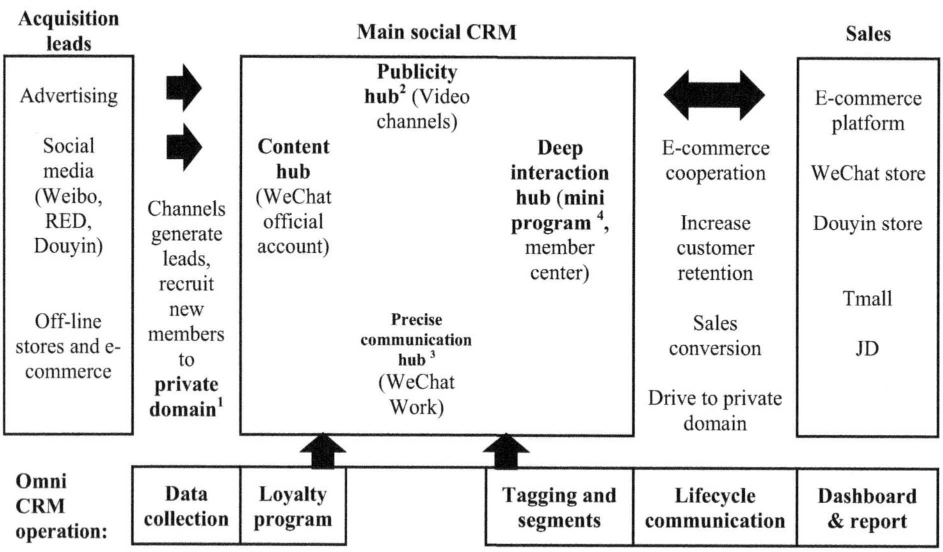

[1] *Digital spaces where brands have direct control over customer interactions and data, typically within proprietary platforms like WeChat where brands can engage with customers more intimately, offering personalized content, services and experiences without the interference or limitations imposed by third-party platforms.*
[2] *Channels within the WeChat ecosystem dedicated to promoting brands through video content, driving awareness and engagement.*
[3] *WeCom is a professional version of WeChat, used for precise communication with customers, allowing personalized interactions through 1V1 chats, group chats and moments.*
[4] *A feature within WeChat that allows brands to create mini programs for deep, interactive engagement with customers, such as personalized services and exclusive offers.*

Figure 5.1 CRM ecosystem in China, based on (Daxue Consulting, 2024, p. 35), simplified and explained by authors.

programs to maintain and enhance customer relationships specifically in the context of the Chinese luxury segment."

The use of data analytics allows luxury brands to offer **customized product suggestions** based on each customer's demographic data, purchase history and behavior patterns. For example, personalized campaigns on WeChat can directly target customers with tailored content, including bespoke private consultations.

A crucial component of CRM in the luxury sector is **loyalty programs**. They often involve tiered membership systems that reward customers with exclusive benefits based on their spending levels. For instance, Farfetch offers a tier-based loyalty program that gives customers access to exclusive discounts, priority customer care and personalized styling services. These programs incentivize repeat purchases and enhance customer loyalty by offering personalized rewards and experiences (Daxue Consulting, 2024).

Integrating CRM systems into omnichannel strategies allows luxury brands to build a unified customer experience across all touchpoints – one that is tailor-made for each customer. Data aggregation is a critical element of this integration because it enables brands to combine customer information from various channels, such as social media, e-commerce platforms and in-store interactions, into a single profile. **WeChat's role as a central platform in China's CRM** landscape demonstrates the power of data aggregation because it combines messaging, social media, payments and business services to facilitate continuous customer engagement.

Liu et al. (2019) suggested that WeChat's integration into luxury brand strategies in China represents a significant shift in how brands manage consumer engagement in the digital era. The platform's ability to combine e-commerce, social media and CRM makes it necessary for brands to maintain and enhance their desirability among digitally-savvy Chinese consumers. Contrary to traditional concerns about the potential for digital channels to dilute luxury brand exclusivity, the study suggests that WeChat can reinforce exclusive brand image and loyalty through tailor-made services that meet the expectations of Chinese HNWIs. The **need for certain cultural adaptations** was also highlighted, including **decentralization of operations to local teams**. In other words, creative content and local cultural credentials that resonate with Chinese consumers are essential. Omnichannel interconnectedness ensures a consistent and high-quality experience across all touchpoints, from in-store interactions to digital communications on WeChat; this is a critical driver of success. Importantly, Liu et al.'s (2019) conclusion emphasizes the **need to thoroughly control e-commerce channels to ensure consistency in brand messaging and product offerings**, and maintain the subtle balance between accessibility and exclusivity (Liu et al., 2019).

5.4 Summary: Evolving dynamics in luxury distribution

The distribution strategies in luxury are experiencing significant evolution driven by technological advancements as well as changes in consumer behavior and demographics. The chapter explores how luxury brands are adapting to new distribution trends, including how they balance their traditional in-store presence while simultaneously expanding and innovating in the digital and social commerce markets. Major luxury groups like Kering SA, LVMH and Richemont have reported substantial increases in online sales, accelerated mainly by the COVID pandemic and the growing purchasing power of younger generations. Despite new technologies, offline retail is still expected to generate most luxury revenues. However, the split may differ by different geographies.

Luxury brands tend to control their distribution channels, and this is considered to be one of the fundamental aspects of a luxury business strategy. Directly operated stores are still gaining importance. Bain & Company's analysis still reports the stable growth of mono-brand stores, which have become critical for luxury brands' post-pandemic recovery and account for a significant portion of total sales. However, this trend is complemented by a rise in experiential retail, where physical stores are evolving to integrate digital and in-person customer journeys.

Younger generations, particularly Gen Z and Gen Alpha, are expected to accelerate the conversion towards social commerce and live shopping. These digital native consumers have a strong affinity for purchasing luxury goods through social media platforms or engaging in live shopping events (especially in some geographies). These channels offer an interactive and personalized shopping experience because the offers are created based on data analytics related to each customer's previous digital behavior. Therefore, brands can respond to the younger generation's need for authenticity in a very personal way.

Key terms

Augmented Reality (AR) in Sales: Technology integrated into luxury shopping to enhance customer experiences.

Customer Journey: The mix of digital and physical touchpoints brands use to engage customers.

Customer Relationship Management (CRM): Systems integral to maintaining and enhancing customer relationships. CRM systems enable brands to collect, analyze, and utilize customer data to deliver highly personalized experiences.

Live Stream Shopping: A form of s-commerce where influencers or brands host live events to promote products.

Luxury E-Commerce: Refers to the digital selling and buying of luxury goods, which accelerated during the COVID pandemic.

Luxury Mono-Brand Stores: Stores that are (typically) directly operated by the luxury brand or group and exclusively sell their own brand's products. Brands maintain control over distribution, branding and client experiences.

Omnichannel: Distribution strategy aiming to create a shopping experience for customers by combining online and offline customer touchpoints.

Personalization: Tailoring luxury experiences to individual customer preferences across digital, physical or omnichannel platforms.

Social Commerce (S-Commerce): The use of social media platforms for shopping and customer interaction.

Discussion questions

1. How did the pandemic affect luxury e-commerce?
2. How does social commerce differ from traditional e-commerce?
3. What is live stream shopping, and why and where is it popular?
4. How do luxury brands use CRM to enhance personalization in customer interactions?
5. What role does WeChat play in luxury CRM strategies and where is it important?
6. What are the key goals luxury brands aim to achieve through live stream commerce, and how do they utilize this strategy effectively?

Reference list

Abdelsalam, S., Salim, N., Alias, R. A., & Husain, O. (2020). Understanding Online Impulse Buying Behavior in Social Commerce: A Systematic Literature Review. *IEEE Access, 4.*

Alibaba Group. (2019, September 30). *Richemont and Alibaba Group Announce the Launch of NET-A-PORTER Flagship Store on Tmall Luxury Pavilion in China.* Retrieved October 2024, from alibabagroup.com: https://www.alibabagroup.com/en-US/document-1491572647861944320

Alibaba Group. (2023, February 20). *Tmall Luxury Pavilion: A Guide to Immersive Shopping.* Retrieved March 2024, from https://www.youtube.com/watch?v=79qxASxxiQU

Alizila. (2024, January 19). *Tmall Luxury Pavilion Brings LVMH's Tiffany & Co. to Digital-First Chinese Shoppers.* Retrieved March 2024, from https://www.alizila.com/tmall-luxury-pavilion-lvmh-tiffany-co-digital-china-shoppers-alibaba/

D'Arpizio, C., & Levato, F. (2022, June 21). *Bain & Company, Inc.* Retrieved September 2022, from Global personal luxury goods market reaches 288 billion in value in 2021 and experienced a remarkable performance in the first quarter 2022: https://www.bain.com/about/media-center/press-releases/2022/global-personal-luxury-goods-market-reaches-288-billion-in-value-in-2021-and-experienced-a-remarkable-performance-in-the-first-quarter-2022/

D'Arpizio, C., Levato, F., & Steiner, A. (2024, January 18). *Long Live Luxury: Converge to Expand through Turbulence.* Retrieved March 2024, from Bain&Company: https://www.bain.com/insights/long-live-luxury-converge-to-expand-through-turbulence/

Daxue Consulting. (2024). *China's Luxury Market in 2024: VICs, Omnichannel & CRM Strategies.* Retrieved August 2024, from daxueconsulting.com: https://daxueconsulting.com/wp-content/uploads/2024/07/Luxury-CRM-2024-final.pdf

Deloitte. (2021). *Global Powers of Luxury Goods 2021.* Retrieved September 2022, from deloitte.com: https://www2.deloitte.com/content/dam/Deloitte/at/Documents/consumer-business/at-global-powers-of-luxury-goods-2021.pdf

Deloitte. (2023, November 29). *Global Powers of Luxury Goods 2023.* Retrieved February 2024, from Deloitte: hhttps://www.deloitte.com/global/en/Industries/consumer/analysis/gx-cb-global-powers-of-luxury-goods.html

Farfetch. (2020, November 5). *Farfetch, Alibaba Group and Richemont Form Global Partnership to Accelerate the Digitization of the Luxury Industry.* Retrieved December 2022, from farfetchinvestors.com: https://www.farfetchinvestors.com/financial-news/news-details/2020/Farfetch-Alibaba-Group-and-Richemont-Form-Global-Partnership-to-Accelerate-the-Digitization-of-the-Luxury-Industry/default.aspx

Farfetch. (2022a). *About Farfetch.* Retrieved December 2022, from farfetch.com: https://aboutfarfetch.com/about/farfetch/

Farfetch. (2022b). *Annual Report 2021.* Retrieved December 2022, from s22.q4cdn.com: https://s22.q4cdn.com/426100162/files/doc_financials/2021/ar/2021-Annual-Report.pdf

Forbes. (2022, August 28). *Richemont-YNAP Deal Puts Farfetch Closer to Being the Global Platform for Luxury.* Retrieved September 2022, from forbes.com: https://www.forbes.com/sites/pamdanziger/2022/08/28/richemont-ynap-deal-puts-farfetch-closer-to-being-the-global-platform-for-luxury/

Jing Daily. (2022, November 2). *From 2017 to 2022: Five Years of Tmall Luxury Pavilion So Far.* Retrieved December 2022, from jingdaily.com: https://jingdaily.com/tmall-luxury-pavilion-five-years/

Kering SA. (2022, February 17). *Excellent 2021 Performances, Well Ahead of 2019 Levels.* RetrievedFebruary2022,fromKeringSA:https://www.kering.com/en/news/excellent-2021-performances-well-ahead-of-2019-levels

Liu, S., Perry, P., & Gadzinski, G. (2019). The Implications of Digital Marketing on WeChat for Luxury Fashion Brands in China. *Journal of Brand Management, 26*(4), 395–409.

LVG. (2022). *Finalists Announced.* Retrieved October 2022, from LVG: https://www.luxuryinnovationsummit.com/luxury-innovation-award/

McKinsey. (2023, July 7). *Ready for Prime Time? The State of Live Commerce.* Retrieved October 2024, from mckinsey.com: https://www.mckinsey.com/capabilities/growth-marketing-and-sales/our-insights/ready-for-prime-time-the-state-of-live-commerce

McKinsey & Company. (2022, May 2). *State of Fashion Technology Report 2022.* Retrieved November 2022, from mckinsey.com: https://www.mckinsey.com/industries/retail/our-insights/state-of-fashion-technology-report-2022?cid=other-eml-mtg-mip-mck&hlkid=4fc80ecd43b54873932d4f25af6a2314&hctky=1711743&hdpid=2aca0cfa-6346–40c1–93d6–48680a8382a4

McKinsey Digital. (2021, July 21). *It's Showtime! How Live Commerce is Transforming the Shopping Experience.* Retrieved December 2022, from McKinsey Digital: https://www.mckinsey.com/capabilities/mckinsey-digital/our-insights/its-showtime-how-live-commerce-is-transforming-the-shopping-experience

Milnes, H. (2022, August 26). *CEO Neves: Farfetch-YNAP Deal Will Be "Transformational" for Luxury.* Retrieved December 2022, from Vogue Business: https://www.voguebusiness.com/companies/ceo-neves-farfetch-ynap-deal-will-be-transformational-for-luxury

Mr. Porter. (2022). *About Us: Discover Mr. Porter.* Retrieved December 2022, from Mr. Porter: https://www.mrporter.com/en-cz/content/about-us/

Net-a-Porter. (2022). *About Us: Welcome to Net-a-Porter.* Retrieved December 2022, from Net-a-Porter: https://www.net-a-porter.com/en-cz/content/about-us/

The Outnet. (2022). *About Us.* Retrieved December 2022, from The Outnet: https://www.theoutnet.com/en-cz/editorial/about-us/

Rambourg, E. (2020). *Future Luxe: What's Ahead for the Business of Luxury.* Vancouver: Figure 1 Publishing, Inc.

Reuters. (2020, November 5). *Alibaba, Richemont to Invest $1.1 Billion in Farfetch with Focus on China.* Retrieved September 2022, from reuters.com: https://www.reuters.com/article/uk-farfetch-investment-alibaba-idUKKBN27L2Z7

Reuters. (2023, October 23). *European Regulator Approves Farfetch Deal for YNAP, Richemont Says.* Retrieved March 2024, from reuters.com: https://www.reuters.com/markets/deals/european-regulator-approves-farfetch-deal-ynap-richemont-says-2023-10-23/

Richemont. (2022a, August 24). *Richemont, FARFETCH and Alabbar Cement Partnership to Advance the Digitalisation of the Luxury Industry.* Retrieved September 2022, from richemont.com: https://www.richemont.com/en/home/media/press-releases-and-news/richemont-farfetch-and-alabbar-cement-partnership-to-advance-the-digitalisation-of-the-luxury-industry/

Richemont. (2022b). *Investor Presentation.* Retrieved September 2022, from richemont.com: https://www.richemont.com/en/home/investors/results-reports-presentations/

Richemont. (2022c). *Richemont: Annual Report and Accounts 2022.* Retrieved September 2022,fromrichemont.com:https://www.richemont.com/en/home/investors/results-reports-presentations/

Richemont. (2023, December 18). *Richemont, FARFETCH and Symphony Global Terminate Agreements.* Retrieved March 2024, from richemont.com: https://www.richemont.com/

news-media/press-releases-news/richemont-farfetch-and-symphony-global-terminate-agreements/

Richemont. (2024, October 7). *MYT Netherlands Parent B.V. ("Mytheresa") and Richemont Sign Agreement for Mytheresa to Acquire Yoox Net a Porter ("YNAP").* Retrieved October 2024, from richemont.com: https://www.richemont.com/media/jxxnx3yq/myt-netherlands-parent-bv-mytheresa-and-richemont-sign-agreement-for-mytheresa-to-acquire-yoox-net-a-porter-ynap.pdf

Robertson, T. S. (2022, September–October). *Selling on TikTok and Taobao.* Retrieved October 2024, from hbr.org: https://hbr.org/2022/09/selling-on-tiktok-and-taobao

Smartzer. (2022). *The #1 Live Shopping & Interactive Video Platform.* Retrieved October 2022, from smartzer.com: https://www.smartzer.com

Smartzer. (2024a). *Bloomingdale's x DIOR | + Live Shopping Masterclass.* Retrieved October 2024, from smartzer.com: https://www.smartzer.com/case-studies/case-studies-dior-x-bloomingdales

Smartzer. (2024b). *VALENTINO | Interactive & Discoverable Runway.* Retrieved March 2024, from smartzer.com: https://www.smartzer.com/case-studies/case-studies-valentino

Som, A., & Blanckaert, C. (2021). *The Road to Luxury: The New Frontiers in Luxury Brand Management* (2nd edition). Wiley.

Tencent. (2024). *Connecting Ecosystems.* Retrieved March 2024, from tencent.com: https://www.tencent.com/en-us/business.html

Vogue Business. (2023, December 20). *Without Farfetch, What's Next for YNAP?* Retrieved March 2024, from https://www.voguebusiness.com/story/companies/without-farfetch-whats-next-for-ynap

YNAP. (2022). *Online Flagship Stores.* Retrieved December 2022, from YNAP: https://www.ynap.com/what-we-do/online-flagship-stores/

Yu, F., & Zheng, R. (2021). The Effects of Perceived Luxury Value on Customer Engagement and Purchase Intention in Live Streaming Shopping. *Asia Pacific Journal of Marketing and Logistics*, *34*(6), 1303–1323.

Chapter 6

Corporate social responsibility and sustainability

The United Nations Environment Program defines a sustainable lifestyle as:

> A cluster of habits and patterns of behaviour embedded in a society and facilitated by institutions, norms and infrastructures that frame individual choice, in order to minimize the use of natural resources and generation of wastes, while supporting fairness and prosperity for all.
> (Akenji & Chen, 2016; from Bengtsson et al., 2021)

Luxury consumers, like any other people or consumers, contribute to the carbon footprint. Research by the United Nations Environment Organization (UNEP) shows **a strong correlation between income levels and emissions** and an unequal global distribution of emissions consumption between high- and low-income people. The report points to a link between income levels and consumption, with the share of emissions of the wealthiest 10% of individuals ranging from 36–49% of the global total, while that of the poorest 5% of the world's population is in the range of 7–15% of the total emissions. To illustrate, the UNEP research gives estimates of changes in emissions to reach the global target of 2.1 tCO_2 per capita by 2030: emissions of the wealthiest 1% would have to be reduced 30-fold and emissions of the richest 10% to about one-tenth of current consumption, while emissions of the poorest 50% could increase threefold (United Nations Environment Programme, 2020).

After some initial hesitation, the luxury sector – supported by the academic community among others – is now embracing social responsibility and sustainability, despite a certain contradiction between luxury and sustainability, stemming directly from the definition of both terms. Luxury is associated with excess, pleasure, showing off, waste and spending, while sustainability, on the contrary, is related to ethics and limitation, meaning the satisfaction of current needs without limiting the ability of future generations to satisfy their own. On the other hand, luxury products are to some extent sustainable in their own, as they are designed to last a lifetime, do not go out of fashion, are often produced in the brand's country of origin and have a smaller environmental impact compared to other sectors. At the same time, especially for younger generations, sustainability is becoming part of their lifestyle, and the question of whether and how to include it in luxury brand communication is part of the strategic decisions of luxury companies.

 DOI: 10.4324/9781003593706-6

Another reason for implementing socially beneficial activities and sustainability into the strategies of luxury companies is the view of investors who are looking for investment opportunities among companies with positive environmental impacts, with so-called positive ESG ratings (environmental, social, governmental). More than half of potential investors in the segment with at least $1 million investable assets (55% of HNWIs) stated that the goal of asset management is to invest in activities with positive ESG impact. A closer look at their age revealed that it is 71% for investors under 40 and 49% for investors over 40. In general, topics related to both the environment and ethical management, and corporate governance as well as the creation of a risk management and compliance frameworks are attractive to HNWI investors (Capgemini Research Institute, 2022).

6.1 Implementation of the UN Sustainable Development Goals

On 25 September 2015, at the UN Summit on Sustainable Development in New York, the global community endorsed the *Sustainable Development Goals* (SDGs), for which national governments are primarily responsible for tracking, reviewing and monitoring progress towards the 2030 target year. The 17 SDGs, with a total of 169 targets designed to be relevant to each country, are continuously integrated into national planning processes and policies. The basis for formulating sustainable goals are three pillars: environmental, social and economic (Figure 6.1), and a sustainable enterprise lies at their intersection.

The social pillar of sustainability is generally based on the attainability of basic human rights and needs for all citizens. A socially sustainable company should have the support of

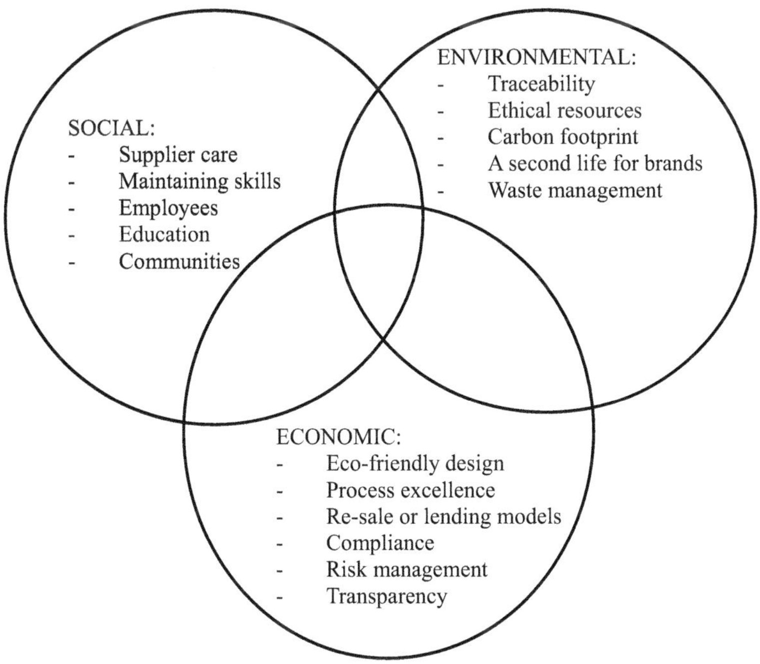

Figure 6.1 Sustainability pillars, modified by the authors according to (Som & Blanckaert, 2021).

employees, stakeholders and the community in which it operates. It should be a good neighbor and member of the community, both locally and globally. In the context of this pillar, the employers include benefits for employees (e.g. work-life balance, longer maternity leave, learning and self-development opportunities), community involvement (sponsorships, scholarships, investment in public projects at the point of production, etc.) or sustainability of the entire supply chain, including monitoring of the sustainable activities of individual subcontractors, in the sustainable goals of the pillar.

For a business to be sustainable, it must be profitable. **The economic pillar** of sustainability is therefore based on the profitability of the company, but it also includes compliance, good corporate governance, transparency, risk management and corporate governance in accordance with the interests of shareholders, society, suppliers and end customers. It is important for investors to know that the company uses transparent accounting methods, that shareholders have a say in important issues, that managers do not have conflicts of interest and that they do not engage in illegal practices. Sometimes this pillar is called governance, as known from ESG reporting.

The environmental pillar is sometimes considered synonymous with sustainability, but it is one of three pillars. Its aim is to keep the planet's environment in balance, where the consumption rate of natural resources adapts to their creation. Many companies are focusing on reducing their carbon footprint, packaging waste and saving water, which can have a positive financial impact and help the planet. For luxury brands, some resources are hard to replace, and through innovation, companies adapt to the requirements of reducing the use of natural resources. The pioneer in this area is the Stella McCartney brand from the Kering Group, which embraces responsibility with a positive impact on people and the planet with the vision of having as little impact on the environment as possible. It strives to co-create state-of-the-art materials and alternatives to raw animal materials, promote circularity and be fully transparent by developing tools for measuring and reporting environmental impact (Stella McCartney, 2022b). A mini-case study on Stella McCartney's journey towards sustainability summarizes the timeline of implementing step-by-step phases to environmental sustainability.

Mini-case 6.1 Stella McCartney: The road to sustainability paved by the strong personality of its founder

Stella McCartney is a luxury lifestyle brand that was launched under the designer's name as a joint venture with the Kering Group in 2001. Before that, the founder was creative director for Chloé within the Richemont Group. Stella's approach to design emphasizes top-notch tailoring and natural confidence with an emphasis on a sexy look. The brand is a pioneer in sharing ethical values and takes responsibility for the resources it uses and the impact it has on the environment. She has long been exploring innovative ways to become more sustainable: from designing clothing to store design and product production. Stella McCartney is a lifelong vegetarian, so throughout her career she has tended to use no animal skin or fur. The brand is represented in women's and men's clothing, handbags, shoes and a range of children's clothing. Her growth was supported by providing licenses for the production of glasses, underwear, swimwear and fragrances as well as through a long-term partnership with the brand Adidas. Stella McCartney collections are currently available in 48 directly owned stores and 28 franchise stores globally, in cities including London, Los Angeles, Tokyo, Hong Kong, Dubai, Milan, Shanghai, Florence, Paris and

New York. The brand also distributes to more than 100 countries with its online shop (Stella McCartney, 2024a).

In 2018, after 17 years, the brand became independent by purchasing its stake from the Kering Group, and one year later, Stella entered into a partnership with the LVMH conglomerate, which had already developed the Stella by Stella McCartney line of vegan beauty products (LVMH, 2022). Table 6.1 shows a timeline for the gradual implementation of sustainable brand activities, showing the gradual removal of natural raw materials for garment creation and their replacement with innovative materials created with less impact on the environment.

Table 6.1 Timeline of the implementation of Stella McCartney's environmentally sustainable activities. Authors based on (Stella McCartney, 2022b, 2024a, 2024b).

2001	Discarding animal skins, feathers, furs.
2008	Transition to organic cotton.
2010	Elimination of PVC.
2012	Introduction of bio acetate into the eyewear segment (Stella Eyewear). Start of using recycled polyester. Launch of the Clean by Design project in Tal factories (a program to improve water and energy use in textile factories). Ban on plastic water bottles. Ensuring certification of the wood used. Joining the Ethical Trading Initiative (ETI), which brings together companies to ensure compliance with international labor standards in its members' global supply chains.
2013	Stop using Angora (rabbit fur). Introduction of Alter Nappa skin replacement. Start of using solar panels and LED lights at the point of sale.
2014	Ensuring certification of all paper and cardboard packaging used.
2016	Ensuring 100% sustainable viscose. Stop using cashmere.
2017	The first garment made of Bolt Threads' Microsilk (a biosynthetic silk-like fiber made by the fermentation process of water, yeast and sugar with spider DNA) has been launched. Introduction of reclaimed nylon under the Econyl brand (made from waste from landfills and the ocean).
2018	Ban on the use of mohair (textile fiber from the coat of an Angora goat). Launch of the Loop sneaker with a commitment to phase out the use of plastic. Launch of Stan Smith's first vegan sneakers. Creation of the first leather handbag grown on the mycelium Mylo from Bold Thread.
2019	adidas by Stella McCartney launched the first garments made from Evrn. NuCycle and fur KOBA Fur Free Fur (sustainably recyclable animal alternatives and made from recycled polyester and plant plastic).
2020	Debut of biodegradable flexible denim Coreva. Introduction of biolenses in Stella McCartney glasses. Bioacetate frames in Stella Kids glasses. Showcase of an innovative sustainable fusion of Stellawear underwear and swimwear made from reclaimed Aquafil Econyl nylon and ROICA elastane.

(Continued)

Table 6.1 (Continued)

2021	Release of Air Slides soles, produced from recycled manufacturing waste sourced directly from the factories they are made in. Launched the garments made from Mylo.
2022	Launch of the Mylo handbag (made of lightly-grained mycelium-based vegan alternative to animal leather). Introduction of Recycrom dye (color powders made from 100% textile waste). Introduction of Humana denim made of recycled textile waste. Introduction of new vegan alternative to animal leather using grape waste.
2023	Introduction of the first parka made from ECONYL designed to be returned and regenerated into new yarn at its end-of-life.

A Fashion House operating in different categories like Stella McCartney, such as bags, clothes and accessories, with strong sustainability and animal-free commitments, has many obstacles to overcome. This requires a significant investment into research and development, the main one being the process of ensuring the sustainability of all suppliers. This is an everyday challenge for Stella and her team, and as stated in the 2023 Impact Report, this is "a work in progress." Among the key tasks for the future is developing a specific strategy for undertaking audits for Tier 1 and Tier 2 product suppliers by setting up a procedure that would be shared with all operations teams and improving supply chain transparency and product traceability by centralizing and standardizing all information from the suppliers. The goal is to do so under the Stella McCartney Sustainability Hub (Stella McCartney, 2024a, 2024b).

Stella McCartney and her brand are leading in sustainable designer luxury fashion. The brand aims to drive positive change across the industry as well with consumer behavior. Activism is fundamental to the brand's identity, as is the founder's personality, which is very authentic in promoting the protection of the planet and cruelty-free practices. The challenges she is facing include advocating for the rights of people within the supply chain, as well as monitoring suppliers. Since its establishment in 2001, Stella McCartney has upheld a unique, cruelty-free standpoint, avoiding animal products such as leather and fur while pioneering sustainable materials such as organic cotton. Through global activism, collaborations with innovators, and participation in key events like the United Nations' COP conferences, the brand seeks to reshape industry policies and practices, championing sustainability, circularity and innovation for future generations, in line with the brand commitment to being an ethical, modern and honest company without compromising on luxury or quality (Stella McCartney, 2024b).

Stella McCartney's approach is an example of the SDG 12 initiatives – to ensure sustainable consumption and production models – which formulate objectives for the sustainable management and efficient use of natural resources, the reduction of waste and, most importantly, encourage large multinationals to adopt sustainable practices and integrate sustainability information into their reporting cycle. Similarly, SDG 8 – with labor and economic growth – is intended to promote sustainable economic growth, full and productive employment, and decent work for all (United Nations, 2015). Work on the SDGs, and in particular Goal 12, is expected to be led by developed countries; the world's leading industries must also be active.

The automotive and food categories are examples of large industries that have significantly integrated CSR and sustainability activities into their planning and strategic processes. Companies such as Unilever or Nestlé are examples that have effectively incorporated the SDGs into their sustainable business strategies (Haski-Leventhal, 2018). Other examples come from the tobacco or fast-food industries, which for various reasons (e.g. usually defending their own business sector from the interference of authorities) have long since crossed the threshold where social responsibility becomes an essential part of a company's strategic management and success (Chandler, 2017).

Table 6.2 provides an overview of the individual SDGs included in the CSR strategies of leading luxury brands and groups. In terms of sustainability strategies of the analyzed companies, most of the selected organizations consider environmental protection (SDG 13) specifically in terms of reducing energy and water consumption, reducing carbon footprint and using renewable energies to be the key axes of their strategy due to their impact on business. The other three most important targets are responsible consumption and production (SDG 12), gender equality (SDG 5), decent work and economic growth (SDG 8) and partnership (SDG 17). Reporting by companies in this area is not yet consistent, and therefore the figure from Table 6.2 is only a preview of the recent situation.

In addition to the United Nations Sustainable Development Goals and the SDGs, luxury sector companies and brands set their own commitments and targets, usually tied to the SDGs, whose achievements they report regularly. As an example, the link between the SDGs and Chanel's social responsibility and sustainability activities is highlighted in the Chanel & Sustainability study, Mission 1.5°.

Mini-case 6.2 Chanel & sustainability: Mission 1.5°

At the end of 2019, Chanel became a signatory to the Fashion Pact, joining fashion companies committed to protecting the environment through science-based goals and strategies. In 2020, it published an official statement of its goals in the fight against climate change under the title **Chanel Mission 1.5°** intending to meet many of the targets set by the 2015 Paris Climate Agreement, which aims to limit the average global heating to no more than 1.5° Celsius compared to pre-industrial levels.

Restricting global warming to 1.5° Celsius is achievable, but it requires a cooperative effort from all stakeholders. Global heating has already reached 1.3°C, and current policies may lead to 2.5°C. But remaining within the 1.5°C limit is critical to avoid severe consequences. Prof. Vanesa Castán Broto, an IPCC author (The Intergovernmental Panel on Climate Change, the United Nations' body for assessing the science related to climate change), acknowledges that although keeping temperature changes under 1.5°C is challenging, it is still possible with determined action, even if it sometimes feels like a daunting task (The Guardian, 2023).

Chanel is committed to meeting its climate commitments (SDG 13) across the brand and its entire supply chain and is continuing broader system measures under Chanel's Mission 1.5° program, according to the 2021 earnings report. The company reported **progress in meeting its science-based targets by** reducing **both Scope 1** emissions (direct emissions from sources owned and controlled by the company) as a result of the company's activities, **and Scope 2** (emissions from the production of purchased energy from a public service provider, that is, all greenhouse gas emissions released into the atmosphere from the consumption of purchased electricity, steam, heat and cooling) by 50% in 2030 compared to 2020. They additionally aim to reduce Scope 3 emissions (all other emissions not included in Scope 2 that occur in the company's value chain, i.e. emissions associated with the company's operations) by 40% by 2030 (Bernoville, 2022). In 2022, Chanel reported 92% of its electricity from renewable sources, an increase of 22 percentage points compared to 2020 (SDG 7), and it plans to source 100% of its energy from renewable sources for all of its operations by 2025 (Chanel, 2024a, 2024b).

Chanel's sustainability report in 2022 also pointed to a 40% global increase in sustainability professionals focused on **managing the Group's sustainability strategy**. To shift sustainability topics into the company's decision-making, the company has established a position of "Sustainability Performance and Reporting" with dual responsibilities – towards the CFO and the Chief Sustainability Officer. Chanel is an ambassador for gender equality (SDG 5) **with regard to its brand identity** created by an independent woman, Gabrielle Chanel (Picture 6.1).

Picture 6.1 Gabrielle Chanel – Inspiration for the brand's support of women's empowerment. By Ilonamay, under the Creative Commons Attribution-Share Alike 3.0 Unported license. Available at (Wikimedia Commons, 2014).

Gabrielle Chanel, a lady herself, had a strong affinity towards entrepreneurship. The company believes that women's empowerment and gender equality are not only a matter of equal rights but are also key to global progress. Chanel is not only a signatory to the UN Women Empowerment Principles (WEPs), but the Chanel Foundation also supports women's empowerment as agents of change in the world by supporting more than 140 projects by 2022. In 2018, the CHANEL Foundation and UN Women launched a partnership to accelerate women's economic empowerment and combat climate change through a multi-year program in Asia. It aims to engage 42,000 women in initiatives aimed at strengthening resilience to climate change through environmentally sustainable methods and training on new technologies. And in 2019, *Gender, Climate and Environment* became one of the key thematic areas of the work of the CHANEL Foundation.

To better understand the implications of the company's impact, Chanel joined the Task-Force on Natural Financial Disclosures Forum, whose mission is to develop and deliver a risk management framework for organizations to support a shift in global financial flows from natural negative to natural positive outcomes (TNFD, 2022). In addition, the firm has entered into a three-year partnership with the University of Cambridge Institute for Sustainability Leadership (CISL), which focuses on educational and sustainability leadership programs, innovative operational projects, as well as providing scholarships to students and thus future sustainability leaders who come from underrepresented or motivated backgrounds (SDG 17).

The company **innovates the materials of its products**, which requires significant investments in research and development. These include recycled glass for a bottle of Chanel No. 5, plant-based lids for the Les Eaux de Chanel collection, and the use of sustainably sourced and certified materials. N°1 DE CHANEL is Chanel's first product line conceived with an integrated eco-design approach including: (1) up to 97% natural origin ingredients and up to 76% camellia derivatives produced with strict environmentally friendly farming practices, (2) eco-packaging in terms of reducing the weight of glass jars and bottles by 30% on average across the entire line, (3) the crème of the same line can be refilled to further reduce impacts and an external life cycle assessment indicates that refilling twice reduces the product's carbon footprint by 50% and (4) recycled materials used for sales promotion materials and merchandising at the point of purchase (Services.Chanel, 2022).

The 2023 report further advanced CHANEL Mission 1.5° towards the company climate commitments to net-zero targets, meaning both the extension of the organizational boundary and a change in scope in terms of categories. Originally, CHANEL Mission 1.5° included all scopes for Chanel Brand and Scopes 1 and 2 for the integrated suppliers within operational control, but as of 2023, the company's net-zero targets include categories of Scope 3 for all integrated suppliers (Chanel, 2024a).

In the cultural field, the company Chanel Limited founded The Chanel Culture Fund to **support cultural innovation**. The Fund's partners include The Centre Pompidou in Paris, The Underground Museum in Los Angeles and Power Station of Art in Shanghai. The Fund has launched the Chanel Next Prize, in which ten artists who radically redefine their fields – from visual arts, dance, music and theater to games and metaverse – can receive up to $100,000 in prize money and additional support in the form of mentoring from Chanel (Chanel, 2020).

Table 6.2 SDGs of selected luxury groups and brands. Authors according to (Lopez & Rangel, 2022; Hermès, 2020, 2021b; Impakter Index, 2022; The Estée Lauder Companies, 2022).

SDGs/Company		LVMH	Kering	Estée Lauder	Richemont	Chanel Limited	Hermès	Chow Tai Fook	Rolex
1	No Poverty	x							
2	Zero Hunger	x							
3	Good Health and Well-Being	x	x	x			x		x*
4	Quality Education	x					x		x*
5	**Gender Equality**	**x**	**x**	**x**	**x**	**x**	**x**		**x***
6	Clean Water and Sanitation	x	x						
7	Affordable and Clean Energy	x				x			
8	**Decent Work and Economic Growth**	**x**	**x**		**x**		**x**	**x**	
9	Industry, Innovation and Infrastructure	x						x	
10	Reduced Inequalities	x		x			x		
11	Sustainable Cities and Communities	x					x		
12	**Responsible Production and Consumption**	**x**	**x**	**x**	**x**		**x**	**x**	**x***
13	**Climate Action**	**x**	**x**	**x**	**x**	**x**		**x**	**x***
14	Life Below Water								x*
15	Life on Land	x	x	x		x			x*
16	Peace, Justice and Strong Institutions	x					x		
17	**Partnership for the Goals**	**x**			**x**	**x**	**x**	**x**	

*Rolex did not publish its sustainability goals until Q4 2022. Their activities to promote climate, life in water and on land, and for responsible production and consumption would assign them SDGs 1, 2, 5, 12, 13, 14 and 15 (Impakter Index, 2022).

6.2 Developing an approach to social responsibility and sustainability in luxury

The luxury industry has not always been a pioneer in paving the way for implementing CSR and sustainability best practices. This is because there was no public pressure to do so, and some found the relationship between luxury and sustainability to be contradictory. CSR marketing, defined as "campaigns that are not directly aimed at selling products or services, but those that demonstrate the values, responsibility, sustainability and reputation of the company" (Haski-Leventhal, 2018, p. 311), means going beyond the conventional marketing mix and communication channels in order to gain a sustainable competitive advantage by communicating sustainable brand activities. This is not yet common in the luxury sector. CSR communication is debatable in every industry, but in luxury, deciding on communication topics is even more difficult due to the specifics of marketing and clientele and the aforementioned contradiction between sustainability and luxury.

Still quite recently, in 2015, Kapferer and Michaut described sustainability in the luxury industry as **"sustainability silence"** because few luxury companies took a proactive stance in sustainable development (Kapferer & Michaut, 2015, p. 8). The luxury sector was aware of the problems but remained discreet, which was interpreted as disinterested.

Over the last decade, the situation has begun to change and there has been pressure to engage luxury companies in sustainability: "The unfavorable press, together with the rapid flow of information through social media, has influenced how consumers perceive luxury fashion brands. In response to stakeholder demands, luxury fashion companies have focused more intensively on adopting more sustainable practices. At a time when competition is huge and information is at the consumer's fingertips, it is essential that luxury brands have a fully sustainable and transparent business strategy." (Franco et al., 2020, p. 55)

However, some previous research has warned that sustainability and luxury are **contradictory** (i.e. incompatible) because luxury itself creates social injustice and harms the environment. The authors pointed to the conclusion that the interest of clients of luxury brands regarding sustainability when purchasing luxury brands is relatively minimal (Kapferer & Michaut-Denizeau, 2014); other authors suggested that involvement of the information about luxury product sustainability has a negative impact on the perceived quality of luxury products with the impact varying according to different countries of origin (Dekhili et al., 2019; Achabou & Dekhili, 2013). To some extent, the **discrepancy between the quality of luxury products and sustainability communication** has been discussed.

Kapferer and Michaut-Denizeau (2014) identified sustainability issues in luxury as those related to hidden parts of the supply chain, such as sourcing raw materials (e.g. control sources of all animal skins, gold, or precious stones), animal treatment (e.g. foie gras lobby, crocodile farms, killing baby seals for fur, etc.), working conditions (e.g. in gold or diamond mines), production methods polluting the local environment (e.g. mercury for tanning leather) and environmental destruction (e.g. endangered tree species used in the luxury furniture industry, exploitation of scarce water resources by luxury golf courses and hotels in poor countries). These sustainability issues specific to the luxury industry align with previously published public concerns about the role of gemstones in financial conflicts, the impact of mining operations, workers' rights in companies and their supply chains and trade with products from wildlife (Bendell & Kleanthous, 2007).

The impact of awareness of luxury brands' CSR activities on the shopping behavior of luxury customers has not been measured or proven for a long time. The conclusions of Hung et al. (2011) supported the strong influence of social context on the purchasing intention of luxury brands, with the role of functional and experiential aspects as weaker but still positively correlated with the purchase intention. The symbolic role correlated negatively with the intention to buy. However, the conclusions were not based on a sample of consumers actually buying luxury brands, which, incidentally, is a frequent weakness in luxury goods research (Hung, et al., 2011). Ho et al. (2016) also identified luxury consumer segments where CSR played a more important role in purchasing intentions, such as those with stronger intrinsic value perceptions. Conversely, it played a smaller role in segments with a stronger external value perception, suggesting that CSR plays a more prominent role in consumers' purchasing decisions than previously reported (Ho et al., 2016).

Aliyev et al. (2019) examined the motivations for luxury and sustainable car purchasing intentions and classified e-cars as an *ethical luxury* (Aliyev et al., 2019). And finally, Amatulli et al. (2018) also concluded that the economic and ethical activities of a firm's CSR policy are less visible to buyers of luxury goods, while external CSR activities increase consumers' willingness to buy. Moreover, this relationship is emphasized among consumers with higher status and a striking orientation towards consumption (Amatulli et al., 2018). However, their sample of respondents also used random samples without specific criteria to eliminate those who are not luxury customers.

6.3 The relationship between knowledge of luxury brand CSR and purchasing behavior

In a study, based on the results of in-depth, qualitative interviews with luxury customers, Olšanová et al. (2018) examined brand CSR awareness as a potential factor influencing purchase intention towards luxury brands. The results indicated a positive relationship between the social responsibility associated with the brand, along with core luxury values and the intention to purchase it. The qualitative research findings have shown that the **lack of knowledge about CSR activities in the luxury industry is not explicitly linked to a specific brand but is weak for the industry as a whole.** However, most respondents also agreed that they feel better when buying from a socially-responsible company. Additionally, it was confirmed that the traditional values of luxury brands (symbolic, experiential, functional and social) have a stronger influence on the purchasing intent compared to the sustainable dimension. While knowledge of specific CSR activities of specific brands was low, respondents from the luxury sector were very open to considering CSR as an added value to their purchases (Olšanová et al., 2018).

The relationship model resulting from the interpretation of qualitative research (Olšanová et al., 2018) was examined in a quantitative survey on data from a sample of 253 respondents with proven purchases of selected brands in the luxury sector, which showed **a significant positive relationship between awareness of the CSR activity of the purchased luxury brand and the consumer's purchase intention.** This means that a consumer of luxury goods who is aware of the corporate social activities of a particular luxury brand is more likely to purchase it. In other words, raising awareness among luxury consumers about a particular brand's social and environmental activities will positively influence their shopping behavior. The results further indicated the positive impact of demographics on the relationship between CSR brand awareness and purchasing behavior, taking into account age and gender. Specifically, it was confirmed that men aged 30–55 have a higher purchase intent compared to other segments when knowing the CSR of a luxury brand, which has already been confirmed outside the luxury sector (Olšanová et al., 2022).

At the same time, it has been shown that the general attitudes of luxury sector customers towards sustainability are not related to the purchase of a luxury brand nor do they significantly impact the relationship between CSR awareness of a brand and purchasing behavior. This finding can be explained by the content of the scales used to measure general attitudes towards sustainability (Kapferer & Michaut-Denizeau, 2014); the statements are rather general in nature and contain items related to the planet, pollution, environment, food and health. Respondents find these too far removed to make a real decision about buying luxury products. Simply said, respondents had difficulties linking their overall attitudes towards sustainability issues to purchasing a luxury brand. Davies et al. (2012) have noted in this context that, for example, the importance of ethical production conditions for customers is significantly lower for luxury purchases compared to products with high purchase frequency, where they feel that they can make a more significant contribution to tangible change due to higher volumes in general purchases during their lives (Davies et al., 2012).

6.4 Implementation of CSR in the luxury sector

Luxury brands feel a growing expectation with regard to their approach to sustainability and social responsibility, especially in the context of younger generations of consumers who are slowly entering the luxury market. Many luxury brands have issued declarations of intent in the past decade to become a means of change for sustainability and will strive to meet these commitments in the coming years. Business executives face the challenge of identifying the clear steps needed to realize these long-term goals at the following points, which form the vision of the future luxury sector:

1. **Redefining a brand's purpose towards sustainability**, with an emphasis on preserving its identity, that is, having a product that is both beautiful and good for people and the planet. The growing demand for more sustainable luxury brands is expected to be structural, rather than a fad. The brand's purpose must be authentic so that the consumer can believe it. The mini-case Chanel & Sustainability – Mission 1.5° is a good example of fit between the brand identity, including the DNA related to the personality of Gabrielle Chanel and its CSR strategy;
2. **Decoupling growth from volume** is a way for a company to produce growing sales without relying on volume increases, thereby minimizing environmental impact. Growing sales figures can come from supporting circular business models such as resale and lease. AI can increase the accuracy of sales forecasts, reducing overproduction and waste. Most unnecessary fabrics can be upcycled into future collections or limited editions at a higher price. Reselling and lending will also help deliver growing sales while maintaining volume. An item borrowed approximately 20 times can generate a margin of more than 40%, which is less than the usual 65% margin on new product sales; however, lending has the advantage of expanding the luxury customer base with new entrants for whom the brand would otherwise be out of reach;
3. **A fully transparent and traceable supply chain** proving the origin of each ingredient of clothing, bag or pair of shoes, as well as the place and date of manufacture. The customer will be able to see not only data on the environmental and social impact of the company's suppliers, but also his/her own environmental impact if he/she makes a purchase of a

certain item. The supply chain should be narrower (fewer suppliers) and evolve towards a more localized one (where possible);
4. **Maximizing environmental and social commitments** towards zero greenhouse gas emissions through introducing renewable energy in offices, factories and suppliers, diversity of the work community, and inclusivity in marketing communication (avoiding outdated beauty standards, including different body types, ethnicities, age, gender, etc.);
5. **The creation of economic value from sustainability,** which is not seen as a source of additional costs, but as a long-term contributor to cash flow. Investments in regenerative agriculture, reforestation and community programs further reduce tax expenses. More generally, KPIs that were previously isolated in silos labelled *sustainability* and *finance* are integrated across the enterprise and are part of the strategy and strategic decision-making. Transparent reporting makes it easier for investors to navigate as they do not have to worry about investing in a company that hides or obfuscates about its environmental commitments or results (D'Arpizio et al., 2021).

The following represent the basic building blocks needed in order to incorporate sustainability into the strategic management of an organization: setting a bold strategic vision and redefining the purpose of the company, creating a transparent basis for key sustainability issues, defining scientifically based and qualitative goals for a positive impact for the following decade, having up-to-date projects for the implementation of the vision and goals, building and promoting the commitment to sustainability through the management of the company and alignment of the organizational and operational model with new challenges.

It is important to approach sustainability in a holistic way, one that involves consumers, employees, suppliers, communities and all corporate departments. This will enable meaningful change while making significant gains in the form of economic rewards for the business. The Hermès case study shows some of the company's tools to develop its sustainability and social responsibility strategy.

Mini-case 6.3 Creating a CSR strategy: The Hermès brand example

The basic principles of CSR strategy creation in the luxury industry are not fundamentally different from the steps taken by other sectors. An illustrative example of the specifics of luxury across the entire CSR strategy spectrum is apparent from the Hermès approach. Hermès created a structured framework of CSR in 2015 and has been using and gradually improving it since then. Corporate social responsibility reports are characterized by a high level of transparency, which makes it possible to verify the company's advanced approach towards CSR.

Since the brand's foundation in 1837, its development has been shaped by attributes of craftsmanship, which – over time – have become core corporate values shared with employees, suppliers and partners. These value attributes have long formed a platform for forming a corporate social responsibility strategy and are intertwined with the individual pillars of CSR, which are:

- **Responsibility**: every handmade Hermès leather product is the work of a single person according to the original production principle of *one person, one bag*, where one individual manages all the steps required to create the bag and is thus responsible for its final quality. The same sense of responsibility applies to the quality of the materials used and the long-term service life of the product;

- **Authenticity**: craftsmen exploit the authenticity of perfect materials in terms of their authenticity, avoiding the use of imperfect raw materials, even if the end result may seem acceptable. The product must be perfect from the inside, not just from the outside. Hermès craftsmen and other employees constantly question every stage of development and production precisely to maintain the pure perfection of the products. Sustainable development is built in the spirit of honesty, perfection and continuous improvement;
- **Urgency**: in the sense of urgent action in case of necessity, not hasty execution. The brand sees time as an ally that allows employees to do their job well, integrate the challenges of all stakeholders and see things from a balanced perspective. In manual production, skipping any follow-up step to save time is impossible. Modes of operations or project management methods support the implementation of responsible procedures and those which combine the demanding production requirements together with efficiency in order to achieve a high-quality end result, all the while maintaining the necessary rhythm to guarantee the final quality (Hermès, 2021b).

Every year, before shaping its sustainability strategy, Hermès reviews the **materiality assessment**, which helps to identify key stakeholder groups along with their needs and expectations and highlights the aspects of sustainability that are essential to the company. The result of the analyses is the so-called **significance matrix,** which then overviews the areas of activities important for the company's CSR strategy. In 2021, for the first time, they used the so-called double materiality analysis, which takes into account two dimensions of values: (1) financial values that are primarily important to investors and (2) social and environmental values that have a broader impact on other stakeholders of the company.

The materiality analysis resulted in identification of 15 topics (Table 6.3), which crystallized after analyzing the results of an anonymous questionnaire survey of a sample of 100 respondents. The sample consisted of both internal sources (representatives of the company's senior management, CSR and sustainability experts from the French headquarters as well as those from foreign branches) and external sources (experts from the luxury industry with knowledge of social responsibility and luxury strategy of the company). The results were analyzed by Hermès' internal commission for sustainable development.

The upper right quadrant of the matrix emphasizes ten priority tasks, or potential problems, that are important to address to the company's CSR strategy. The company further divided all ten potential problems into three areas: the three basic pillars of the CSR strategy, people, planet and communities.

The aspect of people encompasses employee well-being and job fulfillment, know-how and corporate culture, as well as diversity and inclusion. The planet contains ecology and circular economy, sustainable raw materials and their responsible sourcing, animal welfare, climate change and biodiversity. Finally, the community pillar addresses issues from

Table 6.3 Hermès significance matrix (2021), adapted by authors based on (Hermès, 2021b).

Significance for Hermès

Significance to the world

	• Biodiversity	• Ethics and human rights • Employee well-being and job fulfillment • Know-how and corporate culture
• Employer brand: recruiting and retaining employees	• Climate change • Ecology and circular economy • Responsible company • Diversity and inclusion	• Animal welfare • Sustainable raw materials and their responsible sourcing
	• Innovation, research and development • Institutional and non-financial communication	• Resource management: energy, water, waste • Supplier support

identified areas of responsible society, ethics and human rights. In the next phase of CSR strategy development, Hermès created a strategic CSR framework, built on pillars identified through a materiality matrix (linked to the earlier mentioned pillars – people, communities and planet), which they further elaborate into individual measurable activities of each pillar, as illustrated in Table 6.4 with specific challenges and samples of measurements for the People pillar of the strategic CSR framework. The two other pillars are elaborated in a similar way, while the objectives continuously take into account the values of the company mentioned earlier: the responsibility of individuals and society, authenticity and urgency of fulfilling tasks.

The individual challenges for each of the three pillars are further elaborated in detail, linked to the objectives for the next period and to the relevant SDGs, namely for the People pillar: #3 good health and well-being; #4 quality education; #5 gender equality; #8 decent work and economic growth; #10 reduced inequalities; #16 peace, justice and strong institutions; and finally, #17 partnerships for growth.

For the correct setting and continuous fulfillment of CSR objectives, the commitment of top management is important as the only option for serious and long-term linking of the corporate strategy with social responsibility. Figure 6.2 highlights the CSR functions linked to top management. At Hermès, the central department for the design and implementation of CSR strategy is **an independent Sustainable Development Department**, which also oversees the correct implementation of CSR across all operating departments and subsidiaries of the Hermès Group in France and worldwide. It monitors the results achieved, coordinates the activities of various committees (the Committee for Sustainable Development and the Committee for Group Operations) and manages projects between departments and non-financial reporting. One level above the sustainability department in the

Table 6.4 Challenges, objectives and benchmarks for the People pillar; authors based on (Hermès, 2021b).

Priorities	Main challenges and objectives	Specific measurements of results for given year
Well-being and development of employees	Regular comprehensive employee surveys	73% of employees have participated in an employee satisfaction survey in the last three years
	Ensure occupational health and safety	17% decrease in the severity of time-related accidents at work
	Additional financial compensation to salary	€94 million in France split into incentive schemes and profit shares
	Benefits beyond legal requirements	Implementation of maternity policy with compensation maintained, covers 98% of employees in the group and
	Promote diversity	5.68% of company employees in France are people with disabilities
	Promoting gender equality, especially in managerial positions	Signature of the second Disability Agreement in France (in favor of employment and inclusion of people with disabilities) 60% of managers are women 25% of executive positions are held by women, with a view to reaching 40% in the coming year
Savoir-faire and corporate culture	Implement operational and management training	83 trainers covering leather goods for 22 leather workshops
	Cultivation of internal know-how	Worldwide, 423,317 hours of training were provided, 8% more than in the previous year 6,855 leather craftsmen trained over the previous 10 years
	Spreading corporate culture	Creation of an Apprenticeship Center for Leather Haberdashery (with a state diploma) 23 workers awarded the prize for the best French craftsmen (*Meilleurs Ouvriers de France*) 100% of employees receive training on Hermès culture

company's hierarchy is the **Sustainable Development Strategic Committee**, which validates the strategy and then directs and oversees the sustainability department. It consists of 12 members, including three members of the superior Executive Committee, and includes managers from various departments (Human Resources, Industrial Affairs and Distribution, Leather and Textile Workshops and Communication Departments).

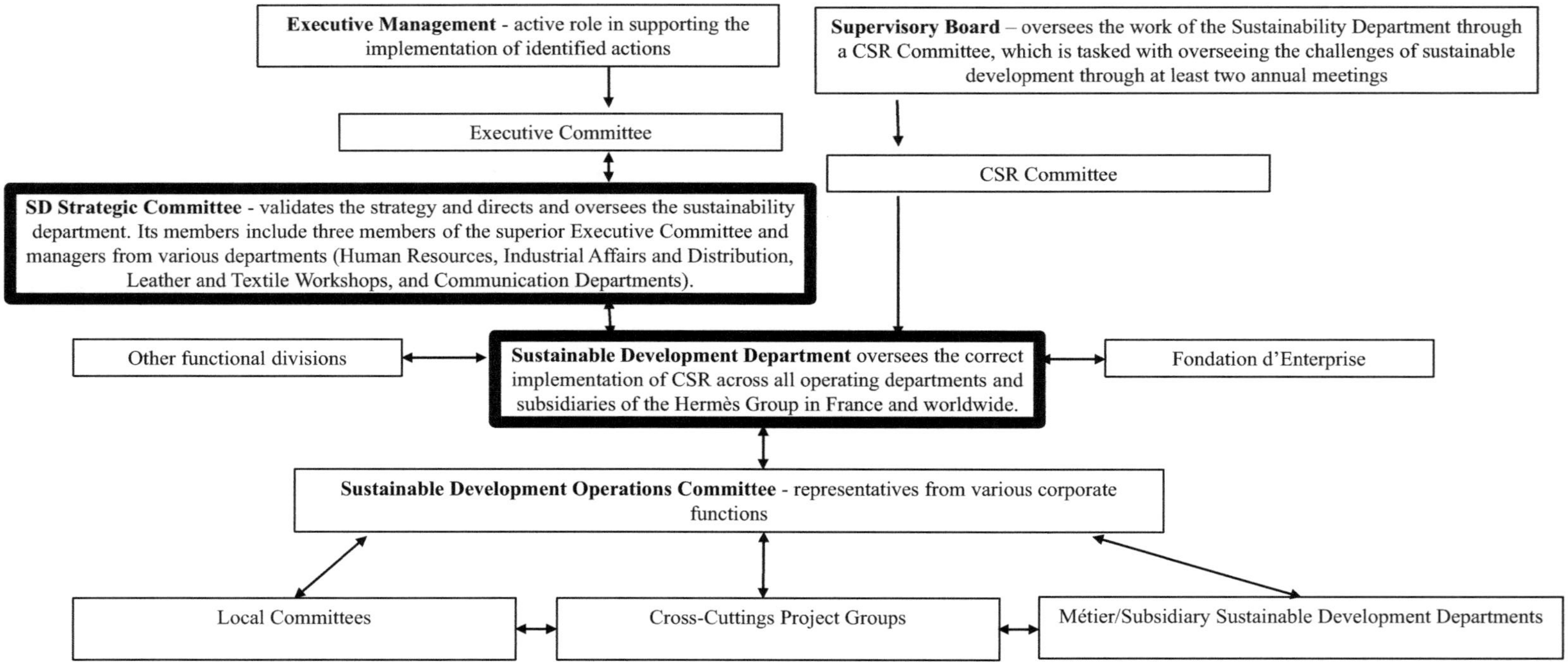

Figure 6.2 Involvement of the sustainability department in the Hermès management hierarchy; authors based on (Hermès, 2021a, 2021b).

In 2021, the members of the **Sustainable Development Strategic Committee** met six times, and the results of their meetings were shared with **the Executive Committee** (hierarchically one level higher) which, together with **the Hermès executive management,** plays an active role in supporting the implementation identified actions.

Since 2019, Executive Chairman Axel Dumas has had a variable remuneration component based on the fulfillment of CSR obligations. The three members of the Executive Committee (who are on the Strategic Committee for Sustainable Development) should inform the Executive Committee of the plans and results of the Committee's work. The work of the Sustainability Department is also overseen by the Supervisory Board through a CSR Committee, which is tasked with overseeing the challenges of sustainable development through at least two annual meetings. This highlights the fact that involvement of top management is absolutely fundamental for the effective and consistent implementation of CSR policy.

The Group's Operations Committee comprises 45 representatives from various corporate functions. It analyzes and validates projects from a technical and functional point of view, and facilitates the sharing of information between departments. Local committees in Asia, Europe and the Americas are regional, initiating and monitoring actions launched and sharing their results during regional meetings. For the eighth consecutive year, the heads of the sustainable development committees in the regions met remotely twice. Environmental initiatives are managed more specifically by the "EEC network" in France, which is run by the Industrial Affairs Department (Hermès, 2021a, 2021b).

This hierarchical structure is an example of good practice for involving top management in the management of socially beneficial activities of the company and a guarantee that CSR goals are linked to the strategic management of the company.

6.5 Luxury and the second life of brands: Circularity enhanced by digital product passports

Another consequence of the shift in the demographics of luxury customers to younger target groups is the shift to new business models. These include shared consumption, renting and second-hand luxury. The second-hand luxury market continues to develop, reaching €45 billion in 2023, thanks to increased demand and growing supply. Overall, the used luxury market grew by 65% between 2017 and 2021, compared to a 12% increase for items in the primary market. In 2023 the growth rates of second-hand luxury normalized to 4–6%, driven by European markets and hard luxury product categories (jewelry and watches), with more than 80% of the items being "pre-loved" (Bain & Company, 2024).

The original intention of new businesses in the second life of brands is usually to promote circular fashion. Unfortunately, many of them only offer unsold inventory in the name of sustainability, which threatens the image of brands. The aspect of sustainable sales is still a big question mark for luxury brands with regard to maintaining the principles of quality and authenticity of their brands (Rathi et al., 2022).

Still, one of the trends stemming from both fashion sustainability and changes in consumer behavior is the growing demand for second-hand luxury goods, as extending the lifespan of luxury products is an effective way for brands, fashion platforms and investors to **demonstrate their commitment to sustainability**. In addition, second-hand sales offer **another distribution channel** that is gaining a share of the larger luxury ecosystem and allowing brands to tap into younger consumer groups. With a relatively new and promisingly growing market, work remains to be done – to create a compelling value proposition, resolve operational complexities, make difficult decisions on branding or rebranding, and ensure the right pricing strategy for oversold items (Bain & Company, 2020). Farfetch's ESG report stated a 153% increase in circular sales, representing 2.1% of the company's total sales. The company's 2030 sustainability targets assume that more than 50% of all items sold or repaired by the company will be circular (defined as second-hand sales or made from recycled or upcycled materials) or those that have been resold, donated, repaired or otherwise had their utility increased through the Farfetch platform (Farfetch, 2022).

The opportunity for luxury brands, trading platforms and investors lies in entering a growing market, demonstrating their commitment to sustainability and, last but not least, implementing a **network-based business** model (i.e. a model in which two or more stakeholders create a common value proposition – some telecommunication companies allow competitors to use their networks, banks connect their ATMs, airlines their reservation systems, etc. (Coyne & Dye, 1998)). There is a unique opportunity for brands and business platforms **to collect customer data** and have at least partial control over the next distribution channel. Brands can also better control the authenticity of resold products, provided they solve the problem of their authentication (Altagamma, 2021). The authentication is either carried out by experts employed in second-hand luxury goods stores (often with errors ending in a luxury brand lawsuit) or by the authentication companies based on advanced data processing technology and the involvement of evolving artificial intelligence. Blockchain technology combined with artificial intelligence is revolutionizing authenticity verification leading towards traceability of the origins and authenticities of luxury items through immutable records stored on the blockchain (Deloitte, 2023).

The acquisition of the British used-watch retailer Watchfinder & Co by the Richemont Group in 2018 is perceived as a significant innovation of the business model towards circularity in the market for used luxury goods. The platform provides a professional, trusted and transparent platform for putting the products of various brands of luxury watches back into circulation. At the same time, it allows the group to obtain important information about when and why a current customer wishes to sell a watch and why a new customer wishes to acquire a used watch, which is a benefit for the companies, customers, individual brands and society.

Daniella Ott, former president of the Swiss non-profit Aura Blockchain Consortium, which brings together luxury groups and brands (more about Aura Blockchain in the section on new technologies in luxury brand management), said the company estimates that over the next decade, physical product sales will account for only 70% of luxury brand sales, 15% for virtual items and 15% for circular sales (Luxury Innovation Summit, Geneva, 2022). In 2024, the Aura Blockchain (with members including LVMH, OTB Group and Prada Group) announced that already 40 million luxury products had gained digital identities through the Aura Blockchain Consortium (Aura Blockchain Consortium, 2022).

The circular model cannot be applied by brands alone. It is a complex system of interdependencies that no company can achieve by itself. Within this ecosystem, luxury companies must collaborate with partner institutions, competitors, researchers and research institutes.

The circular model requires disrupting the traditional linear value chain model and implementing new strategies to (1) promote new business models that increase the use of products (resale, rental, reuse), (2) use new innovative materials that ensure that the use of the material(s) used is minimal or has less negative impact on the environment (biomaterials, biochemicals, etc.) and (3) implement alternative options for converting used products into new or reusable ones (repair, recycling). The transition to a circular scheme must be based on the commitments of large groups in the luxury industry and be supported by digital developments, research and development, and innovation in the form of the creation of biomaterials based on plant resources (e.g. replacing real leather or reducing the use of plastics in clothing, cosmetics or packaging) (Deloitte, 2022).

It is also important to have technology that is able to ensure the authenticity of luxury items, such as digital passports used for the secure resale of original luxury products. The European Commission's proposal for the introduction of the Digital Product Passport (DPP) aims to promote transparency and circularity as it documents a product's entire life cycle, including raw materials and water usage, energy consumption, manufacturing processes, production sites, transport details, sustainability certifications and other relevant environmental impacts. Another tool for securing traceability is a digital ID, such as a QR code inside a product that contains information about its origin(s), care instructions, styling tips, and repair/resale/recycling services (Deloitte, 2023).

Luxury brands should anticipate EU regulations with the roll-out of DPP requirements to begin mid–2027. Initial preparations are taking place already. According to Arianne, the tech provider, there are three main technology architectures for Digital Product Passport, summarized in Table 6.5: centralized, permissioned blockchain and tokenized, differentiated by the forms of accessibility, storage and who can access and edit.

From both operational and business perspectives, tokenization offers significant advantages over other technological options because using a tokenized DPP on a public blockchain ensures high levels of trust, security and integration with other systems. Tokenization naturally supports interoperability, reducing the need for complex IT setups. For brands, it may enhance customer trust in second-hand markets, enable access to additional services, boost brand engagement with minimal data sharing and create a link between physical products and their digital counterparts. For consumers, web3 technology allows them to truly own the digital version of their

Table 6.5 Architecture for Digital Product Passports; authors based on (Arianee, 2024).

	Centralized	**Permissioned Blockchain**	**Tokenized**
DPP Accessibility	Through a web page or app using the physical product identifier	Through a physical identifier and stored in either a custodial or brand-specific central wallet	Through a physical identifier
DPP Storage	**Centralized databases,** managed by a single third-party or linked through a third-party portal	**Private or consortium blockchain,** accessible to platform members Passport usage confined within a closed ecosystem	Stored in either a custodial or non-custodial wallet, DPP **encoded as an NFT on a public blockchain.** Passport intended for use in an open ecosystem
DPP Access	Overseen by a third-party platform	Controlled by ecosystem owner(s)	Managed via encryption keys, passport designed for interoperability with standardized formatting

product, just as they own the physical one. This creates an ongoing, respectful connection between consumers and brands, fostering deeper engagement and interaction (Arianee, 2024).

For example, Breitling, a Swiss watch manufacturer, released in 2022 its first-ever traceable watch – The Super Chronomat Automatic 38 Origins. Each watch owner can access entirely transparent information about their watch, including details of the raw materials, which are verified by Sourcemap (supply chain regulatory software) and securely stored within a third-party-enhanced NFT (Arianee, 2024).

According to research amongst luxury customers conducted in April 2024 by the digital identity tech provider Authentique, the most important attributes luxury customers would most likely use from DPPs are: product information, certificate of authenticity, maintenance and repair instructions, and finally, warranty and resale information. According to Danielle Ott (former president of Arianee) of Vogue Business, the brands should use DPPs as an opportunity for more vital connection with customers: "While currently, brands are focusing on what they have to do to be compliant with the pending regulations, the real opportunity here is to build a more powerful connection with their customers" (Vogue Business, 2024).

Increased digitalization and the use of digital product identifiers are synthesized in Schultz and Seele's (2024) book related to technological trends and the ethical challenges in the Swiss luxury watch business. The use of digital product identifiers (sensors) enable luxury corporations and customers to keep track of their goods throughout the product life cycle, a concept known as *sensored luxury* (Schultz & Seele, 2024).

According to Deloitte's 2022 Luxury Sector Report, luxury companies have come to understand the importance of resale as a strategic solution to reduce negative environmental impact with the increasing importance of sustainability and conscious consumption issues. Due to the growth of the second-hand luxury goods market, where most transactions are done online, new origin verification solutions are a great challenge and a necessity for developing circularity in luxury (Deloitte, 2022).

6.6 Should luxury brands communicate about CSR activities?

Whether and how to communicate the CSR activities of luxury brands is a matter of debate, and it is still difficult for luxury brands to decide on the content of communication about their socially responsible activities. Knowing that luxury consumption is significantly different from non-luxury consumption, it can be expected that consumer reactions to luxury firms' CSR initiatives will also be different. Even with conventional FMCG brands, the success of the brand's CSR communication is not guaranteed. An example of best practice is the Always brand project from the Procter and Gamble portfolio, which, since 2014 (under the name Always#LikeaGirl), has been helping girls overcome puberty problems. Coca-Cola, on the other hand, ran into a problem in 2013 with its efforts to promote social responsibility through communicating its product portfolio and innovations aiming to highlight reduced sugar content and smaller portions. The company withdrew the campaign because neither consumers nor authorities trusted the company's good intentions, since it still generates most of its turnover from selling beverages with high sugar content. Still, CSR research in the non-luxury sectors provides evidence that CSR practices generate positive marketing outcomes, such as favorable consumer attitudes towards the brand (Berens et al., 2005), better company ratings and higher purchasing intentions, as well as a direct positive impact on brand credibility and reputation (Hur et al., 2013).

On the contrary, several published studies show that positive results of CSR communication may not be the case for luxury brands. Consumers may consider luxury brands and CSR incompatible, a paradox that exists between the consumer's self-oriented values of luxury products and the philanthropic values that CSR initiatives often represent. Consumers may undervalue luxury brands that explicitly provide CSR information compared to luxury brands that do not (Torelli et al., 2012), and this is the main reason why some brands are still hesitant to communicate their CSR activities.

In general, the literature already provides evidence that appropriate communication about CSR sustainability activities supports the value of the luxury brand and its positive perception by the consumer, i.e. that awareness of the CSR activity of the brand has a positive impact on the consumer's further purchasing intentions (Olšanová et al., 2022). Research suggests that if a luxury customer knows nothing about a brand's social responsibility, he assumes that the brand behaves responsibly. This assumption is because luxury customers generally have very limited awareness of CSR activities in the luxury sector as a whole (Olšanová et al., 2018). Considering different perceptions of sustainability issues amongst younger target groups, this might be challenged quite soon by Gens Z and Alpha, whose awareness of CSR and sustainability is generally higher.

The content of the luxury brand's CSR communication should be consistent with the brand identity and created with the utmost care to avoid a negative impact on the perception of brand quality. Rolling & Sadachar published the results of an experimental study in 2017, where two randomly selected groups of millennials received a description of the Gucci brand either as a luxury brand only or including sustainable luxury communication, namely *Made from 100% recycled materials*. The results showed that the brand's perception of luxury item communication, including a description of the use of recycled materials, did not change the brand's luxury values compared to pure luxury brand communication. By adding both the recyclable logo and sustainable rhetoric, the perception of Gucci as a luxury brand among survey respondents did not change through measured attributes such as exclusive, prestigious, expensive, elitist, sophisticated, extravagant, emotional, snobbish, attractive or striking. Millennials did not see the brand as less luxurious but rather more sustainable. The authors concluded that brand descriptions that reflect the use of recycled materials do not adversely impact purchase intention and thus encouraged luxury brands to more intensively disclose their sustainability efforts in their marketing communications (Rolling & Sadachar, 2017).

Another study pointed out that a communication message focused on the environmental benefits of the brand led consumers to perceive the CSR of the luxury brand as a genuine interest in improving the social problem, as a public interest, which ultimately elicited a positive rating of the company by consumers and thus provided empirical communication strategies for luxury brand practitioners. At the same time, the results confirmed that the objective character of the communication message, which contains the company's specific activities, further strengthens the relationship between the environmental message and the measured rating of the brand. This means that the current vague information from companies' CSR reports is not able to deliver the meaningful content of brands' CSR communications aimed at luxury consumers. The appealing content of CSR communication in the case of environmental communication must contain **objective and specific facts about the brand's contribution to the planet** (Kang & Sung, 2022).

The last argument for communicating the CSR of a luxury brand has to do with the feeling of guilt when buying an expensive product. Awareness of the socially beneficial activities of an extremely expensive product purchased can help reduce such a feeling. Specifically, Hagtvedt and Patrick (2016) showed that cause-related marketing of a luxury brand coupled with communicating its point-of-sale charitable efforts **reduced consumers' perceived guilt** for purchasing an expensive item. This reduction of the perceived guilt increased their future purchasing intentions by providing an additional (rational) reason to buy an otherwise inexplicably expensive product (Hagtvedt & Patrick, 2016).

Proof that some brands are not afraid of CSR-related communication is evident in the visuals of Stella McCartney's communication campaigns. They contain easy-to-read and understandable sustainability messages for consumers while appealing to customers with sustainable lifestyles. On its Facebook page, which has approximately a million followers, the brand communicates about not only its sustainable products but also its commitment to the environment and its response to public events related to sustainability (e.g. COP 27 in Egypt/2022). In specific stories, Stella explains the benefits of her collections. For example, an advertisement for organic cotton clothing reads: "Conventional cotton accounts for 16% of global pesticide use. Our organic cotton uses no harmful pesticides or chemicals, helping to protect farmers, local communities and planet Earth." Another example is the visual with the new S-Wave handbag: "Made using a vegan alternative to animal skin based on grapes from Italian wine waste, with a carbon impact that is up to 10 times less than that of cowhide. More than 1 billion animals die annually because of the global leather industry. There's a better way" (Stella McCartney, 2022a).

In the fall of 2019, the brand shot a campaign with models known for their positive views on sustainability, communicating simple tips on how everyone can contribute to making a difference with simple ideas like opting for reusable bags, riding public transport, giving up paper coffee cups and getting rid of guns. The models in the visuals pose with alpacas, for example, themselves dressed in faux fur with a drawing of the planet on their faces (Luxury Daily, 2019).

The important question now is not if but rather how luxury brands should communicate their CSR activities to reach the hearts of luxury customers and thus have an impact on their shopping behavior. According to McKinsey interviews with CEOs of industries, the trend towards sustainability and the desire for more responsible consumption is likely to intensify in the post-COVID pandemic crisis period (McKinsey & Company, 2020). The results of the previous study on the impact of luxury brand CSR knowledge on purchasing intentions (Olšanová et al., 2022) have several managerial implications, and highlight the following implications for the management of luxury communications:

1. **Allocating the CSR budget** for marketing communication of socially responsible activities of the luxury brand, which will create space for **strategic** building of awareness of the CSR brand;
2. **The content of brand CSR communication** should be strong and **relevant to the brand in accordance with its identity**, but it does not have to appeal to general customer attitudes to CSR and sustainability issues in terms of general topics such as reducing car use, environmental degradation and companies' compliance with social and environmental regulations;
3. **Targeting CSR communication to men** aged 30–45 and 46–55 is more likely to influence shopping intentions due to the higher affinity of these segments for the relationship between brand CSR knowledge and purchasing behavior, i.e. in a multi-brand portfolio, brands targeting men for CSR communication;
4. The concept of CSR as **creating shared value (CSV)** between the brand and the customer, where CSR activities rectify existing imbalances in the brand value chain. The problem of imbalance needs to be identified and linked to societal needs. In communications, it is important to strike the right balance between the emotional and rational benefits of the

brand and CSR. One should take into account that a brand with a less subtle or challenging strategy may expect a more favorable understanding of its CSR message than a brand with a more intrusive strategy (Janssen et al., 2017); and
5. To overcome the feeling of incompatibility between CSR and luxury values, choose a communication strategy that is based on the so-called **"CSR value instantiation"** (Park et al., 2019), that is, to communicate a personality or brand ambassador who is known to share common values with a brand or to visualize a consumer engaged in philanthropic activities using audio/video media including virtual reality (Olšanová et al., 2022).

The Monica Vinader case study is an example of a jewelry brand whose founder has long striven for circularity in production and sustainability across all parts of the value chain. Digital passports proving the origin of the materials of the selected jewelry collection are proof of an unusually high level of transparency and implementation of social responsibility and sustainability in the strategic management of the brand.

Mini-case 6.4 Monica Vinader: Benefits of certification

Founded in 2002 by Spanish designer Monica Vinader, the British jewelry brand is known for its values of unique design, sustainability and luxury, highlighting true femininity through everyday uniqueness and confidence. In 2021, it received the first Butterfly Mark certification of the Positive Luxury platform, which brings together over 150 luxury brands with a positive approach towards luxury business. The certification process led to further self-reflection with regard to sustainable practices and helped to develop the brand, as commented on by its founder and CEO Monica Vinader: "The Butterfly Mark assessment has allowed us to get an honest and realistic view of where we are on our sustainability journey, including what we have done well and what we need to improve. We have gone through self-reflection and are realistic in setting our goals. The evaluation has given us a better understanding of how we can achieve the most meaningful impact" (Positive Luxury, 2022c). In 2022, the company won the Positive Luxury platform in the category *Responsible Luxury Business of the Year*. According to one of the certification evaluators, sustainability has been systematically implemented across the brand's business with the aim to create a framework for transparency in its supply chain and for building responsible goals. At the same time, the brand has long striven for innovative creativity with a view to increasing positive impacts on the planet and society (Positive Luxury, 2022a, 2022b).

During 2020–21, the company focused on transitioning to a circular business model. The jewelry is made from recycled gold and sterling silver, with recycled silver alone reducing CO_2 emissions by two-thirds. Yet approximately 80% of the world's silver supply is still mined. The firm provides a five-year warranty and lifetime repair service, allowing clients to wear their jewelry for longer, and it offers free recycling of jewelry of any brand. Packaging and bags are 100% recyclable, and they have removed almost 90% of single-use plastics from the supply chain through audits by subcontractors (Monica Vinader, 2021, 2022).

The company applies the following principles in its supply chain:

- before cooperation begins, the supplier must be able to supply recycled gold and silver;
- each supplier must sign a Code of Conduct which obliges it to supply only recycled metals;

- in each factory, a mapping of the individual production stages is carried out for a better understanding of the specifics of the production;
- contractors must audit their subcontractors to check the supply of recycled metals; and
- each supplier must include a declaration of supply of recycled metals on the invoice.

The positive approach to sustainability was also appreciated by Hollywood stylist Kate Young, who works for Selena Gomez and Dakota Johnson. During lockdown in 2021, she and Monica Vinader created a collection of 13 pieces of jewelry completely through Zoom meetings. Combining a sustainable aesthetic with a red-carpet stylist seems like an oxymoron at first glance, but when building a luxury brand, such a seemingly disparate partnership is important not only for publicity and expansion of the consumer base, but also for the brand's identity itself and, last but not least, for the final economic result (Pener, 2022).

6.7 Summary: The evolution of sustainable luxury

Luxury groups and brands have started to more significantly adopt sustainability and social responsibility principles. Younger consumer values and investor expectations are among the forces that promote sustainability. The demand for responsible luxury is growing, and the whole industry is evolving to align its traditional values with a more sustainable and ethical future. In the context of younger consumer groups entering the luxury market and their attitudes towards sustainability (which border on panic anxiety about climate change), social responsibility, sustainability and its communication are an important part of the strategy of companies and brands. Luxury brands and companies often disclose their strategies as part of their reporting, monitor their goals and update them continuously. The communication of a luxury brand's CSR must be approached cautiously, considering the brand identity and all the specifics of the luxury strategy, but its positive benefits in the future will not be negligible.

The second-hand luxury market is another area of notable growth, driven by rising demand and an expanding supply of "pre-loved" items, particularly in Europe. Although the growth rates of this market have normalized in recent years, it continues to be a significant segment of the luxury industry, especially in the hard luxury categories like jewelry and watches.

Luxury strategy is based on rarity, scarcity and skilled high-end craftsmanship. A sustainable economy implies a scarcity of resources. Kapferer and Bastien (2012) wonders if scarcity is just a positive term for inadequacy, bringing luxury strategy closer to being a sustainable one. Luxury is not about surpluses produced on the other side of the world, where unsold stocks are quickly disposed of to be replaced by new fast collections. In this, luxury in itself is sustainable, but it must make this known, because luxury is habitually associated with excess and waste. Luxury products, however, are typically made to last a lifetime. The paradox is that their intrinsic durability contrasts with their associations with overconsumption. However, the luxury industry's link to sustainability is obvious and essential. Younger consumers and investors are driving the shift, with more than 70% of investors under 40 favoring businesses with positive environmental, social and governance ratings. On the other hand, the wealthiest 10% are responsible for almost half of the global emissions. This fact further enhances the need for sustainability efforts in the luxury sector.

The chapter also discusses the alignment of luxury brands with the United Nations Sustainable Development Goals, focusing on responsible consumption, production and climate action. Major luxury groups, including LVMH, Kering and LVMH, have incorporated the SDGs into their strategies, particularly targeting climate action (SDG 13), decent work and economic growth (SDG 8) and responsible production (SDG 12). The approach of Stella McCartney in pioneering innovative, eco-friendly materials and production methods (that align with these global goals) is shown in more detail in the mini-case.

Consumer awareness of CSR efforts plays a role in luxury purchasing decisions. Traditional luxury values such as exclusivity and craftsmanship remain principal, but it has been suggested that awareness of a brand's CSR activities positively influences purchase intent, especially among specific demographic segments. However, the relationship between sustainability awareness and purchasing behavior is still developing. Luxury consumers often assume brands are naturally responsible or they have very low awareness about any CSR activities from the luxury sector as a whole. The chapter also emphasizes circular models in luxury where second-hand markets and innovative approaches such as product rentals are becoming popular. Digital Product Passports are emerging as tools for ensuring product traceability and sustainability, further encouraging adaptations of circular models.

Finally, the chapter addresses management decisions regarding whether and how to communicate branded CSR activities. Consumers expect CSR initiatives from luxury brands, but to avoid undermining their exclusive image, brands should be careful about the contents of the communication strategies. The Stella McCartney and Monica Vinader mini-cases illustrate how CSR can be successfully integrated into communications without detracting from brand prestige.

Key terms

Carbon Footprint: The total greenhouse gas emissions caused by an individual, event, organization, or product. The luxury industry is increasingly scrutinized for its significant carbon footprint, especially among wealthy consumers.

Circular Economy: An economic system aimed at eliminating waste and reusing resources, especially relevant in the luxury industry through second-hand markets, product rentals and resale platforms that extend the life of products.

Corporate Social Responsibility (CSR): Refers to a company's commitment to manage the social, environmental and economic impacts of its operations responsibly; in the luxury industry, CSR activities are increasingly demanded by consumers and investors.

CSR Communication: The challenge of effectively conveying a luxury brand's CSR activities to consumers without diminishing the brand's exclusive image. Luxury brands must balance messaging about sustainability with their reputation for quality and exclusivity.

Digital Product Passport (DPP): A tool (using new technologies) that tracks a product's lifecycle, provides transparency on its origins, materials and environmental impact. This technology is key for verifying the authenticity of luxury goods.

Environmental, Social and Governance (ESG): A set of criteria investors use to evaluate a company's ethical impact and sustainability efforts. ESG ratings are essential for attracting investment in the luxury sector.

Luxury Paradox: The contradiction between traditional hedonistic luxury values (associated with excess and pleasure) and sustainability (focused on ethical production), which highlights the challenges luxury brands face in adopting responsible practices.

Second-Hand Luxury Market: The market for pre-owned luxury goods, which extends product lifecycles. This market has expanded rapidly, driven by younger, sustainability-conscious consumers.

Significance Matrix: A strategic tool companies use to prioritize sustainability issues by assessing their importance to both the company and external stakeholders. It helps luxury brands identify key CSR areas to focus on, such as climate action or ethical sourcing.

Sustainable Development: The overarching framework for global efforts to reduce environmental impact, promote social well-being and ensure long-term economic viability. Luxury brands are integrating sustainable development principles into their business strategies.

Sustainability: The practice of meeting current needs without compromising the ability of future generations to meet their own. Environmental, social and economic factors are the key components. In the luxury sector, this often involves long-lasting products and responsible sourcing.

United Nations Sustainable Development Goals (SDGs): A set of 17 global goals developed to address pressing environmental, social and economic challenges globally. Luxury brands increasingly align their strategies with specific SDGs, such as climate action and responsible consumption.

Discussion questions

1. Explain the *luxury paradox*. Why is the contrast between durability of luxury items and the general associations of luxury being connected to overconsumption challenging for luxury brands?
2. How does consumer awareness of CSR brand related initiatives affect purchasing behavior in the luxury sector?
3. Why are younger consumers and investors particularly influential in directing luxury brands toward sustainability?
4. Explain the role of the United Nations Sustainable Development Goals (SDGs) in the luxury industry. Which SDGs are commonly targeted by luxury brands?
5. How does the model of a *circular economy* relate to the luxury industry, and what are some examples of circularity initiatives?
6. What challenges do luxury brands face in communicating their CSR activities, and what strategies can they use to avoid undermining their exclusive image?
7. Why might some luxury consumers assume brands are inherently responsible, even without explicit CSR communication?
8. What is the purpose of Digital Product Passports (DPPs) in the luxury industry, and how do they contribute to sustainability?
9. How is Stella McCartney contributing to sustainable practices in luxury fashion, and what are some of the brand's specific sustainability achievements?
10. In what ways are luxury brands adapting to meet the sustainability expectations of Gen Z and millennials?

Reference list

Achabou, M. A., & Dekhili, S. (2013, October). Luxury and Sustainable Development: Is There a Match? *Journal of Business Research*, *66*(10), 1896–1903.

Akenji, L., & Chen, H. (2016). *A Framework for Shaping Sustainable Lifestyles*. Retrieved April 2025, from oneplanetnetwork.org: https://www.oneplanetnetwork.org/sites/default/files/a_framework_for_shaping_sustainable_lifestyles_determinants_and_strategies_0.pdf

Aliyev, F., Wagner, R., & Seuring, S. (2019). Common and Contradictory Motivations in Buying Intentions for Green and Luxury Automobiles. *Sustainability*, *11*(12).

Altagamma. (2021, November 11). *Luxury Is Back . . . to the Future*. Retrieved November 2022, from altagamma.it: https://altagamma.it/media/source/Altagamma%20-%20Bain%20Luxury%20Market%20Monitor%202021.pdf

Amatulli, C., De Angelis, M., Romani, S., & Korschun, D. (2018). Consumers' Perceptions of Luxury Brands' CSR Initiatives: An Investigation of the Role of Status and Conspicuous Consumption. *Journal of Cleaner Production*, *194*, 277–287.

Arianee. (2024). *All about the EU Eco-design Regulation and Digital Product Passport (DPP)*. Retrieved August 2024, from arianee.com: https://www.arianee.com/post/digital-product-passports-guide

Aura Blockchain Consortium. (2022, July 21). *Cartier after-Sales Case Study*. Retrieved October 2022, from auraluxuryblockchain.com: https://auraluxuryblockchain.com/case-studies/cartier-after-sales-case-study

Bain & Company. (2020, January 20). *Secondhand Luxury Goods: A First-Rate Strategic Opportunity*. Retrieved September 2022, from bain.com: https://www.bain.com/insights/secondhand-luxury-goods-a-first-rate-strategic-opportunity-snap-chart/

Bain & Company. (2024, January 18). *Long Live Luxury: Converge to Expand through Turbulence*. Retrieved September 2024, from bain.com: https://www.bain.com/insights/long-live-luxury-converge-to-expand-through-turbulence/

Bendell, J., & Kleanthous, A. (2007). *Deeper Luxury: Quality and Style When the World Matters*. Retrieved November 9, 2017, from http://aidagency.typepad.com/good_stuff/files/DeeperluxuryReport.pdf

Bengtsson, M., Akenji, L., Toivio, V., Lettenmeier, M., Fawcett, T., Parag, Y., . . . Kenner, D. (2021). *1.5-Degree Lifestyles: Towards a Fair Consumption Space for All*. Berlin: Hot or Cool Institute. Retrieved September 2024, from: https://hotorcool.org/wp-content/uploads/2021/10/Hot_or_Cool_1_5_lifestyles_FULL_REPORT_AND_ANNEX_B.pdf

Berens, G., Van Riel, C. B., & Vann Bruggen, G. H. (2005). Corporate Associations and Consumer Product Responses: The Moderating Role of Corporate Brand Dominance. *Journal of Marketing*, *69*(3), 35–48.

Bernoville, B. (2022, June 12). *What are Scopes 1, 2 and 3 of Carbon Emissions?* Retrieved September 2022, from plana.earth: https://plana.earth/academy/what-are-scope-1-2-3-emissions

Capgemini Research Institute. (2022). *World Report Series Wealth Management 2022*. Retrieved November 2022, from Capgemini Research Institute: https://worldwealthreport.com/pdf/Capgemini_WWR_2022_VFinal_Digital.pdf

Chandler, D. (2017). *Strategic Corporate Responsibility: Sustainable Value Creation* (4th edition). SAGE Publications Ltd.

Chanel. (2020, March). *Chanel Mission 1.5: Our Journey towards Low-Carbon Future*. Retrieved November 2022, from chanel.com: https://corpo-services.chanel.com/medias/Chanel-Climate-Publication.pdf?context=bWFzdGVyfHBkZnw1NjQ0ODc5fGFwcGxpY2F0aW9uL3BkZnxzeXMtbWFzdGVyL3BkZi9oMTgvaDlmLzg3OTcwNzc1MzY3OTgvQ2hhbmVsX0NsaW1hdGVfUHVibGljYXRpb24ucGRmfDUxMTY2OTIxNDE0MzBiNTllNGU5YzNmZGUwYTN

Chanel. (2024a). *Chanel Mission 1.5: Is our Climate Plan to 2030*. Retrieved March 2024, from https://www.chanel.com/us/sustainability/

Chanel. (2024b). *Sustainability Performance Extract*. Retrieved October 2024, from chanel.com: https://www.chanel.com/puls-img/1723537316984-chanelsustainabilityperformanceextract2023pdf.pdf

Coyne, K., & Dye, R. (1998, January/February). *The Competitive Dynamics of Network-Based Businesses*. Retrieved November 2022, from Harvard Business Review: https://hbr.org/1998/01/the-competitive-dynamics-of-network-based-businesses

D'Arpizio, C., Nieto, D. V., & Capellini, M. (2021, March 10). *Bain & Company*. Retrieved November 2022, from LuxCo 2030: A Vision of Sustainable Luxury: https://www.bain.com/insights/luxco-2030-a-vision-of-sustainable-luxury/

Davies, I. A., Lee, Z., & Ahonkhai, I. (2012). Do Consumers Care about Ethical-Luxury? *Journal of Business Ethics*, *106*(1), 37–51.

Dekhili, S., Achabou, M. A., & Alharbi, F. (2019). Could Sustainability Improve the Promotion of Luxury Products? *European Business Review*, *31*(4), 488–511.

Deloitte. (2022). *Global Powers of Luxury Goods 2022: A New Wave of Enthusiasm in Luxury*. Retrieved December 2022, from Deloitte: https://www.deloitte.com/content/dam/assets-shared/legacy/docs/industry/consumer/2022/gx-global-powers-of-luxury-goods–2022.pdf

Deloitte. (2023, November 29). *Global Powers of Luxury Goods 2023*. Retrieved February 2024, from deloitte.com: hhttps://www.deloitte.com/global/en/Industries/consumer/analysis/gx-cb-global-powers-of-luxury-goods.html

The Estée Lauder Companies. (2022). *Beauty Inspired, Values Driven: Our Fiscal 2022 Social Impact and Sustainability Report*. Retrieved November 2022, from elcompanies.com: https://www.elcompanies.com/~/media/files/e/estee-lauder-companies/universal/our-commitments/2022-si-s-report/sis-report–2022.pdf

Farfetch. (2022). *2021 ESG Report*. Retrieved December 2022, from Farfetch: https://s22.q4cdn.com/426100162/files/doc_downloads/2022/06/Farfetch-2021-ESG-Report.pdf

Franco, J. C., Hussain, D., & McColl, R. (2020). Luxury Fashion and Sustainability: Looking Good Together. *Journal of Business Strategy*, *41*(4), 55–61.

The Guardian. (2023, July 23). *Sunday was World's Hottest Ever Recorded Day, Data Suggests*. Retrieved August 2024, from theguardian.com: https://www.theguardian.com/environment/article/2024/jul/23/world-temperature-records-shattered-hottest-day-climate-crisis

Hagtvedt, H., & Patrick, V. M. (2016). Gilt and Guilt: Should Luxury and Charity Partner at the Point of Sale? *Journal of Retailing*, *92*(1), 56–64.

Haski-Leventhal, D. (2018). *Strategic Corporate Social Responsibility*. SAGE Publications Ltd.

Hermès. (2020). *2020 Universal Registration Document Hermès International*. Retrieved November 2022, from Hermès: https://labrador.cld.bz/HERMES-2020-Universal-registration-document/182/

Hermès. (2021a). *2021 Universal Registration Document*. Retrieved October 2022, from www.finance.hermes.com: https://labrador.cld.bz/Hermes-2021-Universal-Registration-Document/10/

Hermès. (2021b). *2021 Universal Registration Document Including the Annual Financial Report*. Retrieved November 2022, from Hermès: https://assets-finance.hermes.com/s3fs-public/node/pdf_file/2022–04/1650894273/HERMES-URD2021-EN_03.pdf

Ho, H. C., Awan, M. A., & Khan, H. U. (2016). Luxury Brands and Corporate Social Responsibility: A Perspective on Consumers' Preferences. *Journnal of International Management Studies*, *16*(1), 77–81.

Hung, K.-p., Chen, A. H., Peng, N., Hackley, C., Tiwsakul, R., & Chou, C.-l. (2011). Antecedents of Luxury Brand Purchase Intention. *Journal of Product & Brand Management*, *20*(6), 457–467.

Hur, W.-M., Kim, H., & Woo, J. (2013). How CSR Leads to Corporate Brand Equity: Mediating Mechanisms of Corporate Brand Credibility and Reputation. *Journal of Business Ethics*, *125*(1), 75–86.

Impakter Index. (2022). *Rolex*. Retrieved November 2022, from Impakter Index: https://index.impakter.com/rolex/

Janssen, C., Vanhamme, J., & Leblanc, S. (2017). Should Luxury Brands Say It Loud? Brand Conspicuousness and Consumer Perceptions of Responsible Luxury. *Journal of Business Research*, *77*, 167–174.

Kang, E. Y., & Sung, Y. H. (2022). Luxury and Sustainability: The Role of Message Appeals and Objectivity on Luxury Brands' Green Corporate Social Responsibility. *Journal of Marketing Communications*, *28*(3), 291–312.

Kapferer, J.-N., & Bastien, V. (2012). *The Luxury Strategy: Break the Rules of Marketing to Build Luxury Brands* (2nd edition). Kogan Page Limited.

Kapferer, J.-N., & Michaut, A. (2015). Luxury and Sustainability: A Common Future? The Match Depends on How Consumers Define Luxury. *Luxury Research Journal*, *1*(1), 3–15.

Kapferer, J.-N., & Michaut-Denizeau, A. (2014). Is Luxury Compatible with Sustainability? Luxury Consumers' Viewpoint. *Journal of Brand Management*, *21*(1), 1–22.

Lopez, B., & Rangel, C. (2022). How Luxury Fashion Brands Contribute Efficiently to Sustainable Development. In A. Pérez, *Future Advancements for CSR and the Sustainable Development Goals in a Post-COVID-19 World* (pp. 139–161). Madrid: IGI Global Scientific Publishing.

Luxury Daily. (2019, July 25). *Stella McCartney Advertises Action in Eco-Conscious Campaign*. Retrieved November 2022, from Luxury Daily: https://www.luxurydaily.com/stella-mccartney-advertises-action-in-eco-conscious-campaign/

Luxury Innovation Summit, Geneva. (2022, October 24). *2022 Edition – Luxury Innovation Summit and Awards*. Luxury Innovation Summit and Awards. https://luxuryinnovation-summit.com/past_events/2022-edition/

LVMH. (2022). *Stella by Stella McCartney*. Retrieved November 2022, from LVMH: https://www.lvmh.com/houses/perfumes-cosmetics/stella-by-stella-mccartney/

McKinsey & Company. (2020, April 1). *A perspective for the Luxury-Goods Industry During – And after – Coronavirus*. Retrieved October 2020, from Mc Kinsey & Company: https://www.mckinsey.com/industries/retail/our-insights/a-perspective-for-the-luxury-goods-industry-during-and-after-coronavirus#

Monica Vinader. (2021, November). *Monica Vinader*. Retrieved June 2022, from Sustainability Report 2021: https://cfs3.monicavinader.com/pdfs/original/14733543-mv-sustainability-report.pdf

Monica Vinader. (2022, June). Facebook. *Facebook*.

Olšanová, K., Cook, G., & Zlatić, M. (2018). Influence of Luxury Companies' Corporate Social Responsibility Activities on Consumer Purchase Intention: Development of a Theoretical Framework. *Central European Business Review*, *7*(3), 1–25.

Olšanová, K., Escobar Ríos, A., Cook, G., Král, P., & Zlatić, M. (2022). Impact of the Awareness of Brand-Related CSR Activities on Purchase Intention for Luxury Brands. *Social Responsibility Journal*, *18*(3), 597–618.

Park, J. K., Torelli, C. J., Monga, A. B., & John, D. R. (2019, December). Value Instantiation: How to Overcome the Value Conflict in Promoting Luxury Brands with CSR Initiatives. *Marketing Letters*, *30*(3/4), 307–319.

Pener, D. (2022, August 30). *Stylist Kate Young Picks Favorite Pieces from Monica Vinader Jewelry Collab: "I Want to Wear it All the Time"*. Retrieved September 2022, from The HollywoodReporter:https://www.hollywoodreporter.com/lifestyle/lifestyle-news/stylist-kate-young-monica-vinader-jewelry-collab-1235208267/

Positive Luxury. (2022a). *Our Members*. Retrieved June 2022, from Positive Luxury: https://www.positiveluxury.com/our-members

Positive Luxury. (2022b). *Positive Luxury*. Retrieved June 2022, from Awards Winners Report 2022: https://www.positiveluxury.com/content/uploads/2022/04/PL_AwardsWinners Report2022.pdf

Positive Luxury. (2022c). *Monica Vinader*. Retrieved September 2022, from Positive Luxury: https://www.positiveluxury.com/our-members/monica-vinader/

Rathi, R., Garg, R., Kataria, A., & Chhikara, R. (2022). Evolution of Luxury Marketing Landscape: A Bibliometric Analysis and Future Directions. *Journal of Brand Management*, *29*, 241–257.

Rolling, V., & Sadachar, A. (2017). Are Sustainable Luxury Goods a Paradox for Millennials? *Social Responsibility Journal*, *14*(4), 802–815.

Schultz, M. D., & Seele, P. (2024). *Managing Sustainable Luxury and Digitalization: Technology Trends and Ethical Challenges in the Swiss Luxury Watch Business*. New York: Routledge.

Services.Chanel. (2022, May 24). *Chanel Limited Financial Results for the Year Ended 31 December 2021*. Retrieved September 2022, from Services.Chanel.com: https://services.chanel.com/media/files/Press-release-2021-Results-ENG-FINAL.pdf

Som, A., & Blanckaert, C. (2021). *The Road to Luxury: The New Frontiers in Luxury Brand Management* (2nd edition). Wiley.

Stella McCartney. (2022a). *Stella McCartney*. Retrieved November 2022, from Facebook Stella McCartney: https://www.facebook.com/stellamccartney

Stella McCartney. (2022b). *Sustainability*. Retrieved November 2022, from Stella McCartney: https://www.stellamccartney.com/us/en/sustainability/sustainability.html

Stella McCartney. (2024a). *Sustainability – Timeline*. Retrieved March 2024, from https://www.stellamccartney.com/cz/en/sustainability/sustainability-timeline.html

Stella McCartney. (2024b). *2023 Impact Report*. Retrieved March 2024, from https://www.stellamccartney.com/on/demandware.static/-/Library-Sites-StellaMcCartney SharedLibrary/default/dwa4ea4b5c/report/StellaMcCartney_ImpactReport_2023_4.pdf

TNFD. (2022). *About*. Retrieved September 2022, from Taskforce on Nature-Related Financial Disclosures: https://tnfd.global/about/

Torelli, C. J., Monga, A. B., & Kaikati, A. M. (2012). Doing Poorly by Doing Good: Corporate Social Responsibility and Brand Concepts. *Journal of Consumer Research*, *38*(5), 948–963.

United Nations. (2015). *Sustainable Development Knowledge Platform*. Retrieved August 2018, from https://sustainabledevelopment.un.org/post2015/transformingourworld

United Nations Environment Programme. (2020, December 9). *Emissions Gap Report 2020*. Retrieved June 2022, from https://www.unep.org/emissions-gap-report-2020

Vogue Business. (2024, May 28). *Consumers Want More from Digital Product Passports, New Survey Says*. Retrieved October 2024, from voguebusiness.com: https://www.voguebusiness.com/story/technology/consumers-want-more-from-digital-product-passports-new-survey-says

Wikimedia Commons. (2014, January 17). *File:Coco Chanel Tentoonstelling.JPG*. Retrieved October 2024, from commons.wikimedia.org: https://commons.wikimedia.org/wiki/File:Coco_Chanel_tentoonstelling.JPG

Chapter 7

Emerging technologies in the management of luxury brands

New generations of consumers bring progressive challenges to the luxury sector and luxury brands' strategies. Given the differences in their purchasing behavior, the size of new segments and their technological preferences, engaging these consumers in new ways requires consistent preparation and timely implementation. According to McKinsey, fashion companies invested 1.6–1.8% of their revenue in technology in 2021, and that number is projected to rise to 3–3.5% by 2030. Behind the expected growth is the belief that technologies focused on robotics, advanced analytics and applications can help streamline processes, promote sustainability and create exceptional customer experiences (McKinsey & Company, 2022b). By investing in technology, companies are securing an appeal not only to new generations of customers but also to existing HNWIs. A wealth management survey shows that by the end of 2021, 70% of all HNWIs (and 91% under 40) had invested in digital assets; these technological investments can support companies' efforts to create a diversified portfolio of digital and physical product offerings (Capgemini Research Institute, 2022).

The challenges of managing luxury brands include not only technological innovations such as blockchain and NFTs but also others related to new consumers, in particular sustainability and how to integrate it into luxury brand strategy, as well as circularity, online shopping, metaverse, e-commerce and distribution trends, as discussed in previous chapters.

Marketing in the luxury goods sector relies on traditional marketing practices only to a certain extent due to specifics of luxury strategy. The presence of luxury brands or groups on the internet and entry into e-commerce have been have been approached cautiously due to the priority placed on preserving the traditional values of luxury brands. In the case of e-commerce, it meant certain losses for luxury houses, at least at the beginning of the COVID-19 pandemic. New technologies such as blockchain and non-fungible tokens (NFTs), artificial intelligence (AI), machine learning (ML) and virtual reality (VR) will provide luxury brands with novel opportunities to create new consumer experiences at an early stage. This is also due to the growing segment of Gen Z consumers and potential future Alpha customers, who behave differently in the digital environment, are challenging to understand and grasp for older generations, and are also unreachable through traditional media.

In order for luxury brands to retain the interest of younger target groups, it is necessary to either revitalize their image or to add a consumer experience with the brand that will be

DOI: 10.4324/9781003593706-7

more closely connected to people born into the online environment and yet, at the same time, ensure it will not compromise the DNA of luxury brands. In connection with these technologies, the luxury industry is experiencing a historic transformation (Joy et al., 2022), and thus, it has the opportunity to virtually accompany the upcoming generations on their way to future purchases. According to Bain & Company (2022), digital assets and the virtual world (metaverse) will make up 5–10% of the luxury market by the end of 2030. Thus, luxury brands have the opportunity to play a key role in shaping virtual worlds as one of their builders and creators (Bain & Company, 2022).

The largest groups and brands are aware of this. In April 2021, international leaders in the luxury industry co-founded the Aura Blockchain Consortium, a Swiss-based nonprofit that promotes the use of a single global blockchain solution open to all luxury brands worldwide to provide consumers with transparency and traceability when purchasing luxury goods. The founding members include LVMH, Richemont, Prada Group, Mercedes-Benz and the Italian holding company OTB. The founding members contribute to the development costs and have a more significant say in management, while all members pay a license fee for the software services and each manufactured digital twin of the physical product. The platform strives to make blockchain solutions and related technologies simple and accessible for all luxury brands, helping to improve the customer experience of buying, owning, resale and recycling of luxury goods (Aura Blockchain Consortium, 2022).

The consortium's general secretary at that time, Daniela Ott, told CNN Business that the goal of the Aura Blockchain Consortium is to simplify blockchain for luxury brands, which is a really complex and very fast-paced technology. A year after the company's founding, Aura software was used by more than 20 luxury brands, with more than 17 million products registered on the platform. Aura software creates a digital version (called a digital twin) for a physical product, such as a handbag, and creates a report of the material type, manufacturing location and time, and total number of fabricated products for the physical product. This provides consumers with a higher level of protection by acting as a digital authentication certificate with encryption, which cannot be tampered with. The owner can access the digital twin via a website or mobile application. The platform allows brands to control what information they share, and it keeps brand and consumer data safe (CNN Business, 2022).

For example, the Cartier brand manages the after-sales process through the Aura Blockchain in case a previously purchased good needs repair. Here, the customer can access a secure online environment to monitor the product's status and the work in progress. Aura Blockchain verifies the authenticity of all the information that customers have shared, and then the product owner can accept or reject the repair price estimate and track each step of the process online (Aura Blockchain Consortium, 2022).

7.1 Blockchain and NFTs

Owning an NFT means owning an indelible item on the blockchain that cannot be fraudulently altered, falsified, copied or destroyed. It is there forever (CNN, 2022). The creation of NFTs is enabled by blockchain technology, that is, a system of recording information in a way that makes it difficult or impossible to change, hack or otherwise cheat the system (Euromoney, 2021).

It is, therefore, no coincidence that NFTs are used by artists in the digital environment, as the system prevents illegal distribution or copying. Sotheby's views NFTs as a paradigm shift for digital art and other forms of online media by allowing online assets to have verifiable scarcity and some form of ownership without the possibility of manipulation, i.e., elements that add value to physical art and assets in the digital realm. This opens the door to valuable digital art and creates opportunities for artists that did not exist before. Once an artist "knocks out" a unique NFT and a potential collector buys it, usually through an auction, the owner can continue to trade it. The origin of each NFT is always recorded, and collectors can find out its authenticity before buying or bidding at auction (Sothebys, 2021).

Josh Pullan, head of Sotheby's global luxury division, said at the Geneva conference dedicated to luxury innovation in 2022 that they find art forms in unmistakable tokens very promising and that they entered the market at an early stage due to the pandemic. With around 50% of their customers under the age of 40, they see the NFT segment as a new way to capture younger customers (Luxury Innovation Summit, Geneva, 2022). Furthermore, Morgan Stanley estimates that the size of the NFT market in the luxury industry will exceed $50 billion by 2030 (Gurzki, 2022).

Sotheby's auctioned off NFTs from the famous ten-thousand-CryptoPunk series (*CryptoPunk #7523)* in June 2021 for $11.75 million. The extraordinary price compared to others from the same NFT collection is attributed to its uniqueness, as it is the only one in the series to have a mask on its mouth, an earring in its ear and a knitted cap on its head (NFT Evening, 2022) and also one of only nine other Alien types of Punks that achieved meteoric sales due to perceived rarity (Yuga Labs, 2024).

The rarest CryptoPunk in Yuga Labs' (a blockchain technology company that develops NFTs and digital collectables) ownership is, for example, *CryptoPunk #372* (Picture 7.1), one of the 24 Ape Punks in the whole 10,000 Punks' collection. The Apes (like the Aliens) were promptly acquired by the initial purchasers (first *claimers*) as an undeniable illustration of **the concept of scarcity being inherently tied to perceived value,** even in the absence of those rules and standards by the creators at Larva Labs. The link between rarity, scarcity and value has since evolved into a **defining criterion for valuing NFT collections** across the industry (Yuga Labs, 2024).

In another example, the NFT *The Merge* by digital artist Pak (logo or emblem associated with the digital artist Pak whose identity is unknown, Picture 7.2) was sold for $91.8 million in December 2021 (Block, 2021). Unlike most other prized tokens, it was sold to nearly 29,000 collectors, who each bought part of the NFT's 312,686 units (NFT Evening, 2022). The composition of the digital item reveals the interconnectedness of elements – blending art, mathematics or geometry and philosophy. There is a sharp contrast between black and white, which accentuates a duality that is both visually and intellectually engaging. It is also

Picture 7.1 CryptoPunk #372 © 2024 Yuga Labs, Inc. All rights reserved. *Source:* (Reprinted here with permission.)

Picture 7.2 Logo associated with digital artist Pak, author of *The Merge*. By Pmmccurdy, public domain, available at (Wikipedia Commons, 2021).

in line with Pak's reputation for creating thought-provoking digital art. *The Merge* is about exploring new ways of thinking about ownership and the future of art. The ability to merge collectors' individual pieces into a collective whole, symbolizes the evolution of art and emerging communities' connected by NFT's ownership in the digital world. When people purchased the pieces, they were buying individual tokens that could combine with other owners to create a larger mass (Art Explained, 2024).

The worlds of art and luxury are similar in many ways. Values such as authenticity, portability and scarcity – in the sense of a limited supply – are common to both sectors and made possible by blockchain through NFTs. Their value in the world of luxury brands does not reach the astronomical amounts seen in art auctions, but they are already used by some creative directors of luxury brands.

Pierre-Emmanuel Angeloglou, director of fashion and leather goods strategy at Louis Vuitton, told BCG and Comité Colbert research, "Luxury brands and NFTs are based on numerous common concepts that make them compatible: rarity, innovation, sense of belonging and connection to culture" (BCG & Comité Colbert, 2022). In the summer of 2022, Yves Saint Laurent Beauté, of L'Oréal Group's luxury division, announced plans to gradually explore new digital frontiers through the creation of an NFT wallet and custom tokens, the activation of which is linked to a donation to a non-profit organization related to the YSL Beauté community (Arianee, 2022). Back in 2019–20, Louis Vuitton Women's Creative Director Nicolas Ghesquière designed luxury gaming accessories called skins in games for the Riot Games Leagues of Legends online video game, for about $10. The clothing collection called LVxLOS inspired by this game contained about 40 different items ranging in price from $170 to $5,600 for a leather jacket (Meisenzahl, 2019). The fashion house also launched NFTs celebrating the brand founder's bicentenary by depicting various historical moments in building this icon (Opensea, 2022).

NFTs can be expected to connect with the luxury world through the gaming industry, which already has 3 billion players and is expected to maintain a steadily growing number of players through 2024 (Takahashi, 2021). Interestingly, nearly half of the players – or 46% – are women (Bryter, 2020). This is a space where a player's avatar can boast a Louis Vuitton backpack and Dior sneakers from the same luxury group one interacts with in the real world. Thus, it can be an opportunity for synergies within luxury groups as well as a unique way to reach target groups that are difficult to approach through conventional communication channels. Therefore, new projects for the use of unmistakable tokens by luxury brands can be expected.

Mini-case 7.1 "Tiffany goes wild" by collaborating with CryptoPunk

An unusual approach to NFTs compared to other luxury brands was chosen at Tiffany's, where they linked the luxury brand to cryptocurrencies and NFTs. Less than a year after LVMH's acquisition of Tiffany's for nearly $16 billion, Bernard Arnault's 30-year-old son Alexandre announced the release of his own cryptocurrency TiffCoin in a tweet on April 1, 2022. In fact, it was a limited edition of 499 real, individually numbered coins, not real cryptocurrency, but gold or silver coins that can be exchanged for Tiffany jewelry. Still, the tweet aroused curiosity and anticipation.

A week later, Alexandre hinted at a collaboration with CryptoPunk in a tweet subtitled "When punks go wild at @TiffanyAndCo" and had his own CryptoPunk made into a pendant. Finally, Tiffany's offered to make a real piece of jewelry for a limited number (250) of the owners of the existing 10,000 unique NFT CryptoPunks. This piece of jewelry was a pendant lined with 30 diamonds and gems and an 18-karat gold chain. The condition for acquiring a pendant was the possession of at least one CryptoPunk NFT placed on the Ethereum blockchain from the 2017 collection, which was one of the first tokens issued, and some of the unique CryptoPunks are among the most desirable NFTs.

To turn the CryptoPunks' NFT into a pendant, the owners had to purchase one of the 250 NFTiffs' digital passports (Tiffany's own cryptocurrency, which Alexandre had posted about on Twitter the day before the beads went on sale). These could be minted and redeemed in order for owners to get their own pendant based on the NFT's digital artwork. Each customer could purchase a maximum of three NFTiffs, each costing 30 ETH (approximately $50,000 in 2022). The limited offer was sold out on the first day of the sale's launch, August 1, 2022.

The project to merge Tiffany's with CryptoPunks was preceded by an important step for the commercialization of NFTs. In March 2022, Yuga Labs (the parent company for the Bored Ape Yacht Club) acquired all intellectual property (IP) for CryptoPunks and announced plans to grant commercial rights to all CryptoPunk holders. According to Noah Davis, leader of the CryptoPunks brand, owning a token does not mean "just that this JPEG belongs to you" (CNN, 2022) but also the possibility to use other rights associated with ownership. Thus, the owners of CryptoPunks can commission Tiffany to create a new product from their own CryptoPunk, that is, said pendant. By purchasing an NFTiff and linking it to his/her own CryptoPunk, a customer grants "Tiffany and Company, its affiliates, agents and others working for or on its behalf, an irrevocable, non-exclusive, royalty-free license to use your CryptoPunk and its underlying intellectual property" (Tiffany and Co., 2022).

The result? According to an analysis compiled by Stanford student and cryptocurrency researcher Noah Levine for dune.com, of the 250 NTiffs mined (and offered), a total of 224 were redeemed as of September 14, 2022. The 184 NTiffs minted were unique, 164 Cryptopunk owners used more than one NTiff and the average number of redemptions per wallet was 1.4. The total revenue was therefore $12.62 million (based on the ETH exchange rate). By comparison, Nike's NFTs releases were the most successful on the same day, with total revenues of just under $183 million. Unlike Tiffany, Nike has released more than 10 NFT collections that the analyst brings together. Ten brands exceeded $1 million, including luxury brands such as Tiffany, Dolce & Gabbana ($23.7 million) and Gucci ($11.6 million) (Dune, 2022).

During the first half of 2023, many happy CryptoPunk owners linked their *just received* pendants on Twitter (later "X"), thanking Alexandre Arnault personally for the initiative. For example, CryptoPunk #3788 said on Twitter in March 2023: "Beauty is in the eye of the Hodler. #nftiff Still speechless. Special thanks to @larvalabs, @yugalabs, @TiffanyAndCo, @dt_chain and @alexarnault" (X & CryptoPunk #3788, 2023).

Experts' reactions were ambiguous, the success of NFT fashion and luxury brands was surprising for many of them. Crypto entrepreneur Amanda Cassatt, co-founder of web3 services firm Serotonin, wrote for Vogue Business that she is not surprised by the dominance of fashion in the rankings, as these are brands with great traditional appeal that have been able to translate their DNA into the context of web3. Others point out that primary sales volumes and revenue are not the main success criteria for NFT brands. In addition to sales on the secondary market, these include building a community of potential customers with affinity for blockchain, NFTs, cryptocurrencies and the metaverse. In terms of the size of the affected community (Vogue Business, 2022), the first release of Tiffany's cryptocurrency and NFTs cannot be judged as a success but rather as cautious exploration to use these technologies for brand building. From the luxury brand NFT strategy point of view, they contain elements of a very limited offer, and the pendants stimulate the desire to own them.

7.2 Metaverse

The metaverse is not yet ubiquitous, except perhaps among the professional public. Hollensen et al. (2022) characterize the metaverse as a giant laboratory with direct access to younger target groups. In December 2021, Facebook renamed itself Meta with the ambition to "help bring the metaverse to life." A month later, Microsoft said that its proposed acquisition of gaming giant Activision Blizzard provided the basic building blocks for the metaverse (McKinsey & Company, 2022a).

Meta announced a $50 million global investment in 2021 into responsible research of the metaverse development (Meta, 2021). Other platforms are in the development phase, and it is now too early for academia and business to agree on a definition of metaverse. Meta defines it simply as

> A collection of virtual spaces that you can explore and in which you can create, work, play, learn, shop, and much more together with other people who are not in the same physical space as you. It's not necessarily about spending more time online – it's about making the time you spend online more meaningful.
>
> (Meta, 2021)

Since then, Meta has faced mixed financial results, balancing profitability with substantial investments. It was reported in 2024 that so far, Meta has invested $46 billion in the metaverse and AR initiatives, focusing on advancing virtual reality and immersive experiences, and while still committed to the metaverse, Meta is directing twice as much spending toward AI development, indicating a broader technology expansion strategy (Nasdaq, 2024).

According to McKinsey, a metaverse space can be characterized on the basis of the following common features:

- Immersive environments, often (but not always) using virtual or augmented reality technology;
- "Always on" exists in real time;

- Connects the virtual and physical worlds, as well as multiple platforms;
- Powered by a fully functional virtual economy, often (but not always) built on cryptocurrencies and digital goods and assets, including non-fungible tokens (NFTs); and
- Allows people to create a virtual identity, presence and ability to act virtually, including between interpersonal interactions, make transactions, create their own content and build their world (McKinsey & Company, 2022a).

According to the tech website Ars Technica, there is no doubt about what the meaning of the word metaverse is: it's a place where primarily young people develop online lives through avatars that can move, talk and look exactly as their creators wish. They can own property, shop, wear designer clothes and engage online. NFTs can serve as a tool to track and determine ownership of virtual goods as they pass through the metaverse of different companies (Arstechnica, 2021).

Given the amount of investment that companies such as Meta or Microsoft devote to the development of the metaverse, one can assume that it will develop rapidly and create a completely immersive environment that will imitate our life in a 3D environment. At the same time, the level of investment indicates the potential for commercial use in terms of a communication medium aimed at customers among the younger target groups. Both Microsoft and Meta define the metaverse as a virtual world that ushers in the next phase of the internet's development (Wall Street Journal, 2021). The sectors in which the biggest changes can be expected in connection with the development of the metaverse are the education sector, the gaming industry, retail (especially the fashion industry), social networks or platforms and, last but not least, platforms for organizing conferences and conference calls such as Zoom (Jung, 2022).

One interesting example of luxury brand involvement in the metaverse is linked to the gaming industry. Luxury watch brand Hublot, owned by LVMH, has, in line with its DNA involving the fusion of traditional watchmaking and advanced technologies, launched the Big Bang watches line in 2005, followed by **Big Bang e** watches released in 2020. This product was part of Hublot's metaverse debut in 2022 when the brand unveiled its "Hublot Loves Football Metaverse Stadium" to celebrate soccer's 2022 FIFA World Cup in Qatar, which it sponsors as the official timekeeper (Forbes, 2022). For more about Hublot, see Mini-Case 7.2.

Mini-case 7.2 Hublot: Timekeeper of the metaverse: A blend of tradition and forward-thinking

Since its acquisition by LVMH in 2008, Hublot has distinguished itself as a relatively young brand within the luxury watch sector, especially when compared to its more established counterparts. **Founded in 1980** by Carlo Crocco, an Italian watchmaker who diverged from his family's traditional watchmaking practices, Hublot was perceived as a brand that would break new ground in the industry. The name *Hublot*, which translates as *porthole* from French, reflects the nautical design elements that were a source of inspiration for the brand's early designs (Picture 7.3). Hublot introduced a pioneering concept of fusing gold with rubber at the Basel Watch Fair in 1980, and it had an immediate impact. This innovative approach was particularly striking because, at that time, luxury watches predominantly utilized more conventional materials such as gold and leather (Hublot, 2024a).

The essence of the Hublot brand is condensed in the **"Art of Fusion,"** a guiding

Picture 7.3 Porthole of the military sailing training ship Amerigo Vespucci. By Jpbazard. Permission granted under the terms of the GNU Free Documentation License, Version 1.2 or any later version. Available at (Wikimedia Commons, 2019).

philosophy that was notably advanced by Jean-Claude Biver after he joined the company in 2004. Biver, who had previously revitalized Omega, infused Hublot with innovation, and under his leadership the brand introduced the Big Bang collection. This collection rapidly became emblematic of Hublot's dedication to integrating traditional craftsmanship with modern technological advancements. The brand's core values – boldness, innovation and courage to push the boundaries of watchmaking – remain evident in every aspect of its identity and DNA (Hublot, 2024a).

The brand is produced in Switzerland, where teams from various areas of expertise (watchmakers, physicists, chemists and engineers) work under one roof on crafting micro-components to design cases and dials, as well as research related to innovative material. Their combined expertise and synergy drive the creation of exceptional watches, with high levels of technical precision and aesthetic standards (Hublot, 2024b).

Hublot has gained recognition for its continuous innovation within the luxury watch industry. Among its most significant contributions was **material fusion** blending traditional elements like gold with modern materials such as rubber, ceramic and carbon fiber. The Big Bang collection, for example, features a multi-component construction that allows for limitless combinations of materials, and this is what makes each piece unique. Hublot has also finished development of an in-house chronograph (the UNICO movement) underscoring the brand's technical expertise. And finally, Hublot's dedication to innovation was further demonstrated in its Masterpiece (MP) collection, which pushed the limits of horological design. One example in this collection, the MP-05 LaFerrari, is crowned by an unprecedented 50-day power reserve, a new benchmark in the industry (Hublot, 2024a).

In 2018, Hublot became a pioneer among luxury brands by announcing that it would begin **accepting cryptocurrency payments,** initially in Hong Kong and then globally. This move was considered particularly brave within the industry because it linked the brand's entry into e-commerce with cryptocurrency. At the time, this payment method had not yet achieved extensive adoption (Revolution, 2018), and the limited-edition Big Bang Meca-10 P2P was exclusively available via Bitcoin (Hublot, 2024c).

Hublot extended its digital journey in 2022 with the launch of the **Hublot Loves Football Metaverse Stadium.** This virtual environment was developed in collaboration with the architectural company MEIS and the metaverse platform Spatial. The stadium was inspired by the design of the **Big Bang e** watch. It marked a significant step in Hublot's strategy to create immersive digital experiences connecting the brand's passion for football and technology. The gaming experience aimed to appeal to younger consumers who value experiential luxury (Hublot, 2024c) and gaming experiences. The Big Bang e incorporated the latest technology while maintaining the iconic Big Bang design elements. The model was powered by Wear OS by Google, offering functionalities such as a perpetual calendar, GMT and customizable dials (Hublot, 2020).

Beyond its technological and digital projects, Hublot remains actively involved in various **sponsorships, particularly within the sports domain.** The brand has established long-term relationships with prestigious events such as the FIFA World Cup, where it operates as the official timekeeper. Moreover, the brand partners with athletes and teams across diverse disciplines (Hublot, 2024b). Its **digital transformation** was also accompanied by the launch of digital boutiques.

Hublot's evolution from its establishment in 1980 exemplifies its commitment to innovation and bold design. The courage of the brand's creators has been expressed via its "Art of Fusion" philosophy. Hublot has consistently challenged the conventions of traditional watchmaking, introducing new materials, pioneering designs, and even venturing into the digital world with initiatives like the Metaverse Stadium. The dedication to innovations for different age groups ensures its continued appeal to watch enthusiasts and collectors worldwide.

Hollensen et al. (2022) estimate that in the future, the metaverse will revolutionize almost all sectors of society, from healthcare, consumer goods, entertainment and business-to-business technical solutions to payments. In addition, entire new industries, marketplaces and resources will be created to make this future possible, as well as new types of skills, professions and certifications. The aggregate financial value of these changes, they say, will be in the billions and trillions of dollars. The authors also point out that communication in the metaverse takes place between avatars and provide an overview of the eight basic building blocks of the metaverse (Hollensen et al., 2022).

The first building block includes **consumer-oriented hardware** such as virtual reality headsets, mobile phones, haptic gloves (which virtually produce the feeling of grasping) and enterprise hardware used to operate or create virtual or augmented reality environments. These include, for example, industrial cameras, projection and surveillance systems, and sensor sensors. This block does not include computer-specific hardware, such as chips or servers, or network-specific hardware, such as fiber optic cables or wireless chipsets. A consumer set of Meta Quest 2 VR glasses cost approximately $400 in 2022 (Meta, 2022). The evolution towards greater accessibility, higher resolution and greater user comfort is constantly advancing. In 2024, the simplest version of the Meta Quest (3S) was available for $300. The product range also includes a professional version (Meta Quest Pro) at $1,000, providing better technical features and user comfort (Meta, 2024). According to the estimates, AR Insider Meta sold almost 700,000 VR headsets in Q1 2024 (AR Insider, 2024) – still a low number to penetrate the global market, but other competitors are far behind (e.g. Apple's Vision Pro is approximately eight times more expensive compared to Meta Quest 3).

The second building block of the metaverse is **networking**, specifically with regard to three KPIs: (1) bandwidth – expresses how much data can be transferred per unit of time. The requirements for the metaverse are much higher than for most internet applications and games. Other indicators are (2) network latency, the time it takes for data to move from one point to another and back, and (3) reliability, as an expression of quality of service. Netflix, for example, receives all video files hours to months before they are made available to the audience so that it can perform the analyses needed to discard unnecessary information and compress the file sizes to reliably reach end customers.

Another building block is the **availability and development of computing power** when performing diverse and demanding functions such as computation, data alignment and synchronization, using artificial intelligence, projection or motion sensing. The fourth block is **virtual platforms**. Once most users are connected to the metaverse through virtual platforms, accessible from various devices such as web browsers and VR glasses, users will meet, shop, collaborate, build, learn and play, work and relax. This building block includes the development and operation of digital, often three-dimensional simulations that allow users to immerse themselves in environments and worlds and participate in a wide range of experiences (e.g. gaming, education, shopping, listening to music) but also to engage in economic activity between businesses and between businesses and consumers.

The fifth element of the metaverse is the **creation of industry standards** for systems to work together. At this stage of the metaverse ecosystem's development, hardware, computing, networking and virtual platforms already exist. This building block includes a broadly defined category with different technical solutions, protocols, formats and services that enable interoperability, that is, the ability of different systems to work together. Meanwhile, Meta is investing heavily in the metaverse to introduce its own operating system, fight mobile operating systems, and avoid using a standard created by its direct competitors; nevertheless, interoperability with competitors' systems will be important for user convenience.

The form of payment in the metaverse, another building block, is likely to be tied to blockchain and virtual currencies. While blockchain is not necessarily needed to prove or manage ownership of assets or to transfer money safely and quickly, cryptocurrencies are increasingly being used not only for gaming (via NFTs) but also for users' initial payments and to obtain in-game currencies. Finally, the penultimate element is the creation of content, services and assets, which include all services and business based on the metaverse. Brand owners (like Gucci; see the mini-case "Welcome to Gucci Town") play a major role in the metaverse as content providers. This building block contains all businesses and services based on the metaverse. It could also include content independent of virtual platforms or lead to the establishment of many new entertainment franchises and brands aimed at consumers and creating consumer experiences.

Consumer and business behavior is the last building block of the metaverse, and it refers to the observable changes in consumer and business behavior that are directly related to what is happening in the metaverse. Generations Z and Alpha express themselves, learn quickly and constantly socialize through virtual worlds that they can touch and change and where they can interact with others. The capabilities of virtual worlds will grow, their accessibility and ease of use will improve, and a fad or a trendy affair will become a permanent presence in the other world (Hollensen et al., 2022).

How can these new technologies help bring the world of luxury brands closer to younger target groups? Research by Joy et al. (2022) mapped this new territory to find out how advanced technologies are impacting the luxury fashion industry. They ultimately formulated questions for both academia and business as to whether young consumers who live essentially online will buy more fashion products in the digital world than in the real world, and how the fashion industry can create a strategy for the coexistence of digital collections and physical goods.

The answer to this conundrum is not yet verifiable, but Joy et al. (2022) quote an interview from The Business of Fashion Show (2021) with former LVMH digital director Ian Rogers, who says that it is perfectly normal for a younger person to have digital collections that everyone in their digital surroundings can see rather than a physical collection that almost no one will see (Video 7.1). Such an approach by the younger generation may also open the door to purely virtual fashion brands such as the digital brand Dematerialized in the future. This Berlin-based start-up is based on the idea that if more and more of our lives take place online, why not invest in our avatar look by buying digital clothes (The Business of Fashion Show, 2021) (Joy et al., 2022).

Sung et al. (2023) employed a sample of 469 metaverse users from both the United States and South Korea to explore consumer behavior related to blockchain-based luxury NFT purchases in the metaverse, focusing on cultural (individualism vs. collectivism) and psychological factors. The results suggested that both perceived economic and social values are key drivers of consumers' purchase intentions for luxury NFT fashion items in the metaverse. Moreover, consumers value NFTs as digital assets and representations of their ideal self-image and social status within virtual environments. Ownership of luxury NFTs therefore influences both virtual and real-world purchasing behaviors. Interestingly, the study exposed cultural differences between individualistic (U.S.) and collectivist (South Korean) cultures. South Korean consumers, predominantly women, were more concerned about losing social value if they miss out on NFT acquisitions. The U.S. respondents focused more on economic advances. The difference implies that luxury brands must **adapt their tactics to respect distinctive values in diverse cultural backgrounds**. Perceived **authenticity and scarcity of NFTs are crucial** in shaping consumers' evaluations of the benefits and risks associated with purchasing (Sung et al., 2023).

To appeal to younger target groups, luxury brands will try to expand the possibilities of their products, for example, by creating digital twins. Customers who buy a $10,000 watch won't walk around the metaverse with an empty wrist. Simultaneously, luxury brands need to be careful in implementing their digital strategies to avoid making the young consumers feel imposed upon (Vogue Business, 2024a). According to a sample of US Gen Z consumers,

Video 7.1 Interview of Ian Rogers for the Business of Fashion Show, available at (The Business of Fashion Show, 2021).

around only half of Gen Z respondents had created a virtual avatar (52%), used an app filter (49%) or made friends in a virtual game (44%). When asked what would make brands seem "cool," just 32% of Gen Zs said presence in a virtual world like Roblox or Decentraland (versus 28% of millennials). Only 16% of Gen Zs believe that branded NFTs would make a brand seem cooler, compared with 28% of millennials (Vogue Business, 2024a).

Schauman et al.'s (2023) research suggests that digital fashion and other digital substitutes will reshape how material things, cultural meanings and people's daily activities connect, rather than creating an entirely new, separate digital fashion culture. In short, digital substitutes seem valuable because they can enhance and support real-world experiences rather than entirely replace them (Schauman et al., 2023).

Mini-case 7.3 "Welcome to Gucci Town" and further into the metaverse world

Internet gaming platform Roblox, with almost 80 million users in Q3 2024 (Roblox, 2024), introduced Gucci in 2021 with the words: "Welcome to Gucci Town. You'll be surprised to see how the vision of Alessandro Michele [Gucci's former creative director] turns into a fictional story starring the Gucci community. Walk through every nook and cranny of the city, creating, connecting and collecting, Gucci style!" (Roblox, 2022). Roblox players, typically ages 9–15, could get stones with the signature GG logo in the "Gucci Garden," create artwork, learn about the brand's tradition and craftsmanship, show off their own Gucci style in front of others or even visit the Gucci boutique with limited edition virtual Gucci items. Over 20 million users visited the space.

David Baszucki, Roblox CEO, highlighted in his interview for *Harvard Business Review* the **importance of community building** as the primary building block of the company strategy, "Other companies offer creator economies and user-generated content (UGC), but at Roblox, user innovation is not a nice-to-have alongside other things. It's fundamental. We're a community. And for us, community is the path to creating what many now know as the metaverse" (Baszucki, 2022, p. 31). Roblox's community-centric model, according to Baszucki, is a path toward realizing the metaverse as an immersive platform for shared human experiences.

Roblox's focus on community and co-creation helps brands like Gucci tap into a younger audience, build emotional connections and establish long-term brand loyalty within emerging digital spaces. The primary target group of the Roblox platform is the Alpha generation, individuals born after 2010. Luxury brands, like those in other industries, are aware that reaching into the community of future potential consumers is essential to create brand awareness among a generation that has been part of the digital world since childhood. And it is **the community that connects luxury fashion with its future consumers**, of which Alessandro Michele was well aware. Videos and discussions on YouTube and Discord show that Gucci is settling into the alpha community ("What should I do if I've already missed half of my promotions and can't get enough to buy a Gucci Blondie Bag?" (Pandora, 2022).) Players are brand aware and learn the terminology for Gucci-typical items, with their avatar then playing other games and contributing to building the desire to own one of the brand's iconic pieces, even if only virtually.

Gucci also adhered to one of the basic attributes of luxury strategy within Roblox. The games are freely accessible on Roblox, and there is no need to buy anything special in order to participate. However, there were Gucci special **limited-edition items** available, and they were also only available for extremely limited time periods. These two conditions mean they are extremely difficult to get and therefore highly prized. That said, users who cannot obtain them are often willing to buy them on the secondary market. For example, a Queen Bee Dionysus handbag appeared in 2021 for 475 Robux (about $5). The handbag was available for one hour on two different days, which greatly limited the availability and increased demand among Roblox players. One of the handbags ended up costing $4,115, which is more than the physical version of this product that sells in stores for $3,400. What's more, it is not an NFT; that is, the item is usable only within the community of players or their avatars on the Roblox platform. (Luxus+, 2021; Roblox, 2022).

According to Bernard Marr, an expert in business and future technologies, the digital Gucci Garden on Roblox was visited by over 20 million users (Marr, 2022). Gucci's metaverse strategy has evolved from its initial expedition in Roblox into a **multifaceted digital presence** that includes immersive experiences on platforms like The Sandbox, NFT collaborations and integrating emerging technologies. This approach reflects Gucci's dedication to engaging with both existing and future consumers across various digital landscapes. The Sandbox Metaverse allows the users to experience a digital journey through the House's past, present and future. The experience includes various interactive games, the digitized exhibition and the historical pieces highlighting the Gucci codes as well as how they evolved over time while staying relevant to the young audience of Sandbox (Vault Gucci, 2022). Another Gucci Metaverse activity relates to NFT drops of SuperGucci targeted at collectors who are very likely an older target audience compared to Roblox or Sandbox activities. There is a direct link from the Gucci web page to the OpenSea platform, where the famous limited SuperGucci NFT collections are traded. The characters result from a collaboration between Gucci and Superplastic (SUPERGUCCI), co-created by the former Gucci Creative Director Alessandro Michele and synthetic artists Janky & Guggimon (OpenSea, 2024). Double G, as a recognizable brand code, is part of the skin of each character at OpenSea. The same code accompanies the House activities on Sandbox, Roblox and, nowadays, even Gen Z and Alpha's favorite Discord.

The Sandbox platform also includes **Gucci Cosmos Land** – a digital experience mirroring the House exhibition conducted physically in Shanghai, London or recently in the Kyoto KYOCERA Museum of Art. The exhibition traces Gucci House's 100 years of history, highlighting its heritage, history of innovation and creative legacy (Gucci, 2023, 2024).

To further demonstrate a commitment to innovation, Gucci premiered an immersive, mixed reality film using Apple's Vision Pro headset. The documentary *Who Is Sabato De Sarno? A Gucci Story* explores the lead-up to Creative Director Sabato de Sarno's debut collection, enhancing viewer engagement through interactive 3D content. The film is available for headset owners on the Gucci app. While several brands have explored shoppable stores on the Vision Pro, Gucci has prioritized art, entertainment and brand education – Vogue Business (2024b)

Gucci's digital strategy is targeted at engaging younger audiences through experiences in the metaverse. Brand presence on platforms like Roblox and The Sandbox creates interactive environments where users can explore the brand's heritage, participate in virtual events and acquire exclusive branded digital items. This approach builds brand awareness among Generation Alpha and Generation Z and also **cultivates a sense of community and exclusivity.** Collaborations, such as the *SUPERGUCCI* NFT series with Superplastic, further demonstrate Gucci's commitment to blending traditional luxury with digital innovation, ensuring the brand remains relevant and appealing to future customers.

Creating brand-related metaverse worlds has certain advantages. The development of digital items is related to **lower production costs** compared to physical items, allowing for replication and wide distribution at a fraction of the cost associated with physical goods. The metaverse **attracts younger demographics**, and thus it is possible to build brand awareness and cultivate early brand loyalty with them. Experiences with luxury goods in virtual environments can inspire consumers to purchase physical products. Brands can introduce and evaluate new designs in the metaverse, gathering **feedback from the specific communities** before committing to physical production. In addition, digital collections **do not lead to overproduction** or excess inventory like physical items. And last, the metaverse enables brands to revive and monetize archival designs, creating **new income streams** (Marr, 2022).

There is an important factor to be considered – digital objects developed by luxury brands for the web3 environment need to respect the same branding rules as the physical objects do. This means that the brand identity, including the brand DNA and codes, needs to be transformed into the digital world through creating a **digital brand identity**. Currently, there are limited amount of developers experienced in building digital brand identities. At least for now, the digital skills needed to develop a unique digital brand identity respecting the original brand are rare, and luxury houses often perceive it as limitation to their expansion to the metaverse.

One example of a brand with an excellent digital identity, including all aspects of luxury business strategy – product uniqueness, limited availability and distribution, superior product, extraordinary price and so on – is Louis Vuitton VIA.

Mini-case 7.4 Louis Vuitton VIA – Best practices in building digital brand identity

Louis Vuitton has established its brand presence on web3 by launching an ultra-limited NFT collection named *Treasure Trunks*. On June 8, 2023, the company released the digital collection with the quote: "The VIA Treasure Trunk unveils its universe of infinite possibilities. Join the waiting list for a chance to participate in this unique voyage" (Louis Vuitton, 2023).

The VIA Treasure Trunk digital collectible (NFT) is the gateway to VIA, which is the brand's own web3 ecosystem. This NFT is soul-bound, that is, a nontransferable, non-fungible token. This means that after acquiring the NFT, it is connected to the identity of the owner and cannot be sold or transferred to another person. Ownership of the VIA Treasure Trunk NFT allows owners to enter the digital world of Louis Vuitton, which will reveal new, limited products through immersive drops launched at regular intervals (Louis Vuitton, 2024).

Web3 represents the next generation of internet technology, characterized by decentralization, blockchain technology and user interaction. Unlike its predecessor, web2, which focused on user-generated content and social media, web3 emphasizes ownership and security through blockchain because this technology enables the creation and exchange of NFTs, which are unique digital assets authenticated and stored on the blockchain, guaranteeing verifiable ownership and provenance.

The first limited product offer for the owners of the VIA Treasure Trunk was VIA Speedy P9 unveiled during Pharrell Williams' Men's Spring-Summer 2024 show, a design based on the traditional *Maison*'s bag from 1930. Owners had the opportunity to redeem a physical counterpart starting in November 2023. Once the customer submits the claim through MyLV account, an LV Client Advisor will reach out within a few days to coordinate delivery details. The second digital collectible available exclusively for the VIA Treasure Trunk owners, announced during Nicolas Ghesquière's Women's Spring-Summer 2024 show, was The VIA Tile Trunk. The redemption period for the VIA Tile Trunk physical twin started in February 2024 (Louis Vuitton, 2024).

Louis Vuitton aligns NFTs with its brand DNA, particularly with the theme of travel, a core aspect of the **brand's identity**. The VIA Treasure Trunk exemplifies this integration by embodying LV's travel culture and dispersing it into the **digital brand identity**. The unique savoir-faire of LVMH digital developers has ensured that the **brand's identity remains consistent across both physical and digital platforms**.

LV's approach to NFTs involves creating highly unique offerings. The products are not only digital collectibles but also physical counterparts, such as the trunk bag designed by Nicolas Ghesquière. These items are positioned at high price points (e.g. €39,000 for the VIA Treasure Trunk and €6,000 for the physical trunk bag), reinforcing the **brand's luxury status and setting them apart from other digital collectibles**. There were 200 pieces of the Via Tile Trunk available but only to those who already own one of the Louis Vuitton Treasure Trunk NFTs Voque Business (2023). **Uniqueness of the product** as one of the critical aspects of the luxury business strategy is clearly emphasized.

The **rarity of LV's offerings** is a cornerstone of its strategy. The NFTs are released in ultra-limited editions, available only to select customers on waiting lists. This scarcity extends to the brand's digital items, as the NFTs serve as exclusive keys to potential purchases of physical products and future collections. The incorporation of soulbound NFTs, which remain permanently in the owner's digital wallet (and cannot be traded on the secondary market like regular NFTs can) (Forbes, 2023), adds another layer of rarity and exclusivity, ensuring a long-term attachment to the brand).

Louis Vuitton is focused on building a dedicated web3 community, differentiating itself from other luxury brands like Gucci and Adidas, which target broader web3 application communities on the existing platforms like Bored Ape Yacht Club or G Money. By developing its own unique community, LV enhances customer loyalty. The brand's own web3 platforms allow interaction with the clients (unlike other known platforms) because it allows the company to collect personal data about the customers for future communication activities. The brand NFTs are tickets to future brand experiences and collections, fostering ongoing interaction within the brand's web3 ecosystem. Louis Vuitton's digital business strategy emphasizes maintaining a **strong brand identity, creating unique and rare products and building a dedicated community**, all while leveraging advanced digital technologies to enhance the luxury experience.

7.3 Artificial intelligence and machine learning

The use of artificial intelligence is widespread in the world of luxury brands but, regarding their specifics, more limited. Amazon is undoubtedly an example of best practices and a role model for other retailers, but luxury brand managers are more cautious about using AI to communicate with clients. The use of chatbots (a computer program created for the purpose of automated communication to answer people's questions based on pre-defined scenarios) for communication with clients is already common in communication with Estée Lauder or Louis Vuitton, but unlike in non-luxury sectors, it is always ensured that the client can more easily interact with a human consultant, who is still considered more empathetic than a bot or virtual assistant.

However, with the rapid development of artificial intelligence and machine learning, it is possible that the fear of low empathy for virtual assistants will soon be overcome. In addition, AI machine learning will enable a high level of personalization and communication of recommendations tailored to each client (Joy et al., 2022).

Machine learning has played a key role in the development of Serpenti metamorphosis (see the Mini-Case BVLGARI – Serpenti Metamorphosis), which relies on artificial intelligence algorithms "trained" on the vast number of available images, and through machine learning, algorithms can learn to make accurate predictions, for example, about what combinations and sequences of images will be attractive. The machine learning process automatically improves through processing enough experiences. By understanding real-time customer data, such as who buys what, when, at what prices and in which locations, machine learning can help luxury brands offer highly personalized and relevant recommendations for each customer.

Artificial intelligence has the potential to improve customer relationships. Luxury brands have traditionally preferred to welcome the customer to a brick-and-mortar store in the hope that the seller's interaction with them will build a personal enough relationship to make a purchase. With the rise of e-commerce, luxury brands must find new ways to provide **personalized online interaction**. The solution is an **omnichannel marketing strategy**, including the implementation of **artificial intelligence in e-commerce data processing**. This gives customers the opportunity to get personalized online interactions by searching for brand e-shops and then completing purchases in-store. Artificial intelligence applications help provide personalized services, and technology and luxury businesses are increasingly converging. As the volume of data on sales and consumer preferences grows, AI can use this data to improve the shopping experience further, attracting consumers whose digital behavior is more confident. AI can unlock the potential of consolidating shopping history data, from clothing sizes to style preferences for millions of different individuals. This is both a big advance and a challenge for customer service (The Joue, 2021).

In luxury hospitality, AI-powered voice assistants (Alexa or Google Assistant) might be integrated into hotel rooms to help customers control room settings, order services, optimize cleaning services and so on. Chatbots or virtual concierges can help with guest inquiries, bookings, dining or activity recommendations. Predictive analytics can help optimize pricing, resource allocation and, therefore, revenue maximization (Jogarao, 2024). Similarly to luxury hospitality, the luxury customer experience in brick-and-mortar and online stores can be optimized using AI-driven tools, optimizing the data collected from the customers both physically and online.

Image recognition technology can potentially contribute to the fight against counterfeiting, which is estimated to be worth €8–11 billion on the grey market. AI can help brands identify unauthorized sellers on mass e-commerce platforms such as eBay, Amazon, or the Chinese marketplaces Taobao and Tmall. For example, the Cypheme mobile app uses real-time tracking from a scan of product packaging to confirm product authenticity (Heuritech, 2018). With the growing popularity of luxury brands available on the secondary market, the need to identify the authenticity of a product will only increase.

Mini-case 7.5 BVLGARI – Artificial intelligence and Serpenti Metamorphosis

Founded in Rome in 1884 by Greek silversmith Sotirio Bulgaria, with a strong Italian influence, Bulgari became part of the LVMH Empire in 2011, with the Bulgari family still the second largest stake in the newly formed subsidiary. One of the iconic BVLGARI collections is *Serpenti*, with a snake as a symbol of wisdom, rebirth and vitality. This first appeared on bracelet-looking watches made of gold mesh or elastic straps of polished yellow gold in the late 1940s. See Picture 7.4 for a Serpenti representation. The current collection is still based on snake symbolism, with generous creativity emphasizing variability, respectively – metamorphosis (BVLGARI, 2022).

The collection is often linked to the arts and contemporary artists. The most recent

Picture 7.4 Bulgari shop illuminated for Christmas with the iconic Serpenti in Statue Square, Central, Hong Kong. By HAPlipayami. Licensed under the Creative Commons Attribution-Share Alike 4.0 International license. Available at (Wikimedia Commons, 2015).

BVLGARI *Serpenti in Art* capsule collection of handbags celebrates the enduring connection between the iconic serpent motif and the art world. This exclusive series features Serpenti Forever handbags reimagined by three contemporary artists, each bringing a unique perspective to the symbol of transformation, often with nature-related motives, which are part of the brand DNA. Zhou Li, born in Hunan China, is known for dynamic abstractions that begin from natural observation (Ocula, 2024). Her interpretation of the Serpenti Forever top handle bag was titled *Ocean and Forest*. The calf leather handbags are enriched with golden embroidery and intricate applications, adding texture and depth to the pieces (BVLGARI, 2024).

Refik Anadol is a well-known and recognized digital artist, renowned for his innovative use of artificial intelligence to create immersive visual experiences (Anadol, 2022). Over the past decade, his proficiency in mixing art and technology has resulted in collaborations with respected luxury brands and well-known galleries globally. Besides branded work, his achievements include *Dvořák Dreams* an AI-driven installation that transforms the musical legacy of Czech composer Antonín Dvořák into a multi-sensory experience, showcasing his ability to bridge classical art forms with contemporary digital media (Refik Anadol, 2024). The large-scale installation was part of the Dvořák's anniversary celebration in Prague in 2023 (Picture 7.5); it was also later exhibited at the Kennedy Center in Washington DC. Refik Anadol used custom AI algorithms and data-driven processes to interpret Dvořák's melodies, harmonies and rhythms. This resulted in appealing visualizations and a unique soundtrack evoking the essence of the composer in a non-traditional way, incorporating the elements

Picture 7.5 Dvořák Dreams by Refik Anadol at the Rudolfinum (Prague), by Justagallerina, made available under the CC0 1.0 (Wikimedia Commons, 2023).

of nature and cities that were part of the composer's life and work (The Kennedy Center, 2024).

To celebrate the Serpenti collection, Refik Anadol, was invited to create at the intersection of art, science and technology. His installations take various virtual and physical forms. For example, entire buildings come to life – floors, walls and ceilings disappear into infinity – and large expanses of data create a breathtaking aesthetic, giving viewers new perspectives of the world.

In 2021, Refik created an installation of digital art inspired by the Serpenti metamorphosis concept for BVLGARI Serpenti in Milan's Piazza Duomo – a multisensory installation created by artificial intelligence to celebrate the beauty of nature through the transformation of algorithmically processed data from 200 million images of nature, 160 million images of flowers and 120,000 images of snakes (LVMH, 2021) (Video 7.2).

The work symbolizes Bulgari's ability to shape the rarest and most valuable materials into artistic creations. In parallel, artificial intelligence reconstituted images inspired by the colors, patterns and shapes of nature into a living work of art from embedded paintings. At the same time, Refik collaborated with perfume creator Sophie Labbe to produce the first AI-created fragrance *Rainforest Serpenti*, inspired by the scents of nature. The installation, together with the newly introduced fragrance, meant a comprehensive multisensory experience for customers.

Video 7.2 Serpenti Metamorphosis – Milan, available at (BVLGARI, 2021).

Artificial intelligence and machine learning are also used to authenticate products in the luxury industry. For example, Origyn Luxury creates so-called biometric authentication certificates and digital twins of luxury products, primarily jewelry and watches, on the blockchain. It uses artificial intelligence and machine learning, but also industry experts. All data is stored fully on-chain to secure the immutability and transparency of the certificates (ORIGYN, 2024).

Artificial intelligence and machine learning are redefining the luxury industry by enhancing personalization, optimizing customer experiences and safeguarding brand authenticity. As technology advances, integrating AI into luxury brand strategies from retail to hospitality, as well as product authentication, will continue to bridge the gap between digital innovation and personalized human touch. Luxury brands traditionally focus on human-centered experiences. Artificial intelligence now provides sophisticated tools to replicate experiences in digital spaces, allowing brands to retain their magic in an increasingly virtual world. The synergy between art, technology and craftsmanship promises a new era where artificial intelligence supports and elevates the essence of luxury brands in line with their luxury business strategy.

7.4 New technologies in luxury brand management enhance the experience

The innovative design of experiences provided by luxury brands will be an increasingly important part of luxury marketing. In experiential marketing, which has been written about in connection with services and later luxury products since the 1980s, it is about taking the essence of the product and extending it into a set of tangible, physical and interactive experiences that strengthen the brand's offering (Atwal & Williams, 2009).

Figure 7.1 shows four experiential zones divided by customer engagement (measured by the level of interactivity between supplier and customer) and intensity: entertainment, education, escape and aesthetics. Increased *engagement* means that suppliers no longer create an experience for the customer, but the supplier and the customer co-create that experience interactively. *Intensity* refers to the perception of the power of feelings relative to interaction. The four zones are not meant to be mutually exclusive; however, the richness of the experience is a function of the degree to which all four zones are incorporated.

BVLGARI Serpenti Metamorphosis represents a highly aesthetic experience with a strong intensity of perception regarding the interaction between the brand and the customer. CryptoPunks' physical pendants created by Tiffany, designed to match the corresponding tokens, can be perceived as highly aesthetic, with less involvement in creating the experience. Roblox Gucci Town is an interactive game whose important mission, in addition to interaction with the brand, is to educate a younger target group and build brand awareness. Dematerialized fashion, using the example of the brand Dematerialized, provides an escape from reality through exclusively designed dresses for the online world (Dematerialized, 2024).

The case studies in this chapter show the inspiring journeys of luxury brands into deep, immersive experiences. Digital tools bring the customer a new experience with a luxury brand. NFTs in the luxury world build on the tradition of combining luxury and art. Blockchain technology ensures the uniqueness of each NFT, its origin and authenticity. In the case of luxury, it can form the basis of a digital art collection and deepen the relationship between luxury and art.

The metaverse will mean access to a community of new generations whose virtual experiences can represent opportunities for luxury brands in the form of creating virtual events or collections for a virtual, so-called second life. The use of artificial intelligence and machine learning by virtual artists for real or second life is a significant link between luxury and new target groups. Improving customer service and services in both online and physical stores through artificial intelligence is another challenge. At the same time, managers of luxury brands must continue to protect the core values of the brands carefully.

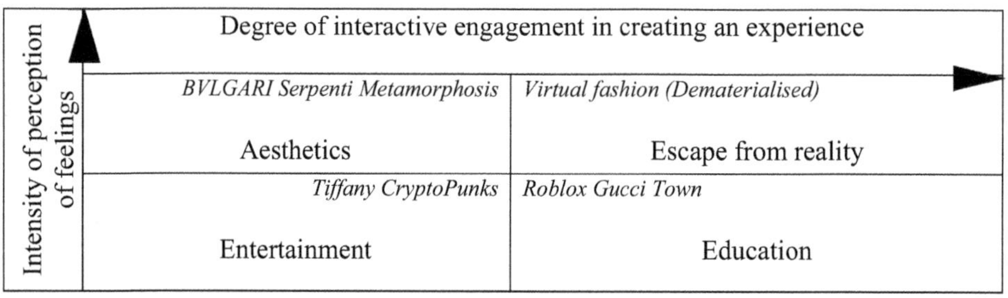

Figure 7.1 Experience zones, adapted by authors and based on (Atwal & Williams, 2009).

A recent study conducted by Murtas at al. (2024) involved four cases in luxury brand management and web3 technology implementation. The cases were selected based on their relevance to NFTs and the metaverse, their recognition as pioneers in technological experimentation, and their active social media presence during the investigation period. These cases included, for example, a Gucci digital exhibition held in the Roblox metaverse, where avatars could explore thematic rooms and purchase limited-edition digital clothes as well as a Louis Vuitton video game launched to celebrate the bicentenary of the founder's birth, featuring exclusive NFTs designed in collaboration with digital artists. The findings suggest that luxury fashion brands should use these technologies to reinforce the perception of scarcity, accelerate the "artification" process and innovatively express their inherited identities. But the authors moderate the expectations of the new technologies by pointing out that when implementing web3 technologies, luxury brands must be **cautious about the risks of expressing their distinctive aesthetics ineffectively** and about "offering experiences that do not align with the highly experiential nature of luxury" (Murtas et al., 2024, p. 90).

In the midst of the current enthusiasm for experimenting with NFTs, there are also other reasons to be cautious. One concern is the environmental impact of blockchain technologies, which underpin NFTs, in particular the energy needed to validate transactions. Cybersecurity is another cause for concern. McKinsey gives an example where a cyberattack on the official website of the artist Banksy caused the collector to pay the equivalent of $334,000 for a counterfeit NFT. Still, embedding luxury brands in the metaverse may promise new ways to engage consumers in brand life, which will require changes in creative branding strategies to create immersive consumer experiences and excitement among in-demand consumer groups (McKinsey & Company, 2020).

The metaverse allows luxury companies to create extravagant experiences in it, building credibility, loyalty and engagement of the user community in the new world. They are able to do this and still maintain brand identity and relevance to a more tech-savvy and younger audience.

7.5 Summary: Integrating emerging technologies in luxury brand strategies

Chapter 7, "Emerging Technologies in the Management of Luxury Brands," explores how digital innovations potentially reshape the luxury sector. The chapter highlights the rise of artificial intelligence, blockchain, NFTs and the metaverse in luxury brand strategies, emphasizing their potential to engage younger, digitally native consumers while preserving traditional luxury brand values regarding its heritage, culture, exclusivity and scarcity. AI and machine learning drive personalized customer experiences, streamline operations and bolster product authenticity, as seen in tools like Aura Blockchain, which enhances brand transparency.

Luxury brands are increasingly cautious yet innovative in implementing these technologies to maintain exclusivity. AI-powered personalization allows brands to replicate high-touch experiences online, while machine learning algorithms enhance design predictions and customer recommendations. Examples include AI-driven art installations, like BVLGARI's Serpenti Metamorphosis, which showcase the synthesis of creativity, technology, art and heritage. Blockchain-enabled NFTs and the metaverse offer new opportunities for building luxury experiences and luxury digital ownership, appealing to younger audiences through unique virtual collectibles and immersive environments. Projects by Gucci and Louis Vuitton illustrate this shift, blending brand heritage with digital expression to maintain relevance.

The importance of creating brand digital identities in line with the brand's physical DNA and codes, is emphasized and showcased in the example of Louis Vuitton VIA and related "phygital" products.

However, the chapter also discusses challenges, including balancing innovation with brand integrity and safeguarding digital asset security. As the luxury sector ventures into web3, a balance between preserving brand DNA, unique brand codes and identities while embracing digital transformation is crucial.

Keywords

Artificial Intelligence (AI): Technology enabling machines to perform tasks like human intelligence. In luxury, AI is typically used for personalized marketing and customer engagement.

Blockchain: A decentralized technology used to secure and verify digital transactions. In luxury, it can be used to ensure authenticity and traceability of goods.

Digital Brand Identity: The online representation of a brand's values, codes and DNA, crucial for luxury brands expanding into virtual spaces – which must be done without damaging the physical product's identity.

Experiential Marketing: Strategy that focuses on creating memorable consumer experiences to strengthen brand loyalty, particularly through interactive and immersive brand interactions.

Metaverse: A collective virtual space created by digital platforms, where luxury brands can create immersive experiences and virtual products. Meta defines it as "a collection of virtual spaces that you can explore and in which you can create, work, play, learn, shop, and much more together with other people who are not in the same physical space as you. It's not necessarily about spending more time online – it's about making the time you spend online more meaningful."

NFT (Non-Fungible Token): Unique digital assets secured on a blockchain. Luxury brands may develop and use it to provide exclusive virtual items and experiences to the clients.

Soulbound NFTs: NFTs that are non-transferable, tied permanently to the owner's identity, used to create exclusive and limited luxury experiences.

Web3: The next generation of internet technology focused on decentralization and digital ownership, enabling brands to explore new consumer engagement strategies.

Discussion questions

1. What is the role of blockchain in luxury brand management?
2. How do NFTs benefit luxury brands in reaching new audiences?
3. Why are luxury brands cautious about implementing AI in customer interactions?
4. How does the metaverse provide new opportunities for luxury brands?
5. What is a digital twin, and how does it impact luxury branding?
6. In what ways do NFTs align with traditional luxury values?
7. What are the benefits of experiential marketing in the luxury sector?
8. How does digital brand identity affect luxury brands entering the digital territory?
9. What challenges do luxury brands face with web3 technology?
10. How can luxury brands ensure authenticity in a digital environment prone to counterfeits?

Reference list

Anadol, R. (2022). *Biography*. Retrieved September 2022, from refikanadol.com: https://refikanadol.com/about

Anadol, R. (2024). *About Refik Anadol*. Retrieved November 2024, from refikanadol.com: https://refikanadol.com/refik-anadol/

AR Insider. (2024, April 29). *How Many Headsets Did Meta Sell in Q1?* Retrieved November 2024, from arinsider.co: https://arinsider.co/2024/04/29/how-many-headsets-did-meta-sell-in-q1/

Arianee. (2022, May 17). *Yves Saint Laurent Beauté Makes a Daring Step into Web3*. Retrieved September 2022, from arianee: https://www.arianee.org/newsfeed/yslbeauty

Arstechnica. (2021, July 11). *So What Is "the Metaverse," Exactly? Will We All Live in the Metaverse Soon? Or Is the Idea Just Second Life Redux?* Retrieved September 2022, from arstechnica.com: https://arstechnica.com/gaming/2021/11/everyone-pitching-the-metaverse-has-a-different-idea-of-what-it-is/

Art Explained. (2024, August 18). *'The Merge NFT' – Quick Explanation Why It's Sold for over $90,000,000!* Retrieved November 2024, from youtube.com: https://www.youtube.com/watch?v=XCtT0HePyYU

Atwal, G., & Williams, A. (2009). Luxury Brand Marketing – The Experience Is Everything! In *Advances in Luxury Brand Management* (Vol. 16, pp. 338–346). Palgrave Macmillan.

Aura Blockchain Consortium. (2022, July 21). *Cartier after-Sales Case Study*. Retrieved October 2022, from auraluxuryblockchain.com: https://auraluxuryblockchain.com/case-studies/cartier-after-sales-case-study

Bain & Company. (2022, June 21). *Global Personal Luxury Goods Market Reaches 288 Billion in Value in 2021 and Experienced a Remarkable Performance in the First Quarter 2022*. Retrieved September 2022, from bain.com: https://www.bain.com/about/media-center/press-releases/2022/global-personal-luxury-goods-market-reaches-288-billion-in-value-in-2021-and-experienced-a-remarkable-performance-in-the-first-quarter-2022/

Baszucki, D. (2022, March – April). The CEO of Roblox on Scaling Community-Sourced Innovation. *Harvard Business Review*, 30–33.

BCG & Comité Colbert. (2022). *BCG and Comité Colbert Luxury Outlook 2022*. Retrieved September 2022, from BCG: https://web-assets.bcg.com/e4/c4/5b3786d44055aa2b31749e98bd9e/bcg-and-comite-colbert-luxury-outlook-2022-final.pdf

Block, F. (2021, December 7). *PAK's NFT Artwork 'the Merge' Sells for $91.8 Million*. Retrieved June 2022, from Penta: https://www.barrons.com/articles/paks-nft-artwork-the-merge-sells-for-91-8-million-01638918205

Bryter. (2020). *Female Gamer Survey*. Retrieved September 2022, from www.bryter-research.co.uk: https://pages.bryter-research.co.uk/hubfs/003-FGS-1603/Bryter%20-%20Female%20Gamers%20Survey%202020.pdf

The Business of Fashion Show. (2021, November 11). *Why the Metaverse Is Fashion's Next Goldmine*. Retrieved September 2022, from YouTube: https://www.youtube.com/watch?v=UBZ6Bd0LDjs

BVLGARI. (2021). *YouTube*. Retrieved October 2022, from Bvlgari Metamorphosis Refik Anadol – Milan Event: https://www.youtube.com/watch?v=CU89Fs8MyBI

BVLGARI. (2022). *BVLGARI Icons*. Retrieved September 2022, from Bulgari: https://www.bulgari.com/en-int/bulgari-heritage-icons.html

BVLGARI. (2024). *Serpenti in Art*. Retrieved November 2024, from bulgari.com: https://www.bulgari.com/en-int/stories/serpenti-in-art.html?story=true

Capgemini Research Institute. (2022). *World Report Series Wealth Management 2022*. Retrieved November 2022, from Capgemini Research Institute: https://worldwealthreport.com/pdf/Capgemini_WWR_2022_VFinal_Digital.pdf

CNN. (2022, August 7). *Tiffany's Sells Out Custom Cryptopunk 'NFTiff' Pendants for $50,000 Each*. Retrieved September 2022, from edition.cnn.com: https://edition.cnn.com/style/article/tiffanys-cryptopunk-nft-pendants-trnd/index.html

CNN Business. (2022, June 30). *Crypto Is Crashing But the Tech behind It Could Save Luxury Brands Bi*. Retrieved October 2022, from edition.cnn.com: https://edition.cnn.com/2022/06/26/business/aura-blockchain-luxury-counterfeit-hnk-spc-intl/index.html

Dematerialized. (2024). *Drmat*. Retrieved November 2024, from thedematerialised.com: https://thedematerialised.com

Dune. (2022, September). *NFT Brands Case Study Overview*. Retrieved September 2022, from Dune: https://dune.com/kingjames23/nft-project-possible-data-to-use

Euromoney. (2021). *What Is Blockchain?* Retrieved June 2022, from euromoney.com: https://www.euromoney.com/learning/blockchain-explained/what-is-blockchain

Forbes. (2022, November 8). *How Hublot Is Bringing the FIFA Soccer World Cup to the Metaverse*. Retrieved November 2024, from forbes.com: https://www.forbes.com/sites/stephaniehirschmiller/2022/11/08/hublot-brings-fifa-soccer-world-cup-to-the-metaverse/

Forbes. (2023, June 7). *Unpacking the Web3 Strategy behind Louis Vuitton's 39k Digital Treasure Trunk NFTs*. Retrieved June 2024, from forbes.com: https://www.forbes.com/sites/stephaniehirschmiller/2023/06/07/unpacking-the-strategy-behind-louis-vuittons-39k-digital-treasure-trunk-nfts/?sh=3914d14823db

Gucci. (2023). *Gucci Cosmos Land*. Retrieved May 2024, from https://www.gucci.com/us/en/st/stories/article/cosmos-london-sandbox

Gucci. (2024). *Gucci Cosmos – An Exploration of Heritage*. Retrieved November 2024, from gucci.com: https://www.gucci.com/us/en/nst/cosmos-exhibition

Gurzki, H. (2022, April 14). *Three Paradoxes Luxury Brands Face in the Digital Era*. Retrieved October 2022, from IMD: https://www.imd.org/ibyimd/luxury/three-paradoxes-luxury-brands-face-in-the-digital-era/

Heuritech. (2018, December 27). *Grey Market: How Can Luxury Regain Control of Its Image?* Retrieved September 2022, from heuritech.com: https://www.heuritech.com/articles/fashion-solutions/regain-control-gray-market/

Hollensen, S., Kotler, P., & Opresnik, M. O. (2022). Metaverse – The New Marketing Universe. *Journal of Business Strategy* (ahead-of-print).

Hublot. (2020, June 2). *Hublot Bing Bang e*. Retrieved November 2024, from hublot.com: https://www.hublot.com/en-cz/news/hublot-big-bang-e

Hublot. (2024a). *40 Years Anniversary Products*. Retrieved August 2024, from hublot.com: https://www.hublot.com/en-cz/40-years/digital-book-products

Hublot. (2024b). *Our World: The Art of Fusion*. Retrieved November 2024, from hublot.com: https://www.hublot.com/en-cz/craftsmanship#cp_preview-2

Hublot. (2024c). *Timekeeper of the Metaverse*. Retrieved August 2024, from hublot.com: https://www.hublot.com/en-cz/hublot-loves-football-metaverse-stadium

Jogarao, M. (2024). AI in the Hospitality Industry. In P. Thaichon, P. K. Dutta, P. R. Chelliah, & S. Gupta, *Technology and Luxury Hospitality*. New York: Routledge.

The Joue. (2021, December 1). *Are Consumers Really Embracing AI in the Luxury Industry?* Retrieved September 2022, from theoue.com: https://thejoue.com/artificial-intelligence-in-the-luxury-industry/

Joy, A., Zhu, Y., Peña, C., & Brouard, M. (2022). Digital Future of Luxury Brands: Metaverse, Digital Fashion, and Non-Fungible Tokens. *Strategic Change*, *31*(3), 337–343.

Jung, B. (2022, April 21). *How the Metaverse Will Change the World*. Retrieved September 2022, from TEDxRockville: https://www.youtube.com/watch?v=ExUovs0n4bA

The Kennedy Center. (2024). *Dvořák Dreams*. Retrieved November 2024, from kennedy-center.org: https://www.kennedy-center.org/whats-on/explore-by-genre/exhibits/2023–2024/dvorak-dreams-exhibition/

Louis Vuitton. (2023). *Our Itinerary*. Retrieved June 2024, from Louis Vuitton: https://us.louisvuitton.com/eng-us/stories/louis-vuitton-via

Louis Vuitton. (2024). *Louis Vuitton VIA International*. Retrieved November 2024, from eu-.louisvuitton.com: https://eu.louisvuitton.com/eng-e1/faq/products/digital-collectibles-int

Luxury Innovation Summit, Geneva. (2022, October 24). *2022 Edition – Luxury Innovation Summit and Awards*. Luxury Innovation Summit and Awards. https://luxuryinnovation-summit.com/past_events/2022-edition/

Luxus+. (2021, May 26). *A Virtual Gucci Bag Sold for More Than Its Physical Version*. Retrieved September 2022, from Luxus-plus: https://luxus-plus.com/en/a-virtual-gucci-bag-sold-for-more-than-its-physical-version/

LVMH. (2021, October 13). *Bvlgari Celebrates Serpenti in Artwork Created Using Artificial Intelligence*. Retrieved from LVMH: https://www.lvmh.com/news-documents/news/bvlgari-celebrates-serpenti-in-artwork-created-using-artificial-intelligence/

Marr, B. (2022, December 13). *Gucci Enters the Metaverse*. Retrieved November 2024, from bernardmarr.com: https://bernardmarr.com/gucci-enters-the-metaverse/

McKinsey & Company. (2020, April 1). *A Perspective for the Luxury-Goods Industry During – And after – Coronavirus*. Retrieved October 2020, from McKinsey & Company: https://www.mckinsey.com/industries/retail/our-insights/a-perspective-for-the-luxury-goods-industry-during-and-after-coronavirus#

McKinsey & Company. (2022a). *Marketing in the Metaverse: An Opportunity for Innovation and Experimentation*. Retrieved September 2023, from mckinsey.com: https://www.mckinsey.com/~/media/mckinsey/email/newsletters/2022-05-24g-daily-read.html

McKinsey & Company. (2022b, May 2). *State of Fashion Technology Report 2022*. Retrieved November 2022, from McKinsey: https://www.mckinsey.com/industries/retail/our-insights/state-of-fashion-technology-report-2022?cid=other-eml-mtg-mip-mck&hlkid=4fc80ecd43b54873932d4f25af6a2314&hctky=1711743&hdpid=2aca0cfa-6346–40c1–93d6–48680a8382a4

Meisenzahl, M. (2019, December 10). *Take a look at Louis Vuitton's New Collection of Video Game Clothes, a Collaboration with 'League of Legends' That Includes a $5,000 Leather Jacket*. Retrieved June 2022, from Insider: https://www.businessinsider.com/louis-vuitton-clothing-league-of-legends-2019–12

Meta. (2021, September 27). *Building the Metaverse Responsibly*. Retrieved September 2022, from fb.com: https://about.fb.com/news/2021/09/building-the-metaverse-responsibly/

Meta. (2022). *Meta Quest 2*. Retrieved September 2022, from meta.com: https://www.meta.com/quest/products/quest-2/tech-specs/#tech-specs

Meta. (2024). *Compare Meta Quest*. Retrieved November 2024, from meta.com: https://www.meta.com/quest/compare/

Murtas, G., Pedeliento, G., & Mangiò, F. (2024). Luxury Fashion Brands at the Gates of the Web 3.0: An Analysis of Early Experimentations with NFTs and the Metaverse. *Journal of Global Fashion Marketing*, *15*(1), 90–114.

Nasdaq. (2024, April 1). *Meta Platforms Has Spent $46 Billion on the Metaverse Since 2021, but It's Spending Twice as Much on This 1 Thing*. Retrieved November 2024, from nasdaq.com: https://www.nasdaq.com/articles/meta-platforms-has-spent-$46-billion-on-the-metaverse-since-2021-but-its-spending-twice-as

NFT Evening. (2022, April 17). *Most Expensive NFT Art: The Highest Value Crypto Art Sold.* Retrieved June 2022, from nftevening.com: https://nftevening.com/most-expensive-nft-art-the-highest-value-crypto-art-ever-sold/

Ocula. (2024). *Zhou Li.* Retrieved November 2024, from ocula.com: https://ocula.com/artists/zhou-li/

OpenSea. (2022). *Louis Vuitton x Beeple SS19 #7 of 10.* Retrieved June 2022, from opensea.io: https://opensea.io/assets/ethereum/0x56215538dd8419a16cd86e22229321cd9826ff33/26

OpenSea. (2024). *SuperPlastic: SuperGucci.* Retrieved May 2024, from https://opensea.io/collection/superplastic-supergucci

ORIGYN. (2024). *Designed to Trust: Products & Tools.* Retrieved November 2024, from origyn.com: https://www.origyn.com

Pandora, Twiisted. (2022, May 27). *How to Get All Items in Gucci Town Event! (Roblox).* Retrieved September 2022, from YouTube: https://www.youtube.com/watch?v=rHHeZhEPPN4

Revolution. (2018, November 8). *A Hublot Watch That You Can Buy Only with Bitcoins: The Big Bang Meca-10 P2P.* Retrieved August 2024, from revolutionwatch.com: https://revolutionwatch.com/a-hublot-watch-that-you-can-buy-only-with-bitcoins-the-big-bang-meca-10-p2p/

Roblox. (2022). *Gucci Town by Gucci Town.* Retrieved September 2022, from roblox.com: https://www.roblox.com/games/7830918930/Gucci-Town

Roblox. (2024). *One Platform: Millions of Ways to Engage.* Retrieved November 2024, from roblox.com: https://corp.roblox.com

Schauman, S., Green, S., & Korkman, O. (2023, Novembeer–December). Sufficiency and the dematerialization of fashion: How digital substitutes are creating new market opportunities. *Business Horizons*, *66*(6), 741–751.

Sothebys. (2021, April 6). *NFTs: Redefining Digital Ownership and Scarcity.* Retrieved June 2022, from sothebys.com: https://www.sothebys.com/en/articles/nfts-redefining-digital-ownership-and-scarcity?locale=en

Sung, E., Kwon, O., & Sohn, K. (2023). NFT Luxury Brand Marketing in the Metaverse: Leveraging Blockchain-Certified NFTs to Drive Consumer Behavior. *Psychology & Marketing*, *40*, 2306–2325.

Takahashi, D. (2021, July 4). *Newzoo: Game Market Will Hit $200B in 2024.* Retrieved September 2022, from venturebbeat.com: https://www-statista-com.zdroje.vse.cz/statistics/748044/number-video-gamers-world/

Tiffany and Co. (2022). *NFTiff Frequently Asked Questions.* Retrieved September 2022, from Tiffany and Co.: https://nft.tiffany.com/faq/

Vault Gucci. (2022). *About Vault: The Experimental Concept Space by Gucci.* Retrieved September 2022, from Vault Gucci: https://vault.gucci.com/en-CZ/story/enter-vault

Vogue Business. (2022, August 24). *Nike Leads NFT Success by Revenue as Fashion Shines over Pepsi, Time Magazine.* Retrieved September 2022, from voguebusiness.com: https://www.voguebusiness.com/technology/nike-leads-nft-success-by-revenue-as-fashion-shines-over-pepsi-time-magazine

Vogue Business. (2023, November 27). *Louis Vuitton Is Selling a 6,000 Digital Mini Trunk by Nicolas Ghesquière.* Retrieved June 2024, from Vogue Business: https://www.voguebusiness.com/story/technology/louis-vuitton-is-selling-a-euro6000-digital-mini-trunk-by-nicolas-ghesquiere?uID=fa44d56a3421e1bd59eeaa0b01a60e5912e32f35339c1ca98294907eebb5d5c0&utm_campaign=newsletter_weekly&utm_source=newsletter&utm_brand

Vogue Business. (2024a). *Gen Z Broke the Marketing Funnel.* Retrieved March 2024, from https://www.voguebusiness.com/story/consumers/gen-z-broke-the-marketing-funnel?uID=fa44d56a3421e1bd59eeaa0b01a60e5912e32f35339c1ca98294907eebb5d-5c0&utm_campaign=newsletter_weekly&utm_source=newsletter&utm_brand=vb&utm_mailing=VB_NEWS_Kirsty_FRI_080324&utm

Vogue Business. (2024b, April 2). *First Look: Gucci's Immersive, Mixed Reality Fashion Film.* Retrieved November 2024, from voguebusiness.com: https://www.voguebusiness.com/story/technology/first-look-guccis-immersive-mixed-reality-fashion-film

Wall Street Journal. (2021, November 12). *Trapped in the Metaverse: Here's What 24 Hours in VR Feels Like.* Retrieved September 2022, from YouTube: https://www.youtube.com/watch?v=rtLTZUaMSDQ

Wikimedia Commons. (2015, December 29). *File:HK Central State Square Night Xmas Decor Bulgari Ring O Snake Lighting CKC BOC HQ Dec-2015 DSC.JPG.* Retrieved February 2025, from commons.wikimedia.org: https://commons.wikimedia.org/wiki/File:HK_Central_State_Square_night_Xmas_decor_Bulgari_ring_O_snake_lighting_CKC_BOC_HQ_Dec-2015_DSC.JPG

Wikimedia Commons. (2019, November 26). *File:Le Grand Voilier Amerigo Vespucci (39).JPG.* Retrieved February 2025, from commons.wikimedia.org: https://commons.wikimedia.org/wiki/File:Le_grand_voilier_Amerigo_Vespucci_(39).JPG

Wikimedia Commons. (2023, September 8). *File:0xCollection Dvorak Dreams.jpg.* Retrieved November 2024, from commons.wikimedia.org: https://commons.wikimedia.org/wiki/File:0xCollection_Dvorak_Dreams.jpg

Wikipedia Commons. (2021, November 24). *File:Pak Image.jpg.* Retrieved November 2024, from commons.wikimedia.org: https://commons.wikimedia.org/wiki/File:Pak_image.jpg

X, & CryptoPunk #3788. (2023, March 3). *X.* Retrieved November 2024, from X: https://x.com/Cryptopunk3788/status/1631700548247224339

Yuga Labs. (2024). *Shaping Web3 through Storytelling, Experiences and Community.* Retrieved October 2024, from yuga.com: https://yuga.com

Index

Note: numbers in **bold** indicate a table. Numbers in *italics* indicate a figure. Numbers <u>underlined</u> indicate a box. Italicized numbers that are also *<u>underlined</u>* indicate a video. Bolded numbers that are also **<u>underlined</u>** indicate a table inside a box.

For Product Safety Concerns and Information please contact our EU representative GPSR@taylorandfrancis.com Taylor & Francis Verlag GmbH, Kaufingerstraße 24, 80331 München, Germany